UFOs and Abductions

UFOs and Abductions
Challenging the Borders
of Knowledge

Edited by David M. Jacobs

 University Press of Kansas

© 2000 by the University Press of Kansas
All rights reserved

Published by the University Press of Kansas (Lawrence, Kansas 66049),
which was organized by the Kansas Board of Regents and is operated and
funded by Emporia State University, Fort Hays State University, Kansas
State University, Pittsburg State University, the University of Kansas, and
Wichita State University.

Library of Congress Cataloging-in-Publication Data

UFOs and abductions : challenging the borders of knowledge / edited by
David M. Jacobs.
    p. cm.
  Includes bibliographical references and index.
  ISBN 0-7006-1032-4 (pbk. : alk paper)
  1. Human-alien encounters. 2. Alien abduction. I. Jacobs, David
Michael, 1942–
  BF2050.U36 2000
  001.942—dc21   00-028970

British Library Cataloguing in Publication Data is available.

Printed in the United States of America
10 9 8 7 6 5 4 3 2 1

The paper used in this publication meets the minimum requirements of the
American National Standard for Permanence of Paper for Printed Library
Materials Z39.48-1984.

To Jack and Addie

Contents

Acknowledgments

I would like to thank my wife, Irene, for the support she has shown during my requests for time and help. Her editing abilities made my contribution readable. Michael Briggs, editor in chief of the University Press of Kansas, has been extraordinarily wise, patient, and insightful in overseeing this project. My admiration for him is profound. My sons, Evan and Alexander, have had to put up with my long hours of sequestering myself while I worked on the manuscript. The contributors to this project have been extremely understanding of my requests for revisions, sometimes against their better judgment. They not only have added to our understanding of the UFO and abduction phenomenon but also, as scholars in this field, have endured pressures in that endeavor that most in their professions will never experience. My gratitude is boundless for their courage and commitment to the search for knowledge.

Introduction

In 1969, James McDonald, professor of atmospheric physics at the University of Arizona, presented a paper at the American Association for the Advancement of Science (AAAS) symposium on the UFO phenomenon. The title of his paper was "Science in Default: Twenty-two Years of Inadequate Investigation." McDonald said that, in his opinion, "The UFO problem, far from being the 'nonsense problem' it has been labeled by many scientists, constitutes an area of extraordinary scientific interest."[1] But few in mainstream science either heard or heeded his implicit call to take UFOs seriously.

McDonald's assessment still applies. After more than half a century, science remains in default; moreover, so do the social sciences and humanities. Indeed, the UFO and abduction phenomenon touches nearly all disciplines that participate in modern intellectual discourse, and yet the subject remains virtually virgin territory.

Granted, much has been said and written about UFOs since 1947, when a pilot in his small plane claimed to witness nine unusually configured objects flying at what he estimated to be extraordinarily high speeds. There has been a passionate public debate fueled by a steady stream of sighting and "experience" reports. Advocates and debunkers alike have had their say. The subject has been included in official records: governments around the world have tracked UFOs; the United States has mounted three air force projects to collect information on UFOs; and all other branches of the armed services, plus the Central Intelligence Agency, have investigated sighting reports.

The scientific community and the rest of academia have remained on the periphery of this debate, content to let the air force handle most investigations in this field. But the air force closed down its last official UFO project in 1969, declaring there was no evidence to indicate that the objects were a direct threat to the national security or that they represented technology beyond that known on earth. The "mainstream" scientific community concurred and took the position that the UFO phenomenon had no "hard" scientific value.[2]

Not surprisingly, UFO researchers have disagreed with this assessment, contending that government-sponsored studies have been inadequate and that the scientific community cannot judge the scientific value of the phenomenon without rigorously studying it. Once the battle was joined, the two sides became hardened in their positions, to their mutual disadvantage. The intellectual struggle continues between, on the one hand, scientists who pass judgment on UFO reports (often with little knowledge of them) and, on the other hand, "untrained" private lay organizations, whose members conduct most of the investigative work (often with little knowledge of how to do science).

Class and education have played an important role in the UFO debate. Academics and professional scientists have maintained that "average" people have difficulty discriminating between fantasy and reality and often misidentify conventional phenomena. Most of that intellectual elite conclude that all UFO sightings are mistakes, due to amateurs' lack of knowledge of what can be seen in the sky and an inadequate knowledge of the human mind's complexities and vagaries.

Central to the debate has been the acquisition of accurate information. In 1977, Stanford astrophysicist Peter Sturrock polled members of the American Astronomical Society about the UFO phenomenon.[3] He found that the more the physicists had read about the subject, the more they thought it deserved further study; conversely, the less they had read about the subject, the less they thought it deserved further study.

To be fair, it has not been easy for scientists to obtain reliable and accurate information about UFOs. Although people from all walks of life (including scientists) have witnessed UFOs, amateur investigators have collected, chronicled, and analyzed the majority of reports and events. As a result, much of the material about the UFO phenomenon is—from a scientific viewpoint—unreliable, inaccurate, and otherwise of poor quality. Nevertheless, there exist a great deal of excellently researched data and a sufficient number of well-investigated sighting reports to make a compelling case that witnesses have observed a potentially extraordinary and significant phenomenon. Most of this research has been published in specialty UFO journals and books and is not normally found in mainstream publications. Thus, despite ongoing attempts by UFO researchers to convince scientists to look at the data, most scientists do not have ready access to it, and, to complicate the problem, they are often ridiculed when they seek such access, which further deters serious primary investigation.[4]

The dearth of scientific study has led UFO researchers to turn inward. They have formed their own quasi-scientific community, including a peer-reviewed journal, protocols for systematic investigations of UFO accounts, and a continually growing database of evidence. However, this has not solved the problem of "building bridges" between them and the scientific community.

The alien abduction phenomenon, an increasingly prominent part of the UFO story, has undergone similar treatment. Since the mid-1960s, when the abduction phenomenon first came to public attention, tens of thousands of sometimes terrified people have reported either being abducted or having strong suspicions that they may have been abducted. Like UFO witnesses, these individuals represent a cross section of cultural, economic, educational, and political levels in society. Most accounts independently share an extraordinary critical mass of common details about abductions.

Accounts of abductions have stimulated an intense and acrimonious debate: Are people accurately recalling real events, or are they generating psychologically based accounts? Whatever their origins, abduction accounts fascinate, and for that reason have been exploited for their commercial value. Abductions and abductees have thus become part of our public entertainment and a "hot" topic for the media. Against this backdrop, the scientific community has been reticent, understandably, about engaging with the abduction phenomenon other than speculating about its possible psychological causes. Not surprisingly, ridicule about abductions in the academic and scientific communities has been much more intense and unrelenting than it has been for reports of UFO sightings.

The slopes of the learning curves for understanding UFOs and abductions have been very different. For UFO sightings, the knowledge grew increasingly rich and sophisticated from 1947 to its peak in the early 1980s. During those years, researchers studied the effects of UFOs on the natural environment, on mechanical and electrical devices, on animals, and on humans. They studied photographs, motion pictures, radar tracings, videotapes, and eyewitness testimony. They amassed hundreds of thousands (if not millions) of sighting reports from around the world. UFOs, it should be noted, are a truly *worldwide* phenomenon, not a particularly American one. The data suggested that witnesses were sighting a strangely behaving phenomenon that seemed to have an objective reality regardless of its origin.[5] But beyond this repetitive confirmation, new insight into the phenomenon has been hard to come by.

The learning curve for the abduction phenomenon has been different. The data are dynamic, increasing in complexity, and, its proponents say, substantive. They claim that the data reveal the motivations of the "entities" or "occupants" and thus can solve the UFO mystery. But most of the data have been collected through a controversial methodology—from "memories" elicited either "consciously" or through hypnosis. So-called physical evidence is largely unavailable. In general, the abduction phenomenon does not provide the photographic, radar, and other forms of nonanecdotal evidence associated with UFO sightings. Nevertheless, researchers have developed enough unexplained abduction cases to suggest that something unusual but very real is happening, be it a new form of mental derangement or evidence of extraterrestrial manipulation.

Like UFO sightings, abduction reports have been subjected to a variety of explanations from a wide spectrum of the academic world. Many of these solutions have been based on speculation rather than on scientific studies. As with UFOs, scientists, academics, and professionals seem largely unfamiliar with the literature on the subject, and most of the serious research has not been published in refereed journals within the mainstream academic community.

Only a small number of scholars have publicly announced that they are interested in studying the UFO and abduction phenomenon.

Most scientific researchers have had little reason to believe that studying the subject would bring anything other than confirmation of conventional explanations as misidentifications of conventional objects or psychologically induced fantasies. Even if the objects or abduction experiences could be better categorized and identified, the chance that these reports would lead to verification of extraterrestrial activity seems extremely remote to mainstream scientists. In spite of all the obstacles, many mainstream researchers have looked into the subject since the late 1940s. By the year 2000, over three hundred scientists and professionals have lent their names as consultants to UFO organizations. Unfortunately, their involvement has had little impact on either their colleagues in the academic and scientific communities or the improvement of scientific research into the UFO and abduction phenomenon.

Serious UFO and abduction researchers are another matter. They have worked diligently to study the phenomenon. Because of a lack of standardized methodology, they are a contentious lot and generally wary of each other. Most carefully question one another's research and take little at face value, which has led to heated debates over cases, theories, and research methodology. From this great debate, researchers have forged methods and protocols that, while not creating consensus, have nevertheless greatly improved the quality of research and helped "flesh out" the phenomenon to a degree few could have guessed possible only a few years ago.

UFO and abduction researchers come from a variety of backgrounds. The contributors to this volume include an artist, a writer, a sociologist, a psychiatrist, a natural scientist, a folklorist, a neurobiologist, a historian, and two psychologists. Each author has conducted serious research into the subject and written extensively on it. Here, Stuart Appelle explores the role that UFO and abduction research has played in the academy. Don C. Donderi discusses the nature of evidence best suited for UFO research. Thomas E. Bullard delineates the relation of myth and legend to the UFO phenomenon, while David M. Jacobs, Budd Hopkins, and John E. Mack tackle the abduction phenomenon in its history, methodology, evidence, and possible meaning. Michael A. Persinger provides an alternative explanation for abductions based on neurology. Michael D. Swords examines the government's initial handling of the UFO phenomenon, and Jerome Clark discusses the early societal response to it on a popular level and the development of the extraterrestrial hypothesis. Ron Westrum analyzes the motivations and resources of a few of the major investigators of the phenomenon both pro and con.

The unifying context for all these researchers is the belief that the UFO and abduction phenomenon deserves the serious attention of scientists, scholars, intellectuals, and public officials. They all share the desire to rid the field of self-promoters, charlatans, and "knee-jerk" debunkers whose goals are antithetical to gaining an understanding of the phenomenon. They have all devoted a significant amount of time and energy to clarify issues, develop and analyze data, investigate cases, discover the etiology of current thought about the subject, and, ultimately, try to solve the UFO mystery.

The UFO and abduction phenomenon has been a part of public debate for over half a century, and there is every indication that the debate will continue. It is difficult to name another subject so quickly identifiable, so widely debated, so easily dismissed, and yet so little understood. This volume strives to encourage the scientific and intellectual communities to begin the process of understanding not only what the phenomenon is but also how the debates have developed over the years and shaped our attitudes toward it.

David M. Jacobs
Temple University

Chapter One

Ufology and Academia: The UFO Phenomenon as a Scholarly Discipline

Stuart Appelle

The growth and development of scholarly disciplines depend largely on their acceptance within the halls of academe. It is here that disciplines achieve the identity and respect that attract funding and draw future practitioners to the field. It is here that an infrastructure is created for the allocation of resources needed to advance and communicate knowledge. With the recognition of the academy comes professional organizations, refereed journals, annual conferences, and discipline-based texts. Without these sources of recognition and support, *avocations* fail to become scholarly *vocations*, and otherwise worthy fields of study fail to flourish.

For "scientific" disciplines, these issues are even more relevant. Since World War II, funding for basic science has increased dramatically,[1] with the bulk of those funds going to university-based researchers. And while research can thrive within industry or government, a field's imprimatur as a "science" is nearly always bestowed through its acceptance by university-affiliated academics.

For these reasons, all new academic areas of interest (conventional or not) strive for membership in the academy. But in this regard, the study of unidentified flying objects (i.e., "ufology") has had little success. To understand why, it is helpful to examine the impediments to any discipline's emergence, maintenance, and evolution, especially for disciplines that aspire to be considered scientific.

7

Among these obstacles are a need for clarity regarding the nature of the discipline, a pervasive resistance to interdisciplinary fields, and acceptance of the discipline's central tenets, hypotheses, and methodologies. In examining these issues, this chapter focuses exclusively on the work of academics. It does this for thematic clarity only, and neither rejects nor is unaware of the many contributions to ufology by professionals, scientists, and laypersons not affiliated with academic institutions.

Discipline Clarity and Interdisciplinarity

Academic disciplines represent collections of related knowledge specialties.[2] There is certainly no shortage of such specialties. Indeed, Crane and Small were able to identify over eighty-five hundred separate knowledge fields in existence by 1987.[3] In principle, then, ufology should be able to find its niche as a knowledge specialty within some established academic discipline. However, while hypotheses abound, little has been verified about UFOs' true nature. For this reason, the discipline to which ufology properly "belongs" (e.g., physics, psychology, sociology) remains unclear. By necessity, then, the study of UFOs requires an interdisciplinary approach.

This necessity creates a problem for ufology if it is to gain a foothold in academia. Jacobs has pointed out:

> When the nature of the UFO controversy is understood . . . and when the interdisciplinary nature of the phenomenon is grasped (no one knows to what discipline the subject belongs simply because not enough yet is known of the subject), a meaningful start can be made on a truly scientific study of the subject, which can then be approached as scientific subjects should be approached—without prejudice or emotional bias.[4]

The problem, however, is not simply one of recognizing ufology's interdisciplinary character. Such recognition creates its own dilemma for ufology. As discussed by Klein, "for much of the twentieth century, the surface structure of academic institutions has been dominated by disciplinarities."[5] Klein refers here to the traditional disciplines on which academic curricula are based and to the resistance to crossing the boundaries those disciplines impose. This influence has been characterized as so fundamental to the academy that it constitutes a "first principle" upon which academic institutions are structured.[6] It is a structure maintained not only by ideology but also by procedures and criteria for professional advancement and accountability.

The interdisciplinary nature of ufology is not unique. Indeed, Klein asserts that knowledge in general is becoming increasingly interdisciplinary.[7] This perception, as well as new interdisciplinary technologies, methodologies, and vehicles for professional communication, blends the boundaries between traditional disciplines and fosters an openness to both interdisciplinary curricula[8] and interdisciplinary research.[9] Notwithstanding, opposition to disciplinary boundary crossing persists at academic institutions, and scholarly activity remains largely cloistered within discrete academic units. This ongoing resistance to interdisciplinary structures represents a continuing obstacle to ufology's acceptance as a discrete area of scholarship. As a consequence, ufology can neither find an existing home in the established disciplines nor create a new one for itself.

Scientific Respectability

Independent of disciplinary issues, ufology has had considerable difficulty gaining recognition as a science. For a variety of reasons, it is viewed by many as a pseudoscience. For example, Edward O. Wilson cites ufology as a classic example of a pseudoscience.[10] Real sciences, he argues, are distinguished from the impostors by meeting the following five criteria: (1) repeatability (confirmation or disconfirmation of results by a series of independent investigations), (2) economy (the ability to yield "the largest amount of information with the least amount of effort"), (3) mensuration (measurement with universally accepted scales), (4) heuristics (the ability to advance discovery that bears upon original principles), and (5) consilience (consistency and convergence of explanations for related phenomena).

Students of ufology can reach their own conclusions about which, if any, of these criteria the field does not possess, but for Wilson, "ufology, sadly, possesses none."[11] More sadly for ufology's proponents, Wilson's perception is extant among academics. Consider the following statement from an article published in the *Chronicle of Higher Education,* academia's premier news periodical, in which Ferris laments some of the consequences of popularizing science for the general public: "We should keep in mind . . . how little progress scientists have made in enlightening the citizenry, nearly half of whom think that their planet is a UFO landing site."[12]

Statements such as these are common, and they indicate that ufology is not simply *rejected* as a legitimate discipline; for many, it is categorically *dismissed*. This is a critical difference. Rejection suggests a conclusion based on close examination and careful reflection. Dismissal is an a priori judgment that close examination is not warranted.

This attitude of dismissal is self-perpetuating. A scientist's initial interest in a phenomenon is typically acquired not by personal familiarity but by exposure to the works of knowledgeable colleagues. In the absence of such works, the attention of the uninitiated is much less likely to be gained.

The problem is exacerbated in another way. Because so few scientists have chosen to examine ufology firsthand, much of the research in the field has had to be conducted by lay individuals who lack scientific degrees or appropriate technical training. To the scientific community—which defines itself not only by its methods but also by the credentials of its members—this sends an implicit message that such activity might put one's professional advancement at risk. As a consequence, the field continues to be ignored by those whose attention it needs most.

Another obstacle to the acceptance of ufology as a science is that one of its central hypotheses (e.g., that UFOs are extraterrestrial craft) is given little credence in the scientific community. Carl Sagan (professor of astronomy and director of planetary studies at Cornell University) and Thornton Page (professor of astronomy at Wesleyan University) noted that "the *public* interest in the subject, but not the *scientific* interest, derives from the idea that unidentified flying objects are space vehicles sent to the earth from elsewhere in the universe."[13] This may seem paradoxical, given that most scientists regard the probability of intelligent life on other planets as exceedingly high. However, scientists reject the notion that extraterrestrials could accomplish interplanetary flight or, if they could come here, that extraterrestrials would choose to avoid overt contact with the earth's inhabitants. Although logical and empirical arguments can be advanced to counter such reasoning,[14] the summary dismissal of this idea, even as just a hypothesis worth testing, continues to prevail. No field will be recognized as a science if its central tenets and hypotheses are not considered plausible.

An additional problem is that the database in ufology is primarily one of UFO reports (sightings). That is, testimony rather than material evidence represents the foundation of the field. This largely precludes repeatable, controlled experimental observation, the kind of methodology that represents the hallmark of scientific investigation. Although this situation is not without precedent in some established sciences (e.g., in regard to many aspects of astronomy), the elusive and fleeting nature of ufological observations makes the gathering of data particularly problematic. Physical evidence does exist (photographs, radar traces, soil and plant effects, physiological effects on witnesses), but most scientists either are unaware of this evidence or regard it as insufficiently probative.

The lack of acceptable hypotheses, methodologies, and credentialed researchers, along with the aforementioned issues of discipline identity, converge as a serious impediment to the acceptance of ufology by the scientific and academic communities. In turn, this lack of acceptance inhibits the development of other discipline-supporting structures. For example:

1. There is only one peer-reviewed journal (the *Journal of UFO Studies*) dedicated to the subject of ufology.
2. There are no professional societies for ufology in which membership or participation reflects upon the credentials of its members. Indeed, what credentials would be appropriate for such affiliation have not been established. There are a number of organizations that serve the interests of both scholars and interested laypersons (e.g., the Mutual UFO Network [MUFON], the Society for Scientific Exploration [SSE], and the J. Allen Hynek Center for UFO Studies [CUFOS], but none of these are true professional organizations. The Committee for Scientific Investigation of Claims of the Paranormal (CSICOP) is a skeptics group composed of many academics (its founder is a philosopher at the State University of New York at Buf-

falo), but, again, membership does not require an academic affiliation.
3. There are no annual professional meetings in ufology. MUFON has an annual convention, but this attracts a primarily lay audience. SSE's annual meetings often include individual papers on ufology, but not sessions routinely dedicated to the subject.
4. There exist no textbooks in the field (a number of scholarly books have been written on the subject, but none serves as an introductory text to the discipline). Indeed, academic presses have had little interest in publishing any books dealing with ufology (the present volume is a welcome exception).
5. Traditional sources of funding are almost nonexistent for UFO research. Although funding from private sources is available (e.g., the Fund for UFO Research), the moneys available are typically very modest, and the peer review process is rarely carried out by academics.

Scholars hoping to change this situation can do so only by slowly chipping away at these attitudinal and situational barriers through contributions of their own. And this requires a perseverance in the face of institutional opposition that more mainstream scholars need not face. Nevertheless, the field of ufology has attracted just such individuals throughout its half century of existence.

The Invisible College

J. Allen Hynek, an astronomer at Ohio State University's McMillin Observatory, and later director of the Lindheimer Astronomical Research Center at Northwestern University, served as the chief scientific consultant and spokesperson for the U.S. Air Force's official investigation of UFOs from 1948 to 1969. Although as air force spokesperson he often generated dismissive explanations for UFO reports, he later became the main scientific advocate for ufology as a legitimate scholarly pursuit. Commenting on the involvement of other academics, Hynek used an analogy with the "Invisible College of London and Oxford," an informal group of scholars whose meetings (in 1645) preceded the founding of the Royal Society of London for the Promotion of Natural Knowledge. The membership of the

Invisible College was made up of followers of Sir Francis Bacon, an advocate of data-driven scientific inquiry, rather than the prevailing science dictated by the dogma of established authority. Hynek suggested that ufologists, like the members of the Invisible College before them, have "to sneak, so to speak, through back alleys"[15] to pursue their interest in a subject outside the scientific establishment:

> I have positive evidence from personal correspondence and conversations with scientists that their interest is increasing but that it is still, in most cases, anonymous. There is truly a growing "Invisible College" of scientifically and technically trained persons who are intrigued by the UFO phenomenon and who, if provided with opportunity, time, and facilities, are most willing to undertake its serious study. They represent an international group ready to accept the challenge of the UFO.[16]

Although there is little evidence that the Invisible College has grown substantially in the fifteen years since Hynek's observations, there is ample evidence that it does continue to exist. This is reflected by the participation of academics in several major scholarly events, and by the independent contributions of academics across a variety of disciplines.

Major Academic Events in Ufology

Perhaps the first major involvement of academics in analyzing the data from UFO sightings was the Robertson Panel. This group, convened in January 1953, was assembled by the U.S. Air Force and the Central Intelligence Agency (CIA) in response to an alarming increase in the number of sighting reports. The panel included a number of academics: H. P. Robertson (California Institute of Technology), Luis Alvarez (a future Nobel laureate from the University of California, Berkeley), Lloyd Berkner (a physicist formerly from MIT), and Thornton Page (at that time an astrophysicist at Johns Hopkins University). The panel spent twelve hours examining six years' worth of data. Although the Robertson Panel was not an academic meeting per se, these individuals set the tone for much of what followed in academic circles, concluding that most sightings had an apparent conventional explanation and that the rest were not worth the effort to investigate.[17]

The University of Colorado Study
(The "Condon Report")

Perhaps the best-known (and most notorious) involvement of academia with the UFO phenomenon was the Scientific Study of Unidentified Flying Objects, an air force–commissioned project carried out under the direction of Edward U. Condon, a professor of physics and astrophysics at the University of Colorado.[18] Condon was a prominent researcher and a former director of the National Bureau of Standards who served on numerous government projects, including the atomic bomb program as district head at the Los Alamos Manhattan Project. Although Condon's staff on the study was composed primarily of faculty from the University of Colorado, there were also representatives from the University of Wyoming, the University of Arizona, the University of Chicago, and the Stevens Institute of Technology. This group represented the disciplines of psychology, astronomy, astrophysics, physical chemistry, meteorology, engineering, psychiatry, and astrogeophysics.

William K. Hartmann, a professor of astronomy at the University of Arizona's Lunar and Planetary Laboratory, carried out an analysis of photographic evidence. Although the vast majority of photographs could be attributed to mundane events, about 2 percent of the photographic cases remained unidentified. Hartmann concluded that none of the unidentifieds were conclusive proof of extraterrestrial activity, but they were "not inconsistent with the hypothesis that unknown and extraordinary aircraft have penetrated the airspace of the United States."[19]

Physical evidence (reputed landing traces, material artifacts, electromagnetic disturbances, radiation, and electrical malfunctions or power interruptions) was examined by Roy Craig, a professor of physical sciences in the Division of Integrated Studies at the University of Colorado. Craig was generally unimpressed with the physical evidence examined by the project, except for alleged malfunction of automobile motors. He noted, "The claim [of vehicular interference] is frequently made, sometimes in reports, which are impressive because they involve multiple independent witnesses. Witnesses seem certain that the function of their cars was affected by the unidentified object, which sometimes reportedly was not seen until after the malfunction was noted. No satisfactory explanation for such effects, if indeed they occurred, is apparent."[20]

Franklin E. Roach, a member of the Astrogeophysics Department at the University of Colorado, examined observations made by U.S. astronauts, a group whose "training and perspicacity . . . put their reports of sightings in the highest category of credibility." Roach highlighted three such sightings he felt were "a challenge to the analyst" and for which "we shall have to find a rational explanation or, alternatively, keep it on our list of unidentifieds."[21]

Despite these statements from its own academic staff (and the fact that nearly one-third of its analyzed case studies remained "unidentified"), the official conclusion of the Condon Report was that "further extensive study of UFOs probably cannot be justified in the expectation that science will be advanced thereby. . . . UFO phenomena do not offer a fruitful field in which to look for major scientific discoveries."[22] This obvious disconnect between the findings and conclusions of the Condon Report remains a source of controversy, and dissenting opinion has come not only from independent readers of the report[23] but also from its participating academic staff.[24]

AAAS Symposium

The controversy over the Condon Report had its impact on a second major event. The American Association for the Advancement of Science (AAAS) sponsored a symposium on UFOs in Boston during December 1969. Originally the symposium had been planned for the year before, but it was postponed so the Condon Report could be available to its participants. Presenters at the symposium included faculty from the University of California at Los Angeles (UCLA), Cornell, Harvard, the University of Arizona, Northwestern University, the Massachusetts Institute of Technology (MIT), Wesleyan, and the University of Hawaii and represented the disciplines of psychology, medicine, physics, astronomy, and sociology. Carl Sagan and Thornton Page, editors of the book based on these proceedings, note

that the study of UFOs by scientists is important, if only to aid in a
public understanding and acceptance of science:

> All of us who teach at colleges and universities are aware of a
> drift away from science. Some of the sensitive, intelligent, and
> concerned young people are finding science increasingly less
> attractive and less relevant to their problems. . . . We all agree
> that this drift is deplorable. It must be due in part to their mis-
> understanding of what science is about. . . . There seems to us to
> be an . . . important area which has not been adequately stressed,
> namely, the application of scientific thinking to problems of
> human interest.[25]

Sagan and Page suggest that the subject of UFOs is certainly one
of these topics, and that "it seems to be unprofitable [for science] to
ignore it."[26] In the same spirit, Page provided an overview of some
selected UFO cases and a defense of ufology as an opportunity to
"take advantage of public interest in UFOs to correct public miscon-
ceptions about science."[27]

William Hartmann and Franklin Roach, two participants in the
Condon project, provided perspectives (respectively) on the history
of UFOs and astronomers' views about them. J. Allen Hynek, an
astronomer who made his own significant contribution to the history of ufology, described his twenty-one years of studying UFO
reports for the U.S. Air Force's official UFO investigation. In doing
so, Hynek set forth the fundamental arguments for interest, importance, and open-mindedness that academic ufologists have continued to champion:

> Reports of UFO observations remain after we delete the pro-
> nouncements of crackpots, visionaries, religious fanatics, and
> so forth. A large number of UFO reports are readily identifiable
> by trained investigators as misperception of known objects and
> events. A small residue of UFO reports are [sic] not so identifi-
> able. . . . They are made by competent, responsible, psychologi-
> cally normal people—in short, credible witnesses. These reports
> contain descriptive terms, which collectively do not specify any
> known physical event, object, or process. And, furthermore, they
> resist translation into terms that do apply to known physical

and/or psychological events, objects, and processes. . . . Although I know of no hypothesis that adequately covers the mounting evidence, this should not and must not deter us from [being] curious, capable of being astonished, and eager to find out.[28]

Empirical support for Hynek's position was provided by James E. McDonald, a professor of atmospheric sciences and senior physicist with the Institute for Atmospheric Sciences at the University of Arizona. Echoing Hynek's complaint of academic neglect, McDonald titled his presentation "Science in Default" and presented an unapologetic condemnation of the scientific community's failure to give the subject proper attention:

No scientifically adequate investigation of the UFO problem has been carried out during the entire twenty-two-year period between the first extensive wave of sightings of unidentified aerial objects in the summer of 1947 and the convening of this symposium. Despite continued public interest and frequent expression of public concern, only quite superficial examinations of the steadily growing body of unexplained UFO reports from credible witnesses have been conducted in this country and abroad. . . . I believe science is in default for having failed to mount any truly adequate studies of this problem.[29]

McDonald was equally critical of the Condon Report, which he felt did not provide "anything superior to the generally casual and often incompetent level of case analysis that marked [the official air force investigation's] handling of the UFO problem."[30]

Not all participants agreed with Hynek and McDonald's assessment of ufology's importance. For example, Sagan argued that an examination of the UFO problem was not "the most efficient method" to search for extraterrestrial intelligence (an activity which, in contrast, he deemed "exceedingly important [for] both science and society").[31] Robert M. L. Baker, a lecturer at the School of Engineering and Applied Sciences, UCLA, found much of interest in photographic evidence, although not necessarily consistent with the traditional concept of a "UFO." The data, he felt, provide "substantial evidence to support the claim that an unexplained phenomenon . . . is present in the environs of the earth, but that it may not be 'flying,' may not always be 'unidentified' and may not even take the form of substantive 'objects.'" Accordingly, Baker argued that "experiments should be devised, and study programs should be initiated" to investigate these anomalies, but that it was unnecessary to justify this in terms of presuppositions about extraterrestrial intelligence.[32]

Of the sixteen conference participants, only Donald H. Menzel (professor of practical astronomy and professor of astrophysics at Harvard University) was openly hostile to ufology, presenting his long-established dismissal of the UFO phenomenon as "a modern myth." Other participants presented valuable perspectives on matters related to the study of UFOs. Robert L. Hall, a professor of sociology at the University of Illinois at Chicago, discussed sociological perspectives of UFO reports. In particular, Hall emphasized the importance of the UFO phenomenon, regardless of its cause:

> The very strength of our resistance to the evidence on UFOs suggests . . . that there is clearly a phenomenon of surpassing importance here. It is going to force some of us to make some fundamental changes in our knowledge and this is a good definition of scientific importance. The [question is] who has to change. . . . Do the physical scientists have to accept the existence of such a puzzling and anomalous physical object . . . ? Or do the behavioral scientists have to accept the puzzling and anomalous fact that hundreds of intelligent, responsible witnesses can continue to be wrong for so many years?[33]

Rounding out the discussion, Douglass R. Price-Williams (professor of psychology, UCLA) and Philip Morrison (professor of physics, MIT) discussed methodological problems in studying UFO reports; Lester Grinspoon and Alan D. Persky (both of the Harvard Medical School) discussed UFO reports from the perspective of psychoanalytic theory; and Frank D. Drake (professor of astronomy, Cornell University) discussed the limitations and frailties of human perception.

Although the conference did little to solve or soften the UFO controversy, it had at least one positive outcome. Acknowledging the "potential value" of the air force's records on UFOs, the conference presenters, along with the president of the AAAS (the conference sponsor) joined in requesting that the air force files be preserved, declassified, and made accessible to physical and behavioral scientists. This request reinforced the philosophy of science as a system of open and careful inquiry, and for ufology as a legitimate area of scholarship.

Abduction Study Conference at MIT

The extraterrestrial hypothesis for UFOs has led to an even more controversial hypothesis, namely, that the occupants of the UFOs are engaged in the practice of kidnapping earthlings for their own unearthly purposes. As implausible as such an idea may seem at first analysis, the "alien abduction experience" is seen by those who believe in the extraterrestrial origin of UFOs as a logical explanation for why such travelers would choose to carry out their visitations covertly.

In response to literally thousands of alien abduction accounts, an Abduction Study Conference was held at MIT in June 1992. The proceedings of the conference have been published as a nearly seven-hundred-page volume of divergent opinion on what has emerged as one of ufology's most talked about phenomena.[34] The conference featured presentations by over fifty participants, including mental health practitioners in private practice, abduction experience investigators, and academics from a wide range of disciplines and institutions.

Among the academics contributing case studies or discussions of methodology were Stuart Appelle (professor of psychology, State University of New York, College at Brockport); James Harder (professor of mechanical engineering and civil engineering, University of California, Berkeley); and David Jacobs (professor of history, Temple University). In the physical sciences, David E. Pritchard (professor of physics, MIT) described a preliminary investigation of a reputed "implant" obtained from an abduction experiencer; the results were consistent with a terrestrial biological origin. Paul Horowitz (professor of physics, Harvard University) and Michael D. Papagiannis (professor of physics, Boston University) discussed their involvement in the search for extraterrestrial intelligence by radio telescope and their reasons for skepticism regarding the current presence of alien life-forms on earth.

In the behavioral and social sciences, papers on the psychology of the abduction experience were presented by John Mack (professor of psychiatry, Harvard Medical School); Susan Powers (Woodstock Academy); Norman Don (a neuropsychologist in the Department of Psychiatry at the University of Illinois at Chicago); Don Donderi (professor of psychology, McGill University); and Maralyn Teare (clinical instructor of psychiatry, University of Southern California School of Medicine). Sociological perspectives were addressed by Ron Westrum (Eastern Michigan University); Mark Rodeghier (University of Illinois at Chicago); and Robert Hall (University of Illinois at Chicago). Gerald Eichhoefer (professor of computer studies and philosophy, William Jewell College) and J. Gordon Melton (Department of Religious Studies, University of California, Santa Barbara) discussed theological issues related to the abduction experience, while Thomas E. Bullard (Indiana University) and David Hufford (Pennsylvania State College of Medicine) presented papers on folkloric aspects of the phenomenon.

In all, the conference provided an unusually rich variety of evidence and opinion, an opportunity for academics and other professionals to openly discuss their observations and conclusions, and an occasion for considerable attention from the media.[35] It also led to development of an ethics code for investigators and mental health practitioners as a guide for research and therapy with abduction experiencers.[36] This document complements those in the established professional disciplines for other work with human subjects and patients.

Physical Science Review Panel

Although the abduction phenomenon may provide a theoretical rationale for surreptitious UFO activity, it is based almost exclusively on testimony. The evidence for UFO sightings themselves is also largely testimonial, but here physical evidence in support of such reports has been much more forthcoming. Recognizing the evidential limitations of testimony alone, a panel was convened in the fall of 1997 to focus exclusively on physical evidence of UFOs. Through the efforts of Project Director Peter Sturrock (Center for Space Science and Astrophysics, Stanford University), the meeting was organized under the aegis of the Society for Scientific Exploration, an organization dedicated to meaningful examination of scientific anomalies. The steering committee responsible for planning this workshop included (in addition to a number of scientists affiliated with research, rather than academic, facilities), Robert Jahn (professor of aerospace engineering, Princeton University), David E. Pritchard (professor of physics, MIT), Charles R. Tolbert (professor of astronomy, University of Virginia), and Yervant Terzian (Department of Astronomy, Cornell University).

Physical evidence was provided by eight experienced investigators of the UFO phenomenon in the categories of photographic and video evidence, aircraft equipment anomalies, radar evidence, automobile engine anomalies, physical injury to witnesses, spectroscopic data, ground traces, and effects on vegetation. The group of academics asked to study this evidence included Von Eshleman (Emeritus Professor of Electrical Engineering, Stanford University), J. R. Jokopii and H. J. Melosh (professors of planetary sciences and astronomy, University of Arizona), James J. Papike (head of the Institute of Meteoritics and professor of earth and planetary sciences, University of New Mexico), and Bernard Veyret (Bioelectromagnetics Laboratory, University of Bordeaux).

Although the panel found no evidence to convince its members that unknown physical processes or extraterrestrial intelligence was involved, it did conclude (1) that the UFO problem is not simple, nor is any simple explanation likely to be universally applicable; (2) that unexplained observations provide learning opportunities for science; (3) that some form of "formal, regular contact" between the UFO and physical scientist communities could be productive; and (4) that institutional support for research in ufology should be provided.[37] These conclusions, like those that emerged from the earlier AAAS symposium, were at odds with the conclusion of the Condon Report that the scientific study of UFOs is unjustified.

Contemporary Ufology in Academia: Theoretical and Empirical Contributions Across the Disciplines

Beyond these organized activities, academics working independently have made numerous scholarly contributions to the study of UFOs. The Invisible College to which J. Allen Hynek referred has remained active throughout the phenomenon's fifty-year history and continues to be active today. Reflecting the field's interdisciplinary character, the Invisible College's faculty (a number of whom, not surprisingly, are contributors to the present volume) represent a wide range of disciplines and have treated the subject of UFOs from a variety of perspectives. Certainly, not all of these scholars regard themselves as "ufologists." The subject in general may not reflect their primary areas of interest and, indeed, does not represent the traditional academic disciplines with which they identify (as has been argued, academia has yet to accept ufology as a discipline). Regardless, their contributions are many. A sample of contemporary work is presented in the following (this sample aims to be representative rather than comprehensive).

The Natural Sciences

Astronomy/Astrophysics. Perhaps the best-known academic commentator on UFOs was the late Carl Sagan, who wrote frequently on what he perceived as logical and empirical fallacies regarding UFOs and the abduction experience.[38] Sagan rejected an extraterrestrial explanation for the phenomenon but felt there were both empirical and pedagogical benefits to examining UFO reports and that the subject was, therefore, a legitimate topic for study.

The attitudes of astronomers in general were studied by Peter Sturrock (Stanford University Center for Space Science and Astrophysics), who polled over one thousand members of the American Astronomical Society to determine their views on possible causes of UFO reports. Sturrock's survey suggested that the typical member of this society shared views not dissimilar from Sagan's. In summary, Sturrock reports that "scientists have thoughts and views but no answers concerning the UFO problem [and] although there is no consensus, more scientists are of the opinion that the problem certainly or probably deserves scientific study than are of the opinion that it certainly or probably does not."[39] Mark Rodeghier (a sociologist at the University of Illinois at Chicago) obtained similar findings from a group of respondents representing a much wider range of academic disciplines. Presumably this attitude accounts for the widespread (albeit limited) involvement of the Invisible College in matters ufological.

Botany. Physical evidence sometimes includes reports of effects to the fauna or flora in the immediate vicinity of the reported UFO. These may take the form of effects on the human observers, nearby animals, or plants and soil. Michel Bounias, a botanist at the University of Avignon (France), has applied the technique of biochemical traumatology to investigate a significant sighting case that left anomalous ground traces associated with the reported object's landing.[40]

The case in question involves a 1981 report of an anomalous object observed outside the village of Trans-en-Provence, France. The reported landing occurred at a site where two concentric circles, 2.5 to 3 meters in diameter, were left on the ground. Based on his analysis of plant samples taken from within and outside this area, Bounias concludes that "something unusual did occur that might be consistent . . . with an electromagnetic source of stress"[41] and that the "influence of the unidentified source" of these anomalous findings "decreased with increasing distance from the epicenter" of the ground trace.[42]

Physics. Edward Zeller and Gisela Dreschoff, physicists at the Radiation Physics Laboratory, Space Technology Center, University of Kansas, conducted an analysis of UFO report frequency as a function of radiation in the earth's atmosphere.[43] The authors found a positive correlation between the frequency of UFO reports and particle radiation in the form of galactic cosmic rays, whereas there was little relationship between sightings and solar radiation. Although the implications of these findings are not clear, they do demonstrate the kind of meaningful analysis that physicists can bring to bear on the UFO phenomenon.

David Pritchard, a professor of physics at MIT and one of the chief organizers of the Abduction Study Conference at MIT, has used his expertise to examine a reputed "alien implant." The object came from an abduction experiencer who reported it had spontaneously dislodged after having been placed within him at an early age by his alien captors. Using the sophisticated technology available in his laboratory (scanning electron microscopy, Auger electron analysis of an object's elemental composition, secondary ion mass spectroscopy), Pritchard was able to demonstrate that the object in question had properties consistent with that of terrestrial organic matter. Pritchard also provided a valuable theoretical commentary on the limitations of physics in settling questions regarding the alien origin of any reputed artifact, the need to demonstrate such an origin through an object's function rather than its composition, and the burdens of doing research in this field. Referring to the "amazing amount of time and money" involved, Pritchard observed:

> Properly analyzing an artifact like this demands a multidisciplinary group with chemists, biologists, and material scientists of various sub-specialties as well as several experts on each of the various machines and techniques used in the analysis. . . . However, the fact that abduction-related implants are not on the mainline scientific agenda means that [one] can't possibly get enough support and help to do an analysis of the requisite quality.[44]

Pritchard's personal observation is a snapshot of the obstacles academics face when studying the UFO phenomenon. His work in the area, however, is testimony that the Invisible College continues to contribute in spite of these obstacles.

Another physicist, Charles B. Moore (Professor Emeritus of Atmospheric Physics at the New Mexico Institute of Mining and Technology) examined one explanation for the notorious report of a crashed UFO at Roswell, New Mexico. Moore had been project engineer for research and development related to Project Mogul, a classified project involving weather balloons to monitor atmospheric effects related to nuclear testing. In this capacity, Moore gained considerable knowledge about the secret project later to be identified by the U.S. Air Force as an explanation for the Roswell incident. Using his direct personal experience, Moore provided considerable background information for a book about this incident.[45]

Jack Kasher, a professor of physics at the University of Nebraska at Omaha, has carried out an extensive analysis of anomalous images appearing on TV camera footage taken from the space shuttle *Discovery*.[46] These images, suggestive of glowing objects within the vicinity of the shuttle, have been explained by NASA as "orbiter-generated debris illuminated by the Sun against a dark background." Specifically, Kress suggested that these particles were "ice dislodged from the surface of the spacecraft [either from] water dumps [or] oxygen ice from residual liquid oxygen."[47] Based on a frame-by-frame examination of the videotape and on data from shuttle structural and performance characteristics, Kasher presented five mathematical proofs that demonstrate the ice particle explanation is not tenable. He suggested that the images represent physical evidence of UFO activity in earth's near orbit.

As noted earlier by the Physical Science Review Panel, scientists need physical evidence if they are to make contributions in their fields. The preceding examples indicate that such evidence does exist and that, by examining it, physical scientists can make meaningful contributions to the knowledge base in ufology.

Behavioral and Social Sciences

Cultural Anthropology. Charles Ziegler and Benson Saler, cultural anthropologists at Brandeis University, have looked at the Roswell case from the perspective of their discipline. They argue that Roswell "can be best understood as an example of a modern myth" and, accordingly, in terms of the theories and concepts of cultural anthropology.[48] In the process, they make some valuable observations about the evolution of Roswell accounts by witnesses and investigators, its impact on belief systems, the role of the media in shaping those beliefs, and relationships between UFO lore and folklore.

Another researcher with a background in folklore studies is Thomas E. Bullard, of Indiana University. Bullard's dissertation, "Mysteries in the Eyes of the Beholder," examined the UFO phenomenon from a folkloric perspective. Extending this perspective to the abduction phenomenon, he writes:

> The question before us is not whether UFOs are folklore. They certainly are, and just as certainly resemble other folklore in form and function. The question of greater concern must be what else are UFOs, if anything. The coherency of abduction reports stands out as the most unequivocal piece of evidence that folklore scholarship contributes to the UFO mystery. What fails to act like a fictitious or well-circulated narrative is probably not altogether fictitious or well circulated. Something more than familiar folkloric processes seems responsible for these reports.[49]

Psychology. The UFO phenomenon is characterized by reports of unusual observations, that is, by behavior and perception. Because the study of behavior and perception is a primary focus of academic psychology, one might expect that psychologists would be contributing widely to the study of UFO reports. However, they have made relatively few contributions of this kind, perhaps because psychologists' special understanding of anomalous experience and behavior leads them to have especially low expectations that new knowledge will emerge from its study.

One exception to this rule is Michael A. Persinger, a professor at Laurentian University, who has published extensively on a neuropsychological basis to UFO reports. One theory he has promoted suggests that tectonic strains in the earth's crust (earthquakes and other stresses) generate anomalous lights that are mistaken as UFOs.[50] Moreover, Persinger argues that tectonic stresses may generate electromagnetic fields that could cause electrical instability in the human brain. This, in turn, could result in anomalous perceptions interpreted by the affected individual as a UFO or even an abduction experience.

The abduction experience, unlike UFO sightings themselves, has received a good deal of attention from the psychological community. For example, Nicholas Spanos (Carleton University) used an extensive battery of psychological tests to study the characteristics of persons reporting close encounters with UFOs or aliens. He and his colleagues found "no support whatsoever for the hypothesis that UFO reporters are psychologically disturbed [and] the onus is on those who favor the psychopathology hypothesis to provide support for it."[51]

Alternatively, Robert Baker, a psychologist at the University of Kentucky, has attributed abduction experiences to a variety of anomalous psychological factors, including sleep paralysis, hypnogogic hallucinations, and the effects of hypnotic suggestion.[52] Kenneth Ring (University of Connecticut) looked for personality factors associated with the phenomenon and found unusual personality characteristics in the absence of pathology. Comparing individuals with close encounters to those reporting near-death experiences, Ring found many similarities between these two populations. He interprets this fact as suggesting a common propensity for such experiences across these two groups.[53] These and many other psychological explanations for the abduction experience have been reviewed by Appelle, who concludes that "no theory yet enjoys enough empirical support to be accepted as a general explanation."[54]

In addition to these psychologists, a number of investigators with a background in psychiatry (e.g., John Mack, Department of Psychiatry, Harvard Medical School; David Gotlib, Department of Psychiatry, Johns Hopkins University Hospital) have studied abduction experiencers from a clinical perspective.[55] These writers have provided insight into treatment for the emotional and behavioral sequelae of the abduction experience. One of the most extensive analyses of UFO reports from a psychoanalytical perspective was done by Carl Jung, one of the founders of psychoanalytical theory.[56]

Sociology. UFOs influence not only their observers but also society in general and the community of researchers who study the phenomenon. Charles F. Emmons (Department of Sociology, Gettysburg College) explores the reaction of government, academia, and the media to the study of UFOs, and the relationship between established science and ufology.[57] His treatment of ufology, from the viewpoint of the sociology of science, provides insight into the dynamics of social influence when the "establishment" reacts to a phenomenon outside of establishment science (what Emmons calls "deviant" science).

Australian sociologist Robert E. Bartholomew (James Cook University) has coauthored a book with psychologist George Howard (University of Notre Dame) in which they examine UFO reports throughout history, especially UFO waves or "flaps" (periods of intensified sightings). The authors evaluate these reports from the perspective of the sociological influences of the time, and how those influences can affect human thought, symbolism, and fantasy.[58]

Other sociologists have used that discipline's survey methodologies as a means of learning more about the UFO phenomenon. Ron Westrum (Department of Sociology, Eastern Michigan University) collaborated on the development of a Roper poll designed to assess the prevalence of abduction experiences among the American population.[59] The authors concluded that the phenomenon is extremely widespread, involving perhaps millions of Americans. Alternatively, sociologists Robert Hall and Mark Rodeghier criticized the survey's methodology and argued that no meaningful interpretation regarding abduction experience prevalence could be derived from the data.[60]

Humanities

History. The UFO phenomenon has been of continuing interest to academic historians. David Jacobs, a professor in the Department of History at Temple University, has provided one of the most comprehensive volumes on early UFO history.[61] More recently, he has changed the direction of his attention from the sightings of UFOs to reports of alien abductions.[62] Although his interpretation of these reports is controversial, his historian's perspective has provided perhaps the most detailed description and taxonomy of abduction report content. Also, according to Jacobs, he offers one of the few (perhaps the only) regular curricular courses on the subject in the United States. Jacobs's course represents another connection between ufology and academia.

One of the most prolific contributors to the ufology literature is Michael Swords, a science historian by training and a professor in the Department of Science Studies at Western Michigan University. Swords's careful examination of historical records has provided important insight into such events as the Condon Report, the U.S. Air Force's Project Sign, and the influence of Donald Keyhoe, one of ufology's earliest popularizers, on Pentagon policy.[63]

Philosophy. Michael E. Zimmerman's interest in ufology focuses on the alien abduction phenomenon. Zimmerman, a professor of philosophy at Tulane University, asks "why this phenomenon is not examined more closely by those in a position to provide a satisfactory explanation of it." To answer that question, he considers the abduction experience as an example of "forbidden knowledge of hidden events"—events that "conflict so sharply with accepted views about 'reality' that the event can scarcely be brought up in polite society, much less made an object for publicly funded research."[64] Zimmerman analyzes this attitude in terms of scientists' lack of interest in the phenomenon, their failure to recognize the phenomenon as something new, their fear that overt interest in the phenomenon would be an obstacle to career advancement, or their avoidance of phenomena that might require a drastic revision of what is accepted as "truth" and "reality." Although answering neither these questions nor the more fundamental one about the phenomenon's true nature, Zimmerman concludes that the abduction experience is "a possible challenge to perceived received views about the nature of 'experience' and 'consciousness' as well as about humanity's place in the cosmos," and he "encourage[s] open minded debate about possible explanations for this unusual phenomenon."[65]

Political Science. John C. Hickman, a professor in the Department of Political Science at Berry College, conducted an analysis of news coverage of UFOs. Looking at coverage in the *New York Times* during the period 1947–95, Hickman and his colleagues examined the hypothesis that UFO news coverage is biased. Using a content analysis of news events reported in the *New York Times*, the authors found that news reports that simply describe a sighting express minimal negative or skeptical quality. However, pejorative and critical comments increase as the article becomes larger and more narrative, a trend that has become more pronounced across the decades of UFO coverage. In general, the news coverage examined by these researchers suggested a "general pattern of profound skepticism on the part of the press."[66]

In addition to finding support for the hypothesis of bias, Hickman and colleagues comment on the implications of this situation: "If news coverage decisions made by elite newspapers like the *New York Times* matter, it is because they affect elite opinion, general public opinion, and the news coverage decisions of [other] broadcast media."[67] It might also be added that such biased coverage influences the opinion of academics as well, including their decisions to pursue or avoid their own scholarly study of the reported phenomena.

Jodi Dean (Department of Political Science, Hobart and William Smith Colleges) has studied the alien motif and its influence on and by social, technological, and political structures in our culture. For Dean, ufology is a political issue "because it is stigmatized. To claim to have seen a UFO, to have been abducted by aliens, or even to believe those who say they have is a political act. It may not be a very big or revolutionary political act but it contests the status quo."[68] From this perspective, Dean argues that "the aliens infiltrating American popular cultures provide icons through which to access the new conditions of democratic politics at the millennium."[69] Her analysis is an important contribution to political theory and to ufology, helping explain how the concepts of UFOs and aliens relate to contemporary democratic politics.

Conclusion

Much of the work in ufology (in particular the investigation of sight-ing reports) is conducted by lay investigators whose credentials and affiliations remain well outside the halls of academe. Although some of this activity is amateurish and embarrassing, a good deal of it remains valid and important, perhaps even critical to the work of those better connected to the academic community. Similarly, there have been many contributions to ufology from credentialed research-ers affiliated with industrial, governmental, military, or medical es-tablishments. This chapter has not addressed these contributions, not because they lack value but because if ufology is to gain a foot-hold in academia, it must be embraced by academics themselves.

This will be difficult to accomplish given the obstacles in its path. Nevertheless, there are reasons for optimism. Ufology's most con-troversial hypothesis (that UFOs are spacecraft) is based on a premise (the existence of extraterrestrial intelligence) that has become increas-ingly more accepted in both academic and lay communities. In addi-tion, theoretical solutions to the technological problems associated with interstellar travel continue to be advanced. Similarly, the ob-stacles to interdisciplinary fields are diminishing, both in terms of the ever-increasing interdisciplinary nature of knowledge itself and in regard to "political" pressures arising out of a rethinking of tra-ditional approaches to higher education.

But perhaps the most meaningful reason for optimism is the persistent activity of the Invisible College. Its contributions have created an interdisciplinary field of scholarship in the absence of formal recognition. In time, as these scholars continue to develop its database, test its theories, and perfect its methodologies, ufology may indeed become accepted as a recognized field of knowledge, a field respected by academics for addressing issues acknowledged to be interesting, important, and mysterious.

Chapter Two

Limited Access: Six Natural Scientists and the UFO Phenomenon

Ron Westrum

In principle, science allows the systematic study of anything. Just apply the "scientific method," and the results are objective. Following this principle, one might almost imagine that science could have, in the phrase of two martial arts experts, a "mind like the moon," which shines down equally on everything.[1] A person who believes this image of science will find it difficult to understand the way scientists—pro and con—have approached UFOs. And this model of "dispassionate curiosity" has little to do either with scientists' approaches to UFOs or in fact with scientists' behavior in most areas of endeavor.

Science in the making is dynamic. Science may be objective in the long run, but in the short run scientists are *oriented*. This is true of the routine practitioners, but even more so of those who push scientific progress. Scientists can be compulsive searchers or passionate entrepreneurs, extending their theories and their research as far as their physical and social resources will take them.[2] They can also be remarkably rigid, protecting their theories and results against new knowledge.[3] Researchers with different styles of work and varying opinions war unceasingly with each other.[4] Rebels challenge orthodoxy only to establish new orthodoxies, which in turn are challenged by new rebels.[5] Institutions compete for funds and for top minds, as the top minds in turn seek to make key discoveries and gain fame, jobs, and money.

31

This dynamic quality is seen particularly in those changes of framework Thomas Kuhn has called *paradigm shifts*, in which one mode of thought is replaced or challenged by another. During critical periods, when all is in flux, science seems anything but dispassionate or objective. Emotion, invective, and overt competition rule the day. The disembodied image of science so often printed in textbooks seems to apply mostly to routine science, but even here the same forces are at work, if at a lower intensity.

When scientific opinion is challenged, from either the inside or the outside, champions of orthodoxy will respond to the external threat. Some scientists even go so far as to argue that disagreement with current scientific opinion is an attack on reason itself, a false and dangerous claim. Reason is not the exclusive possession of science (or of any other discipline), nor do scientists always play by textbook rules. Most studies of controversies over anomalies such as UFOs show that the lawyer's methods become as important as the scholar's.[6]

The way key scientists responded to UFO reports and the UFO controversy shows this dynamic quality in operation. Influential scientists who went on record for or against the reality of UFOs were not dispassionate; they worked hard to promote or degrade UFOs. No doubt those on each side felt that the situation required vigorous and definite action. And perhaps they were right. The costs of controversy have nonetheless taken a heavy toll. Still, the controversy has also forced each side to marshal its arguments and seek evidence that supports them. We would like to believe that out of the struggle truth will emerge and our knowledge of the external world will progress.[7] This is to take the long-run view; but lives as well as careers exist within a more limited horizon.

And scientists' careers are a major force in shaping research into controversial subjects such as UFOs. While curiosity and idealistic fervor are powerful drivers, few scientists can afford to be indifferent about the impact of such inquiries on their future prospects. If involvement in such an area is to provide career advancement, there must be the promise of progress and discoveries. Further, involvement by itself should not decrease scientists' prospects of career success. Yet, frustratingly, UFO research seems to suffer from both of these drawbacks. And strong pressures against free inquiry have sharply limited the activities of scientists in studying UFOs. Limitation has occurred both by narrowing entry into the field and by restricting debate within it. The net result of the social pressures has been less knowledge about UFOs. To illustrate how these pressures have operated, I will look at the intersection of the careers of six important researchers and the UFO phenomenon.

The UFO Controversies

Some background is necessary before plunging into details. The history of the UFO controversy can be divided into three stages. I will characterize the first stage, lasting about twenty years (1947–67), as "scientists versus sighters." During this period, virtually all pro-UFO writings were offered by laymen, including some from the contactee fringe. Both large and small amateur UFO organizations grew up during this period, the largest being the National Investigations Committee on Aerial Phenomena. But the scientific community, led by Donald Menzel of Harvard, was uniformly against the special reality of UFOs. This situation existed in spite of a number of scientists who had personal UFO experiences.[8] During the second period, which I call the "great UFO debate," many scientists who had done research on the subject wrote books and articles supporting the reality of UFOs. The period, which lasted about fifteen years, started with two books by Jacques Vallee,[9] soon followed by one written by J. Allen Hynek.[10] During this time, highly committed nonscientist debunkers, such as science writer Philip J. Klass of *Aviation Week*, came to prominence, and in 1969 the notorious Condon Report was published. The third period, "the abduction debate," began in about 1980 and has continued until the present time.

The abduction debate has changed the ground of inquiry. Now not only is the reality of UFOs at issue but also the existence of human abductions by aliens. The stakes in the debate have risen. Are aliens intervening to reshape the human population, or is the abduction phenomenon simply a psychological and sociological problem? Is there a far-reaching "hidden event" taking place, or is society experiencing one of the most powerful mass psychology manifestations of modern times? In either case, science is expected to act as an "early warning system," to tell us how things really are. Yet, as we will see, the reactions of science in this case seem to depend on such frail human forces as individual inclinations and institutional dynamics. The scientist is therefore not simply a passive recipient, a camera that snaps a picture of reality, with better lenses every year; rather, he or she is an active seeker, full of hypotheses, orientations, and questions to answer.[11] And most scientists are tied to the dynamics of their careers.

This chapter will consider a half dozen major figures whose influence has been important in shaping the terms and process of the debates. Not only did these men have a strong effect on the controversy, but in many respects they encapsulate the action on each side.* I will consider three issues: (1) what influenced their entry into the controversy, (2) the strategy they chose, and (3) their impact on the field. All but one are Americans, which reflects both the United States' preponderant role and also the accessibility of their biographies for the purpose here.

Donald Menzel (1901–76)

A Harvard astronomer for most of his adult life, Donald Menzel represents a curious contradiction. A distinguished astrophysicist, Menzel wrote or coauthored three books attacking the validity of the UFO phenomenon: *Flying Saucers* (1953), *The World of Flying Saucers* (1963), and *The Truth About Flying Saucers* (1977).[12] These books did little to advance our scientific knowledge of the UFO phenomenon, but no doubt they were influential in discouraging Menzel's scientific colleagues from concerning themselves with UFOs. The paradox is that his UFO books represent quite shoddy science, in contrast with his better-known work in astrophysics.[13] During Edward U. Condon's University of Colorado UFO study project in the late 1960s, for instance, Menzel tried to explain some of the puzzling cases, but

---

*Those interested in less influential participants should consult the general survey by Charles F. Emmons, *At the Threshold: UFOs, Science, and the New Age* (Mill Spring, N.C.: Wild Flower Press, 1997), and autobiographical works by Harley D. Rutledge, *Project Identification: The First Scientific Field Study of UFO Phenomena* (Englewood Cliffs, N.J.: Prentice-Hall, 1981), and Frank B. Salisbury, *The Utah UFO Display: A Biologist's Report* (Old Greenwich, Conn.: Devin-Adair, 1974).

air force UFO consultant J. Allen Hynek found the project personnel completely unimpressed with Menzel's explanations of some of
the cases. Jacques Vallee wrote in his diary in 1967 that when Hynek
had dinner with the project coordinator, Robert Low, and his secretary, Mary-Lou Armstrong, "they discussed Menzel's recent trip
to Boulder. Mary-Lou laughed so hard as she recalled Menzel's
speeches that she fell from her chair and landed flat on her back on
the restaurant floor. Menzel's explanations for the cases were so
ridiculous that only propriety and respect for a senior colleague
prevented the members of the team, including Condon, from laugh-
ing openly in his face."[14] Since Menzel's efforts to debunk UFOs were
continuous, why were they not conducted at a level commensurate
with his main body of scientific work?

Menzel's involvement in the UFO debates began with a personal
sighting on 12 May 1949, which he reported in a confidential memo
to the air force and then, following an interview in *Time*, Menzel
blithely explained the whole business away two years later in a popular magazine article. Evidently Menzel found this an interesting topic,
and he soon wrote his first UFO book. This probably was the reason
the air force consulted him during the Washington flap in July 1952.
And in none of his books was there any ambiguity about the explanation of UFOs—it was all a case of misperception. Menzel enjoyed
being in the limelight and scoring apparent "hits" on UFO sightings
he believed were faulty. In a lecture at Harvard on the subject in 1964,
he lampooned the "saucer boys," as he called them. But his strong
opinions were not based on any profound research into the phenomenon, a situation very similar to that of Carl Sagan, whose influential opinions will be explored later.

Menzel's role in the UFO controversies was that of the first professional debunker. He treated UFOs as a side issue and devoted very
little actual research time to them. Nonetheless, thanks to a kind of
halo effect, Menzel's reputation in astronomy buttressed his loosely
put together scientific arguments. In this role, Menzel assumed the
role of speaking for the scientific community and therefore allowed
other scientists to disregard UFOs.

In spite of his work's low quality, Menzel's involvement had a
large impact. It discouraged work by other scientists who otherwise
might be interested. He also went beyond his simple expression of
opinion. At one point he tried to have Project Blue Book taken out

of the hands of the air force and given to a private corporation.[15] When he found sympathetic Blue Book managers, he assisted them in analyzing their cases, although, as far as one can tell, he did little fieldwork.[16] By suggesting that the subject of UFOs was nonsense, Menzel discouraged further inquiry not only by scientists but also by science writers and others who might be interested in the subject.

Yet why did he care? Why write three books on this subject if one was enough? J. Allen Hynek, in a 1973 interview, suggested that Menzel liked to win, and, having once expressed an opinion, he could not let the subject go.* This may be so, but Menzel's level of commitment to this subject is curious and remains unexplained.†

Carl Sagan (1934–96)

One of the public's best-loved scientists, Carl Sagan was the planetary astronomer par excellence. A professor of astronomy and director of laboratory studies at Cornell University, Sagan published over six hundred scientific papers, wrote many books, and developed the television series *Cosmos*. He was a theorist about extra-

---

*UFO researcher Stanton Friedman, the first to discover that Menzel had a top secret, ultra clearance (a matter apparently unknown to many colleagues and some of his military contacts in the Air Technical Intelligence Center), suggests the explanation lies in Menzel's membership on the hypothetical Majestic-12 (MJ-12) team. The MJ-12 group was purportedly a high-level and supersecret government committee steering investigations into UFOs, having been started in the aftermath of the Roswell crash (Stanton T. Friedman, *Top Secret/MAJIC* [New York: Marlowe, 1996]). Most ufologists consider the MJ-12 affair a hoax, but if it were true, Menzel would have led a curious double life as public debunker and secret sharer in the greatest of all military secrets. And Menzel did lead a double life in the sense that he was used to operating both in the academic community and in the black world of military secret projects; he kept the two strictly separated (Friedman, *Top Secret*). Whether Menzel's black projects included UFO work, we do not know.

†Aviation writer Philip Klass has had a similar negative relation to UFOs, but his cause is more personal: he thought he had an explanation. When his explanation was pooh-poohed by James McDonald, however, he made the cause personal. And like Menzel, he never let up.

terrestrial life and wrote extensively on the subject. He was also extremely active in assisting NASA on space missions, such as *Voyager* and *Viking*.[17] In addition to this research activity, he was one of the most sought-after speakers on space subjects and also a powerful public advocate of the Search for Extraterrestrial Intelligence (SETI), which in practice meant searching for alien electromagnetic signals.

According to his biographer, Keay Davidson (personal communication), Sagan was interested in UFOs early in his scientific career. In 1964 Vallee recorded that Hynek had met Sagan at a meeting of the American Association for the Advancement of Science (AAAS), and it was Hynek's impression that Sagan was much more interested in UFOs than he appeared to be.[18] By 1966 Sagan was still curious, but he then claimed that interest in UFOs was largely religious, an opinion he held until his death.* The topic of UFOs is not even mentioned in a long *New York Times* obituary.[19] Yet Sagan, because of his prominence in SETI and his extensive research in extraterrestrial biology, was seen as a natural "keeper of the problem" in regard to UFOs.[20] Thus, while UFOs meant little to Sagan, his opinion about UFOs was widely sought. Sagan also helped to create a symposium on UFOs given at the AAAS meetings in 1969.[21]

Sagan spent very little time researching UFOs, but he did devote one section of his *Cosmos* television series to the UFO problem, focusing on the Betty and Barney Hill abduction case. The series had some four hundred million viewers, and his opinion was distributed worldwide. He thought that little evidence existed to show that the UFO phenomenon represented alien spacecraft, believing instead that the motivation for interpreting UFO observations as spacecraft was emotional. This opinion persisted in the face of abduction reports, which Sagan interpreted in a *Parade* article and in a later book as mass contagion.

The high point of Sagan's treatment of the UFO question was the AAAS's symposium in 1969.[22] A wide variety of educated opinions on the UFO question were offered by a large panel of participants, including not only proponents such as McDonald and Hynek

---

*I spoke to him about the subject in 1966 when I was taking a class from him at Harvard.

but also skeptics such as astronomers William Hartmann and Menzel. The roster of speakers was balanced, and it is to Sagan's credit that this event was presented in spite of pressure from Edward Condon not to hold it.

Sagan did much to popularize the idea of intelligent life elsewhere and to suggest mechanisms by which it might evolve. He was also influential in promoting the search for signals from such intelligent life. However, he did not believe that aliens were likely to arrive here on earth and (apart from the AAAS symposium) did little to encourage the study of UFO reports. One might think it curious that someone so intent on looking for one kind of haystack-hidden needle would not be open to searching out another, but SETI research was highly vulnerable to political forces, which could remove funding on slight provocation. Sagan may have been eager to distance SETI from the much less acceptable UFO phenomenon.[23] What happened to James McDonald no doubt hardened such resolve.

James E. McDonald (1920–71)

James Edward McDonald was an eminent atmospheric physicist and one of the founders of the Atmospheric Research Institute at the University of Arizona, where he spent most of his academic life. Of all the scientists who became involved in the UFO controversies, McDonald's involvement in the last five years of his life was the most passionate. Beginning with a personal sighting in 1954, McDonald was intrigued by the UFO phenomenon and started active investigation in 1958, when he began quietly looking into Arizona cases. He continued this private UFO investigation for eight years, when he went public with his work and his opinions. From 1966 until his death, he was probably the strongest proponent of UFO research one can imagine, both in personal qualifications and in intensity of effort. He accused Hynek of not having given correct information to the public as an air force scientist; he attacked Menzel's scientific qualifications and the work of Condon's committee. He frankly described the scientific community's overall treatment of UFOs as "science in default."[24] But he was also critical of the low standard of most nonacademic UFO investigation.

A careful investigator with high standards, McDonald personally studied hundreds of cases, including many radar/visual cases originally taken from air force Project Blue Book. These cases, McDonald felt, constituted an irrefutable body of evidence that something unusual was taking place. He presented his opinions in every public and scientific forum available to him from 1966 to 1971, including one arranged by U Thant, secretary-general of the United Nations. While his immediate impact on the scientific community appeared slight, he provided great encouragement for many serious UFO investigators, some of whom he knew personally.

Unhappily, McDonald's passion made him few friends, and a very dangerous enemy in writer Philip J. Klass. Klass, canceled from a ball lightning conference on McDonald's recommendation, conducted what amounted to a personal vendetta against McDonald, which he pursued through public and privately circulated writings, and eventually through letters to McDonald's scientific sponsors. These letters were influential, it would appear, in McDonald's loss of a navy research contract, which he had used partially to pursue his UFO interests. Such "bootlegging" is probably more common than it would appear and has been associated with some very important work.[25] However, according to political scientist Paul McCarthy, it apparently offered a perfect target for Klass's revenge.[26]

Later, in March 1971, McDonald was publicly embarrassed in front of a congressional committee to which he was testifying on the atmospheric impact of a supersonic transport (SST). McDonald, a recognized expert on this subject, found his UFO interests brought up before the committee and used to discredit his testimony. Shortly thereafter, he became seriously depressed and took his life on 13 June 1971, at age fifty-one.[27]

McDonald's bitter end shows the dangers of active UFO involvement for the prominent scientist. Unlike Hynek, whose UFO work occurred largely after his main scientific work was finished, McDonald tried to pursue mainstream scientific work and UFO investigation at the same time, and he found that the latter could seriously harm the former. Reputation is not only the outcome of successful scientific work, but it is a vital resource to carry on such work. Damage through taint to reputation can seldom be repaired, and McDonald realized after the congressional hearing that his credibility would not recover from the blow. By contrast, J. Allen Hynek went on quietly with his UFO research until his major mainstream work was finished.

J. Allen Hynek (1910–86)

Josef Allen Hynek was a quiet man with scientific and administrative abilities that would impress his colleagues and speaking skills that would endear him to the public. After receiving a Ph.D. in astronomy in 1935, he joined the faculty of Ohio State University and eventually served as associate dean of its graduate school. He was a competent and effective astronomer who participated in several key federal projects and acted as head of Project Moonwatch, which trained amateur astronomers to assist in optical tracking of satellites. He arrived at Northwestern University in 1960 as department chairman of astronomy and soon improved that department's quality and reputation.

Hynek originally came to public attention when the air force hired him as a consultant in 1948 to help sort out UFO cases from astronomical events. For the most part, his involvement was both lucrative (he got a consulting fee) and fun—he liked being "on the inside."[28] Hynek recognized that some of these cases were difficult to explain, but apart from a paper in the *Journal of the Optical Society of America* in 1953, he simply did his work and handed in the results to the air force. It would appear that Hynek explained away some "good" cases, whether through caution or complicity. As a result, McDonald would later accuse Hynek of being "the original Menzel."[29] But Hynek kept a low profile until the 1960s, realizing, he said, that making waves would immediately have ended his usefulness and his consulting. It might also have spelled an abrupt end to a promising career.[30] He later said he was disturbed by the casual way in which his assessments were handled, but he made no waves until an unsettling incident in 1966.

Hynek investigated a series of cases in Michigan in March 1966 and, at a Detroit Press Club conference, stated that he had found explanations for most of them.[31] Among the explanations offered was that methane, or "marsh gas," seemed to be a good fit for some cases. The reporters present quickly focused on this particular explanation, and "swamp gas" became a national joke.[32] This was too much for the public, which had already been treated to one too many questionable explanations from the air force. It was too much for Hynek as well. He realized that whatever the explanation for the Michigan cases, it was time to state that there were other cases not so easily explained. In his opinion some UFO cases were definitely more than mistaken identifications.

Hynek's opinions had undergone a slow change during the 1960s, which he described as a "rising curve" of interest in UFOs.[33] He had been meeting privately with a small "Invisible College" that included colleagues William Powers and Fred Beckman and graduate student Jacques Vallee, who felt he was influential in changing Hynek's approach.[34] This small group nudged Hynek toward a more open public stance on UFOs, which he took fully when he published *The UFO Experience: A Scientific Approach* in 1972. Hynek's book was much more cautious than either of those previously written by his colleague Jacques Vallee but was based to a greater degree on in-depth personal investigation.

In 1973 Hynek founded the Center for UFO Studies at Northwestern, which became a center of UFO research. He published or co-authored two additional books, but neither was as influential as his first. His real value was to act as an anchor for UFO research. Unfortunately, in spite of all his previous caution, he sometimes chose to speak at gatherings with an occult or metaphysical orientation. Hynek's reason for doing this can only be guessed at, but such appearances undercut the scientific credibility he had worked so hard to achieve. Nonetheless, his accomplishments in the UFO field were substantial, especially in legitimating such inquiry.

Still, like other scientists, he paid a substantial price for being outspoken. One distinguished colleague, Robert Machol, asked for an opinion of Hynek, said, "He's a nut. What else could he be?" And no doubt Machol was not alone in this opinion. Like McDonald, Hynek had little apparent impact on opinions of the scientific community, but he may have emboldened a few others. Founding the Center for UFO Studies, however, was a key move in encouraging research into UFOs.

Jacques Vallee (b. 1939)

Born in France and trained as an astrophysicist (M.S., Lille 1961) and a computer scientist (Ph.D., Northwestern, 1967), Jacques Vallee has been a prolific theorist of the UFO phenomenon. Vallee had been aware of the wave of sightings in France in 1954 and had a personal UFO sighting as a young man in September 1958. What precipitated his involvement with the UFO phenomenon, however, was reading Aime Michel's book *Mysterieux Objets Celestes* (1958). Michel believed that UFO sightings occurred along straight (great circle) lines, but Vallee was eventually able to show that Michel's data could be explained by chance. He soon developed an extensive correspondence with Michel and began work on two UFO books. When Vallee came to Northwestern University in 1963 to work for a doctorate in computer science, he had already written two science fiction books, and his two UFO manuscripts were well under way. And on a previous visit he had met J. Allen Hynek.

Soon Vallee and Hynek started meeting regularly with like-minded colleagues in what Hynek called the "Little Society," a kind of Invisible College to study UFO cases. In 1965 Vallee published his first book on UFOs, *Anatomy of a Phenomenon,* and later another entitled *Challenge to Science* (1966).[35] These were the first of at least ten UFO books, but in contrast to later writings, his first two books took a strict natural-science approach to UFO study. Vallee's later works, starting with *Passport to Magonia* (1969), espoused interest in a variety of approaches, including occult and conspiracy theories, and contained a catalog of reported UFO landings. Interviewed in 1973, Vallee indicated that he was not sure that a natural-science approach was necessarily the right one, and that researchers should also consider others. Still, in contrast to the works of many popular writers such as Donald Keyhoe, Vallee's initial books firmly situated ufology as a potential branch of natural science.

Vallee did not pursue a standard academic career. He has never had a professorship but has worked in a variety of influential staff positions inside universities, think tanks, and private corporations. Because he did not pursue a career in the academic world, he was less vulnerable to pressure than were some of his professorial counterparts. He was able to pursue his UFO interests without jeopardizing his standing as a computer scientist professional. His work on computers and technology (including his book *The Network Revolution*)[36] has thus existed side by side with extensive UFO theorizing and writing. He has become one of the best-known theorists on UFOs.

Edward U. Condon (1902–74)

Edward Condon's contact with UFOs was not a lengthy one, but it was fateful. A former head of the National Bureau of Standards and onetime director of research for Corning Glass, he had many academic distinctions and was a distinguished member of the scientific community. He had the additional virtue of having stood up for intellectual freedom during the McCarthy era and in the turbulent sixties seemed like a perfect person for the air force to use in putting an end, once and for all, to its public involvement with UFOs. At the time of his involvement with the air force study that soon became known as the University of Colorado Project, he was a professor of physics at the University of Colorado. He gave no indication that he had ever given UFOs a serious thought.

Through the efforts of the air force, however, Condon was soon to be fatefully entangled with the UFO phenomenon. At this time, in 1966, Robert Low, assistant dean of the Graduate School at the University of Colorado, was a key player in convincing Condon and the university to take on the job. Low was convinced that the university could investigate UFOs without damage to its reputation. What the investigation might do to or for UFOs, Low never considered.* Condon's friend Hugh Odishaw, another high-profile physicist, with whom he coedited the *Handbook of Physics* (1958), advised Condon not to become involved in the investigation, but he did so nonetheless. Under Condon's leadership, the University of Colorado accepted an air force contract to complete a study of the UFO phenomenon.

It is important to understand that the air force, by 1966, was tired of the expense and public controversy associated with Project Blue Book, a vast headache that was producing little of value to the air force. The lack of progress was the result of the air force assigning few resources, including scientific talent, to the project. The outcome was predictable: most officers heading Blue Book thought their role was to explain as many UFO sightings as possible, largely dismiss

---

*Low's role has suffered more from adverse publicity than apparently he deserved (Michael D. Swords, "The University of Colorado UFO Project: The 'Scientific Study of Unidentified Flying Objects,'" *Journal of UFO Studies*, n.s., 6 [1995–96]: 149–84).

the rest, and look forward to their next billet. With this kind of bias, it is hardly surprising that little work of scientific value emerged. Hynek, the principal consultant, was aware of this bias but felt he could do little to change matters and thus made little effort to shift the project's direction.[37] Nonetheless, there was strong congressional pressure on the air force not to rest content with Blue Book's output but to seek outside scientific scrutiny for the cases investigated. To the air force the Colorado project appeared to be the perfect solution: it would end congressional pressure and allow the air force to close Blue Book.

Condon's attitude, which soon became evident, was just what the air force sought. Far from having an open mind, Condon was convinced the subject of UFOs was silly. Much to the embarrassment of Colorado project members, from the first day of the study he began to make statements regarding his opinions, even in public forums. During the investigation itself, he appeared to favor "kook" cases and spent little time in serious study. When his report appeared in late 1968, its conclusion was a strong negative: there was nothing to UFOs, it said, and nothing would be gained by further investigation.[38] A review of the report by the National Academy of Sciences seemed to vindicate Condon's opinion. It appears that the panel involved was largely handpicked by Odishaw.[39] Needless to say, the air force was satisfied with this verdict. It soon closed Blue Book and (at least on the surface) ended its study of UFOs.

Shortly after the report's release, however, a minority report appeared in book form, arguing that Condon was biased and had not really considered the data.[40] There had already been a furor earlier in February 1968 over a memo written in August 1966 by Robert Low, in which Low had advised the university to take on the project, since the study could be made to appear open-minded while in fact the expectation was a null finding.

> Our study would be conducted almost exclusively by nonbelievers who, although they couldn't possibly *prove* a negative result, could and probably would add an impressive body of evidence that there is no reality to the observations. The trick would be, I think, to describe the project so that, to the public, it would appear a totally objective study but, to the scientific community, would present the image of a group of nonbelievers

trying their best to be objective but having an almost zero expectation of finding a saucer. One way to do this would be to stress investigation, not of the physical phenomena, but rather of the people who do the observing—the psychology and sociology of persons who report seeing UFOs. If the emphasis were put here, rather than on examination of the old question of the physical reality of the saucer, I think the scientific community would quickly get the message.[41]

The intersection of the search for scientific truth and institutional pressures is striking. It seems certain that in this instance internal and external social forces were encouraging the university to take on this project not so much as an open-minded search for truth but rather to confirm a null hypothesis.

Project members David Saunders and Norman Levine were fired for complicity in the memo's public release, but this simply added to their motivation to publish a minority report. Condon himself, after writing a summary that was far more negative than the report's contents justified, was to argue a year later that any public school teacher who taught about UFOs ought to be publicly horsewhipped. Other scientists, however, had very mixed reactions to the Condon Report, and a committee of the American Institute of Aeronautics and Astronautics severely criticized it.[42]

Quantity and Styles of Work

What is the character of the work these men did? While quantity of writing can be assessed objectively, quality of investigation is more elusive, and the evaluation is inevitably subjective. It may be most valuable to summarize my opinions in a table, then to discuss them.

Scientist	Quantity of Work	Typical Sources
Donald Menzel	High	Literature
J. Allen Hynek	High	Personal investigation
Jacques Vallee	High	Literature
James E. McDonald	High	Personal investigation
Carl Sagan	Low	Literature
Edward U. Condon	Medium	Literature

Doing personal investigations depended on both preference and opportunity. Hynek and McDonald preferred to investigate personally, in Hynek's case because he was initially paid to do so, and in McDonald's because he made the time to do so. Both were concerned about reliability and were not easily satisfied with the answers they got. And they had to face the reality that their work would be examined closely by skeptics like Klass, whose no-holds-barred style of investigation and presentation would leave no stone unturned and no epithets unflung. If Sagan or Menzel had faced this kind of scrutiny, they would have had to do better work or leave the field.

While Hynek and McDonald did extensive personal investigation of cases, the others typically did research from their desk rather than in the field. Vallee often covered cases in detail in his books, but these cases were based largely on reading rather than on firsthand investigation. Upon further investigation, some of these cases turned out to be hoaxes, such as the disappearance of a regiment into a cloud during World War I. Only in later years did Vallee do extensive work on the physics of some of the cases.[43] Sagan and Condon had very little exposure to cases, though in Condon's situation he had resources that allowed him unusual access.

Hynek and Vallee offer an interesting study in contrasts. Vallee, a natural theorist, used a large amount of secondary material, some of it untrustworthy, but was able to use this material to propound laws, principles, and theories. Hynek, by contrast, was far more careful, using only cases with which he was intimately familiar for his 1972 book. Hynek took a Baconian approach and for the most part did not propound any sweeping hypotheses. In his book *The UFO Experience*, he used only cases he knew well. In contested areas such as UFOs, it is often critical to know the "personal equation" of the researcher. For Vallee these concerns generally took a backseat to theoretical speculation.

However, while Vallee was the most theoretical of the researchers mentioned, he was not responsible for the paradigm shift into abduction research. Credit for the paradigm shift belongs to artist Budd Hopkins and historian David M. Jacobs.[44] Hopkins, a meticulous researcher, was able to use hypnosis to probe beneath the surface of conscious awareness, thus eliciting materials whose accuracy is still in question, but which have changed completely many researchers' views of the nature of the phenomenon. Perhaps because

Hopkins was *not* a scientist, he was willing to use a tool that all the others viewed skeptically. Jacobs learned from Hopkins and expanded the investigations into new directions with greater detail.

Surprisingly, the laboratory played a very small role in the work these men carried out. While physical investigations of, for example, landing traces have been carried out, they have seldom played a key role in guiding hypotheses. Similarly, computer analysis, although initially promising, has not proved of major value, although it may play a more important role in the future. A 1997 scientific symposium, emphasizing physical evidence of UFOs and its interpretation, also left out the extensive biological evidence, for example, in regard to abductees.[45] Part of the reason for the low emphasis on physical evidence has been the search for the ufological Holy Grail, a "smoking gun" piece of evidence that would prove, once and for all, to be extraterrestrial. Researchers have mounted separate studies on such subjects as car-stopping,[46] landing traces,[47] and physiological effects,[48] but progress from physical evidence has been incremental, and the physical artifacts badly need comprehensive collection and organization.

Forms of Leadership

Intellectual leaders shape opinion through several kinds of activities. First, they can pose key questions and thus guide investigation; they can set the terms of debate and persuade others regarding what is important. Second, they can carry out critical studies and thus in principle decide key research questions. Third, they can act as exemplars and inspire others to do the same kind of research. Fourth, they can initiate research enterprises that generate data helpful to those in the field. These men variously carried out these roles, which I will consider in turn.

Posing Key Questions

Key questions are those whose answers constitute scientific progress. The critical questions in a field are those that link empirical observations with theory. Theories are important because they

unite disparate observations, arrange them, and relate them caus-
ally to other orders of events. For instance, in the late-eighteenth-
century controversy over the existence of meteorites, the key moves
were those that established meteorites as a separate category and
united them both with theory and with particular kinds of observations.[49] The linking up of empirical patterns in the data with supporting theory "nests" the field of study with respect to science.

This group, however, tended to take the terms of reference for
granted and instead spent most of its time arguing about cases.
Hynek had the most systematic approach.[50] He separated observations into six types (nocturnal lights, radar/visual, physical trace,
and three types of close encounters). Yet this was a classification
of forms of observation rather than of forms of UFO behavior.
Vallee was the most persistent theorist of the group, but he seldom
rested with a particular theory long enough to encourage a long-
term research program. He made a number of suggestions about
observation patterns, such as the moon illusion, the law of the
times, and so on. Unhappily, each of these "laws" tended to be
advanced once but not further developed. Vallee would go on to a
new set of insights, rather than refining and recasting those he had
previously propounded. The results were stimulating but ultimately did not build a comprehensive picture. And unfortunately,
Vallee's critics were far better at finding his weaknesses than building on his strengths.

By contrast with Hynek and Vallee, the others present a far less
theoretical picture. Menzel tried to fit many observations into his
"mirage" explanation but did not succeed. Condon did not take the
phenomenon seriously enough to search for patterns. Sagan's processing of UFO data was casual at best and largely driven by analogy. McDonald, apparently a very bright man, concentrated on cases
and did little to suggest overall patterns.

The ordinary understanding of science sees the scientist building up a store of cases, then propounding a general law or theory.
Actually, in science there is a constant interaction of theory and observation. While it is true that observations can lead to theory, it is
just as true that theories can lead to observations. In any case, just as
observations can validate theory, theory can validate observations,
as in the case of continental drift[51] and meteorites.[52] The key is in
finding theories and observations that fit each other and nest with

other scientific knowledge. The failure to provide such interlocking theories and evidence is one of the key reasons that UFO research is still in limbo.

Contributions to Empirical Knowledge

If propounding key questions is one aspect of intellectual leadership, performing critical research is another. Controversies can be turned into scientific knowledge through performing what come to be seen to be critical experiments or studies. Darwin's *Origin of Species* was not the first work to suggest evolution, but it was the first to unite that suggestion with a fully fleshed-out body of data and theory. A comparison of this group's data collection and analysis yields some interesting insights.

We can quickly dispose of Sagan, who did little data collection, and Condon, who did little analysis. Menzel certainly built up a data set, though his analysis was unsatisfactory. Vallee's *Magonia* catalog was one of the first databases, but it was far from complete. Nonetheless, the works of Vallee form an imposing body of cases to examine, even though some now appear to have been accepted too easily. McDonald built up the most carefully conceived data set, representing extensive personal investigations over many years.

The common problem that all these data sets face is that they were assembled without reference to a critical test. On one hand, the proponents have tried to convince by marshaling a large number of cases that appear to have no conventional explanation. On the other, the skeptics have argued—often using the same cases—that even the best evidence is susceptible to explanations other than alien origin. But while such cases are often persuasive (especially if one reads the literature of only one side), the touchstone that could turn the cases into tests of key hypotheses remains elusive.

A great deal of time has been spent looking for a "smoking gun" case that would decide the controversy once and for all. Should such a case appear, its scientific impact would be small compared with its social and political fallout. But it appears more likely that resolution will come through searching for patterns in the data. It is hard not to wonder if at some later time the thread that unites much of the unexplained data will be found, and the various aspects of this confusing phenomenon will largely fall into place.

Exemplars

The people at the tip of the UFO investigation iceberg were influential in shaping the terms of the UFO debate. Whether they spoke at UFO conferences, wrote articles in the popular press, or influenced others through writing books, they caused other researchers to enter or abstain from the fray. Hynek, McDonald, and Vallee became models for others to imitate. Sagan's views must have provided answers for innumerable science teachers.

With Menzel and Condon, however, there was another effect. Because they appeared to have "handled" the UFO problem, this meant that other scientists felt they did not have to bother with it. Condon and Menzel were thus quite influential in discouraging others from risking their careers and reputations in this contentious area.

These men also influenced each other. Vallee and other members of the "Little Society" encouraged Hynek to go public; so did McDonald's accusations of "flinching" on the data. Vallee encouraged the interest of Peter Sturrock, a plasma physicist at Stanford, who would also become influential. Menzel's impact on Sagan must remain hypothetical, but the fact that both men worked in an organization run by Menzel (the Harvard Observatory) is probably an overlooked influence. Otherwise Sagan might have been more tempted to look more carefully at "astronauts" who were less "ancient."*

It is important to emphasize that Hynek and Vallee were not the only exemplars for styles of case investigation. These developed from the personal styles of the top investigators, among whom I would certainly rank Budd Hopkins, David Jacobs, Richard Hall, Ray Fowler, and Walter Webb. The art of "UFO investigation" developed in much the same way that psychic investigation did at the turn of the century, a tradition of amateur science that deserves a study of its own.

---

*Sagan did write about the possibility of extraterrestrial visitation in ancient times.

Most casework in UFO investigation is carried out by people less eminent than the scientific leaders. These six men were the most visible, but behind them were innumerable others who also contributed. Their work can be seen through such documents as the National Investigations Committee on Aerial Phenomena's book *The UFO Evidence* (1964);[53] the periodical journals of such organizations of the Aerial Phenomena Research Association, the Mutual UFO Network, and the Center for UFO Studies; the work of countless individual investigators; and the international (especially French, English, and Belgian) counterparts of these organizations and individuals. Many other scientists such as Frank Salisbury (biologist) and Harley Rutledge (physicist) carried out their own investigations.[54] Without the spadework of this large number of people, much of the data would not be available. In addition, many of the best and most detailed investigations have been carried out by those with less scientific training, who devoted time to prolonged investigations.[55] If the key scientists have seen far, it is because their work is predicated on the efforts of many others, less visible but no less valuable.

Creating Intellectual Enterprises

Often scientific leaders influence not only through their own studies but also through the creation of intellectual enterprises. Organizing a research center or a study group may have far-reaching effects. J. Allen Hynek founded the Center for UFO Studies, for instance, and he was able not only to carry out his own research but also to enlist some very talented associates. One of them, Allan Hendry, conducted a large number of investigations and wrote *The UFO Handbook* (1979)[56]—a very helpful aid for anyone embarking on field investigations. Hendry's book was more systematic than the Condon Report and has more useful information, about both explained and unexplained cases.

A research center may provide funding, personnel, and laboratory as well as intellectual resources that can aid in continuing investigation. Such institutes can also act as the point of contact with other research facilities, such as universities and industrial laboratories. Had James McDonald lived, he might have been able to provide more access to the resources of atmospheric science, including better analysis of photographs, more sophisticated weather interpretation, and use of databases designed for another purpose.

Ironically, the person who had the most access to such resources, Edward Condon, cared the least about the subject. His greatest failing was his preconceived opinion. His investigation was supposed to be headed by someone impartial; obviously, he was not. Condon did not build on any of the previous insights or turn to the UFO community for some of the best previous cases, which might have steered the work of his field investigators to more fruitful territory. Instead, like the inspector in the film *Casablanca,* he "rounded up the usual suspects." And when he was done, he actively discouraged others from doing further research.

Condon's attempt to solve the UFO problem shows the dangers of a crash effort as opposed to a continuous, systematic one. While his field investigators received a valuable education,[57] Condon did not allow for continuation of the research program. He naively thought that his study would be the final word on the subject. This was a most serious underestimation.

Barriers to Entry and Limitations on Inquiry

The work of these men was shaped by the preconceptions of their professional community. This community's beliefs provided a strong barrier to entry in this field. One evidence of this barrier is that five of the six did this work in their spare time. All except Hynek pursued other more conventional research while the UFO work was being carried out. Only Hynek could afford, in the last decade of his life, to devote himself exclusively to this area.

UFO work also hurt the reputations of those who did it. Of the six men considered, only one (Sagan) emerged unscathed from his involvement. Stigma is a real risk for those entering taboo research areas. A variety of restrictions, from informal pressures (evident in the case of Hynek, inferred in the case of Sagan) to outright sanctions against research in this area (McDonald), are evident. Evidence of these pressures is available through the words and actions of participants.

Hynek's early involvement with the field is a case in point. Brought in by the air force as a consultant in 1948, Hynek recognized the pressures brought to bear not only on himself but also on the air force project (successively Projects Sign, Grudge, and Blue Book). Hynek knew he was supposed to keep a low profile, and he did. Only later, as a department chair of astronomy at Northwestern, and thus in a basically unassailable position, was he persuaded by the Invisible College (in support) and James McDonald (in accusation) to make a positive position public. He stated during a 1973 interview that he knew that any other course of action would have ended his participation and sidelined his career.[58] Vallee was able to pursue his own researches because he was on the fringe of academia and was not subject to the same pressures as Hynek.

Another facet of the barrier to entry is lack of funding, which can doom an area of investigation. This was less true earlier in the century but has been something to reckon with in the last decades. Unless one was willing to say that UFOs would be investigated as mirages or social phenomena, money to research them was simply not present. One of the reasons that the University of Colorado qualified for air force funding was its adequate supply of the right kind of psychologists to explain the sightings away as psychological events.[59] Thus a preconception of the problem shaped the kind of funding available to study it.

One can get around the funding problem by bootlegging funds. James McDonald piggybacked some of his UFO research on funds committed to other research. As we have seen, however, this not only was an insecure source but also could lead to potentially serious sanctions if someone wanted to make an issue of it, as did Philip Klass. And bootlegging requires expending energy to conceal the bootlegging, which takes effort away from the actual research.

A third limitation on inquiry is apparent when one considers the SETI community. Scientists involved with SETI who were interested in UFOs were well advised not to mention it and to do only vicarious research through reading. The threat to SETI's research funding if it became entangled with UFOs was serious, as McDonald's humiliation showed. Similar pressures at Harvard may explain Sagan's strong interest in "ancient astronauts" while his interest in UFOs seemed underdeveloped. Yet SETI-oriented astronomers, I discovered through interviews, are perfectly capable of taking an interest in, for example, alien bases in the solar system. Such interests, however, are kept carefully under wraps. It does not help that figures such as Edward Condon ridiculed any involvement with UFOs. Nor did it help that SETI scientists might face the nasty tactics of Philip Klass if they betrayed public interest in UFOs. The existence of Klass and those like him was by itself a barrier to public involvement.

The discouragement is all the more interesting in that scientists, including astronomers, sometimes have UFO experiences themselves and are also likely to come across colleagues and others who have convincing experiences.[60] Hynek discovered in an early informal survey of astronomers that five out of forty-five had seen something unusual themselves.[61] In my own research I came across several cases of scientists whose colleagues or respected friends had seen something quite unusual but kept quiet about it. Nor is the current trend toward treating UFOs as myth, folklore, or revitalization movements likely to increase scientific interest in this frustrating and elusive subject.

Conclusion

This chapter has examined some of the key players in the UFO controversy. The debate is still in progress. Efforts to resolve the debate have led to a standoff in which each side has created a strong, but incomplete, case. The "pros" have assembled an imposing dossier, which is exciting to dip into and must certainly intrigue the open-minded inquirer. This dossier may contain as-yet-unspotted correlations or patterns that would aid a future analyst in pinning down explanations. In spite of some excellent partial analyses,[62] however, the UFO evidence is still a "cabinet of curiosities."

The "antis," meanwhile, have taken what they believe to be the scientific high ground, and at times have been able to portray the proponents as part of a general movement in favor of the irrational. This activity, led by Klass and other members of the Committee for Scientific Investigation of Claims of the Paranormal (CSICOP), has convinced many outside the controversy that the UFO evidence does not deserve consideration.[63] This dismissal has had the effect of discouraging inquiry, if not blocking it.

The doubters also point to the large number (say 90 percent) of reported cases that have yielded to analyses, most of them done by proponents![64] And it is all too tempting to say, given this record of disappointments, that the unexplained cases are actually similar to those explained and would also be explained if we had just a bit more data. Statistical analysis, however, does not always bear out this expectation. In an earlier government report, the Battelle Memorial Institute found that the unexplained cases, for instance, tended to have more reliable observers than the explained cases![65]

So the chasm remains. These two worlds seldom, if ever, communicate. On rare occasions they may appear at the same conference, but the off-line informal talks necessary to share ideas and find commonality are absent. The SETI group, somewhere in the middle, could act as broker, but, to avoid being associated with ufology, it does not.

The UFO phenomenon remains elusive. The sightings, the puzzling physical effects, and the apparent abduction experiences raise many questions. These questions will not be answered without further research. As this study has shown, however, there are many barriers to the conduct of this research. They are likely to remain, even in the face of serious efforts to elicit more scientific interest.[66] When the subject is difficult and preconceptions are strong, truth does not easily emerge. So the debate continues.

Chapter Three

Science, Law, and War: Alternative Frameworks for the UFO Evidence

Don C. Donderi

Air force jets, ball lightning, balloons, birds, earth lights, experimental aircraft, false memories, hallucinations, landing lights, masochistic delusions, meteors, neurosis, planets, publicity seeking, psychopathology, social conformity, stars, suggestion, sundogs, temperature inversions, and wishful thinking—this is a partial list of possible natural, engineering, and psychological causes that have been suggested to explain UFO reports. Contradicting the hypothesis that these reports are evidence of extraterrestrial technology is the skeptic's argument that they are nothing more than misidentified natural or human phenomena.

Fifty years of accumulated evidence subject to routinely critical scrutiny[1] means that the basic UFO report (metallic-appearing objects, radical maneuvers) has already passed the test of researchers who are just as anxious to eliminate observations of natural, engineering, or psychological origin as are the skeptics.[2] One of the goals of this chapter is to explain why this large and consistent body of UFO evidence, which almost shouts "extraterrestrial technology," is still either attacked or ignored by the scientific community.

Science is not the only profession that collects and analyzes evidence. To put the almost complete rejection of the UFO evidence by scientists into perspective, I contrast the goals and methods of the scientific community with those of two other professional communities: the legal profession and the profession of military intelligence analysis. Lawyers and military analysts use evidence differently and have different rules for understanding it. Comparing law and military intelligence with science highlights the weaknesses of the scientific method and suggests that lawyers and military intelligence analysts are trained to do a better job than scientists when it comes to evaluating the UFO evidence.

I first outline a modern interpretation of the scientific method that is based on the work of Thomas Kuhn. I conclude from Kuhn's analysis that, as a result of their rigorous but narrow approach to understanding nature, "good" scientists simply cannot deal effectively with entirely new phenomena like UFOs. Then, switching to psychological science, I discuss the phenomena of recovered memory and hypnosis, and consider the real and imagined difficulties that these phenomena produce in dealing with eyewitness testimony about UFOs and UFO abductions.

Then I favorably contrast the open, conservative, but adversarial legal method of dealing with evidence to the scientific method and conclude that UFO evidence would be better received in court than by the information gatekeepers of science. Military intelligence, unlike the law, is neither open nor conservative, but military analysts are trained to react immediately and fully to any information about novel technological developments of their adversaries, whether or not these developments have any standing in "science." The military intelligence analysts of the world have probably already digested the UFO evidence and drawn the proper conclusions—but because their work is secret, we will never know.

Scientific Paradigms

In *The Structure of Scientific Revolutions,* Thomas Kuhn argued that scientists routinely limit their interest to only those natural phenomena that can be explained by extending or modifying the general theories that underlie the field of study with which the phenomena are associated.[3] Kuhn called these general theories *paradigms.* Simultaneously restrictive and liberating, paradigms focus attention on problems that intelligent people can solve using the tools and resources of their scientific specialty. Kuhn compared scientific problems to crossword puzzles, because the rules are clear and yet the solution requires both patience and specialized knowledge.

During periods of what Kuhn called *normal science,* scientists spend their time applying existing general theories like Newtonian mechanics or Mendelian genetics to explain more and more of the phenomena of the natural world. But the phrase *scientific revolutions* in Kuhn's title illustrates his interest in the transition between normal science under the influence of one general theory, for example, Newtonian mechanics, and a later theory, for example, relativity theory. Kuhn wrote that normal science becomes less structured and less effective during scientific revolutions. An "essential tension" (Kuhn's phrase) exists between the principles of a general theory and the phenomena that cannot be explained by that theory. As more phenomena are investigated, the old theory often comes to explain the new observations less well. Additionally, old observations that were discrepant with the theory but were ignored become more salient as they are repeated and verified by more researchers.

When this happens, the original theory may have to be broadened or loosened to accommodate the new observations, so that it becomes a less consistent and therefore less satisfying explanation of nature. Alternative theories are suggested, and if a new general theory is proposed that explains both the old and the new observations, it will be accepted.[4]

According to Kuhn, the practicing scientist always seeks a paradigm within which to work. If there is "tension" generated by the inadequacies of one paradigm, that tension is reduced by modifying or extending the paradigm at the cost of reducing its unifying power and its intellectual appeal. This will continue to the point where almost everyone in the field sees that such modifications can no longer succeed. At this point someone may introduce a new paradigm that reorganizes the data and, according to Kuhn, makes it practically impossible for the practicing scientist to see the entire set of data, new and old, in the old way again.*

---

*Although Steven Weinberg reminded us recently ("The Revolution That Didn't Happen," *New York Review of Books,* 8 October 1998, pp. 48–52) that Newtonian mechanics is still both used and understood by students of postrelativity physics.

Kuhn is insistent that scientists work within paradigms, and that "there is no such thing as research in the absence of any paradigm. *To reject one paradigm without simultaneously substituting another is to reject science itself"* (my italics).[5] Kuhn even suggests that "some men have undoubtedly been driven to desert science because of their inability to tolerate crisis. . . . that rejection of science in favor of another occupation is, I think, the only sort of paradigm rejection to which counter-instances by themselves can lead."[6] To paraphrase Kuhn, scientists take no interest in phenomena without paradigms. If they take an interest in a phenomenon without either trying to subsume it under an old paradigm or trying to build a new paradigm to explain it, they are no longer behaving as scientists.

Suppose that Kuhn is right: What does this mean about scientists' attitudes toward UFO phenomena? The answer, as Jacobs noted in 1975,[7] is that within "normal science," UFO reports must be explained as phenomena from the fields of atmospheric physics, engineering, or psychology. To use J. Allen Hynek's well-known classification scheme,* "nocturnal lights" must be misperceptions of stars or planets caused by a well-known visual phenomenon called *autokinesis*, which makes stationary objects in a uniform field appear to move. A variety of nocturnal phenomena associated with UFOs were classed as "ball lightning" by Philip Klass, "mirages" by Donald Menzel, or "piezoelectric discharges" by Michael Persinger.[8] Hynek's "daylight disks" were explained as optical phenomena ("sun dogs") by Menzel. Radar-visual sightings were explained away as temperature inversions and mirages (Menzel, Klass). UFO close encounter reports by groups or individuals were explained as either mutual suggestibility and sensation seeking, on the one hand, or psychopathology (hallucinations), on the other. The general interest in UFOs was explained in the cultural context of myth and folklore,[9] and the existence of this cultural context was accepted as a paradigm that apparently includes all of the motivational influences that led people to repeat and believe other people's stories about UFOs.

---

*NL = nocturnal light, DD = daylight disk, RV = radar-visual, CE I = close encounters of the first kind (no physical evidence), CE II = close encounters of the second kind (physical traces), CE III = close encounters of the third kind (humanoids), and (as a posthumous extension to Hynek's system) CE IV = close encounters of the fourth kind (abductions).

I deliberately exclude the possibility that the UFO evidence can trigger a real paradigm shift accompanied by a scientific revolution. The reason is that, to my knowledge, no physical science theory published in the open literature comes anywhere near explaining the UFO phenomenon. Therefore, in complete consistency with Kuhn's idea that "once it has achieved the status of paradigm, a scientific theory is declared invalid only if an alternate candidate is available to take its place,"[10] for the foreseeable future reports of UFOs will be subsumed as puzzles to be explained away by using natural, engineering, or psychological processes. Barring a dramatic, attention-riveting change in the UFO phenomenon or an even more unlikely reduction in general scientific hubris, scientists will not agree that UFOs are real until there is an accepted theory about how to make a machine that will do what UFOs have been repeatedly observed to do. Before then, the scientific community will be unanimous that it is simply "premature" to so much as acknowledge the existence of facts that no general scientific theory can explain.*

Back to the Future

Eighteenth- and nineteenth-century science was enriched by making observations and collecting specimens to record both the curiosities and the regularities of nature.† Twentieth-century philosophers of science have argued that collecting things or observing phenomena, and then reasoning inductively from them, cannot *prove* scientific theories.[11] Nevertheless, novel phenomena do provide an empirical basis on which to attack old theories and to develop, if not to prove, new ones. Like many of my colleagues interested in UFOs, I have read hundreds of UFO reports and have collected a score of

---

*A clear example of this attitude is expressed by this quote about UFOs from Albert Einstein: "These people have seen something. What it is I do not know and am not curious to know" (Einstein, quoted in David Jacobs, *The UFO Controversy in America* [Bloomington: Indiana University Press, 1975], p. 81).

†Sir Joseph Banks (1743–1820) is an example. See Patrick O'Brian, *Joseph Banks, a Life* (London: Collins Harvill, 1987).

them myself, in good nineteenth-century fashion. My understanding of the UFO phenomenon is also influenced by my familiarity as a research psychologist with the phenomena of visual perception and memory and by my knowledge about how these processes influence the reliability of UFO witnesses. But if Kuhn is right, this will lead me nowhere as a scientist, because there is no scientific paradigm available to explain the UFO evidence.

Abduction Memories

While the classic UFO evidence itself has been subjected to intense analysis by UFO scholars and critics, the more recent UFO abduction evidence has not. Ignoring, for the moment, paradigm shifts or even the question of science as a framework for the UFO evidence, I would like to briefly consider UFO-related abduction reports from the perspective of one of my own main research interests, the psychology of human memory.

In the seventeenth century, many women in England and in the American colonies were arrested, tried, imprisoned, and burned as witches. In the late twentieth century, the accusations and accompanying legal persecution of many completely innocent people as satanic ritual child abusers took on the proportions of a mania.[12] During both the witchcraft mania and the satanic abuse mania (which academics call the *recovered memory/false memory debate*), some of the falsely accused, under intense pressure to admit their crimes, actually began to believe that they were guilty and confessed to crimes that they demonstrably did not commit.

The fact that social pressure led some people to incriminate themselves with untrue accounts of physical and sexual abuse does not, of course, alter the fact that some children are abused by adults. Westrum described how child abuse was first suspected when physicians began using X rays and found that the long bones of the legs and arms of some children had been repeatedly broken, although parents denied the children had fallen or had been hit. It took years before pediatricians, social workers, and the courts accepted that some parents did beat their children, and sometimes beat them to death.[13]

Abduction Narratives as Self-Persuasion

UFO abduction narratives began to attract widespread attention at the same time the satanic abuse mania was at its height. Not
surprisingly, academic psychologists saw only similarities between
the false "recovered memories" of people who narrated stories of
alien abductions and the false "recovered memories" of the alleged
victims and perpetrators of satanic abuse.[14] From the academic critics' point of view, recovered abduction narratives are produced following a vague cue of "missing time" plus feelings of distress that
drive the narrator to consult a credulous therapist. Critics claim that
this mobilizes all of the therapist's power of suggestion, the hardly
surprising therapeutic outcome being an abduction story constructed
from widely available media accounts and shaped by the therapist's
leading questions. In other words, the UFO abduction narrative is
simply a false "recovered memory." That this does considerable
injustice to both the perspicuity of therapists and the strength of
the evidence is argued later in this section.

The detailed alternative explanations for abduction narratives
include the simple false memory syndrome, birth trauma re-creation,
masochistic escape fantasy, fantasy-proneness, and temporal-lobe
lability.[15] Persinger's temporal-lobe lability theory holds that UFO
and abduction narratives result from a subclinical epileptic hallucinatory seizure that affects some people with susceptible temporal
lobes.[16] All of the other academic explanations purport to show how
constructing and believing in an abduction narrative satisfies a psychological need. To buttress the simplest (false memory) case, it has
been shown that people can be persuaded by other people who are
important to them that something happened to them that did not
really happen. With the help of parents and a brother, Loftus persuaded a fourteen-year-old boy that, contrary to fact, he had been
lost in a shopping mall when he was five years old.[17] Lawson proposed that abduction imagery, like long tunnels and creatures with
large heads, was relevant to birth experiences, and that the form
of abduction narratives suggested a psychological mechanism involved in coming to grips with birth trauma.[18] The fantasy-proneness
argument of Bartholomew, Basterfield, and Howard was based on
the idea that some normal people have a rich fantasy life and that
they cannot discriminate well between external events and their own

imagination. However, Spanos et al. showed that UFO observers were not more fantasy-prone than a comparison sample of non-UFO observers.[19] Newman and Baumeister proposed that the helplessness and violation found in many UFO abduction narratives are masochistic fantasies that provide emotional relief from the responsibility and achievement demands of Western society.[20] These fantasies become beliefs because they fulfill a strong motivational need.

Many of the leading participants in the recovered memory/false memory debate wrote invited comments about the Newman and Baumeister masochistic fantasy article. Without distinguishing minor differences in detail, the consensus of ten of the twelve commentators was that Newman and Baumeister were right that UFO abduction narratives were false recovered memories, but that their masochism fantasy hypothesis was wrong. The ten commentators all agreed that known mechanisms of social reward for believing false recovered memories, plus the widespread availability of the "UFO abduction script," were sufficient to explain all UFO abduction narratives.

The two dissenting commentaries by McLeod and Hall cautioned against assuming that all UFO abduction narratives were false recovered memories.[21] Both said that many of the assumptions about the quality of UFO abduction reports made by critical commentators were wrong. Both said that the original article and the ten concurring comments proposed inadequate "normal science" explanations for highly unusual phenomena. One reason to give due consideration to abduction narratives is that not all abduction memories are recovered: some were never lost. Another reason is that not all recovered memories are false: some have really been dissociated or repressed. Memory repression has been known to psychologists since Freud first developed a theory to explain it.[22] I now turn to these phenomena at the center of the controversy.

Memory Repression and Dissociation

Academics were not the first to realize that beliefs could be changed by suggestion. George Orwell and Arthur Koestler described both in fact and in fiction how mass media propaganda influences the beliefs and behaviors of entire nations.[23] There is nothing new in the idea that people can be persuaded to believe something that is not true, and a belief becomes a "memory" as soon as it can be attached to a specific time and place.

But psychologists who have absorbed the current suspicions of false "recovered memory" may have forgotten that there are also true recovered memories. The process by which past events are kept out of consciousness was called *repression* by Freud[24] and *dissociation* by Janet.[25] *Repression*, the stronger term, conveys an "effortless and regular turning away of the psychic process from the memory of anything that had once been painful." Modern writers frequently use the term *dissociation* to describe the same turning away from memory, but with the weaker assumption that remembered pain is only one of the causes that prevent some experiences from being consciously recalled.

The recovery of lost memories has been demonstrated both naturally and experimentally. The clearest experimental example is hypnotic amnesia. A hypnotized observer can be told not to recall certain events until or unless a later command from the hypnotist returns them to consciousness. Hypnotic amnesia and its recovery can be demonstrated in the laboratory, which allows the accuracy of memories recalled following amnesia to be assessed.[26]

Many case studies show that people may recover true memories of traumatic events without hypnosis. English Bagby includes an example of repressed memory associated with a phobia in his early psychology textbook.[27]* A young girl developed an apparently inexplicable fear of any form of running or splashing water, and "it can be imagined that her life was very seriously interfered with by this disorder." When she was twenty, an aunt came to visit. At their first meeting since childhood, the aunt said, "I have never told." This sentence reinstated the relevant memory. As a seven-year-old, the young woman had gone on a picnic with her mother and the same aunt. Her mother left the picnic early and gave the child strict instructions to obey the aunt. The child and the aunt went into the woods for a walk. The girl ran off and then slipped and fell into a stream, where she was trapped, wedged among the rocks, with a waterfall pouring over her head. When rescued by the aunt, she was screaming with terror. They went to a nearby

---

*I thank John Kihlstrom for telling me about this example.

house, where she was dried off, and then returned to her home, with the aunt promising "I will never tell" so that the girl would not be punished for her disobedience. The aunt confirmed the events as the young woman recited them, and as they were recalled, the phobic symptoms disappeared.

Joseph Wolpe, a pioneer behavior therapist, described another case of repressed memory recovered under hypnosis. A thirty-seven-year-old man was referred to Wolpe for extreme anxiety associated with marital unhappiness, and a total amnesia for the previous four days. Working first on the anxiety and then on the marital situation, Wolpe suggested positively reinforcing behavior to his client so that, ten days after treatment had begun, the anxiety had been reduced, but he was still suffering from total amnesia for the previous four days. Under hypnosis, the client remembered having made a long journey to visit the rival for his wife's affection, intending to kill him; he had been unable to do so, had another emotional confrontation with his wife, and had finally gone to his sister's house and collapsed there. He was told that he would remember the events on awakening; he did so, and expressed "slight amusement at it and surprise at having remembered."[28]

Schooler, Bendiksen, and Ambadar presented a thorough analysis of four recent recovered memory cases.[29] They described the recovery experience, the type of forgetting that occurred, the evidence of abuse that led to the dissociation, and the evidence that the recovered memory had actually been forgotten. They concluded that all of the cases were true recovered memories on the basis of the evidence available for each case.

Evaluating the Truth of Abduction Memories

The false-recovered-memory explanation for abduction narratives is that they result from a combination of common knowledge about alien abduction stories, a troubled client seeking help, and a credulous professional who is ready to identify the client's difficulties as caused by an abduction. According to this explanation, it does not matter whether the abduction suggestion originated with the client or with the professional, because each of them provides positive feedback and validation to the other.

The mutual suggestion theory does not eliminate the possibility that some alien abduction narratives are true. Real repressed memories can be recovered. Not every recovered memory is necessarily true, but neither is every recovered memory necessarily false. Other considerations: the quality and reputation of the therapist, the consistency of the report, the possibility of independent confirmation, and the evidence of amnesia for the recovered experience are all necessary to properly evaluate an individual claim of recovered memory.

Abduction narratives like those described by Fuller, Carpenter, and Hopkins provide enough information so that each case can be considered on its merits.[30] In many of these accounts there is independent confirmation of missing time—emotionally stable people arriving hours late after long or short automobile journeys. There is independent confirmation of abduction events reported under hypnosis, sometimes by nonhypnotized observers and sometimes by other hypnotized witnesses. These UFO researchers are well aware of the problems of leading during hypnotic questioning, and their protocols reflect their concern to avoid this situation. Reading these cases with an understanding of the careful investigative methods that have been described in articles by Haines, Carpenter, Jacobs, and Hopkins strengthens the argument that a "normal science" explanation for all abduction narratives is unlikely.[31]

Clinical psychology is a practical art based on fundamental science. The practice of clinical psychology teaches us that each case must be analyzed on its own merits. The art of clinical psychology is to apply the principles of fundamental science correctly in each case. After each case has been evaluated, one begins to look for consistency across cases. And although we will not pursue the evidence in this article, the already sizable collection of methodologically secure and consistent abduction cases is where the serious study of the abduction phenomenon begins.

UFO Evidence and the Law

The standard of proof in criminal law is "beyond a reasonable doubt." The standard in civil law is "the preponderance of evidence" or the "balance of probabilities." In an experiment reported by Feinberg, sitting judges were asked to translate these phrases into the probability of guilt (in criminal trials) or of liability (in civil trials).[32] The median probabilities from over three hundred judges were 90 percent for "beyond a reasonable doubt" and 55 percent for "the preponderance of evidence."

Legal evidence must be *relevant, material,* and *admissible.* Relevance is based on the connection between the evidence and the fact to be proved. If the evidence does not bear on the fact to be proved, it is irrelevant. In law, the connection of evidence with fact is based as much on experience as it is on logic, and the relevance of evidence is a matter of the trial judge's discretion. Evidence must be related to a question that is at issue in the case, or else, regardless of how good it is, it will be rejected as immaterial. And to be admissible, evidence must have been obtained by procedures that conform to the rules of evidence. These rules, among other things, either exclude or severely limit character derogation as well as hearsay testimony, which is a report at second hand of what someone else said happened.[33]

The UFO Evidence on Trial*

Viewing the UFO evidence in the context of civil law means evaluating the relevance, materiality, and admissibility of that evidence to assert the proposition that UFO phenomena are evidence of extraterrestrial technology. Imagine a trial in which an ex-employee is suing his former employer for wrongful dismissal. The defendant has fired the plaintiff because the employee was the director of a local UFO investigation group. The employer said that the plaintiff's public statements that "UFOs are extraterrestrial" made him unsuitable for continued employment on the grounds of mental incompetence. The fired employee says that there is nothing mentally incompetent about his claim, and that on the balance of probabilities, his statements are true. He sues the employer to recover his reputation and his job.

---

*I practice as an expert witness in civil and criminal cases, and so have some experience with court procedure that is reflected in the fictional narrative that follows.

How Would This Be Tried?

The first act of the employee's attorney would be to produce a psychiatrist to testify that the employee (the plaintiff) was of sound mind. The attorney for the employer counters with the assertion that public endorsement of UFOs as extraterrestrial was prima facie evidence of an unsound mind. The employer's attorney then calls as expert witnesses several psychiatrists who testify that an obsession with UFOs demonstrates a retreat from reality into a subjective world of power and subordination fantasies. The psychiatrists might even describe case studies of paranoid schizophrenics with dangerous delusions based on UFO imagery and "space aliens."

The employee's lawyer then counters with written evidence that many other people of demonstrably sound mind endorse the extraterrestrial hypothesis. He would name a long list of people who do so, including academics, professionals, and retired military officers.

Legal Theory Versus Scientific Theory

Before continuing to narrate the case, it is necessary to explain a very important difference between the way the word *theory* is used in science and in the law. Jurists use the word *theory* when they narrate their hypothesis that explains the evidence presented at a trial. There is a plaintiff's theory and a defendant's theory. But the relevance, materiality, and admissibility of evidence do not depend on the status of that evidence in *scientific* theory. Unlike the scientific method, as described by Kuhn, in which a fact without a paradigm is essentially no fact at all, the legal system is built on a foundation of alleged facts presented in evidence, and *the legal theory follows from the evidence*. Legal reasoning is largely inductive.[34]

Some Testimonial Evidence

I now return to the case. The fired employee's attorney calls "Professor X," who has never before told his story in public.* He describes how he and his family were driving home to his university

---

*Based on a case investigated by me and reported in a local UFO magazine.

from a summer posting, how they all saw a large, illuminated object stationary and low on the distant horizon, how they first thought it was a lighted water tower, but how, as they drove nearer, the "water tower" flew directly over the road and directly over their car, and they saw windows in the object and humanoid figures silhouetted against the windows.[35]

The attorney then calls two more witnesses.* The first is a junior college student who, while driving north from Montreal late on a winter night, saw a luminous object hovering over a ski hill. Intrigued by what she saw and familiar with the vicinity, she left the expressway, took local roads to the foot of the ski hill, got out of her car, and watched a glowing disk fly down the hill and directly over her car. The second witness is another UFO investigator who a few days later visited the ski hill, questioned the employees, and recorded the testimony of the driver of a snow-grooming machine who said that he had seen the luminous disk. In this case, the junior college student is presenting testimonial evidence, while the UFO investigator is presenting what is called "hearsay" evidence, backed up by his notes taken at the time.[36]

The employee's attorney then calls another university professor: me.† I testify about another UFO sighting in Quebec. Two young men were thinking about buying a camp located on a lake in northern Quebec. They visited the site in March 1978, before the snow melted. Intending to pitch a tent and spend the night, they had just lit a fire at a site along the lakeshore when a large, luminous object descended and hovered over the lake. Frightened, they retreated to their car, which they had left along a road at the entrance to the camp. Before they left, one of them took several pictures of the object.

When the men returned to Montreal, they developed the pictures and then contacted a local newspaper, which printed them.‡ A colleague and I interviewed the witnesses. We borrowed the original photo negatives and the camera. A university photographic expert examined the negatives microscopically and verified the intensity of the light source by observing the bleaching of the silver grains in the negative. Under microscopic examination he could not

---

*Another case from my files.
†A third case from my files, also reported in a local UFO magazine.
‡They received no money for their photographs.

detect any evidence of superimposition or double exposure. Then we took the camera and went to the campsite. We took photos of the same scene, from the same spot, at a variety of lens openings and shutter speeds. We were able to match the foreground and background with the foreground and background in the UFO photos. By considering lens apertures, shutter speeds, and image blur, we were able to estimate both the maximum and minimum distance and the maximum and minimum size of the UFO.[37]

Cross-Examination

The employer's attorney now cross-examines the plaintiff's witnesses, starting with "Professor X." The professor would be asked if he had not been extremely sleepy after a long drive, and might he not have imagined what he saw? The defendant's attorney would dismiss the professor. But on reexamination the plaintiff's attorney would elicit from the professor the fact that in addition to being an acknowledged scientific expert in his field, he was also an air force reserve pilot with many hours of flying experience; that he knew what a DC-9 looked like; that this was not a DC-9; and that (hearsay evidence again) his whole family had seen the UFO.

The employee's attorney now calls me to the stand. I would explain how a colleague had come across correspondence about this case in a government research agency file; how the colleague had asked me to follow up by speaking to the professor; how I approached the witness; how my wife and I were invited to dinner by the witness; how, after dinner, the witness and his wife recounted the entire story to us with increasing agitation and emotion.

The defendant's attorney would then in turn cross-examine the junior college student and the UFO investigator. He would try to demonstrate either that the witnesses were unreliable or that they were reliable but mistaken. Since he would be unable to show that the witnesses were unreliable, he would try to show that they were mistaken. Did they not simply see a low-flying airplane? The college student would answer that neither an airplane nor a helicopter looks like a self-luminous disk skimming low over a ski hill. Airplanes and helicopters are noisy, and this object, even though seen at close range, was quiet.

Closing Arguments

The attorney for the dismissed employee (the plaintiff) closes by saying:

Your honor, my client was dismissed because the defendant believed his public statements about UFOs showed him to be mentally incompetent. We have established that there is a large body of testimony that supports my client's statements. This evidence shows that UFO reports are not the result of unsophisticated, diseased, or disingenuous minds—instead they are very often the result of highly sophisticated minds looking for conventional explanations of what they have seen but cannot explain as airliners, advertising planes, satellites, planets, stars, or a host of other earthly or atmospheric phenomena. Experienced UFO researchers know very well that a large proportion of UFO sightings are nothing more than honest misinterpretations of human activity or natural phenomena. But that is where the problem begins, not where it ends. Beyond that 85 to 90 percent of misinterpretation, there is some 10 to 15 percent of UFO reports unexplained as natural phenomena or human activity. These phenomena might very well be the result of extraterrestrial technology. My client is simply reporting to his public—the town in which he lives—his evaluation and appreciation of this evidence. The defendant has introduced no evidence to challenge my client's mental capacity, nor has he succeeded in impugning the credibility of the many witnesses I have brought to the stand. In short, the other side has brought forward no evidence to support the alleged mental incompetence that was the basis of this unlawful dismissal. The balance of evidence clearly supports my client's public statements that UFOs represent an advanced, extraterrestrial technology. I therefore urge you to find for the plaintiff.

The attorney for the defense then turns to the judge and says:

Your honor, the witnesses called by my learned friend claim to
have seen impossible things. You cannot see impossible things.
Therefore they didn't see them. They behaved here on the wit-

ness stand just as did the plaintiff while in my client's employ. My client did not want his former employee to continue working, because after his public remarks about extraterrestrial UFOs, the employer had ample evidence to decide that his employee was no longer exercising sound judgment. This is a dangerous trait. People cannot be relied on if they claim to see things that cannot be seen. Therefore, my client had every good reason to terminate the employee, and the employee's case against my client is without merit. Please deny his suit for wrongful dismissal and affirm that my client acted properly in terminating the employment of someone who made such outrageous and unlikely public statements.

I leave the judge's decision in this hypothetical trial to your own imagination.

Military Intelligence and UFOs

Time is neutral toward science and the law, but time is an adversary to military intelligence. It is almost never acceptable to do "another experiment" to resolve a doubt about the enemy. Although there may sometimes be a penalty for deciding too soon, there is always a penalty for deciding too late. Science may be dilatory, justice should not be delayed, but military intelligence must be prompt.

There has been a long and probably continuing military intelligence interest in the UFO phenomenon. The earliest public record of this interest is the CIA's Robertson Panel report of 1952.[38] The conclusions of this panel are well known: the UFO phenomenon is a menace to national defense, not from the (nonexistent) UFOs but because public "hysteria" about UFOs might clog the defense communication channels and so permit a Soviet air attack to sneak in undetected.

How would military intelligence deal with the UFO-related information that is now so widely known to the UFO community? Reginald V. Jones, an Oxford-trained physicist, was the head of British Air Scientific Intelligence (a branch of M.I.6) during World War II. As a young man, he organized and directed Britain's effort to understand and defeat Germany's high-technology weapons, including electronic navigation beams, radar, the V-1 flying bomb, and the V-2 rocket. Incidentally, he also wrote a highly skeptical appendix to the Condon Report.[39]

In *Most Secret War* Jones described how people sometimes attribute causality to random events; how people habituate to and then ignore events and phenomena that are gradually introduced; how superstition and belief influence perception and judgment; and, most particularly, how people ignore evidence that contradicts theories to which they are emotionally attached.[40] Jones's practical lessons in *Most Secret War* provide a marvelous guide to the difference between science and scientific military intelligence. The following passage goes to the heart of the matter:

> An intelligence organization bears many resemblances to the human head, with its various senses. These will generally be on the alert, each searching its own domain and then as soon as the ears, for example, hear a noise and the signals are received in the brain, the latter will direct the eyes in the appropriate direction to supplement the information from the ears by what the eyes can see. So, if one kind of Intelligence source produces an indication, the Intelligence organization should then direct other kinds of source to focus on the same target.[41]

I established earlier that the scientist working within a paradigm has no professional interest in facts that are not explained by the present paradigm, or that cannot help to develop another paradigm. Jones's description makes it clear that, unlike the scientist, the successful military intelligence analyst must pay attention to and follow up all the available facts. As soon as an anomaly is noted, the intelligence organization devotes all its resources to finding out more about it, regardless of whether it fits an existing paradigm or whether it might lead to a new one.

One of the most interesting accounts in Jones's book describes the intelligence analysis of the V-2 rocket. It is important to remember that the V-2 was a technological first. Small liquid-propelled rockets had been built in the thirties, but the Allies had no one trying to develop a liquid-propelled rocket that could carry a one-ton warhead into the stratosphere and drop it two hundred miles away. The Germans were developing the totally new V-2 weapon at the end of the war under what were, fortunately for the Allies, trying circumstances.

Jones's V-2 intelligence sources included decrypted radio messages, rocket parts retrieved by Polish resistance fighters, fallen rocket parts provided by the Swedish government (a neutral in World War II), and photographic reconnaissance. But some respected British scientists who were called in to advise the government following Jones's intelligence discoveries had difficulty imagining that such a weapon was possible. Jones realized that their understanding of rockets was limited to what he called the "Guy Fawkes rocket": a solid-propellant cylinder with a pointed cap, launched from a stick stuck into the ground. These British scientific experts were relying only on what they themselves had done or had thought about, and they were not sufficiently familiar with the developments in rocket propulsion to realize that Jones's intelligence sources were correct. They had not realized that a rocket motor could be attached to the end of a lightweight chassis, and that fuel and oxygen could be contained in tanks fitted into the chassis and fed to the motor by pumps. They did not understand that the rocket could be steered by deflecting its jet stream with heat-resistant rudders, and that these rudders could be set to change the rocket's course in response to a time-of-flight or an altitude signal.

Jones and his intelligence organization knew *all* these things. Before the first rockets fell on Antwerp and London, they had published correct performance specifications for the range, warhead, method of propulsion, method of guidance, and probable blast effect. The scientists called in to advise the government, following the initial discovery of the rocket, did not have a coherent picture of the rocket because, instead of evidence, they relied on what little they knew theoretically about how rockets could or could not work. They discounted the existence of the V-2 because they did not understand how such a rocket could be built.

Of course, not all of Jones's intelligence information was reliable. He had to sift out what was reliable from what was not by using internal checks on his informants' data. For example, when evaluating intelligence reports on the weight of the warhead, he used only reports that correctly identified one of the two propellants as liquid air or liquid oxygen. Jones said, "This provided a touchstone, since it showed that any report that mentioned it had at least one element of truth, and might therefore reflect the knowledge of someone who had a fairly direct contact with genuine information."[42] Since Jones had enough previous evidence to be certain about the method of propulsion, he could dismiss as unreliable later reports that erred about the method of propulsion. Using this screening technique as well as decrypted information from other sources, Jones was able to accurately estimate the warhead size. If he had given equal weight to all the reports, his estimate would have been inaccurate.

Jones describes another incident in which a scientist disregarded evidence that did not fit his preconceptions. In 1940, during the Battle of Britain, an electronics specialist was called on to evaluate the evidence, collated by Jones from prisoners and from captured documents, that the Germans were using radio navigation beams over England. The specialist said that the beams were nonexistent because his theoretical calculations showed that beams could not follow the curvature of the earth from the transmitting stations in France and Germany. He was wrong, and he might have been deadly wrong, because he backed his opinion with the recommendation that the air force pay no more attention to Jones's alleged beams. Fortunately, Jones got the air force to fly airplanes to listen for the beams; the beams were found and then were "bent" when the British set up their own counterfeit beams to misguide the bombers.

One lesson to be learned from Jones's personal history of military intelligence is that scientific experts are prone to disregard facts that do not fit an existing paradigm. The bias against facts without a paradigm was mentioned earlier in the discussion of what Thomas Kuhn called *normal science*. Another lesson from military intelligence is that successful analysis requires a careful collation of multiple sources of information. The pedigree of each piece of information, including the trustworthiness of the supplier, its internal consistency, and its consistency with other information, must be very carefully evaluated before it becomes accepted as forming a part of the intelligence picture. In summary, military intelligence warns us that *one's own preconceptions of what can be* are absolutely no evidence for what *is*.

Occam's Razor

Occam's razor ("hypotheses are not to be multiplied unnecessarily") is a cutting instrument much praised by R. V. Jones and by some philosophers of science.[43] For, as Jones says, "if you start allowing more complicated explanations than are essential to explain the facts, you can launch yourself into a realm of fantasy."[44] Critics have used Occam's razor as a weapon to attack the extraterrestrial UFO hypothesis. They claim that the hypothesis is unnecessary, since "normal science" of atmospheric physics, physiology, or psychology can explain all the UFO and UFO-related evidence without it.[45] This chapter does not review in detail the technical inadequacies of "normal science" explanations for the UFO and UFO-related evidence. I assume for my purposes here that "normal science" cannot explain substantially all the UFO and UFO-related phenomena.

As discussed earlier, Kuhn described the usual response to new and anomalous scientific evidence in *The Structure of Scientific Revolutions*. The existing paradigm is modified to subsume the new evidence. Eventually, if the new evidence is sufficiently well replicated and sufficiently anomalistic, and theorists are sufficiently clever, the old paradigm will give way to a new one, which explains the new evidence and replaces the old paradigm. On the other hand, remember that Kuhn also states that new evidence that cannot be placed in the context of either an existing or a new paradigm is not really scientific, since "to reject one paradigm without simultaneously substituting another is to reject science itself."[46]

UFO critics have an intellectual style that guarantees the accuracy of this quote. They wield Occam's razor with what might be called procrustean abandon. They first stretch "normal science" to unbelievable lengths to at least verbally explain the anomalous phenomena, and then they lop off and ignore the remaining scientifically undigestible evidence because there is no imaginable scientific paradigm that could include it. This was demonstrated very clearly by the contrast between a polemic written by Donald H. Menzel that dismissed UFOs in general terms as optical or atmospheric anomalies,[47] and a detailed rebuttal of the vague references to "ionospheric reflections" and "temperature inversions" that explained away several Condon Commission cases, written by atmospheric physicist James E. McDonald.[48]

Comparing the Three Approaches

The military, legal, and scientific perspectives on evidence represent three different routes to an understanding of the world. The job of military intelligence is to protect us from surprise attack from enemies we may not have suspected and by weapons we may not have imagined. The military intelligence analyst needs timely evidence about foreign developments that threaten the nation. The analyst cannot assume that the scientific theorists and weapons designers of his own country know what is possible and what is not. The intelligence history of rocket propulsion and electronic navigation during World War II shows that military intelligence analysis fails if it ignores evidence that friendly scientific experts cannot explain.

While the goal of military intelligence is to protect the state, the goal of law is to regulate the relations among citizens and the state. Law is a deliberate and largely traditional set of rules that keep us at least one step away from the nasty, brutish, and short life of a state of war or of nature.

Legal evidence does not require the imprimatur of scientific theory. It stands or falls on the basis of its contribution to understanding a case: "Relevant evidence means evidence having any tendency to make the existence of any fact that is of consequence to the determination of the action more probable or less probable than it would be without the evidence."[49] And the trial judge, using common sense and logic, but not subject to the limitations of scientific theory, decides (subject to appeal) whether evidence is relevant or not.

While military intelligence is aggressive and one-sided, law is deliberate and two-sided. It is supposed to be evenhanded between two private adversaries or between the citizen and the state. Therefore, the practice of law constrains the collection and use of evidence. Evidence that impugns the character of a defendant, unless it is directly related to the question at issue, is usually forbidden in court. Evidence about what people say other people said or did is hearsay evidence and is accepted in court only with severe limitations. All evidence presented in court is open to criticism by the other side, and the Anglo-Saxon adversary system provides a forum in which the relevance, materiality, or admissibility of all evidence can be directly challenged and tested. Like military intelligence, the law invites all relevant evidence, but in the interest of fairness, the relevance of evidence is constrained by rules that must be obeyed by all parties to a dispute, including the state.

The goal of science is to develop a consistent understanding of the inanimate and the animate world. Science is a social luxury compared with military intelligence or the law. Science flourishes in advanced, stable societies that have a surplus of income to support the universities, laboratories, journals, and associations that form the scientific community.

Military intelligence and science differ in one vital way. As Napoleon put it, in war it is a sin to "form a picture" of the enemy,[50] that is, to come to a conclusion about the enemy based on your own inclinations and predispositions. Military intelligence has to be brutally empirical. There can be no a priori theoretical reason for a military intelligence analyst to discard evidence. The only justification for doing so is a direct conflict between two sources of evidence, in which case the more consistent evidence takes precedence over the less consistent.

However, as Kuhn pointed out, *the entire business of science is to "form a picture" of nature.* Scientists understand that no picture of nature is ever complete and that science modifies the picture of nature in a manner consistent with Kuhn's description of the progress of scientific revolutions. But, according to Kuhn's analysis, scientists find it both necessary and convenient to ignore evidence. In Kuhn's analysis, as paradigms grow stale and new ones develop, *facts that fit neither the old paradigm nor the developing new paradigm are not scientific facts at all.* Certainly the data that help shape a new paradigm will be fully weighed and considered, but, according to Kuhn's analysis, there is no place in science for facts that can neither be explained under the old paradigm nor used as counterexamples that contribute to building a new paradigm. Therefore, according to Kuhn, practicing scientists are in the habit of ignoring empirical evidence—

facts—that neither fit an old paradigm nor help them to develop a new one. This is why scientists are among the people *worst* suited to accept and accommodate facts that have no place in current theories nor relate to developing theories of nature. Scientists are actually trained to be incapable of dealing with truly anomalous evidence.

Therefore, of the three professions discussed here (military intelligence, the law, or science), *I argue that science is the least fitted to uncover and present radically new facts about nature.* Science can be the most protective of the "picture of nature" it already possesses, the most conservative about adopting a new "picture of nature," and the most ready to ignore facts that do not fit either the existing picture of nature or the one that science finds itself capable of developing.

The second-best profession under which to uncover and present radical new facts about nature is the law. But there has not yet been a place in the law courts for UFO evidence. Until someone's car is damaged by a UFO and an insurance claim is contested, or, as in my fictional trial, someone is "wrongfully dismissed" for publicly advocating the extraterrestrial hypothesis, it is unlikely that the courts of law will have any reason to recognize the UFO evidence. I cannot claim that the extraterrestrial UFO hypothesis could be upheld "beyond a reasonable doubt" in a criminal case, but I believe that before a civil magistrate the "balance of evidence" in favor of the extraterrestrial hypothesis would prevail.

The profession best suited to observe, analyze, and recommend action on the UFO evidence is military intelligence. Given the heavy weight of public evidence that supports the extraterrestrial UFO hypothesis, and given the much greater sensing and data-collecting resources of military intelligence, it is inconceivable to me that some members at least of the military intelligence community are not fully aware that the UFO phenomenon demonstrates extraterrestrial technology.

Since secrecy is central to the use of military intelligence, it is no surprise that what military intelligence knows about UFOs, military intelligence will not tell. The Freedom of Information Act and similar acts in other countries do not really interfere with the exercise of military intelligence, since documents obtained under that act may be so thoroughly censored that they provide effectively no information at all. And whole sets of documents, even if they are known to exist, can simply be concealed for reasons of national security.

Conclusion

The UFO and UFO-related evidence, viewed from the three perspectives of science, law, and military intelligence, leads to three different courses of action. Scientists can help to clarify the UFO evidence. The scientist who understands UFO evidence and who also understands the complexities of human perception and memory knows that much of the observational UFO data do not result from natural, engineering, or psychological phenomena understood by "normal" science. Scientists and technicians can and do verify the reliability of instrumental observations that often accompany human UFO testimony. And scientists and technicians can also help to eliminate the "noise" in the UFO data by identifying the "normal" engineering, natural, or psychological causes of many mistaken UFO reports.

But the residual clarified and verified observational UFO data do not fit an existing paradigm of nature, nor do they fit any currently evolving paradigm of nature. The phenomena suggested by the observations are simply too disparate from the artifacts that our own science has been able to imagine or construct. The UFO data are scientifically inexplicable. Thus, except to supply criticism or clarification, no action at all about the UFO evidence is expected from scientists or from science.

The legal profession would be forced to take a more integrated approach to the UFO evidence, should this evidence ever come before the courts. Legal evidence is not constrained by scientific theory. The "theory" of a case is a hypothesis about the course of events that explains the facts alleged in support of it. The practice of courtroom law consists mostly of arguing about the relevance, materiality, and admissibility of facts. But the facts come first in law, and the theories follow after. I believe that the inductive character of legal argument, which first establishes facts in order to build a legal "theory," would produce a more sympathetic courtroom hearing for the entire body of UFO evidence than would the learned journals of almost any scientific specialty. But until such evidence becomes an issue at law, the legal profession can of course take no action at all.

The military intelligence analyst expects to find things that science cannot explain because the military intelligence profession looks for things that friendly scientists have not yet learned to make. Military intelligence is the only one of the three professions discussed here that may actually be doing something about the UFO evidence, but if it is, the public will not know—at least not right away. Scientists' work is openly discussed and criticized by colleagues, and the practice of law is often a public courtroom contest, but the intelligence analyst works in secrecy.

Nevertheless, the military intelligence analyst is the professional most likely to be able to make sense of the UFO evidence. Military intelligence analysts do not "make pictures" before the evidence is in. They do not dismiss evidence because they do not understand it. They know how to combine ambiguous evidence from various sources to develop a clearer understanding of the complex and often unexpected reality that faces them. And these are the skills needed to make sense out of the complex picture of UFO and UFO-related evidence that confronts us.

It is a serious error to assume that professional scientists are the best evaluators of the UFO evidence. The Philip Morrisons and Carl Sagans[51] of the scientific world, when faced with UFO and UFO-related evidence, are like the British scientists who scoffed at R. V. Jones's intelligence about navigation guidance beams and the V-2 rocket. Despite the scientific disbelief, guidance beams were real, V-2s were real, and they both performed as Jones said they would. The critical, empirical attitude of a skilled attorney and the alertness and open-mindedness of a military intelligence analyst will both produce a clearer understanding of the UFO evidence than the theory-driven closed-mindedness of the professional scientist. And between them, the attorney and the analyst might just persuade the scientist that there is something here that merits paying attention.

Chapter Four

UFOs, the Military, and the Early Cold War Era

Michael D. Swords

UFOs and the cold war have an unusual history, and one still largely hidden.* Enough, however, is known through government documents and other valid sources to paint an accurate picture. It is the story of a secretive phenomenon (UFOs) interfacing with a secretive human activity (military intelligence) at a time of maximum concern and confusion. The new evidence reveals a fluidity of outlook in the early confrontations with the phenomenon that hardened into a negative attitude that dominated government thinking about the subject for years to come.

During the cold war, what perhaps should have been an idealistic venture into scientific research and discovery became possible evidence of danger. Strange phenomena in the skies were wonders to the naive, but they were portents of threat to the armed service personnel who grimly watched over a world of building tensions. UFOs were *never* viewed benignly by those who first began study-

*I wish to thank the institutions and staffs of the J. Allen Hynek Center for UFO Studies, the American Philosophical Society Library, the University of Colorado, the California Institute of Technology, and the University of Arizona. I would also like to thank my fellow ufologists Barry Greenwood, Jan Aldrich, Mark Rodeghier, Richard Hall, Wendy Connors, Michael Hall, Jerry Clark, Loren Gross, and Sharon Stayonovich.

ing them, nor by those who set the policies for handling information about the UFOs. The cold war attitude that security, not science, was preeminent was applied to the UFO problem immediately following the end of World War II and continued at least until 1969 when the air force discontinued its last formal UFO investigative project, Blue Book. This attitude had a powerfully distorting impact on UFO research that lasted throughout the twentieth century.

Ghost Rockets

In 1946 the West and the Soviet Union were on increasingly hostile terms. One war had ended only to be replaced by a situation rapidly building into another horrific threat. Although the United States was dismantling its large armed forces and its major scientific-technological teams (e.g., the Manhattan Project and the Massachusetts Institute of Technology [MIT] Radiation Laboratory), top-level government scientists abhorred this trend and pushed for what they felt was necessary to maintain military superiority. Exactly where that superiority would come from was in debate, but it was generally assumed that it would come from the air.

Within the not-yet-independent U.S. Air Force, Gen. Henry (Hap) Arnold created Project RAND (Research and Development) as a think tank to pursue these future routes to superiority, as well as to provide an incentive to retain some of the wartime expertise that was exiting the services. The first RAND report was *Preliminary Design of an Experimental World-Circling Spaceship*, published in May 1946.[1] The theoretical study, which involved a team of high-level scientists and technologists in academia and industry, was authored primarily by RAND missiles expert James Lipp. The RAND study was inspired by a similar one initiated by the navy's Bureau of Aeronautics about a half year earlier.[2] Both the air force and the navy thought that space platforms would afford a nation a nearly invulnerable power in intelligence gathering, as well as striking power. The launch vehicles would be the precursors of intercontinental ballistic missiles (ICBMs). And, the report speculated, imagine the impact on the citizens and leaders of the world if the United States were to accomplish this.

The Americans and the Soviets were both putting captured German scientists to work building their rocket programs. In the spring of 1946 "our Germans" launched the first of sixty-three V-2 rockets. Around the same time, the USSR "restored" V-2 production in its occupied territories. At Oak Ridge National Laboratories, a program to pursue nuclear-powered engines was launched. In a second report from RAND, Lipp wrote that the Russians would see the power in this, too.[3] Distrust was compounded when Stalin, frustrated that the Allies had taken high-level rocket scientists to U.S. military laboratories, shouted at his General Serov, "We defeated Nazi armies; we occupied Berlin and Peenemunde; but the Americans got the rocket engineers. What could be more revolting and inexcusable? How and why was this allowed to happen?"[4]

The first modern UFO wave, the ghost rockets of Scandinavia, came about in this atmosphere. The sightings began in Sweden in May 1946, peaked in August, and were largely ended by fall. Although some descriptions are reminiscent of meteor bolides, many of the best reports indicate non-self-luminous objects shaped like cigars, rockets, planes, or even birds. The official summary of the Swedish Defense Staff indicated approximately one thousand reports.[5]

Sweden quickly set up a high-level military and technology group to investigate the stories and attempt to pin down the origins and destinations of these objects. Norway issued a media ban on discussion of the overflights, apparently on the premise that the issuing power would gain information about how their *missiles* were doing from the newspaper reports. It did not take long for the Pentagon to go on alert. A memo to the State Department said that the "Swedes profess ignorance as to origin, character or purpose of missiles but state definitely they are not launched by Swedes. Eyewitness reports state missiles came in from southerly direction proceeding to northwest. Six units Atlantic fleet under Admiral Hewitt arrived Stockholm this morning [July 11]."[6]

Inside the Pentagon, the mood was tense. U.S. Army Air Forces chief of intelligence, Gen. George C. McDonald, had been collecting ghost rocket reports from military attachés and Department of State representatives for a memorandum to his superior, Army Air Forces commanding general Carl Spaatz, and his chief advisers, Generals Partridge and LeMay. McDonald worried about several things: no known meteor showers were predicted for the relevant time period, and the Russians might be launching rockets to impress other nations with their power.[7]

The U.S. intelligence community tried to fill this gap in information. Key Pentagon intelligence gatherers, such as Lt. Col. George Garrett in the air force's Collections Branch, reported that pressure had come down from above continuously over a long period of time.[8] During that period Secretary of the Navy James Forrestal, on 16 July 1946, and Generals James Doolittle and David Sarnoff, about one month later, visited Sweden allegedly on routine government and business matters.[9] This was downplayed as coincidence, but the ghost rockets were discussed.

The press reflected the cold war worries about the objects. On 14 August Undersecretary of State Dean Acheson was quoted in the *New York Times* as being "very much interested" in what was going on. Around this same time, British intelligence was working with key Allied intelligence figure R. V. Jones to try to solve the problem. *Newsweek* printed a Scandinavian map with Soviet rocket planes flying from Peenemünde across Sweden and Finland. The article warned direly of "the Soviet Challenge" and the past war's evidence of the astounding progress in missiles: "Public sympathy and public funds must be poured into this work in an unending stream to meet Russia's challenge." The *Christian Science Monitor* claimed that, according to military and technical sources, these overflights were surely part of a "war of nerves" perpetrated by the Soviets. But it will not work, it proclaimed, because we (the United States) are the masters of the air, and we are already far beyond anything that others can fly, and we are going farther. The article continued:

The Army Air Forces have boasted they are developing giant rockets designed to whoosh 130 miles or more into the stratosphere. They said they could zoom a spaceship to the moon or beyond, if they wanted to. The Navy, not to be outdone, began describing pilotless aircraft, now on its drafting boards, which could carry atomic bombs. It added that only a bit further ahead were satellite vehicles, circling earth hundreds of miles up, like moons, and interstellar space ships.[10]

Far from being able to link the objects to the Soviets, the *London Daily Telegraph* revealed that the Soviets were wondering whether the United States was perpetrating this hoax to make them look bad.[11]

By the end of 1946, the observations had essentially stopped. The agencies remained as confused as ever. The Swedish Commission made its final, puzzled report in December. U.S. interest continued well into 1947. An article in the January 1947 *Intelligence Review* (a classified publication of the War Department's Division of Intelligence) admitted confusion about both the nature of the phenomenon and the "contradictory attitude" of high Swedish officials. But it seemed clear that a few, at least, overflights of technological devices had occurred.[12] When the U.S. flying disk wave hit in the summer of 1947, and Wright-Patterson Air Force Base's Air Matériel Command (AMC) was brought in to aid in the analysis, one of the first things that AMC director of intelligence, Colonel Howard (Mack) McCoy, did was to ask for the Pentagon's ghost rocket files. The flying disks did the same thing for McCoy and his investigators as they had for the Swedes and the Pentagon. They tantalized, they confused, and they remained unsolved.

The 1947 U.S. Wave and Its Impacts

In 1946 Josef Stalin had stated that there can never be a lasting peace between the USSR and capitalism. President Harry Truman agreed and sent large amounts of money to defend Greece and Turkey from the thrust of Soviet communism. The Truman Doctrine and the Marshall Plan acted, in part, to permanently hem in the USSR while building a capitalist economic wall against the Iron Curtain. Two incompatible ideologies now existed side by side across the geographic results of World War II.[13]

Responding to the increasing competition with the Soviets, American scientists and engineers were developing innovative air technology. Research on nuclear rockets began at the Nuclear Energy for Propulsion of Aircraft (NEPA) project at Oak Ridge. A nearly noiseless airplane was unveiled by NASA's predecessor, the National Advisory Committee for Aeronautics (NACA). Long-range pilotless flights were achieved. Muroc Field (later Edwards Air Force Base) became the center of advanced U.S. flight technology, and in 1947 the Bell X-1 plane first broke the sound barrier there. At Wright-Patterson Air Force Base, an intelligence engineer, Alfred Loedding, was designing disk-shaped aircraft. At Cal Tech, Theodore von Karman, renowned scientist and chairman of the air force's Scientific Advisory Board, was interested in the Coanda Effect, a propulsion technique for levitating a disk-shaped plane. In the Soviet Union, the push was on for an intercontinental ballistic missile.[14]

In the summer of 1947, into this increasingly tense climate of unspoken war and technological threat, came the second great wave of unidentified flying objects: the flying disks of the United States. Although many earlier cases have been found, the first UFO sightings to come to public attention originated with the Kenneth Arnold sighting of nine disks over the Mount Rainier area of Washington on 24 June 1947. The sighting, later confirmed by a ground witness, is still unexplained.[15] For the first few days of the summer of 1947 reports, the Pentagon seemed slow to respond. But that attitude changed.

The cause of the change was understandable: military pilots and scientists began reporting disk encounters as well, often in the vicinity of high-security installations.[16] Muroc Field itself had at least three reports; secret project balloon scientists in New Mexico made a sighting; other pilots and ground personnel added reports. Now the Pentagon looked at the subject in earnest. Lieutenant Colonel Garrett of the Intelligence Collections Branch was to be the focus person in these matters. He had the cooperation of the other services and agencies such as the FBI. Pressure came down from high-level officers just as it had during the ghost rockets scare. What were these things?

The immediate concern was that they could be Soviet technology. Was it possible that the Soviets were flying something over U.S. airspace? If so, for what reason? The disks were beginning to attract media attention as well. From 6 July through 9 July, they were front-page news almost everywhere, every day.[17] Was this a direct military threat or some sort of psychological warfare? Wright-Patterson's Intelligence Division (T-2) was brought in to assist Garrett and the Pentagon. They searched in Wright-Patterson's secret libraries and found the report "German Flying Wings Designed by Horten Brothers" (5 July 1946). They wondered if the Soviets had expropriated advanced Nazi technologies of the Horten brothers, a pair of brilliant aeronautical engineers far in advance of their U.S. counterparts. They wondered if thin disklike aircraft—missiles or gliders—were operational. T-2's Alfred Loedding contributed his disk-craft ideas, and this material was sent to Garrett in the Pentagon.[18]

Garrett reported to the chief of collections, Col. Robert Taylor, and through him to the executive office of air force intelligence in the Pentagon under Gen. George McDonald. McDonald did not address the flying disk issue himself. He gave that task to Brig. Gen. George Schulgen, chief of intelligence requirements and sometimes substitute for McDonald. On 9 July, at the apex of the concern about the disks, Schulgen brought the FBI formally into the investigation. He requested assistance because:

the thought exists that the first reported sightings might have been by individuals of Communist sympathies with the view to causing hysteria and fear of a secret Russian weapon. . . . [Schulgen] desired the assistance of the Federal Bureau of Investigation in locating and questioning the individuals . . . to ascertain whether or not they are sincere . . . or whether their statements were prompted by personal desire for publicity or political reasons.[19]

J. Edgar Hoover said that he would be willing to investigate but only if the FBI was allowed access to any disks recovered. Hoover knew of one disk that the military had "grabbed . . . and would not let us have it for cursory examination." He was also concerned about the crashed disk in Roswell, New Mexico, where the military claim that it was a balloon had not been borne out when the FBI investigated.[20] But despite concern over military openness and cooperation, an agent from FBI headquarters, S. W. Reynolds, was assigned as liaison to Garrett on the flying disk beat.

In the intensity of the first week and a half of July, the Air National Guards of the Pacific Coast States were mobilized to create "saucer patrols." In Oregon, eight P-51 fighters and three A-26 bombers with telescopic cameras were making flights.[21] A guard unit in North Dakota pursued a reported disk but could not make contact. On 10 July, one of the last days of the wave that produced thousands of reports, mechanics at Harmon Field, Newfoundland, saw a bright disk with powerful contrail "cut" through the clouds, and took a picture of the result. By that date, General Schulgen and the Pentagon were so concerned that they contacted T-2 (AMC's Intelligence Division at Wright-Patterson) chief, Col. Howard McCoy and ordered him to send two investigators to Newfoundland and to report directly to him at the Pentagon.[22] McCoy also contacted ex-German lighter-than-air specialist Hugo Eckener (then at Goodyear) to inquire about possible German/Russian blimp technology and whether "pick-a-back" (piggyback) motherships with small assault planes were a possibility. Two of T-2's senior officers went to Harmon Field, thus beginning Wright-Patterson's active investigations into the UFO phenomenon. Much of this was considered important security information and thereby classified. Capt. Edward Ruppelt, who was chief of Wright-Patterson's UFO project in 1951–53, said that the correspondence of the 1947 era indicated that the UFO problem was seen as "very serious," and that security was tight on it sometime in July.[23]

Meanwhile, Garrett was going about his task. By the end of July he and the FBI's Reynolds had noticed something peculiar: Pentagon pressure had diminished. Garrett knew that from his viewpoint the mystery of the disks was far from solved. He and Reynolds came to the same conclusion: the very highest levels of the Pentagon must know what this is.[24] To test this hypothesis, and to relieve the air force and the FBI of a lot of useless chasing about, Garrett assembled a document, roughly what the military calls an "estimate of the situation," based on what he considered to be his sixteen most credible and useful cases.

The assessment concluded that the reports were of a low-aspect (thin) disklike aerial technology of very high performance characteristics.[25] He and Reynolds then began to send this estimate around to U.S. intelligence and research agencies, to ascertain whether this was our technology. They were astounded to receive back the consistent answer: no. They then sent the estimate to Wright-Patterson's commanding general, Nathan Twining, who had Howard McCoy convene the experts and return the message: the objects appear to be high-performance air technologies, and they are not ours. Twining said to continue the investigation as a formal secret project at AMC's T-2. In September 1947 Garrett transferred his files to T-2 and left the UFO job to Howard McCoy and Alfred Loedding.[26]

In the fall and winter of 1947, Wright-Patterson and the Pentagon gathered far-flung UFO reports and investigated the Soviet-Nazi theory as best they could. T-2 operative Lt. Col. Malcolm Seashore hand-carried essential intelligence requirements (i.e., what to look for) about possible Soviet use of Horten technology to intelligence operatives in Europe.[27] The lower levels of the intelligence community were split on the flying disk hypotheses: Soviet-Nazi technology, U.S. top secret technology, human error, and extraterrestrials. The American people, according to a Gallup poll, had heard about flying saucers widely and considered them to be the middle two.[28] The military was split in the opposite way: it was the Soviets or the extraterrestrials. According to Ruppelt, by the end of 1947, at Wright-Patterson's T-2 Intelligence Division, the USSR had been practically eliminated in their minds as an explanation.[29]

In December of that year, an official exchange of letters took place in the Pentagon, which established Project Sign, a formal U.S. Air Force UFO study project at Wright-Patterson.[30] This action formalized the work led by engineer Alfred Loedding since September. Capt. Robert Sneider was appointed military chief, and the secret official project began in late January 1948.

Projects Sign and Grudge

The year 1948 saw the continuance of the Marshall Plan and the U.S. policy of containing the Soviet Union both militarily and economically. The Soviets responded in June with the Berlin Blockade. During this period, the Americans were very interested in Soviet technological development. The CIA, accordingly, began sending a series of secret picture-taking balloon flights over Soviet territory, a procedure that continued until the development of the U-2 spy planes of the later 1950s. The United States did not yet know that the Soviets had embarked on a path toward building big single-stage ICBMs with capabilities well beyond the lifting thrust of German V-2 devices.[31]

Meanwhile, the United States tested successfully the Northrup flying wing and the Bell X-1, which was pushing one thousand miles per hour. At White Sands Proving Grounds, Werner von Braun and his German rocket team launched a V-2 that carried primates into the upper atmosphere. And Secretary of Defense James Forrestal announced that the American military establishment was seriously engaged in a satellite program.[32]

While military and intelligence eyes were fixed upon the skies and space technologies, the experts in Project Sign at Wright-Patterson Air Force Base began to study UFOs. The core personnel for the project were probably the most talented group to work on UFOs until the air force ended its investigation in 1969. Aiding chief officer, Capt. Robert R. Sneider, were two outstanding aeronautical engineers, Alfred Loedding and Albert B. Deyarmond. Loedding was the designer of the aforementioned disk-shaped aircraft. Deyarmond was a World War II colleague of T-2 chief Howard McCoy and an MIT graduate. Completing the core group was nuclear and missiles expert Lawrence Truettner. Many others helped, and the full facilities of T-2 were at their disposal.[33] The quality of these people indicates the seriousness (and the comparative difference in later years) with which the air force considered the flying disk problem.

The project members looked at about two hundred cases, some of which had happened prior to its inception. A major incident was the Mantell case, wherein a National Guard pilot and war hero lost his plane and his life "chasing a UFO." This casualty, which usually has been thought of as the result of an unfortunate error involving a large secret-project balloon, was quite confusing and spectacular at the time. Mantell was quoted as saying that the thing was fast (at least as fast as his plane) and "metallic" and "of tremendous size." Much later, the air force stated publicly that Mantell had chased Venus, but inside Project Sign no one believed this. But what could he have been chasing? Cold war secrecy about American balloon projects helped to confuse the investigation by covering up classified balloon launches.[34]

The Mantell case was part of a rush of reports from all over the globe. Could they all be Soviet weapons? What was apparently an odd meteor bolide over Kansas brought reports, but also a theory by an amateur as to whether UFOs happened more frequently during close approaches of heavenly bodies. The project later decided to plot this possibility and discovered, strangely, that there *was* a correlation. More reports by scientists occurred. One group saw unusual things at Holloman Air Force Base; they were balloon experts and knew the difference. Loedding investigated this case and went on to Phoenix, Arizona, to interview a man who had photo-graphed a low-aspect disklike craft in July 1947.[35] Because Loedding believed such designs could fly, the photos were of special interest to him.

There were a handful of unexplained cases in May and June 1948. The project engineers did not believe that there was a reason-able mundane explanation for any of them, but most were listed in later years under various categories of known phenomena. Much of this was due to the imagination of J. Allen Hynek, whom the air force hired as an astronomy consultant from Ohio State Univer-sity later in the fall. Hynek thought that when other explanations failed, establishing low-probability explanations was part of his job.[36] Throughout most of 1948, members of the Sign team, how-ever, did not accept any such "stretched" explanations. To them many cases were profoundly puzzling. And the feeling was grow-ing that the United States and the Soviets had nothing to do with them.

Then, on 24 July, the Chiles-Whitted case occurred. Clarence Chiles and John Whitted were veteran commercial pilots who had a spectacular nighttime close encounter with "something" in the skies over Alabama. The object seemed to them to be a large, wing-less, cigar-shaped flying fuselage with two decks of windows and a jet exhaust. The case was reported to their boss, and then to the papers, the following day. Then the men received a phone call from the Pentagon telling them to keep quiet or they would be "in real trouble."[37] New Director of Intelligence Charles Cabell then called Project Sign and ordered it to send investigators immediately to interview the pilots. Loedding and Deyarmond were on a plane that same day.

The Sign investigators were impressed. The quality of the ob-servers, the closeness of the encounter, and the agreement of gen-eral physical details convinced them that this finally was the sort of case that could yield insight into the flying disks. They also located a military ground witness to what was apparently the same object. In addition, a report a few days earlier over The Hague seemed to describe a flying fuselage-shaped object very similar to the Chiles-Whitted device.

The project members reasoned that they had several dozen aerial observations that they could not explain, many of them by military pilots and scientists. The objects seemed to act like real technology, but their sources said that they were not ours. The flying fuselage encounter intrigued them. The Prandtl theory of lift indicated that such an odd shape *can* fly, but it would need some form of power plant advanced well beyond what could be built (e.g., nuclear). Nothing indicated that the Soviets were near having anything like that, and risky overflights of their advanced technologies would seem an insane strategy on their part. The objects were real, with high-performance characteristics, but neither the Soviet Union nor the United States could make them. Thus, the investigators concluded that the flying disks were extraterrestrial.

This theory of the disks was not as incredible in intelligence circles as one might think. Many Pentagon and AMC personnel were pilots, engineers, and technical people. They tended to think that one could build things that worked, that advances were possible, but that certain things were not yet available. This "can-do" attitude contrasted markedly with many scientists' characterization of such concepts as impossible, unthinkable, or absurd. One school of thought in the Pentagon was sure the disks existed; some thought they were Soviet, some thought extraterrestrial, some simply mysterious. Another school took the "total bunk" view, and a third school felt that regardless of the ultimate explanation, it was the duty of intelligence to investigate everything.[38]

The influence of the science community in this debate was contradictory. New theories of planetary system formation suggested that planets were common in the universe, and that life "out there" was likely.[39] Publication of these opinions increased the amount of public commentary about Mars and what the changeable markings on its surface were all about. However, many outspoken scientists (e.g., Irving Langmuir, Harlow Shapley, and Donald Menzel) were worried about "pathological science" and tides of "unscientific" irrationality that were detrimental to America and even to human destiny.[40] Irrational ideas must be eliminated for the good of us all. Flying disks, always referred to as "saucers" by such men (to increase their seeming ridiculousness), were one of their several targets. Many of these "science impossibilists" were persons of influence in the military and intelligence communities. In this atmosphere, some military people sided with the "possibilists" and some with the "impossibilists."

Project Sign felt that it had good evidence, even without an alien craft and body to show off. The team wrote its estimate of the situation, the formal intelligence summary that every project must submit when it feels that it has something important to conclude. The report concluded that the flying disks were extraterrestrial spacecraft.[41]

Captain Sneider and the Sign team worked on the Chiles-Whitted case during August 1948, and Colonel McCoy went to the Pentagon on the twenty-third. Personnel in the Pentagon who were opposed to the extraterrestrial hypothesis were apparently reactivated at this time.

Just after the Chiles-Whitted event, Director of Intelligence Cabell had contacted his chief of Air Intelligence Requirements (AIR), Colonel Walsh (AFOAI), to prepare a study to "examine the pattern of the tactics of the flying saucers." Walsh gave the job to Lt. Col. R. N. Smith in Air Estimates (AFOAI-AE). Smith passed it on to Maj. Aaron J. ("Jerry") Boggs of Defensive Air (AFOAI-DA). Boggs, who had written almost all the intelligence directives concerning saucers for the Pentagon in the past few months, was anti-extraterrestrial and just vaguely tolerant of the notion that the disks were real at all. Boggs was the Pentagon's "saucer killer."[42]

Boggs was a key element in a cadre of antisaucerites in the Directorate of Intelligence that included Brig. Gen. Ernest (Dinty) Moore, Brig. Gen. Walter Agee, and Col. E. H. Porter, one of Boggs's superiors.[43] Boggs's papers on the flying disk problem were consistently negative. For these men, the disks probably did not exist, but there was an outside chance that some sightings were of Soviet weaponry. Boggs went to work briefly on Cabell's request. When Project Sign's extraterrestrial estimate arrived in late September, they readied a counterdocument (AIR 100-203-79). This contrary study, which had the cooperation of the Office of Naval Intelligence as well, stated that although the disks did seem to be real, they were not extraterrestrial, and some observations might be of Nazi technology upgraded by the Soviets.[44]

In early to mid-October, Air Force Chief of Staff Hoyt Vandenberg "batted" the Sign estimate back down. Perhaps he felt that the Soviet threat that was featured in the alternative AIR 100 document seemed too real. Project Sign had received an August sighting report from Moscow of a flying fuselage-shaped object and a report stating, "The

Central Party is making a special secret study of the American 'flying saucer' story and the 'rockets over Sweden' incident." When an alleged close encounter and "touchdown" of a small saucer was reported in Minnesota, both the air force and the FBI looked for a communist-inspired hoax.[45]

What were Boggs and the antiextraterrestrialists worrying about? Within the AIR document there was discussion of Soviet interest in German flying wing aircraft and design genius Guenther Beck, whom the Soviets had "appropriated." The AIR report said it was possible that the Soviets may have achieved "greater overall performance assuming the successful development of some unusual propulsion device such as atomic energy engine(s)." If this was true, then AFOAI and Naval Intelligence came up with reasons that the disks were flying so publicly:

TO NEGATE U.S. CONFIDENCE IN ATOM BOMB AS THE MOST ADVANCED AND DECISIVE WEAPON. If the objects have been used in a propaganda sense, it would be reasonable to assume that the Soviets would choose first to frighten pro-American nations in Europe with the appearance of a radically new weapon to counteract the ability of the U.S. to obtain full propaganda effectiveness with the atom bomb. It will be remembered that strange objects first appeared over the Scandinavian countries in 1946. The objects observed there had unusual range and unusual performance characteristics. As this demonstration over the Scandinavian countries occurred the U.S. was making a vigorous campaign for the economic and political alignment of these nations with other pro-American Western European nations. When these incidents subsided, strange flying objects began to be observed at an increasing rate over the U.S. The conclusion on this point is that flying objects may have been used to frighten both European nations and the U.S. by the appearance of a new device, and that failure to identify such a Soviet object would give them invaluable indication that U.S. development is far behind that of the Soviets. Except for this indication, it is believed that the use of the objects to promote fear has been worthless in that the U.S. public has tended to characterize these incidents entirely as hallucinations by "crackpots," misidentification of conventional objects, or that they represent a secret American project which should not be publicized. Any fear that might result from Soviet use will come only by a discovery that the objects have been Soviet aircraft and that they involve radical developments which are in advance of our own accomplishments.[46]

The conclusion that the disks were of psychological danger more than directly military pointed to a solution. As long as the public viewed them as misidentifications or the hallucinations of crackpots, they had no power. While these conclusions were being discussed in the Pentagon, the first case of radar tracking with corresponding visual confirmation came in from pilots in Fukuoka, Japan. The radarman said, "In my opinion, we were shown a new type aircraft by some agency unknown to us."[47]

Despite Vandenberg's negative reception of the estimate, Project Sign personnel did not back off. They investigated an unusual "dogfight" between a National Guardsman and a UFO in Fargo, North Dakota. They checked his plane for excess radiation, trying to test their advanced propulsion theory. General Cabell, meanwhile, asked them for another opinion—*not* extraterrestrial. In a cleverly worded response, Sign wrote back saying not extraterrestrial in print but strongly implying it between the lines. This led to a confrontational meeting in late November at the National Bureau of Standards. Boggs and Sneider were there to debate the two views. When the smoke cleared, Boggs and AIR 100 were the victors. Project Sign was ordered to send all its analyses and views from now on to Boggs and to the Scientific Advisory Board for overseership. Project Sign's name was changed to Project Grudge. Ruppelt later wrote that the negative name was deliberate.[48] The project was now to attack and destroy the concept of saucers. To ensure this behavior, in relatively short order all the key project members were either transferred or reassigned to other duties at Wright-Patterson. Soon even the two top people in the intelligence division, Col. Howard McCoy and Col. William Clingerman (both sympathetic to UFOs), were replaced. McCoy's replacement was one of the most anti-UFO persons in the air force, Col. Harold Watson. The war of the schools had ended in victory for the antiextraterrestrialists.

A very different message was now given in the Pentagon and at Wright-Patterson: flying disks were errors, hysteria, and even psychopathology or hoaxes (possibly even treasonous ones).[49] But in November a top secret Swedish report arrived stating that "fully technically qualified people have reached the conclusion that these phenomena are obviously the result of a high technical skill which cannot be credited to any presently known culture on earth."[50] Adding another irritant, Sidney Shalett of the *Saturday Evening Post* was contacting the highest levels of the Pentagon, including Secretary Forrestal, for cooperation in doing an article on the flying saucers.[51]

The air force then decided on a policy of news management. The *Post* publicity was deemed not only undesirable but also "harmful to the national interest." General Cabell, writing to Forrestal, said that a "degree of guidance" in the preparation of such news stories was appropriate.[52] But the Pentagon was concerned that its degree of guidance might not be enough to effectively manage the impact of the Shalett article on public opinion. The *Post* article was due in late April 1949, and the Directorate of Intelligence decided to release a coincident informational document to blunt its effect. Its prereading of Shalett's piece indicated that it contained details "inimical to the interests of the National Military Establishment, and therefore might affect national defense."[53] Meanwhile, someone in the Pentagon leaked information from the top secret AIR 100 study to radio newsman Walter Winchell. To the directorate's dismay, Winchell broadcast on 3 April that "the flying saucers, never explained by anyone in authority, are now definitely known to have been guided missiles shot all the way from Russia."[54]

In response to queries by the USAF Scientific Advisory Board, Boggs wrote that while the concept of UFOs as "foreign devices becomes more remote, . . . there are many incidents reported by reliable and competent observers which are still unexplained." Boggs added, "It seems unlikely that a foreign power would expose superiority of power by a prolonged ineffectual penetration of the United States."[55] Boggs's reasoning was identical to that of Project Sign and the extraterrestrialists, who tended to accept the observations and build their deductions on them. Boggs's school tended to selectively reject some observations on undefined grounds, while accepting others.

Somewhat surprisingly, the remnants of Project Sign wrote the accompanying piece to Shalett's *Post* article. It was completed by mid-April and coordinated through the AMC and Pentagon public relations offices, which viewed it as a press release. Boggs reviewed it. With the support of his superiors, he suggested it should *not* be a press release, but an information document that could be read at the Pentagon by inquiring reporters. He wanted to limit the access, and consequently the volume of coverage, and he wanted the removal of certain speculations about space travel and life in the universe, which had been contributed by science consultants to the original Sign report.[56]

But the two changes did not happen. The "press release" of 27 April came out with an even more sympathetic tone toward UFOs than Shalett's two-part article, which it was meant to "correct."[57] Some readers of the release were puzzled. Why would the air force make Shalett look bad and flying saucers look good? The most intrigued reader was former marine major Donald Keyhoe, doing research on an article for *True* magazine. He thought that something about the flying disks must be very interesting yet covered up. He sensed that something big must be happening deep within the Pentagon concerning UFOs. His article and initial books would inspire many civilians to take notice of UFOs, which the Pentagon considered not in the best interests of the nation. The Pentagon's attempt at news management was not working out as it had hoped.[58]

Nevertheless, it still tried. Inside the military, Boggs in the Pentagon and Watson at AMC were openly giving the impression that the whole flying saucer business was ridiculous. Project Grudge became a meaningless exercise of derision and sloppy filing. Boggs was so enthusiastically antisaucer that General Cabell ordered General Moore to create a more proper atmosphere of skeptical respect toward the reports and their observers.[59]

Cabell was helped in this endeavor when Edward R. Murrow created a balanced radio report on the saucers in the summer of 1950. The assistant chief of staff to Vandenberg commented very negatively, but several witnesses and technologists buttressed the saucers' reality. Murrow also featured an interview with Donald Menzel, an astronomer at Harvard Observatory. With Menzel's claims that reports were entirely illusions, hallucinations, and general incompetence, the first arch debunker entered the battle. Interestingly, Menzel's superior at the observatory, Harlow Shapley, had earlier *assigned* him the task of publicly debunking the dangerous irrationalism of flying saucers.[60]

The Pentagon's position about UFOs had been crystallized by an opinion from its Office of Psychological Warfare (OPW) that fed directly into cold war fears. Both the Sign and Grudge reports had requested a psychological warfare analysis, which was completed in early 1950.[61] The office believed that flying disks *could* be used for such purposes, especially in creating mass hysteria. The exploitation of this potential source of hysteria, particularly given the closed system of press in the USSR, would require so much precision planning as to make it impractical. However, the OPW reasoned that big balloons might be a good vehicle for such a ploy. It recommended that other agencies interested in such matters be informed of the relevant facts and studies to get their views.

The Pentagon also created a specific statement for Colonel Watson or Grudge to repeat to anyone inquiring about a UFO case: "The opinion of the Air Force is that all reports of flying saucers are considered to be mythical and are of no concern to the national security at present." Brigadier Moore also ordered a standard response to the public: "We have investigated and evaluated (whatever it was) incident, and have found nothing of value and nothing which would change our previous estimates on this subject."[62]

With Harold Watson in place at AMC, Grudge officers George Towles and Lt. Howard Smith simply filed cases and kept quiet. Their replacements, James J. Rodgers and Capt. Roy James, were even sloppier and more ridiculing.[63] At the Pentagon, with the school of Boggs, Porter, and Moore holding sway, the air force press spokesman, Maj. DeWitt Searles, was pictured in the papers holding his phone, arms outstretched and eyes up to heaven, saying, "No, no, a thousand times no. As far as the Air Force goes, there's no such thing as a flying saucer. Further, there are no such things as flying chromium hub caps, flying dimes, flying teardrops, flying gas lights, flying ice cream cones, or flying pie plates. Thank you and good-by." Searles's office number became the reference point for all inquiries, even by Congress, for "information" on flying disks.[64]

The policy to downplay the disks seemed well managed. In the larger society, however, forces were working against this attempt. In 1950 several popular books about UFOs by civilians were published; one, *The Flying Saucers Are Real*, by Donald Keyhoe, was a rather sensational but accurate account of the matter.[65]

Furthermore, the phenomenon refused to go away. For example, the scientists of navy commander Robert McLaughlin's top secret balloon-launching team at White Sands Proving Grounds had tracked UFOs with their theodolites. He reported the sightings to the newspapers in 1949. Although Boggs and the air force disapproved, McLaughlin wished to write an article for *This Week* magazine, a nationwide Sunday newspaper insert. *This Week* backed out, but the piece was published by *True*. In "How Scientists Tracked a Flying Saucer," McLaughlin unambiguously stated that the device was real, vastly superior to our aeronautical technology, and extraterrestrial, probably from Mars.[66]

Other aspects of 1950 were increasing cold war tensions: fear of the new Russian A-bomb and Communist China; the Korean War; spies and spy trials; McCarthyism; and vicious rivalries for funds between the services. UFOs played their role even here. Representative Mahon complained of the size of the defense budget for 1951: "Our enemies want us to spend ourselves into defeat," and whenever appropriations time comes up, "we begin to hear of flying saucers."[67] All this increased stress on the military to learn precisely about what the Soviets really had in their arsenal. The Far Eastern Air Force (FEAF) and Continental Air Command (ConAC) both had UFO incidents, and they were confused and perturbed about how the Pentagon was handling intelligence on these matters, which they considered far from ridiculous. They complained to Cabell.[68]

General Cabell agreed. He felt that he and his advisers had been overreactive in making the flying disks appear not a serious topic inside the military. Obviously, they were a serious investigative concern. AMC should still be doing that, formally. AMC had even discontinued Project Grudge at the beginning of 1950. Cabell now wanted it activated, but he also wanted the *public* to continue to believe that this was *not* serious. Thus, he wished to do nothing to attract publicity. All sightings outside the military were to be investigated quietly, even though Cabell's advisers were against the policy of investigating outside cases at all. Just in case the flying disk phenomenon had substance, Cabell wanted to be able to show the public that the air force had acted responsibly. Symbolic of the change Cabell wished to institute, he directed an order to destroy

all copies of AIR 100-203-79, the report that had opposed the conclusions of the estimate of the situation.[69] Years later, he told a
civilian organization that he always believed there was something
significant in UFOs. But Watson at AMC did not think so. He viewed
Cabell's change of mind as a nuisance, and Project Grudge continued as a mere formality, not taken seriously by its assigned officers
or its director.

The Ruppelt Era, 1951–53

By 1951, General Cabell felt that a rational intelligence approach to
UFOs had been reestablished, even though Colonel Watson continued to treat them like nonsense (without telling Cabell, of course).
In addition, the public's attitude and the media's treatment of the
subject were changing. With the publication of popular books and
articles and the release of two major movies in 1951 (*The Day the Earth
Stood Still* and *The Thing*), the public and the press were alert for
anything new. Pressures continued to build both at AMC and at the
Pentagon for UFO information. The public's interest in UFOs was
beginning to organize along a spectrum from scientific interest to
bizarre cults. The first civilian UFO clubs or discussion groups
formed, some of them around religious and paranormal themes.[70]

But this "crazier" aspect of public interest in UFOs and the
negative comments and writings of "name" scientists like Irving
Langmuir, Donald Menzel, Royal Astronomer H. Spencer Jones,
and Urner Liddel were having an early impact on the academic
community. Typical was AMC aeromedical psychologist Paul Fitts,
an adviser for the Grudge report, who wrote that all UFO sightings
were the result of misperception, hallucination, or worse. Rarely, a
scientist like Arthur C. Clarke or Walter Orr Roberts would write
that there might be something of interest in UFOs.[71] But for the most
part it was the scientists who had seen UFOs themselves (astronomers
Clyde Tombaugh and Seymour Hess, meteor expert Lincoln LaPaz,
and General Mills balloon experts John L. Kramer and Charles Moore)
who would briefly be quoted positively and then retreat to the qui-
eter confines of their intellectual lives. The door was already closing
on the possibility of academics publicly admitting that they took the
UFO mystery seriously. Without the reinforcement of positive state-

ments from the appropriate military investigators, it was difficult for most academics to view the phenomenon as serious. This situation would establish the intellectual atmosphere surrounding the subject until the present day. It was an atmosphere that suited the Pentagon's cold war concerns well.[72]

The phenomenon did not seem to be affected. Whatever it is, it displayed itself to future astronaut Deke Slayton in 1951, and he, weighing the situation, did not formally report it. A localized wave of UFOs took place in Lubbock, Texas. Many people, including several intensely interested Texas Tech professors, saw them. Project Grudge bungled the investigation, but the professors continued to try to figure it all out. As time passed, some psychological closure to the case became more and more desirable. They eventually decided that they had seen a normal natural phenomenon—moths. But they and the air force would not state this publicly. To announce that the professors had mistaken moths for flying disks would be embarrassing to them, and the incredible moths explanation stood secretly. Project Grudge went forward with this "solution" despite a separate study by a Tech mathematics professor who had triangulated the objects and found them relatively high, large, and fast. His letter to AMC was never read.[73]

At the beginning of 1951, two individuals arrived at AMC and at Pentagon intelligence who would play major roles in UFO history. At AMC, Lt. Edward Ruppelt would lead the last genuine effort to analyze UFOs at Project Blue Book. In the Pentagon, Gen. William Garland joined General Cabell's staff, replacing one of the more UFO-negative people, Gen. Ernest Moore, as "assistant for production," AFOIN-A. And, Garland had seen a UFO.[74]

General Garland started a sequence of events that would change the face of things. It was rumored that *Life* magazine was interested in a feature article about UFOs. Garland contacted writer Robert Ginna and gave him some ideas. How would Ginna like to visit AMC and the UFO project himself? The Pentagon's Office of Public Information asked AMC a seemingly innocent question: Is everything going well with Project Grudge? Rodgers and Watson said, rather disingenuously, that everything was under control. The second wire from the Pentagon said: wonderful; a *Life* reporter is on his way, which, Ruppelt later said, caused "bedlam in the raw."[75]

The research trip did not go well for Robert Ginna. He later told Ruppelt about how poorly the work was done under Rodgers. Whether Ginna's *Life* article or General Garland's attitude was responsible, Rodgers was shortly reassigned and the UFO job given to Lt. Jerry Cummings, who tried to take it seriously. Other shifts occurred. The negative Jerry Boggs was reassigned in the Pentagon. An interim officer, Lt. Col. M. D. Willis, took over Boggs's spot as UFO intelligence analyst but was at best a mediocre station keeper. But he, too, soon would be gone, replaced by the very UFO-friendly Maj. Dewey Fournet. Over Fournet, and insulating him from the negative influences of longtime UFO basher and member of the Intelligence Analysis Command Staff, Col. E. H. Porter, were Col. Weldon H. Smith (sympathetic to UFOs) and Col. William A. Adams (enthusiastic about UFOs). Most important, perhaps, Watson was out at AMC, and the professional, sympathetic Col. Frank Dunn was in. By the fall of 1951, the change was nearly complete.[76]

A case came in from Fort Monmouth, New Jersey, in September 1951, which resulted in the removal of the last of the negative old guard at AMC. The arrival of this report at AMC caused a disagreement between James Rodgers and Jerry Cummings about whether and how the case would be investigated. The Pentagon settled the dispute. Rodgers was out and Cummings was in.

After the investigation of the Fort Monmouth case, Cummings had to report directly in person to Cabell at the Pentagon. Cabell's staff was present, along with a scientist (Brewster) from Republic Airlines, which was sponsoring a short-lived project to study frontier physics (unified field theory) for possible clues to advanced propulsion systems.[77] At the meeting, Cabell was upset and suspicious about AMC's handling of UFOs. He wanted a frank assessment from Cummings. Cummings, who was leaving service anyway for an advanced degree at Cal Tech, gave him one. Cabell exploded, "I want an open mind; in fact, I *order* an open mind! Anyone that doesn't keep an open mind can get out, now! . . . Why do *I* have to stir up the action? Anyone can see that we do not have a satisfactory answer to the saucer question." He angrily told his staff of colonels, "I've been lied to, and lied to, and lied to. I want it to stop. I want the answer to the saucers and I want a good answer." Col. E. H. Porter responded that he thought the reports were all matters of misinterpretation, impressionable emotionalism, and crackpots. Cabell pointedly informed him that he did not consider himself a crackpot, and that he had a lot of doubt in his mind about what UFOs were. He then characterized the very antisaucer Grudge report as the "most poorly written, inconclusive piece of unscientific tripe" that he had ever seen.[78]

In 1951 Jerry Cummings left, and Edward Ruppelt became project leader; for about one year the UFOs began to be treated seriously again. In August 1951 Watson had formally requested that AMC abandon the disk analysis business.[79] After Cummings's meeting, Cabell immediately ordered a clarification of the worldwide reporting mechanisms and ordered the Air Technical Intelligence Center (ATIC—the new name for AMC's intelligence division) to respond seriously to these reports. Colonel William Adams asked for a complete scientific investigation of all current UFO files. This was approved and ultimately was accomplished by the Battelle Memorial Institute. General Garland requested that three areas of the country be equipped with some form of constant monitoring field equipment, but lack of funding and the intermittency of the phenomenon thwarted any data retrieval from this effort.[80]

At the end of 1951, General Cabell moved up to the number two position in the CIA and was replaced as director of intelligence by John Samford. Samford was open-minded about UFOs, and in January 1952 he was briefed on the topic by General Garland. The briefing did not feature tales of extraterrestrials.[81] It discussed Nazi aerotechnology, Soviet rocketry and delivery weapons, and whether it was possible that the USSR could build a novel aircraft with nuclear bombs. Samford was convinced that the subject warranted a serious effort if for no other reason than for its national security implications.

Coincidentally with Cabell's and Samford's views about a serious effort, the Pentagon created the USAF Special Study Group. This was a flexible study project to take on ad hoc tasks of special interest or timelines that did not necessarily fit within the institutional structures of the directorate. The military chief was Lt. Col. E. Sterling. The acting director was Stephan Possony, a Georgetown political science professor and a psychological warfare specialist. The group's first task was to study Soviet air and space technology and delivery systems, and to decide how they related to the flying disk mystery.[82] The members were going on a six-week survey in Europe to gather data.

Possony returned from Europe convinced that the UFO phenomenon was real, but it was not Soviet aerospace vehicles. What was it, then? He and his assistant, Les Rosensweig, did several draft studies, such as what the power source of the objects could be and how one might best contact them. Shortly thereafter, Major Fournet began a study on the motion characteristics of UFOs. Possony also kept his mind open to the possibility that these sightings were of artificially contrived light or plasma effects, deliberately manufactured to achieve some possibly psychological goal. Meanwhile, as George Garrett had done back in 1947, Colonel Dunn asked General Samford to survey all U.S. high-technology projects to determine whether we were responsible for the flying disks after all. As before, Samford reported "No."[83]

Despite these internal changes, the air force's public face was to be noncommittal, unemotional, but more respectful of witnesses and possibilities. It would admit that there were objects that were not "reasonably explained," but it would not encourage further speculation. In an April 1952 Office of Public Information memorandum, Col. William Adams wrote that the public should know that the UFO phenomenon was not "considered a joke or something which can be brushed off lightly as readily explainable, but rather it is considered to be something which warrants constant vigilance and thorough Intelligence analysis in an attempt to provide a satisfactory solution."[84]

The damage from previous air force stances had already been done to the academic community, however. Astronomer J. Allen Hynek was now assigned as a permanent consultant to the UFO project. On his travels around the country, he polled many colleagues about UFOs and found that a surprising number of them had witnessed UFOs, or at least were interested.[85] But he did not get this response when several astronomers were in the same room, especially if a loud senior scientist was present. Upon listening to Gerard Kuiper denigrating UFOs for several minutes, Hynek became amused at the realization that several of Kuiper's staff in the same room had told him privately of their observations.

Other scientists looked into the subject only surreptitiously. The U.S. Air Force Scientific Advisory Board chairman, Theodore von

Karman, always spoke skeptically about UFOs but had regular, private UFO discussions with University of Southern California biophysics and space medicine expert Leslie Kaeburn. Kaeburn joined with a group of technical experts, largely aerospace industry engineers, in a discussion club about UFOs. Another such organization formed at the Jet Propulsion Laboratory, and another at Los Alamos. These groups were common but quiet. In the Civilian Saucer Investigation group of Los Angeles, only one of its technical people, the noted aeronautical engineer Walther Riedel, was willing to be named.[86]

As spring 1952 turned into summer, there began a torrent of UFO cases nationwide. The UFO project, now named Blue Book, was busy but also ambitious. Plans were being made to expand the project to include a dozen or more of the most prestigious scientists in the nation, as a high court of experts who would work closely with Hynek and Blue Book investigators to help solve the mystery.[87] Contained in the reports were many interesting "unknowns," but two events became paramount: the Tremonton, Utah, motion picture film, and the Washington, D.C., sightings.[88] These events were embedded in a flood of others so great that Blue Book and air force communication channels in general were swamped with phone calls by civilians, which created a three- to four-hour communications clog, delaying response to many aspects of normal air force business. This swamping of channels was immediately recognized as a national security issue.

The surge of reports culminated in banner headlines of saucers seen visually and on radar, complete with scrambled jets, over high-security areas in the nation's capital itself. President Truman placed calls to find out what was going on. Truman had been getting quarterly reports on UFOs and their national security implications from his military aide, Gen. Robert B. Landry, for the past four years. Landry made the call to the Pentagon for Truman. Ruppelt was in Washington and took the call. At a loss over what to say, Ruppelt instructed Landry to tell the president that these sightings, which involved multiple radars plus ground and air visual verification, might have been caused by meteorological anomalies. Even though the witnesses vehemently disagreed, the "temperature inversion" theory became the centerpiece of a big U.S. Air Force press conference featuring Samford, Ruppelt, Roy James, and several other officers.[89] James, the arch UFO skeptic, led the debunking. Ruppelt noted that people like Fournet (or Garland) and the local radar experts "were extremely conspicuous by their absence."

Having weathered this public relations crisis, Samford decided, almost certainly through the urging of Fournet, Adams, Garland, and perhaps even Possony, to open up more information to responsible writers.[90] Only one writer, Donald Keyhoe, seems to have taken full advantage of this. He began being fed, through UFO-sympathetic press desk employee Al Chop, all manner of unsolved UFO reports and details. He was even provided with radar cases and radar information, which indicated that the temperature inversion idea for the sightings was impossible. This new openness was the pro-UFO Pentagon forces' last attempt to get the subject out in the open. They failed, and the CIA played a major role in that failure.

After the wave, Project Blue Book spent August and September trying to catch up on its backlog of cases, and doing so in the mood of a project "on the grow" in an exciting field. In the Pentagon, the pro-UFO forces were looking forward to the promised analysis of the Tremonton film. This film was important because *as film,* and as taken by an experienced military photographer, the issue of hoaxing was nonexistent. Even though the photographer had to stop his car and set up his camera, he still shot about seventy-five seconds of film showing a dozen or more objects "flying" in apparent chaotic motion but in a general direction. When the objects had been closest to the car, he and his wife saw them as disks, like two pie pans, one inverted on the other. This photographic evidence seemed to be what the air force had been waiting for. Major Fournet arranged to have the film analyzed by the Naval Photographic Interpretation Center (NPIC), which worked long on the film and on another that showed two objects flying near a ball field in Montana. Regarding Tremonton, the analysts were surprised to discover that the motions of the dozen or so objects were not individual and chaotic, but that groups of objects were moving in separate circular patterns.[91] This study became the centerpiece of Major Fournet's draft study on UFO motions, which supported the possibility that the flying disks were not terrestrial in origin.

However, another movement was occurring in the Pentagon, just as exciting but of much greater pragmatic concern. The air force's response mechanisms had been swamped by a three- to four-hour delay caused by UFO reports. After the Washington events, President Truman requested that the CIA look into the UFO problem, estimate its seriousness, and decide what could be done.[92]

The CIA Intrudes

On 28 July President Truman, at the National Security Council, asked the CIA to look into the problem of the UFOs. CIA chief Gen. Walter Bedell Smith set the agency to work on it the next day. Deputy Director of Intelligence Robert Amory passed the project on to his Office of Scientific Intelligence and his chief science adviser, H. Marshall Chadwell. Chadwell would anchor the CIA UFO study through its completion in January 1953. Chadwell's deputy, Ralph Clark, and their operations chief, Philip Strong, were also involved. The actual project was called a special study group, located in the CIA's Physics and Electronics Division. A CIA specialist in chemicals and rocketry, Fred Durant, immediately began gathering information within the Pentagon.[93]

Durant worked quickly. By 1 August there was an informal report to Clark from one of his colleagues in the Weapons and Equipment Division. The report was relatively negative toward UFOs but serious about the need for CIA surveillance of the subject. Possibly reflecting Fournet's flexible viewpoint, it stated that "interplanetary aspects and alien origin [were] not being thoroughly excluded from consideration."[94]

The study group spent August trying to get a grasp on the UFO situation and the way the air force and Blue Book were handling it. It consulted Possony, and psychological warfare concerns began to surface. General Smith was briefed about these views. He told his "Psychological Strategy Board" that he was informing the National Security Council of these dangers and suggested that it "discuss the possible offensive or defensive utilization of these phenomena for psychological warfare purposes."[95] Buttressing this, the agency's Foreign Documents Division was unable to find mention of the subject in the Soviet press. It reasoned that this suspicious silence possibly indicated that the Soviets were well aware that the subject had disruptive potential and were censoring it. A recent cable from

Budapest accused the American government of using the flying saucers idea to fan war hysteria.[96]

In the fall of 1952, the study group's interest began to center at the higher CIA echelons around Chadwell, Strong, and Durant. Chadwell's memorandum for Smith in early September showed a much clearer awareness of the problem and Blue Book's activities. He had already brought in some of the country's most important scientists to consult with. Julius Stratton, vice president of MIT, was one of them; although not mentioned by name, Howard P. Robertson of Cal Tech, an on-call CIA consultant in 1952–54, probably was another. Chadwell's tentative conclusions from all his sources were as follows:

The flying saucer situation contains two elements of danger which, in a situation of international tension, have national security implications. These are:

(1) *Psychological*—With world-wide sightings reported, it was found that, up to the time of our investigation, there had been in the Russian press no report or comment, even satirical, on flying saucers, though Andre Gromyko had made one humorous mention of the subject. With a State-controlled press, this could result only from an official policy decision. The question, therefore, arises as to whether or not these sightings:
(a) Could be controlled,
(b) Could be predicted, and
(c) Could be used from a psychological warfare point of view either offensively or defensively.
The public concern with the phenomena, which is reflected in the United States press and in pressure of inquiry upon the Air Force, indicates that there is a fair proportion of our population which is mentally conditioned to the acceptance of the incredible. In this fact lies the potential for the touching-off of mass hysteria and panic.

(2) *Air Vulnerability*—The United States Air Warning System will undoubtedly always depend upon a combination of radar screening and visual observation. We give Russia the present capability of delivering an air attack against us, yet at any given moment now, there may be current a dozen *official* un-

identified sightings plus many unofficial. At any moment of attack, we are now in a position where we cannot, on an instant basis, distinguish hardware from phantom, and as tension mounts we will run the increasing risk of false alerts and the even greater danger of falsely identifying the real as phantom.

Chadwell recommended psychological warfare studies, a national policy on how to speak to the public about the phenomenon, and serious concern by the National Security Council.[97]

It was not merely the appearance of flying disks and the possibility of public panic that were encouraging this nervousness in the intelligence community. The United States was entering an era in which the accurate and rapid identification of unknown air traffic was an extremely vital and yet weak link in its national defense. The nation's vulnerability in this area was the concern of many of the elite scientists from the wartime MIT Radiation Laboratory, which focused on radar and electronic detection work. It had been a project as important as, and in manpower even larger than, the Manhattan Project. A cluster of these scientists, such as Julius Stratton, Alfred Hill, and George Valley, maintained a center at MIT and formed what was nicknamed the "Beacon Hill Group." In the early fall of 1952, both Marshall Chadwell and Edward Ruppelt had, separately, briefed and been briefed by them.[98] The group was just coming off its summer project, which was to lead to the establishment of Project Lincoln, and ultimately the Lincoln Lab whose job was to devise an early warning system against surprise attack. Lincoln and Beacon Hill were interested in possible unidentifiable technologies penetrating U.S. airspace. George Valley had even written a sympathetic appendix on extraterrestrial life and interstellar travel for the old Sign and Grudge reports when he was chief air force scientist in 1948–49. Stratton told Chadwell that the CIA should assign the task of scientific study of UFOs to them.[99]

At this same time, Ruppelt, Garland, and Blue Book were continuing under the impression that their work was so important that the higher echelons would initiate directives to supply elite scientific help at any moment. With Garland now at AMC as the head of intelligence, Ruppelt received a very supportive superior. Second in command, Col. John O'Mara, had drawn up an impressive list of scientists, including Edward Teller, James Van Allen, and Irving

Langmuir, for the advisory body.[100] With Beacon Hill and the CIA both showing intense interest, surely something good was coming for air force UFO research.

Ruppelt and even Garland were naive. By October and November, more information coalesced in Chadwell's, Strong's, and Durant's hands. ATIC–Blue Book gave a formal briefing in person. The CIA had essentially discarded the theory that the USSR was flying technology of such sophistication as was reported, but it was still interested in what the USSR knew about the phenomenon, and how it might use that knowledge.[101] By the end of November, Chadwell had reached the conclusion that the phenomenon was neither American nor Soviet. Chadwell also realized that "sightings of unexplained objects at great altitudes and travelling at high speeds in the vicinity of major U.S. defense installations are of such nature that they are not attributable to natural phenomena or known types of aerial vehicles."[102]

Chadwell reported to General Smith that they were organizing a prestigious consulting group to "convince the responsible authorities in the community that immediate research and development on this subject must be undertaken." Such a high-level project required a National Security Council Intelligence Directive (NSCID) for coordinated research. Smith approved. Chadwell presented the plan to the Intelligence Advisory Committee (IAC), chaired by the CIA, which approved it. General Samford promised full air force cooperation.[103]

The CIA now needed to form the evaluating committee to decide who would be on the scientific panel. Stratton had met again with Strong on 2 December, and he continued to insist on Beacon Hill–Lincoln getting the task.[104] If not them, maybe Cal Tech could do it. The actual decision regarding how the panel was to be formed is not known, but the panel that was formed was not one in the vision of Garland, Ruppelt, and Blue Book, nor of Chadwell, nor of Beacon Hill. Ruppelt expected an ongoing group of scientific helpers. Chadwell expected a serious working group leading to an NSCID of ongoing force. Beacon Hill wanted an ongoing, but secretive, investigation of the highest order. What they got was something very different.

The decision was made almost immediately following the IAC meeting to go inside the agency for the CIA consultant (and former chief scientist of the CIA) Howard P. (Bob) Robertson, to chair the panel, which eventually bore his name. Also, immediately, a second scientist was named, Thornton Page. Robertson was a mathematical physicist and an expert on nuclear bombs. Page was an astronomer and an expert on operations research. The other members were unknown as yet. What Robertson and Page knew about UFOs can be judged by their recommended reading discussed with one another: an article from the 6 September issue of the *New Yorker*.[105]

Robertson was a good friend of Donald Menzel and of R. V. Jones, a British scientist and military intelligence expert, who was constantly debunking UFOs in elite circles in Britain. Menzel, writing to the coauthor of one of his anti-UFO books, Mrs. Lyle Boyd, described Robertson as "basically a scientist, a man who does not want to waste his time on trivia. He was convinced from the start that flying saucer reports were not well authenticated (perhaps we had better not mention this point)."[106]

Sometime in mid-December, Chadwell, Durant, and Robertson visited Ruppelt at Blue Book to see its operations. A fourth visitor, according to Ruppelt, was an astronomer, and could have been Page or even J. Allen Hynek. The group stayed about two days and recommended that the formal plans for a panel go forward. Robertson and the CIA then began to fill out the panel. The group of five was not complete until early January, just days before the proceedings. The radar expert (Luis Alvarez), the nuclear physicist (Samuel Goudsmit), and Lloyd Berkner came on board. To say that they were reluctant would be putting it mildly. Alvarez and Goudsmit arrived considering the subject a waste of time. Berkner did not arrive at all until the proceedings were essentially over. Ruppelt commented that "Goudsmit was probably the most violent anti-saucer man at the panel meeting. Everything was a big joke to him which brought down the wrath of the other panel members on numerous occasions."[107]

These men, apparently ignorant of the phenomenon, were to decide on the future of a subject of grave concern to Project Blue Book, the CIA's Office of Scientific Investigation, the Beacon Hill–Project Lincoln Group, and the UFO officers of the U.S. Air Force in the Pentagon. Of these five men, Berkner did not show up for any of the presentations; Goudsmit and Alvarez felt that they were wasting their time; the chairman, Robertson, was convinced a priori that the reports were no good; and Thornton Page was marginally open-minded yet still ridiculed the phenomenon during the meeting. The men would spend less than twelve working hours listening to experts like Ruppelt, Hynek, and Fournet and reviewing reports. Hynek said that the atmosphere of scientific elitism permeating the room was oppressive to the point that he could barely raise objection to some of the commentary. The conference was brusque. Weighing and considering were not on the agenda; dismissal was. Even though Hynek was by far the most UFO-knowledgeable scientist in the room, he was timid and awed by the panel's aura of authority, and he did not object to the proceedings. Hynek found "an absolute odor of superciliousness . . . a Daddy Knows Best attitude."[108]

Ruppelt was still unaware of the CIA's primary objective in the panel. He thought that it was a science advisory group that would recommend stronger ongoing discovery methods. Hynek thought similarly but at least sensed something terribly wrong in the room. Both had thought that the panel's main concern would be science and a search for the truth. But Ruppelt and Hynek were naive. The panel's concern was national security and the cold war.

Lloyd Berkner arrived on the afternoon of the third day in time to miss all the presentations of evidence and hear Robertson charge himself with writing a draft report.[109] By early the next morning, the draft was not only written but somehow Berkner had read it, and it was already in the hands of the air force's director of intelligence.

The panel's conclusions and recommendations had no mention of science. The report focused on the direct and indirect challenges to national security and on means of meeting those challenges. The panel concluded "that the evidence presented on Unidentified Flying Objects shows no indication that these phenomena constitute a direct physical threat to national security."[110] Part of this conclusion seems to have grown out of preconceived notions. Robertson and Alvarez had been involved with the "foo fighter" phenomenon during World War II (balls of light that appeared and chased or paced Allied planes). Whatever these were, they caused no harm. UFOs seemed similar. The panel was under the mistaken impression that UFOs were almost entirely an American phenomenon, and, if so, that alone was preposterous. Extraterrestrials surely would spread their interest around, they said. Despite an admission that several important cases and facts (e.g., fast tracks on Air Defense

Command radar; enigmatic clustering effects) were unexplainable, the panel waved them aside. They brought up the Books of Charles Fort—the writings of a turn-of-the-century collector of anomalous reports about almost anything. The panel suggested that people had always reported odd things in the sky, and we had not been hurt by it. It also implied that people interested in such things (Forteans) were suspect in their judgment. *Forteans* was a convenient term of derision.

Concerning indirect challenges, the panel concluded "that the emphasis on the reporting of these phenomena does, in these perilous times, result in a threat to the orderly functioning of the protective organs of the body politic." It enumerated specific dangers: (1) mass reporting of the phenomena could create an environment in which it was more likely that defense personnel would misidentify real enemy artifacts (e.g., missiles, planes); (2) as happened with the three- to four-hour delay during the Washington, D.C., events, it could overload vital communications channels with misdirecting information; and (3) it could enhance a public tendency toward mass hysteria, which would increase the United States' vulnerability to some psychological warfare ploy. For these reasons, and possibly others, it was a mistake for the military to have fostered an atmosphere that encouraged citizens to report strange aerial observations through intelligence channels. Something had to be done to rectify this inappropriate status of civilians being interested in the phenomenon and feeling that it was their duty to communicate their observations.

The panel gave two recommendations to counter the danger, the first of which was an education and training program within the military. It recommended "that the national security agencies institute policies on intelligence, training, and public education designed to prepare the material defenses and the morale of the country to recognize most promptly and to react most effectively to true indications of hostile intent or action." Although this recommendation mainly concerned in-service personnel, it was a tribute to the rushed nature of the report that a different sort of "public education" enfolded within it. The recommendation was aimed primarily at sharpening military abilities to deal with reports of potential enemy action and to rapidly distinguish that from UFOs. The "public" education program came in the second recommendation and specifically involved manipulation of the subject and "debunking." The panel recommended "that the national security agencies take immediate steps to strip the Unidentified Flying Objects of the special status they have been given and the aura of mystery they have unfortunately acquired."

For the panel, such a recommendation could mean many things: (1) we should embark on a program to reduce the public interest in UFOs, using mass media such as television, motion pictures, and popular articles; (2) these would feature only cases that have been solved, which would make the public less gullible and more aware of tricks that could be played on them; (3) experts in mass psychology could be employed to advise on how best to manipulate this information; (4) popular figures, such as Arthur Godfrey, and film-making experts, such as Walt Disney, could create entertaining and trusted vehicles for spreading this message; and (5) schools and clubs could be venues for reaching many people, and amateur astronomers could help "spread the gospel."

It was very important to use real cases. First, intrigue everyone with the mystery and then solve it. After about two years of this debunking, "the dangers related to flying saucers should have been greatly reduced if not eliminated."

One element, though, remained: the civilian saucer organizations that had begun to spring up, which could keep interest in UFOs alive. The panel felt that there was danger in these organizations:

> The Panel took cognizance of the existence of such groups as the "Civilian Flying Saucer Investigators" (Los Angeles) and the "Aerial Phenomena Research Organization" (Wisconsin). It was believed that such organizations should be watched because of their potentially great influence on mass thinking if widespread sightings should occur. The apparent irresponsibility and the possible use of such groups for subversive purposes should be kept in mind.

Within the month, the FBI was investigating Los Angeles's Civilian Saucer Investigations, and Walther Riedel was being pressured to resign. Robertson shortly wrote to Marshall Chadwell: "That ought to fix the Forteans."[111]

The Impact

Although there was a period following the Robertson Panel when its policies were slowly percolating through the intelligence system, sooner or later these attitudes toward the UFO problem insinuated themselves everywhere. The panel's view, and the power of CIA influence, put a stop to the shifting tides within the air force intelligence community, not on an individual basis of belief but in terms of a formal, fixed institutional position. The logic of the position was simple: if concern with national security is the panel's only function, then secrecy and what can only be termed "public thought management" is the correct approach to duty. The panel concluded that the UFO phenomenon has utilizable psychosocial impacts (apparently unrelated to its essential nature) that are potentially dangerous to national security. The dangers lie in the way the public thinks and feels about the phenomenon. Therefore, the military must "change" that thought process, regardless of what the phenomenon actually is.

The Robertson Panel's impact was enormous in a variety of ways within the intelligence community. The CIA's plan for a major high-level investigation via the NSCID proposal, which it had rendered to the National Security Council, was scrapped.[112] Project Blue Book's hopes for a more scientific advisory board presence to aid in the proper analysis of cases were dashed.[113] The UFO-sympathetic school in the Pentagon had proceeded with plans for further UFO data releases to the public centered around a press conference on the Tremonton, Utah, film and analysis; this effort was stopped.[114]

Project Blue Book began to be downgraded. Fewer personnel were assigned. The investigatory duties were shifted entirely off-base to representatives of Air Defense Command (the 4602d Air Intelligence Service Squadron).[115] In principle, this shift of duties might have been a good one. In fact, it was otherwise. The 4602 "UFO officers" were poorly trained, in a position with low respect, and ideally geared to treat UFOs as "public relations, not science."

By chance, Ruppelt, Fournet, and Pentagon information official Al Chop were all leaving the air force's UFO operations in the normal course of their careers. They were not replaced by people of similar attitude or behavior. The Pentagon public relations desk began issuing similar Robertsonian press releases. Ruppelt was replaced in the interim by his colleague Lt. Bob Olssen, but the permanent replacement was to be Capt. Charles Hardin. Ruppelt later wrote:

Chuck Hardin is running Project Bluebook at the present time. Since the operation of the project has changed and the 4602nd has taken over the legwork, he doesn't have much to do. By his own admission, he has a good deal at ATIC and he is playing it for all it is worth. General Watson doesn't like UFOs, so Hardin is keeping things just as quiet as possible and staying out from under everyone's feet. In other words, being a regular Air Force, he is just doing as little as possible because he knows how controversial the subject is and his philosophy is that if you don't do anything you won't get hurt. He definitely doesn't believe in UFOs, in fact he thinks that anyone who is even interested is crazy. They bore him.[116]

By 1954 the UFO-sympathetic Gen. William Garland had been replaced as ATIC commander by the arch saucer hater Harold Watson. It was back to the days of Project Grudge in almost every way. Before Hardin's turn was complete, even the filing of cases had once again become sloppy and incomplete, just as in the 1949–51 era.

When it became clear how viewpoints had changed, many of the UFO-sympathetic "losers" became upset with both the new attitude and what they perceived as CIA meddling.[117] Allen Hynek's view was much more personal. He could not see how the new arrangements would allow any real scientific investigation, making his job even more of a guessing game sham than it had been. When this was added to the harassment he was getting from fellow scientists for even being involved with UFOs, his future continuance on the project made little sense. He wanted to quit. Hynek said to Capt. Cybulski of the 4602d:

Put yourself in my position. I am being ridiculed by members of my profession for chasing these imaginary objects, and when I went into this, I went into it sincerely, because I thought that both from the astronomical standpoint and also from the scientific value, I could disprove these things. In so doing I would be rendering my profession and my country some service.

However, in the past, I have not been able to get support from the Air Force. It seems that they all think this is a hot subject, and they want to drop it. They don't want to have anything to do with it. No one wants to be quoted.[118]

Hynek stayed on the job, frustrated and harassed until the project folded in 1969. He was deeply unsatisfied with the new procedures, insisting that he was not getting all the cases nor many of the best cases to even read, let alone analyze. The new procedures made it easier for many cases to be stopped at Air Defense Command and to be shunted off elsewhere.[119]

Hynek's problems with his academic and scientific colleagues is indicative of the Robertson Panel's impact beyond the intelligence community. An important dimension of this negative atmosphere was that people were becoming discouraged at the idea of reporting their experience with a UFO. In 1953 Ruppelt wrote about an unofficial conference he had with a group of civilian airline pilots. They were mad as hell at the air force for its treatment of pilots who had made UFO reports. One expressed their general feeling: "If I saw a flying saucer flying wing-tip formation with me and could see little men waving—even if my whole load of passengers saw it—I wouldn't report it to the air force."[120]

The public's nonconfidence in the military (even among military pilots) continued to grow through the 1950s and 1960s. By the time of the Colorado "Scientific Study of UFOs" project in 1967, David Saunders noted that if someone reported a UFO to a civilian UFO organization, he or she did not simultaneously tell Blue Book about it.[121] During the post-Robertson fifties, this trend was getting so far out of hand that the inspector general of the air force had to issue an operations order to all base commanders reminding them that "Unidentified Flying Objects must be rapidly and accurately identified as serious Air Force business."[122]

The civilian research groups, often merely small, enthusiastic clubs of unsophisticated individuals, rose to fill in the gap created by air force policy. But the Robertson Panel had decided that these groups' influence was potentially dangerous, and they too felt the panel's impact. Coral Lorenzen, director of the Aerial Phenomena Research Organization (APRO), was visited by Allen Hynek and Blue Book chief Robert Olssen.[123] They queried her about where she and her organization stood on the UFO problem; she was informed that undue publicity about saucer sightings was troublesome to the air force, and that they would like to minimize this. She was encouraged to finish a book she was writing, and to include in it much scientific fact to educate her readers about what things were *not* saucers. In addition, it would help if her organization would break down the sightings in the air force way: balloons, meteors, planets, and so forth.

Civilian Saucer Investigation (CSI) of Los Angeles, composed mainly of employees of aerospace industries, was almost immediately investigated by the FBI. In 1952 CSI had issued a public bulletin describing an earlier briefing from Edward Ruppelt and one of his associates, Lieutenant Colonel Kirkland. The bulletin also said that the next issue would feature a report on a case of a rapidly accelerated Geiger counter rate coincident with several UFO flyovers. The rumor of the Geiger counter's excursions and the possibility of a radiation link to the UFOs was considered important enough to be described by Ruppelt to the Robertson Panel. The next CSI bulletin carried no such feature.[124] One paragraph, vaguely worded, addressed the subject minimally. After Robertson targeted CSI, and the FBI reported on attempts to pressure Walther Riedel to resign, the third CSI bulletin (July 1953) announced that the organization would "go on stand-by status." It disbanded in October.

Meanwhile, another group calling itself CSI (Civilian Saucer Intelligence of New York) quietly arose, mainly from the herculean efforts of three talented UFO researchers: Isabel Davis, Lex Mebane, and Ted Bloecher.[125] They, with APRO, would serve as focus points for public collection and dissemination of information on UFOs. They were tough analysts, very difficult to fool with trivial cases. Even Hynek would later secretly go to meet with them and exchange UFO information both ways.[126] CSI–New York was often his main source of information on cases coming from overseas. When Donald Keyhoe's National Investigations Committee on Aerial Phenomena appeared, an all-out war developed between it and the intelligence community.[127] Keyhoe's organization was "flameproof" because of an array of prominent retired military people on its board of directors, including the former head of the Central Intelligence Group (the CIA's predecessor), Adm. Roscoe Hillenkoetter. Many CIA members drifted in and out of the NICAP organization, several on the board itself. But there is no evidence that they had any influence on NICAP policy. Keyhoe's administrative assistant and de facto executive, Richard Hall, however, remembers specific formal CIA interest in his and NICAP's activities.[128] There is no question whatever that the intelligence community would rather have had the NICAPs, APROs, and CSIs just go away. In 1960 air force Col. Philip G. Evans, for the House of Representatives Armed Services Sub-committee hearing, issued a hostile statement that characterized civilian UFO organizations as being driven by "either financial gain, religious reasons, pure emotional outlet, ignorance, or possibly to use the organization as a cold war tool."[129]

As the 1950s and 1960s wore on, the actual words of the Robertson Panel Report (e.g., no evidence of any direct threat to national security; remove the aura of mystery surrounding UFOs) regularly appeared in press releases, briefings, and policy statements. The panel personnel themselves kept a lower profile. Alvarez, Goudsmit, and Berkner responded only rarely to inquiries about UFOs, and then usually with unveiled hostility. Robertson returned from intelligence work overseas in 1957 and was briefed by ATIC about how his panel's recommendations were working. Robertson said that he "was very pleased to see how the project is being conducted." The panel had been discussed at the briefing, and the possible declassification of the report was referred to the CIA.[130]

The final member of the panel, Thornton Page, had remained more openly curious about the subject and used it in college classes that he taught. When a great UFO wave burst across the United States in 1966, CBS decided to create a "documentary" narrated by Walter Cronkite.[131] It asked Page to help design the show and to appear on camera. The program included "loaded commentary," extremely negative senior scientists giving explanations for why UFOs are not really UFOs, and a merciless exposure of one person's "true" UFO. Later in 1966, Page wrote fellow Robertsonian attendee Fred Durant that he had organized the show "around the Robertson Panel recommendations."[132]

Such work, plus the somewhat inexplicable and constant public debunking by Donald Menzel, worked well with Robertsonian policy to keep scientists out of the fray until the air force funded a new UFO study project at the University of Colorado. That project, wherein the chief scientist created conclusions diametrically opposed to the views of at least twelve of its top fifteen personnel, produced another strange page in the scientific obituary of UFOs. However, that is beyond the scope of this chapter.[133]

The cold war had a marked, unhelpful impact on the study of the UFO phenomenon. The tension between the United States and the Soviet Union required that the subject be treated as a security matter rather than one of scientific research. As public interest grew too great, it was necessary to manage the subject to defuse its potential use as a psychological warfare tool. This stance, crystallized by the CIA's 1953 Robertson Panel but foreshadowed by the U.S. Air Force's much earlier concern, was very successful. Perhaps the most important accomplishment of the resultant policy was to effectively remove scientists and other academics from a serious concern with studying the mystery. UFO study has not recovered to this day. The subject is a popular culture laughingstock, and one of the greatest mysteries of any era goes wanting for serious personnel, research, and facilitation.

Chapter Five

The Extraterrestrial Hypothesis in the Early UFO Age

Jerome Clark

To all appearances, the UFO phenomenon is a recent historical occurrence, apparently no more than two centuries old.[1] From the early years of the nineteenth century, occasional reports surfaced in newspapers and scientific journals.[2]

So far as is known, the first mention of an extraterrestrial spacecraft was published in the 17 June 1864 issue of a French newspaper, *La Pays*, which ran an allegedly real but clearly fabulous account of a discovery by two American geologists of a hollow, egg-shaped structure holding the three-foot mummified body of a hairless humanoid with a trunk protruding from the middle of its forehead. In June 1884 a weekly newspaper published in Holdrege, Nebraska, reported that a band of cowboys had seen a strange vehicle crash to earth near Benkelman. Investigators and spectators subsequently viewed the remains of what Lincoln's *Daily State Journal* thought "must be an air vessel belonging originally to some other planet." Soon, however, the *Nugget*'s anonymous Benkelman correspondent informed readers that during a blinding rainstorm the "queer object melted, dissolved by the water like a spoonful of salt"—presumably the substance with which the story was to be taken.[3]

The great wave of "airships"—cigar-shaped UFOs in modern parlance—began in northern California in November 1896 and ended in the Midwest and East in May 1897. It brought with it a new rash of speculation about extraterrestrial visitation, including numerous hoaxes playing to the idea.[4] But in subsequent airship scares in the United States and elsewhere, such speculations were little heard, with most theories concerning the objects' origin focusing on spies or secret inventors,[5] though a letter appearing in the 29 July 1909 edition of New Zealand's *Otago Daily Times* attributes local airship sightings to "atomic-powered spaceships" from Mars.

One curious feature of the post-1897 airship waves was the failure of each to stick in historical memory. Although 1909, for example, brought a flood of sightings worldwide and attendant discussion and speculation, contemporary accounts do not allude to the hugely publicized events of little more than a decade earlier. Consequently, airship and other sightings of UFO-like manifestations were treated as if discrete occurrences, with no sense that they could be part of a larger phenomenon spread over time and space.

It would take a failed novelist, obsessed bibliophile, and chronic curiosity seeker to make the connection. Charles Fort (1874–1932), a talented but commercially frustrated fiction writer, took to whiling away his days in libraries in New York (and then in London), where he explored oddities of nature and behavior through newspapers, scientific journals, and other printed sources. "I undertook the job of going through all scientific periodicals, at least by the way of indexes, published in English and French," he recalled.[6] When seen in their entirety, these data exposed a pattern of reports of anomalous structures in the sky, which he discussed in three books published between 1919 and 1931.

Essentially a satirist hugely skeptical of human beings'—and especially scientists'—claim to ultimate wisdom, Fort offered up a kind of theory about extraterrestrial visitation in asides and jokes, not always making it entirely clear when he was serious and when he was not. But a close reading of the books, plus his other writings (notably four letters to the *New York Times*, written in straightforward prose),[7] shows that Fort anticipated many ideas that would come into prominence decades later, after concepts such as "flying saucers" and "unidentified flying objects" had entered the popular vocabulary.

Fort speculated that beings from other planets had been observing the earth for many centuries. Evidence of their presence in ancient times could be discerned in certain enigmatic archaeological artifacts. Possibly extraterrestrials influenced human evolution. Legends of ghosts, gods, and other supernatural entities are distorted accounts of encounters with space people. The extraterrestrials, who come from a variety of worlds, have different motives and missions. Some are only passing through; others have a more intimate interest in the earth and its inhabitants. Esoteric societies may be in contact with extraterrestrials, who may be responsible for mysterious disappearances of people and ships. Some of the eerie shapes seen in the sky may themselves be life-forms—space or atmospheric animals, in other words.

Fort died in 1932, but the Fortean Society (brought into being by Tiffany Thayer the year before) continued collecting reports of anomalous physical phenomena, including unknown aerial objects, in the *Fortean Society Magazine* (later *Doubt*).[8] Although the Fortean Society's membership was small, the influence of Fort's ideas was felt in the popular Ziff-Davis science fiction magazines *Amazing Stories* and *Fantastic Adventures* under the editorship of the flamboyant Ray Palmer. One regular contributor was Vincent H. Gaddis, who two decades later would invent the "Bermuda Triangle."[9] The magazines carried articles on "true mysteries," some—recycling Fort and Fortean Society material—dealing with evidence for space visitation. In the April 1947 issue of *Amazing*, Palmer remarked that only the naive could doubt that "responsible parties in the world governments" are aware of "spaceships visiting the earth."

The Occult Tradition: Contactees Before the Age of Flying Saucers

Since at least the time of Emanuel Swedenborg (1688–1772), mystics had claimed encounters and communications with people from other planets.[10] In *Earths in the Solar World* (1758), Swedenborg recounted his astral travels to other planets and the moon, each inhabited by intelligent beings with whom he was able to engage in fruitful discourse. Each Martian, for example, "lives content with his goods, and everyone with his honor, in being esteemed just, and one that loves his neighbor."

The Spiritualist craze of the nineteenth century brought with it a rash of extraterrestrial communications, the most famous those associated with Catherine Elise Muller, given the pseudonym "Hélène Smith" in Theodore Flournoy's *From India to the Planet Mars* (1899). In trance, sleep, or waking consciousness, Muller interacted with denizens of the Red Planet and observed the landscape, which she held to be crisscrossed with canals, reflecting the much-publicized— and subsequently discredited—theories of American astronomer Percival Lowell.[11] She also produced a Martian language, which Flournoy found to be "an infantile travesty of French."[12]

Around the same period, an American woman whom the pioneering psychical researcher James Hyslop identifies only as Mrs. Smead began receiving communications, via automatic writing, from her three deceased children and a brother-in-law. Mrs. Smead learned that the adult and one child, Maude, had removed themselves to Mars. Soon Maude produced a Martian map showing, among other features, the canals.[13]

Such astronomical gaffes underscore what religious studies specialist J. Gordon Melton calls "the central issue of contactee claims . . . the rather parasitical relationship that occult religion has to . . . popular science." In other words, seeking scientific validation, it ties itself to what often prove to be ephemeral scientific possibilities, such as Martian canals or intelligent beings on nearby worlds. Melton remarks with amusement on Swedenborg's failure, while traveling through the solar system, to note the presence of then-undiscovered outer planets such as Uranus, Neptune, and Pluto.[14]

The most influential of the nineteenth-century occultists was Helena Petrovna Blavatsky (1831–91), founder of the theosophical movement. She proposed a complex supernatural order with a hierarchy of "ascended masters." These include the Venus-based "Lords of the Flame," about whom Blavatsky had relatively little to say but who would figure prominently in the revisionist theosophy of the I AM movement, the brainchild of the notorious Guy and Edna Ballard. In the 1930s the Ballards drew a small army of followers through doctrines that combined popular occultism and native fascism.[15] Guy Ballard claimed that in 1932, in the Grand Teton Mountains, he met twelve "tall masters from Venus." Melton observes that Ballard was "the first actually to build a religion on contact with extraterrestrials."[16]

Another theosophy-influenced (albeit more benign) figure, N. Meade Layne of San Diego, founded Borderland Sciences Research Associates in February 1945. Layne, also a member of the Fortean Society, hoped through theosophical principles to explore alternative energies and to explain a broad range of anomalous and paranormal phenomena. In his efforts, Layne drew on the channelings of medium Mark Probert, who allegedly communicated with such discarnates as the five-hundred-thousand-year-old Tibetan wise man Yada Di' Shi'ite.[17]

On 9 October 1946, between 7:25 and 9:00 P.M., as San Diego residents stood outside watching a meteor shower, some reported seeing a huge object. In many ways reminiscent of phenomena from the airship era, the object—dark except for two red lights along the side—was long and tube-shaped, with huge wings, which observers thought looked like a bat's or butterfly's. Among the observers was Probert, who phoned Layne. Layne urged him to attempt telepathic contact with the ship's crew. Probert reported success. The vehicle was a spacecraft known as a "Kareeta," the product of an alien civilization seeking peaceful relations with earth. "They have very light bodies," Probert said.[18]

Layne agreed. A few years later, after flying saucers had entered the popular imagination, he offered an explanation for craft like these:

The aeroforms are thought-constructs, mind constructs. As such, they are, in effect, the vehicle of the actual entity who creates them. Just as our own terrestrial minds rule and become identified with our bodies, so does the entry of the Etheric world make for itself a body or vehicle out of etheric substance. This body may be of any shape or size, any one of a hundred *mutants*— such as the indefinite and changing shapes reported by observers of flying saucers throughout the world. The shape may be a wheel, a globe, a fusiform or cigar shape, a fireball, vapor or gasses. It may have any density, any rate of vibration desired. The impenetrable steel of landed discs is, as it were, a sort of etheric isotope of our terrestrial steel, or we may call it "etheric steel." The shapes and vehicles and the entity operating them form one being, just as a human being is a psychophysical mind-body unity. The body of this Etherian entity is a thoughtform which can go anywhere, and penetrates our earth and sea as easily as our air.[19]

In the Wake of 24 June 1947

In the spring of 1947, R. DeWitt Miller devoted a chapter of his book *Forgotten Mysteries* to "Enigmas Out of Space." Most of the "enigmas" had nothing to do with interplanetary visitation, but he made brief reference to "modern speculation"—namely, Fort's—that "conscious beings from other worlds have actually reached this earth and navigated our skies in space ships." The June issue of *Amazing Stories* carried an article by Vincent Gaddis titled "Visitors from the Void." Gaddis, a Fortean Society member, cited reports of unusual aerial phenomena as evidence of an alien presence.[20]

On 23 June the *Hartford Courant* took note of the remarks of Lyman Spitzer Jr., associate professor of astrophysics at Yale University, on New Haven's WTIC radio the previous evening. Spitzer speculated that Mars may have been civilized for millions of years; if so, it was possible that Martians have "visited the earth. . . . [U]nless they had spent some time in a large city or had landed sufficiently recently to be photographed, we would have no record of their having been here. . . . [A]ny few men who had seen them would probably not be believed by anyone else."[21]

Spitzer's remarks, which received only local publicity, could not have influenced the pivotal event that would occur the following day: the sighting by Kenneth Arnold, a private pilot from Idaho, of nine shiny objects "flying diagonally in an echelon formation between the first four and the last five" at an apparent speed of seventeen hundred miles per hour.[22] The sighting, which took place over Mount Rainier, Washington, was apparently independently witnessed by prospector Fred M. Johnson.[23]

Because it was widely publicized and because a worldwide wave of sightings followed it,[24] the Arnold sighting, never satisfactorily explained, ushered in the age of flying saucers and more than five decades' worth of theory and debate about the meaning of UFO sightings. Arnold, who knew nothing of Fort and to whom, of course, such concepts as flying saucers and UFOs were unknown, struggled to find a framework in which his experience made some sort of sense. The notion that the objects, whose motion he characterized as resembling that of saucers skipping across water (he did not use the phrase "flying saucers"), might be extraterrestrial spacecraft did not occur to him, at least not at first.

Nonetheless, two days later an International News Service (INS) wire story, datelined McCord Field, Tacoma, Washington, opened with these words: "Nine 'saucer-shaped Martian planes,' reported seen over southwest Washington at 10,000 feet late Tuesday by a Boise, Idaho, airplane pilot, were 'out of this world.' They could not have come from the northwest, according to base operations at McCord army airfield."[25]

The story does not make clear why "Martian planes" and "out of this world" are placed within quotation marks. Most likely they are scare quotes, words spoken by nobody but set in quotes to stress their outlandish nature. The account also has Arnold, erroneously identified as a "forest service employee" (he sold fire equipment for a private firm), referring to the objects as "flying saucers," which he would not have done. In fact, this article—whose author is unknown—may be the first to use the expression.

In any case, the INS dispatch is a curious historical anomaly, the sole—and first—known printed allusion to spacecraft theories in the immediate wake of the Arnold sighting. Aside from this brief and seemingly inexplicable reference, what would become known as the "extraterrestrial hypothesis" simply does not figure in early speculations. For example, in a 28 June piece, Bill Bequette of Pendleton's *East Oregonian* summarized the assorted theories being advanced to explain the flying disks. They ranged from "heated circular exhaust pipes of jet airplanes," to guided missiles, to light reflected off aircraft wings, to war nerves, to mirages, to "whisperings of Russian secret weapons." Spaceships are not mentioned.[26]

Nor would they be until 3 July, when a letter published in the *San Francisco Chronicle* declared flatly that the "flying disks are oblate spheroid space ships from the older planets and other solar systems. . . . Their present local headquarters is on the unseen side of our moon." The correspondent, Ole J. Sneide, wrote from the authority of personal experience; he had learned these things while teleporting himself "hither and yon in and beyond our galaxy." As a follow-up article in the *Chronicle* made clear, Sneide, an occultist and professed out-of-body traveler, was serious.[27]

By now even the less esoterically inclined were beginning to wonder about an unearthly origin for the saucers. On 4 July a short INS item quoted an unnamed Detroit meteorologist's suggestion that maybe the disks were "signals from Mars."[28] Extraterrestrial speculations came to the fore a few days later, on 7 and 8 July, with two widely circulated press-wire stories. The first, implicitly challenging popular wisdom that saw the phenomenon as a new development, reported that "reports of flying discs had similar counterparts in the past," with all that implied. The source for the assertion was identified as "a rare book in Chicago's Newberry Library"—Fort's *Book of the Damned*.[29] The same day, American Rocket Society president and Fortean Society member R. L. Farnsworth told a United Press (UP) reporter that sightings had taken place "in the last century, and plenty of other times, too. Nobody ever found out what any of the objects were. . . . I wouldn't even be surprised if the flying saucers were remote-control electronic eyes from Mars."[30]

On 8 July, in a UP story out of Los Angeles, DeWitt Miller noted the existence of sightings as far back as the early nineteenth century. "There are at least 100 cases in which the queer objects were said to have a 'disk-like' form," he wrote. These and the objects currently being reported could well be vehicles from Mars or other planets, perhaps even "things out of other dimensions of time and space."[31]

By the tenth, however, the ridicule that would dog the subject of UFOs forever after had begun to dominate press coverage. President Truman equated flying saucers with the notorious "moon hoax" of 1835,[32] and Ole Sneide's yarns about his interactions with the "rulers of creation" and spaceships parked behind the moon garnered much tongue-in-cheek coverage,[33] making it seem as if extraterrestrial theories were fit only for cranks.

In a study of the 1947 UFO wave two decades later, ufologist Ted Bloecher found that only two witnesses "openly expressed the opinion that the objects seen could have been 'space ships.'"[34] The first Gallup poll on the subject, released on 14 August ("now that the uproar over the 'flying saucers' has subsided"), found so few respondents mentioning outer-space explanations that they went unlisted in the results. When asked their opinions about saucers, 33 percent didn't know; 29 percent suspected they were illusory, 10 percent a hoax, and 15 percent "U.S. secret weapon, part of atomic bomb, etc." The other 13 percent were divided among "weather forecasting devices" (3 percent), "Russian secret weapons" (1 percent), and "other explanations" (9 percent). Even in this last category, spaceships seem to have gone unmentioned; opinions focused on biblical interpretations on one end, commercial products or "radio waves from the Bikini atomic bomb explosion" on the other.[35]

Opinions had not changed much by 1951, when *Popular Science* released the results of its own poll of UFO witnesses. Asked to choose what they deemed the most probable explanation of what they had seen, only 4 percent said "visitors from afar." Fully 52 percent thought they had observed "manmade aircraft," and 16 percent believed it was "something commonplace."[36]

The Influence of Donald E. Keyhoe

Public skepticism of extraterrestrial theories notwithstanding, within military circles—more attuned to the realities of current aviation technology than average citizens—space visitation was considered a distinct possibility. In fact, a significant faction within the first U.S. Air Force UFO project, Sign, was sufficiently persuaded that in the fall of 1948 it prepared a top secret "estimate of the situation" and sent it up the chain of command. The estimate concluded that the best evidence indicated an interplanetary origin for UFOs. Air force Chief of Staff Gen. Hoyt S. Vandenberg rejected it on the grounds that it lacked proof,[37] though not before it had fueled debate and controversy within the Pentagon.[38] It was declassified and all copies ordered burned. Its existence was not revealed until 1956, in a book by a former UFO project head,[39] though for years afterward the air force denied there had ever been any such document.[40]

Embarrassed, the air force drove the extraterrestrial proponents out of Sign, which was reorganized on 11 February 1949 as Project Grudge, a debunking operation in which, according to its last director, Edward J. Ruppelt (who oversaw its further reorganization and its renaming as Project Blue Book in March 1952), reports were now "being evaluated on the premise that UFOs couldn't exist. No matter what you see or hear, don't believe it."[41] Except for a brief period of neutral investigation between the fall of 1951 and mid-1953, when Captain Ruppelt left the project, this would represent the air force's posture until it left the UFO business in December 1969.[42]

Not a great deal was known publicly about the air force's UFO investigation in 1949. Even its name was classified, so it was known popularly as "Project Saucer." To answer public demands for information and also to underscore the project's assurances that it had the UFO situation well in hand, Grudge cooperated with journalist Sidney Shallett, who wrote two debunking pieces for the popular *Saturday Evening Post* in the spring of 1949.[43]

In the meantime, the men's magazine *True* had been conducting its own inquiries but getting nowhere. Suspecting a cover-up, editor Ken Purdy decided to turn the assignment over to a retired Marine Corps major and much-published writer, Donald E. Keyhoe, who had extensive Pentagon contacts. Keyhoe accepted the assignment in May and spent the next several months researching the story. He announced his conclusion in the title of the piece: "The Flying Saucers Are Real."

In what UFO historian David M. Jacobs has described as "one of the most widely read and discussed articles in publishing history,"[44] Keyhoe proposed that "living, intelligent observers from another planet" had watched the earth for the past 175 years. They had stepped up their efforts after they observed atomic bomb explosions on the earth's surface. He went on to outline what he believed to be the "pattern of authentic saucer reports":

1. First, the world-wide sightings. Then concentration on the United States, the most advanced nation.
2. The numerous small disks seen in the first part of the scare, which some think were "observers," remotely controlled.
3. The frequent sightings at Air Force bases.
4. Later sightings of larger disks, and space-ship types, after the first disks outspeeded and outmaneuvered our planes.
5. Low-altitude appearances . . . which could provide atmospheric samples.
6. The increase of mystery-light sightings, and night encounters, and decrease of reliably witnessed day sightings (when the scare had become nation-wide, and day operations might seem less wise).[45]

Keyhoe insisted that there was no evidence of "belligerence" on the part of the visitors; their intentions, he believed, were benign, even in the face of unfriendly responses from the world's military, which dispatched planes to intercept them. In the *True* article and the best-selling paperback book that followed it, he expressed certainty that the air force knew the truth but was concealing it to prevent mass panic. [46]

In another saucer book published that year in England (the American edition appeared in April 1951), Gerald Heard, a mystically inclined Englishman living in Los Angeles, expressed similar views but added to them some exotic speculations: that the saucers' pilots were probably superbees from Mars, "of perhaps two inches in length . . . as beautiful as the most beautiful of any flower, any beetle, moth or butterfly." [47] Like Keyhoe, Heard implicitly assumed that no one had ever seen the occupants of UFOs; therefore, one could only speculate about their appearance. Heard's "theory" drew on an off-the-cuff, tongue-in-cheek remark by astronomer and UFO disbeliever Gerard Kuiper, who had told a reporter that the only intelligent life one could expect on Mars would be a race of advanced insects. [48] Heard would be heard from no more.

A third saucer book from 1950, by *Variety* columnist Frank Scully, reported—on the authority of what proved to be extremely dubious sources—that the U.S. government had recovered three downed spacecraft in the southwestern desert. [49] Such rumors had been circulating since the summer of 1947, [50] but Scully's book gave them their widest currency. According to him, the craft flew along "magnetic lines of force" and housed crews of small humanlike beings "dressed in the style of 1890" and apparently from Venus.

Keyhoe had already looked into this story and rejected it as a hoax, and two years later *True* writer J. P. Cahn exposed its origins in a complex confidence scheme of which the naive Scully had been but one of the victims. [51] For a long time thereafter, no self-respecting ufologist would listen to a tale of a UFO crash, [52] though such stories became part of the folklore of the age of flying saucers.

Another casualty of the Scully hoax was, for some, *any* report of UFO occupants. These "close encounters of the third kind" (CE IIIs), as they would be called many years later, [53] emerged in the wake of the Arnold report (one allegedly took place the same afternoon, at a rural location near Pendleton, Oregon), [54] but to the extent that they received any attention at all, they contributed to the growing ridicule surrounding the notion of UFOs, now associated with "little green men." Witnesses were describing beings that were small and, for the most part, male, but they were seldom green. Still, the phrase stuck.

Keyhoe would go on to become one of the most influential figures in the history of ufology, leading the field over the course of the 1950s and into the early 1960s. His advocacy of the extraterrestrial hypothesis (ETH), both as best-selling author and as director of the National Investigations Committee on Aerial Phenomena (NICAP) between 1957 and 1969, measurably affected popular attitudes toward the UFO phenomenon.[55]

Keyhoe's influence as a UFO proponent owed much to his relative conservatism. His was a cautious view of extraterrestrial visitation. UFOs were things that citizens of solid reputation—scientists, pilots, police officers, members of the clergy—reported in good faith. They were lights and structures in the sky and seldom seen at close range. If they landed at all, it was only briefly, and if occupants were glimpsed, it was only as shadowy figures in passing craft. Though it was conceivable that one day they might reveal themselves, for now they avoided contact with human beings.

The Contactees After Arnold

This was decidedly not the view of a movement growing out of southern California, out of the same occult underground that spawned Meade Layne and Mark Probert. The first of the new "contactees" to draw significant attention to himself was a longtime occult teacher, "Professor" George Adamski. (He already had some small renown in California esoteric circles for his theosophically oriented "Royal Order of Tibet," founded in the 1930s.) Adamski, among the witnesses to the 9 October 1946 manifestation described earlier, began producing photographs of alleged flying saucers and publishing them in the popular paranormal and occult magazine *Fate*.[56]

Adamski's claims underwent a significant escalation in November 1952, when he supposedly met a Venusian named Orthon in the California desert. His account, with photographs of interplanetary "scoutcraft," was appended to an already existing manuscript by Irish occultist and ancient-astronaut theorist Desmond Leslie and published the following year,[57] electrifying esoterically inclined saucer enthusiasts around the world. A follow-up book[58] two years later told of further encounters with "Space Brothers"—friendly Venusians, Martians, and Saturnians—and cemented Adamski's reputation as "earth's cosmic ambassador."

Slightly less well known but arguably even more influential in the contactee movement, George W. Van Tassel was taking psychic messages from space people (operating out of the Council of Seven Lights on the planet Shanchea) as early as January 1952. A year later he held regular public sessions at his home in Giant Rock in California's high-desert country. His misleadingly titled *I Rode a Flying Saucer!* (at that time, Van Tassel's contacts were purely psychic, though later they became physical as well) preceded Leslie and Adamski's volume by a year and so became the first contactee book in the modern sense.

Just as important, Van Tassel more than anybody helped give shape to the emerging movement. The annual Giant Rock conventions (the first of them held in 1954, the last in 1977)[59] provided a congenial atmosphere for space communicants and their followers (known as "saucerians"), and in that environment a theology for the age of flying saucers developed, based on a complex (if less than entirely consistent) cosmology.

As the contactees saw it, a federation of planets across the galaxy (or, as some had it, the universe itself) governs the cosmos. There are enlightened races and unenlightened ones, locked in physical and spiritual conflict. The earth is considered a backwater, populated by foolish and warlike inhabitants unable to use their technology for productive purposes. Space people are here to oversee our spiritual evolution, which will lead to full cosmic citizenship, though only after great calamities that will destroy many lives and alter the planet's landscape. The contactees are chosen by the space people to give advance word to those who will listen.

Messages came through direct face-to-face encounters or via nonphysical means: dreams, automatic writing, voices in the head, or visions. The physical contactees, who included Adamski, Daniel Fry,[60] Truman Bethurum,[61] and others, often provided what was alleged to be evidence or proof: photographs, witnesses, and the like. The psychic contactees, on the other hand, depended on the authority of the messages themselves, and on the majesty of the alleged communicants, for validation.

If the psychic contactees' claims were impervious to falsification (even, for the believers, when prophecies of apocalypse or mass landings failed, as they invariably did),[62] the same could not be said for the physical counterparts. Because he made the largest claims to confirmation, Adamski in particular saw himself the target of unfriendly investigations that caught him in falsehoods and exposed his photographs as almost surely faked.[63]

The Ufologists Versus the Saucerians

The ufologists who came in Keyhoe's wake were—given their conviction that UFOs were real and intelligently controlled—a cautious lot, and if many (though by no means all)[64] thought the extraterrestrials had no malevolent intentions, they rejected the idea that they were here to save us.

Most went beyond Keyhoe and accepted as credible at least some reports of occupants, though not of humanlike occupants who looked like handsome and beautiful space angels of contactee lore. Such early UFO groups as Civilian Saucer Investigation (formed in 1951), the Aerial Phenomena Research Organization (1952), and Civilian Saucer Intelligence (CSI) of New York (1954) took reports of "little men" seriously, reasoning that objects reported to have portholes were likely to have crews to look out of them. A spate of occupant reports from France in the fall of 1954 made the question of their existence unavoidable for all but NICAP, which for most of its life under Keyhoe continued to ignore such cases.[65]

Ufologists implicitly and explicitly rejected religious approaches to the UFO phenomenon. Though representing a broad spectrum of human beings, from the naively enthusiastic to the scientifically sophisticated, they assumed UFOs to be amenable to study, investigation, and analysis; through the proper methodology and the careful accumulation of evidence, the "UFO mystery" would be solved. The more educated ufologists tended to take a pragmatic approach and indulged in relatively little speculation about the nature and motives of presumed extraterrestrials.

Contactees and saucerians infuriated ufologists, already struggling to overcome the derision the very concept of UFOs engendered in some influential corners. Media already inclined to treat UFOs as fringe material gave prominence to the most extreme claims and claimants, as if to show that the subject belonged only on the fringes. Keyhoe and NICAP denounced contactees, even challenging the most prominent of their number to take polygraph tests to prove their sincerity.[66] Keyhoe was profoundly embarrassed when an employee gave Adamski and six other contactees NICAP membership cards; she was promptly fired.[67]

In a blistering assault on the claims of contactees, Isabel L. Davis of CSI, New York, stressed the unbridgeable differences between ufologists and saucerians:

All flying saucerdom is now divided into two irreconcilable groups. One group believes that human beings have had direct communication with extraterrestrial beings; the other group rejects all such reports as the product of conscious or unconscious fraud.

The split between believers and skeptics is, and should be, a real and permanent one. For to the skeptics, flying saucers still deserve the name of UFOs—*Unidentified* Flying Objects. To the believers, on the other hand, thanks to the extensive information they claim to have received from their extraterrestrial friends, the saucers are no longer UFOs but IFOs—*Identified*, fully identified, Flying Objects. The two terms are mutually exclusive. An object cannot be identified and unidentified at the same time.[68]

Publications such as NICAP's *U.F.O. Investigator*, *CSI News Letter*, and the gossip-oriented *Saucer News* scoffed at and debunked contact claims at every opportunity.[69] Ufologists saw the contactee movement as consisting of little more than fraud and social pathology; its participants were, in ufologists' estimation, either crooked or crazy.

The Decline of the ETH

In the 1960s the distinction between CE IIIs, imaginable in the ufological universe, and contact claims, which were not, became less certain. Ufologists, Davis wrote in the latter 1950s, "reject all cases that involve the *two-way exchange* of ideas or information between earth people and 'space people'" (italics in original). The credible occupant reports involved beings who looked "humanoid, not super- human; their behavior is quite incomprehensible; and they never *communicate* at all. They utter no lofty messages, no explanations of ancient riddles, no admonitions, warnings, reassurances, proph- ecies, or esoteric doctrine. Even when they are said to 'speak,' what they say is as unintelligible as what they do."[70]

But an incident that allegedly occurred on 18 April 1961 seemed on some level to defy attempts neatly to delineate CE IIIs from contact claims. A rural Eagle River, Wisconsin, man named Joe Simonton reported seeing a UFO land just outside his house late that morning. When he went outside to look, he stared inside the craft and saw three "Italian"-looking crew members. Via gestures, one indicated that they wanted Simonton to fill a jug with water. In exchange he was given four "pancakes."[71]

NICAP dismissed the story as an absurd contact claim unwor- thy of further consideration,[72] generating heated criticism both from contactee advocates[73] and from pro-CE III/anticontactee partisans.[74] In retrospect, it is hard to understand how anyone could have taken Simonton to be a contactee. Unlike contactees, he had no background in occultism (or, for that matter, confidence crime), and his UFO crewmen had no messages of cosmic uplift, in fact (or in allegation), no spoken messages of any kind. Moreover, whatever the nature of his experience, practically no one doubted his sincerity. Even Blue Book resisted labeling him a hoaxer; it judged that Simonton had suffered a "hallucination followed with delusion,"[75] less because evidence pointed definitively to such a conclusion, apparently, than that the alternative was inconceivable.

The Simonton story portended the explosion in close-encounter cases that would characterize the 1960s. As early as 1964, even NICAP was remarking on the "unprecedented number of landing, near- landing and close-approach cases."[76] Some of these were highly strange and defied easy categorization.

One was a story told on 24 April 1964 by an apparently sincere Newark Valley, New York, farmer named Gary Wilcox. Wilcox's alleged experience was even more outlandish than Simonton's. As he told it, he spotted a silvery, egg-shaped object on his property that morning, observed its two occupants, four-foot-tall spacesuit-clad humanoids, and engaged them in conversation on mundane subjects, including manure. The beings identified themselves as being "from what you know as the planet Mars."[77] Wilcox later said he thought somebody, possibly from the television show *Candid Camera*, was playing a trick on him.

Wilcox, who sought no publicity, confided the experience only to friends and family members. Eventually, the sheriff's department and a local newspaper heard about it. The first reporter who approached Wilcox was rebuffed, though eventually he did agree to an interview.[78] No one ever charged Wilcox with being a profiteer or a publicity seeker—family, friends, and acquaintances all swore that he had an excellent personal reputation—and a year and a half later, when a newspaper did a follow-up story, it noted, "Mr. Wilcox did not seem particularly happy to see a reporter show up at his farm."[79] Though Wilcox's account was unbelievable, there seemed no doubt that *he* believed it. Nor did he fit the profile of a flamboyant, headline-hunting, occult- or profit-obsessed contactee.

In 1964, however, no rational observer would have credited the idea of intelligent life on Mars. Wilcox's tale made no sense whatsoever; yet it foreshadowed many to come, incidents so weird that they refused to lend themselves to so materialist a notion as extraterrestrial visitation. An early critic sounded a theme that would become familiar: "The reality behind the saucer phenomena [*sic*] transcends our immediately perceptible world, thereby not availing itself to our scientific methods of proof which are geared to the physical world."[80]

The ETH was best suited to reports of lights and structures in the sky, to radar/visual cases, and to those close encounters in which humanoids were fleetingly observed and communication, if any, was minimal. It was harder to apply to the sorts of reports occult journalist John A. Keel began collecting in the mid-1960s, of menacing "Men in Black," monstrous creatures like "Mothman," and various other surrealistic interactions with otherworldly entities.[81] A new generation of ufologists grew ever more taken with paranormal "theories" about UFOs. Such notions, embraced by the influential British publication *Flying Saucer Review* under the editorship of the relatively restrained Charles Bowen and, later, the deeply paranoid Gordon Creighton, amounted to a thinly disguised demonology, in which malevolent shape-shifting entities pretended to be friendly extraterrestrials in order to manipulate or even destroy their naive human contacts.[82]

Ufologists disenchanted with the ETH but unwilling to follow the demonologists into this flight from reason eventually forged the "psychosocial" school, which sought to explain such experiences as visionary in nature and shaped by psychological and cultural processes.[83] But in focusing on the most exotic—and least evidential— UFO claims, the psychosocial advocates failed to deal adequately with ufology's most interesting questions, which brought it into being in the first place and with which the early extraterrestrial hypothesizers had grappled: namely, those related to physical evidence, instrumented observations, and multiply and independently witnessed events.

By the end of the 1960s, the consensus that had guided ufologists through the early years of the UFO controversy had broken down. Though to outsiders ufology was still assumed to be synonymous with belief in visitors from outer space, within ufology three schools of thought had begun to compete for dominance: the materialists (ETH partisans), the occultists (followers of Keel and Jacques Vallee),[84] and the culture commentators (psychosocial theorists), who professed to find existential themes expressed in UFO reports, which were presumed to be subjective experiences.

The ETH had gone unchallenged in ufology's early years because the phenomenon had seemed a straightforward proposition, or—for that matter—a "phenomenon" as opposed to "phenomena." Even in its later period, including the present, advocates have operated from the unspoken assumption that something so complex and irreducible as UFOs may be subsumed under a single explanatory framework. Ufologists have tended to reject pluralistic approaches that make room for a variety of explanatory possibilities—in other words, concede that what we call "unidentified flying objects" may be a range of things with little or no relationship to each other. Hobbled by its chronic problems—its fringe reputation, its continuing appeal to the naive, undisciplined, and unhelpful, its lack of access to funding and experts—ufology continued to have difficulty getting its case heard outside the tabloid press and television.

Still, some degree of progress had been possible. Organizations such as the Fund for UFO Research and the J. Allen Hynek Center for UFO Studies (CUFOS) have sponsored and published serious, scholarly work on the subject. CUFOS issued the refereed *Journal of UFO Studies* approximately yearly. The historically oriented Project 1947, headed by Jan L. Aldrich, encouraged research into the early years of the UFO controversy and added significantly to our knowledge of sightings, official policy, and popular culture responses to the phenomenon. Loren E. Gross published and distributed privately a series of monographs titled *UFOs: A History*, a day-by-day chronicle that at the end of 1999 had reached early 1959. The abduction phenomenon, which came to ufologists' attention in the mid-1960s and which ever since has remained a prominent element in discussions about UFOs, received a measure of attention from psychologists, historians, and physical scientists. One consequence was a conference held at the Massachusetts Institute of Technology in June 1992. Here, scientific and medical professionals mingled with ufologists and abductees for an airing of all points of view on this contentious question.[85]

A particularly significant development occurred between 29 September and 4 October 1997, when an international panel of physical scientists met at the Pocantico Conference Center in Tarrytown, New York, to listen to a small group of ufologists present physical evidence cases which they held to be particularly well documented and puzzling. In a report issued in June 1998, the panel, while distancing itself from the ETH, agreed that "unexplained observations" exist and urged further scientific investigation into those "cases which include as much independent physical evidence as possible and strong witness testimony."[86] Perhaps indicating a loosening of skepticism about UFOs in traditionally hostile major media, the report received sympathetic, sometimes front-page treatment in newspapers as widespread as the *Washington Post* and the *San Jose Mercury News*.[87] Whether fluke or portent, this continuing public interest underscored the UFO controversy's remarkable durability.

Chapter Six

UFOs: Lost in the Myths

Thomas E. Bullard

Ask for the preeminent mystery of the twentieth century, and an answer of UFOs could hardly go wrong. UFOs have invaded modern consciousness in overwhelming force, and endless streams of books, magazine articles, tabloid covers, movies, TV shows, cartoons, advertisements, greeting cards, toys, T-shirts, even alien-head salt and pepper shakers, attest to the popularity of this phenomenon, its ability to hold public attention, and, yes, to sell.[1] Gallup polls rank UFOs near the top of the list for subjects of widespread recognition—in fact, a 1973 survey found that 95 percent of the public had heard of UFOs, whereas in 1977 only 92 percent could identify Gerald Ford in a poll taken just nine months after he left the White House.[2] Only sex Web sites outscore UFOs for popularity on the Internet.

Now ask what thriving cultural concern academic scholars seem determined to neglect, and UFOs would again be a sound answer. For all the burgeoning literature of the humanities and sciences, for all the scholarly enthusiasm to pry into the minutest corners of nature or culture, only a thin sheaf of studies treats UFOs. Natural scientists venture little more than unsubstantiated opinions, psychologists and sociologists pay infrequent attention, and even historians, folklorists, and students of religion usually shy away from a subject that ought to attract them in droves.

Why a mainstay of popular culture should remain a wallflower at the frenzied dance of modern scholarship amounts to a puzzle in its own right. Perhaps UFOs are victims of their own success. This suggestion is not meant in the shallow sense that academics shun any subject exciting enough to deserve study, but in the sense that those very characteristics that win UFOs their popularity also complicate the subject until it becomes too daunting to approach, in political as well as methodological and conceptual terms.

The UFO mystery begins with personal experiences, millions of them since 1947, according to the polls, with tens of thousands of reports on record. These experiences and claims of experience—the sightings, waves, landings, crashes, abductions, and contacts old and new, domestic or foreign, trivial or intriguing—have sustained and renewed the phenomenon these past fifty years as an independent variable, subject only to loose influence by the pronouncements of advocates or scoffers. UFO reports would seem to be a straightforward subject for scientific investigation, but little about UFOs emerges as straightforward. The reports themselves mingle many cases of mistaken identity with the occasional case that stops curious persons dead in their tracks. Genuinely puzzling reports resist easy explanation and set a hard core of anomaly at the center of the mystery, but the inquiries and disputes about UFOs seldom zero in on this core. It shares center stage with—or loses it to—supposedly related phenomena like ancient astronauts, the Bermuda Triangle, Men in Black, the face on Mars, crop circles, cattle mutilations, and innumerable conspiracy theories, where the kinship is tenuous and often fanciful. Also clamoring for attention are the disputational pyrotechnics of interested parties pro and con, theorists with intellectual axes to grind, UFOs as the mass media and popular culture represent them, and the circus of feuds, hoaxes, absurdities, and eccentricities that have dogged the subject from its dawning day.

Such proliferation of parts testifies that UFOs mean all things to all people, or something to almost anyone. Human interest has absorbed the UFO experience into layers of popular belief about UFOs, a welter of observations, narratives, beliefs, associations, themes, factions, and baggage with little coherence or direction, but rich in appeal to emotion and imagination. Familiar for over fifty years, the subject increases in popularity rather than wears out its welcome. Though often overused, the designation of mythic seems built to order for such a flexible phenomenon. An onlooker familiar with religion, mythology, and folklore comes to feel more and more at home with UFOs over the course of their development. Today UFO beliefs crystallize around such age-old mythic motifs as otherworldly visitation, diminutive supernatural beings, the end of the world, and cosmic salvation. Even the archaic pattern of initiation and elements of fairy folklore reappear among abduction reports. UFO tales look to a distant past even as they bridge the gulf between long ago and things to come, expressing in technological idiom certain religious needs and supernatural themes otherwise lost in a secular age.

In a sense the myth has fared all too well. It hides the fact that the UFO mystery is not a single question but two, one about the nature of the UFO experience, the other about the human meanings of UFOs. To overlook this distinction leads to dismissal of the whole phenomenon as a cultural reality and nothing more, without any careful reckoning with the experiential core. Many people are perfectly willing to brush aside scientific questions altogether, while others who want a scientific understanding confuse the phenomenon and the myth. A separation of the two begins with awareness of the basic religious and mythical dimensions of the phenomenon, why they flourish in an age seemingly hostile to supernatural beliefs, and how human needs for hope, meaning, and purpose transform the experiential truth of UFOs into social and psychological truth.

The Religious Face of UFOs

A classic effort to define religion declares it a belief in spiritual beings.[3] An even broader conceptualization identifies religion with any manifestation of the sacred, that is, basic awareness of a reality set apart from the profane.[4] The sacred represents a separate, transcendent order. It is true reality, powerful, pure, and changeless, in contrast to the transient, defective everyday world. Religion concerns the relationship of humans with powers greater than their own, perhaps conscious powers and perhaps blind forces, not necessarily far removed from the commonplace but always distinct from it.

Sacred powers need not be supernatural or otherworldly, but in many religious traditions the separation of sacred and profane widens until the two realms coexist only as worlds apart.

Rudolf Otto's famous formulation of the sacred or holy emphasizes an experience beyond the grasp of reason, unique and "wholly other," at once overpowering, mysterious, awe-inspiring, fascinating, and beautiful. He designates such an encounter as *numinous*, evocative of a mental state or feeling, but also a fundamental property of the mysterious "other" that breaks into the awareness of the experiencer from outside.[5] This concept of the sacred stresses the importance of personal experience and the profound emotions it arouses in the creation and sustenance of religious faith.

Substitute up-to-date technological terms for outmoded supernatural ones, and the relationship between religion and UFOs becomes a union made in heaven. UFOs have been synonymous with visits from otherworldly beings for ufologists as well as Hollywood since about 1950, and in every depiction these alien pilots, not of this earth and not necessarily of human appearance, possess a technological power so advanced it does indeed appear to be magic. UFOs remain the most democratic of mysteries. Anyone, from astronomers and airline pilots to motorists and backyard barbecuers, sees these objects as they suddenly intrude and just as suddenly withdraw, leaving no trace in the physical world as a rule, but stamping a deep impression on the witnesses themselves. Their testimonies ring with emotional aftertones:

> I don't know how long I watched the thing. I began to conjecture: the earth's movements are so mysterious, maybe this is some axis-turning sight only the few—the awake and the curious—are privileged to see. Like another world setting.[6]

> Three or four minutes later, the object started moving away. . . . I got a little upset. I said to myself, "Oh, please don't go, I want to look at you some more." At that split second, it stopped, made a complete turn. . . . Then it started moving toward me. . . . I wanted it to come closer, but I was getting frightened.[7]

> I wished it would come again. It was beautiful. I could feel the life pulsating from it.[8]

Today we seldom hear such language as these witnesses speak. Beauty, mystery, longing, fear, awe, power, interaction with a sentient other—UFO reports provoke expressions of a naked, unguarded wonder that is a hallmark of numinous encounters, and reason to allow as a possibility worth investigation that these descriptions reflect extraordinary experience.

Efforts to associate UFOs with religion and mythology started early in the history of ufology as various writers promoted an interpretation of mythical gods as aliens and the Vimanas, or flying chariots, of Hindu epics as spaceships[9]—speculations already deeply rooted in UFO literature when Erich von Daniken popularized "ancient astronauts" in the early 1970s. Even Carl Sagan, usually the complete UFO skeptic, toyed with the idea that myths of the aquatic being Oannes might preserve hints of aliens bringing civilization to ancient Sumer.[10] Rather than rewrite spiritual history in terms of extraterrestrial intervention, other authors have spiritualized technology out of the phenomenon. Psychologist C. G. Jung recognized UFOs as harbingers of a space-age religion in his influential book, *Flying Saucers: A Modern Myth of Things Seen in the Sky* (1959), and 1950s contactee accounts of meetings with Space Brothers expressed with naive transparency the yearning for a savior to arrive from the sky.

A still more speculative strand has joined both the intellectualizing and the spiritualizing impulse to seek an underlying cause for all extranormal experiences, something more complex and elusive than technologically advanced aliens. In his 1969 book, *Passport to Magonia*,[11] Jacques Vallee compiled an impressive list of similarities between traditional fairy lore and UFO accounts of meetings with "little men." Many readers mistook the parallels for more evidence of ancient astronauts, but the message was actually subversive of this standard view and the beginning of a new perspective on UFOs, one that diminished them from the answer for all mysteries to just one offshoot of a larger mystery encompassing religion, mythology, folklore, and paranormal experience. The suggested source of all mysteries ranged from a cosmic control system manipulating or conditioning human thought[12] to psychological and cultural forces, perhaps the actions of Jung's archetypes of the unconscious,[13] or hallucinations, dreams, and other altered states of consciousness shaped by cultural stereotypes.[14]

The relationship between UFO beliefs and religion has remained friendly ground for humanistic interest in UFOs, even leading to a scholarly anthology published by a university press, *The Gods Have Landed: New Religions from Other Worlds.*[15] This scholarship identifies the religious themes shot through UFO lore—the parallels between aliens and previous supernatural entities, whether angelic or demonic; the emotions roused by an encounter with the otherworldly, feelings of mystery, transcendence, and perfection; the hopes and fears that gather around this phenomenon, most notably apocalyptic beliefs and the wish for salvation; the effort to reconcile religious and scientific worldviews, made possible by the notion of alien intervention in human history; and traditional patterns of spirituality restored in terms of the UFO experience, such as rebirth, initiation, or spirit quest.[16] Abduction reports are especially ripe with suggestions of religious themes. The elaborate but recurrent pattern of these reports corresponds to accounts of shamanic initiation and the ordeals of desert saints, while the overall conflict these stories portray embodies the basic religious struggle between good and evil, darkness and light.[17] More and more authors treating religious or mythical themes in modern culture pause to mention UFOs. They have become inseparable from discussions of nuclear fear,[18] the romance of space exploration,[19] current preoccupations with apocalypse,[20] and disputes over sexual abuse and satanic ritual abuse.[21]

An Unlikely Fellowship

The fact of close entanglements between UFOs and religion is undeniable but surprising all the same. At first glance UFOs seem the least likely candidates in the known universe to share anything with religion and mythology. The alien spaceship—streamlined, metallic, the product of a technology surpassing earthly ken—surely belongs to realms of futuristic science light-years removed from archaic, backward-looking credulities of religious and mythical thinking. One reflects the triumph of intellect over limits imposed by nature, the other, man's accommodation to forces beyond his control.

History bestows low odds on this union as well. The aerial prodigies and portents of ancient and medieval times signaled divine anger, comets prophesied war for thousands of years; but by the eighteenth century these old religious associations died, and anything strange in the sky belonged to categories like meteors or meteorological phenomena, of the anomalous subspecies to be sure, but still located squarely in scientific territory. From about 1880 through 1946, witnesses reported a stream of aerial mysteries— phantom airships, mysterious airplanes, foo fighters, and ghost rockets—that reflected technological expectations of the day or looked one step ahead.[22] The phantom airships of 1897 played to human hopes by heralding that man could fly at last, whereas foo fighters as supposed enemy secret weapons during World War II and ghost rockets as possible Soviet missiles at the onset of the cold war fueled human fears of destruction from the sky.

UFOs before 1947 looked, acted, and inspired popular concerns very like subsequent UFOs, yet for sixty years technological mysteries of the air struck sparks of interest without ever catching fire as myths of their time. The technology advanced and inspired wonder, but it remained machinery, man-made and confined to the boundaries of human know-how. Flying saucers started out under the same handicap. In 1947 conventional wisdom took for granted that they were secret weapons, and when the conventional preference shifted to spaceships a few years later, they still held the line as well-behaved spacecraft should, demonstrating that scientific aliens explored our planet in the same way we planned to explore theirs someday.

The metamorphosis of UFOs from machinery to myth happened in a hurry. By the early 1950s, flying saucers brought the Space Brothers; by the late 1960s, these objects acted in such mysterious ways that many thoughtful ufologists abandoned the extraterrestrial hypothesis in favor of paraphysical speculations about alternate universes and materialized psychisms.[23] Somehow, modern UFOs intercepted the right historical moment to soar off into the wild blue yonder of popular imagination, where their predecessors barely got off the ground. Since then, not even the sky has been the limit. Why a nuts-and-bolts transport vehicle should break out of its technological mold to act in ways at odds with technology, or even hostile to it, calls for attention to the religious crisis of modern times.

News of a Demise Greatly Exaggerated

The age of UFOs nests within an era outwardly unfriendly toward myth, an attitude evident in the ongoing throes of religious uncertainty and change. God is dead, say both atheists and theologians. His demise is well known to university students and to followers of modern intellectual trends. If few representatives of elite culture borrow the dramatic terms of Nietzsche's heresy, many contribute to the epitaph, sparing the name of God while they bury the supernaturalism in which gods make sense.

No intellectual movement has battered the authority and relevance of the divine more forcefully or famously than science. The Copernican revolution, the trial of Galileo, T. H. Huxley's defense of Darwinism against Bishop Wilburforce, and the Scopes "Monkey Trial" of 1925 stand as milestones on the road of retreat for the religious worldview. The claims of biblical literalism no longer have a leg to stand on with most educated people, now that astronomy has exposed the insignificance of the earth, geology its age, biology the evolution of humans from lower animals, and social sciences the relativity of morals and values. Even the argument that science and religion address mutually exclusive problems has fallen on hard times. In fact, science has answers for many big religious questions such as the afterlife, the origin of morality, or man's place in the universe—but answers the aspiring believer seldom wishes to hear.

Students with no interest in natural science can listen to the same message worded more to their taste from almost any other academic direction. Religious myths rank with mistaken beliefs due for replacement by reason and science in Auguste Comte's positive philosophy, and linger into modern times as survivals from the primitive stage of culture according to pioneering anthropologist E. B. Tylor. For Marxists, religion is the opiate of the masses; for existentialists, a denial of human responsibility; for Freud, an illusion. Where once stones, trees, rivers, and animals were sacred, the process of secularization has driven the gods from the earth, and over the past four hundred years even the sky has ceased to be a refuge, just a vastness of space scattered with stars, planets, and natural forces. The disenchantment of the world, to use Max Weber's phrase, has become an established principle of history, an epic of the progressive triumph of naturalism and materialism over magic, miracle, and spirit. H. L. Mencken celebrated the march: "One by one the basic mysteries yielded to a long line of extraordinarily brilliant and venturesome men. . . . The universe ceased to be Yahweh's plaything and became a mechanism like any other, responding to the same immutable laws. . . . Heaven and Hell sank to the level of old wives' tales, and there was a vast collapse of Trinities, Virgin Births, Atonements and other such pious phantasms."[24]

Religious scholars have mounted an internal assault on supernatural belief that is as brutal as any critique by outsiders. Biblical scholarship undercuts the revelatory claims of Scriptures by tracing their mutations as manuscripts, and their affinities with the folklore of the ancient Near East. Theologian Rudolf Bultmann argues that much of the Bible is mythological, and such concepts as the Second Coming, Satan, heaven, and hell cast transcendent realities in concrete, this-worldly images—images no longer credible from a modern, scientifically informed perspective. According to Bultmann, "For modern man the mythological conception of the world [is] over and done with. Is it possible to expect that we shall make a sacrifice of understanding . . . in order to accept what we cannot sincerely consider true—merely because such conceptions are suggested by the Bible?"[25] Sociologists of religion see this demythologizing program already accomplished, since "the supernatural as a meaningful reality is absent or remote from the horizons of everyday life of large numbers, very probably of the majority, of people in modern societies."[26]

What had remained a cloistered debate among theologians for decades burst into public awareness during the 1960s in a variety of guises—liberation theology, radical theology, situation ethics, expressive ethics, the death-of-God controversy, the New Social Gospel, religion for a secular age, ecumenicalism. By any name, these new trends heralded secularization, a rejection of the supernatural in favor of human understanding and a realization that this world matters rather than any otherworld.[27] This Copernican revolution in theology reversed the focus of religion from inner life toward society at large. True worship became political and humanitarian action, a dedication to making a difference in this world. Secularity splintered the unitary religious worldview and dismissed the certitudes of archaic supernaturalism and absolute values, imposing on the laity an obligation to think more about their faith and obey less, to embrace the moral variety of mankind rather than pass judgment.

In an academic environment the old-time religion seemed routed on every side. A few writers still defended the supernatural in a rarefied version, allowing for transcendence—the experience of a reality beyond the material world—but without the full house of anthropomorphic entities and powers that crowded an unrecoverable past.[28] Most theologians were simply glad to ring out the supernatural like a dark night that overstayed its time. Rejection of mythical elements allowed them to reconcile the modern knowledge they could not deny with the intellectual honesty and rigor they professed, sparing them the need to carry the burden of outmoded tenets through ever more tortured apologetics. Writings from the 1960s effervesced with a newfound sense of freedom, revitalization, and purpose for the religious enterprise. The intellectual leaders pronounced a new crusade, and churchgoers heard modernization espoused from the pulpit as the future direction of Christianity.

The 1960s spokesmen of secularization foresaw resistance, but they belittled its significance. They anticipated that the ignorant, the poor, and the disenfranchised would seek refuge from a world where they did not fit in by clinging to old beliefs and gathering in enclaves for mutual support.[29] In the end such resistance was doomed. The mythical worldview was broken, never to be put back together again, and no one could deny it had passed forever. Sooner or later, the currents of modernity would sweep the holdouts from their backwaters into the mainstream, and supernaturalism would disappear once and for all.

Taking refuge in the past was supposed to happen only among marginal churchgoers and leave mainline churches unscathed. The intellectual leaders expected the flock to follow where the shepherd led. Instead, the unexpected happened—the sheep set out on their own. If some clergymen eyed the dutiful church attendance of the 1950s as better evidence for conformity than for piety, they looked with alarm as the mainline churches emptied by 20 to 40 percent of their membership between the 1960s and the 1990s. During this same period, religious affiliations once considered marginal—the evangelical, fundamentalist, Pentecostal, and charismatic movements—scored dramatic gains in membership, with the number of Pentecostals soaring 183 percent.[30] Public opinion polls show a high level of belief in

God or a universal spirit (96 percent in 1994), heaven (90 percent), miracles (79 percent), angels (72 percent), and the devil (65 percent), with such beliefs gaining ground over the past decade.[31] A monitoring of the popular pulse through recent books, movies, and TV series about angel encounters attests that this idea has taken wing, and books by Betty Eadie and Dannon Brinkley about heavenly visions during near-death experiences have become best-sellers.

The devil gets his due these days as well. Satan and demons loom large in the theology of enthusiastic religious movements,[32] but they hold sway as well in parts of the modern world remote from revival meetings or heavy-metal rock. During the 1980s, claims of satanic ritual abuse spread nationwide, implicated in child abuse trials of day care operators and in the recovered memories of mature women accusing their parents of sexual abuse.[33] The accusations of satanic ritual abuse stood up well enough in courtrooms to send some defendants to prison[34] and provoked local panics as people feared that satanists would kidnap their children for sacrifice.[35] Satanic rumors flourished even though the evidence was almost nonexistent and the allegations claimed fantastic supernatural elements—but elements once again persuasive enough to win credulity in the new uncritical climate.

Those academics who pronounced the demise of supernatural religion thirty years ago arrived at their own great awakening when they realized that, for large masses of people, God was neither missing nor presumed dead. The most outmoded elements of faith, the very myths struck down most forcefully by science and humanism, not only survived but grew in appeal and displayed every sign of lively good health in the midst of a secular world, while liberal churches with this-worldly agendas continued to fade. The liberals who came to bury old-time religion learned belatedly that the funeral they attended was their own.

Folk Culture and Elite Culture

Why mythical beliefs take such a beating yet flourish so well in the modern world is a problem to puzzle or even bewilder the secular observer. One explanation advances the throwback hypothesis—that people adrift in an impersonal modern world seek meaning and identity through revival of the past. Historian of religion Martin E. Marty describes these "new traditionalisms" as nostalgic longings for a simpler and homogeneous world, an expression of discontent with chaotic pluralism, and a rejection of the moral anomie of modern society.[36] This answer is true enough, but not enough. It dwells on the negative side, sees only the victimized state of believers and the regressiveness of their beliefs, but fails to honor the independence, creativity, and vigor of their solutions. The supernatural revival testifies to the usefulness of the extraordinary in fulfilling human needs, and ultimately bears on the enduring fascination of UFOs.

If a supernatural resurgence in the lap of a scientific age seems oddly out of place, a reorientation to the cultural perspective of believers reduces the confusion. What appears unlikely from the top down may look quite different from the bottom up. Modern society does in fact have a top and a bottom, along with a great many cultural currents and countercurrents awash in between. Anthropologist Robert Redfield distinguished the "great tradition" of official, systematic knowledge instilled through formal education from the "little tradition" of informal customs and beliefs passed on by word of mouth.[37] Elite or high culture of the great tradition encompasses the scientist, scholar, and academic, the people most likely to leave written records of their thoughts. Elite thinkers wrangle with evidence and consistency to build a tested, argued structure of consensus knowledge, the official standard for truth in the secular world. Ideas and the pursuit of knowledge exist in an independent sphere, obedient to the rules of inquiry and the ideal of an objectivity isolated from the wishes and desires of the inquirers. Supernatural myths face rough handling in this camp.

At the lower or grassroots end of the scale lies folk culture, where tradition is the basis of knowledge, hearsay the medium of transmission, and belief the bottom-line criterion of truth. Folk culture is unofficial culture,[38] its knowledge unsanctioned by official authority and sometimes in opposition to it. In addition to cultural elements long on traditional pedigree, the little traditions of the modern world may draw on the commercial products of mass and popular culture for images and ideas, while the mass media voice the new "word of mouth" and spread it worldwide in an instant. Religion as people actually practice it gathers elements unsanctioned by an institutional church to create a folk or popular religion,[39] with magic and the supernatural brought in to handle needs the official belief system cannot satisfy. This same process leads to folk medicine and even to what might be called folk science, both of them based on faith, opinion, tradition, and unsubstantiated observation blended with selections from the official version. Folk knowledge springs from the heart more often than from the head to answer human concerns with little regard for confirmation or proof. From this perspective, the subjective comes first, and the superhuman is no stranger.

The philosopher David Hume saw unknown causes as the root of religious belief. Their uncertainty becomes the focus of hopes and fears, as well as the source of suppositions that sentient beings direct nature and human destiny.[40] Anthropologist Bronislaw Malinowski concluded that religion and magic owe their perpetuation in primitive societies more to social and psychological utility than to intellectual satisfaction or mystical appeal. The challenges of life divide into the familiar and manageable on one hand, the unexpected and uncontrolled on the other. "The first conditions are coped with by knowledge and work, the second by magic."[41] Today, as in the past, people experience needs an official belief system cannot satisfy, and pursue a quest for fulfillment into the fluid, responsive subsystems of unofficial belief. When vital needs go unmet by natural means, supernatural resources make up the difference.

A Fearful New World

The contemporary search has intensified under a double threat of increasing need and diminishing official resources to meet it. A fast-paced and crowded society overwhelms many people with an awareness that they have little power or control, little importance in the scheme of things. Uprooted, anonymous, shorn of absolute values and left without satisfying answers for ultimate questions, these people turned to the church for security, community, and purpose, only to find that the modernized church shut out the individual in favor of society and left values to personal choice, or personal confusion. The formality of mainline churches chilled the excitement of worship and exemplified "one of the most glaring features of the spiritual crisis of our era, what one writer has called the 'ecstasy deficit.'"[42]

It was not just religion that failed its adherents. So many other cultural pillars tumbled from the 1960s onward that the rank and file had good reason to distrust all social institutions. The civil religion faltered as government, the press, the military, the police, the legal system, and the educational system fell from grace; family and community ties unraveled while familiar sexual norms and gender roles disintegrated; and employees found themselves disposable commodities who saw little relationship left between effort and reward. Science and technology have fallen perhaps hardest of all. Forty years have seen their transformation from a secular religion promising utopia through progress into a threat to be feared and a scapegoat for multiple social wrongs.

The buoyant optimism of the 1950s looked forward to atomic energy making electricity "too cheap to meter," wonder drugs to cure all ills, and space as the heroic new frontier. Though much of the old admiration for science endures, the present is an age of ambivalence as suspicions and doubts with little rational basis dim the former optimism. Some academics demonize science as racist, sexist, and destructive of the environment;[43] activists decry any innovation from cloning to a plutonium-powered space probe as a menace. An abiding source of malaise is the nature of scientific knowledge itself. Ever more esoteric, specialized, remote from everyday experience, this knowledge leaves public understanding ever farther behind. Science delivers genuine wonders but dehumanizes them with its arcane and sterile discipline, gives and takes away as progress also brings the upheaval of change. For now progress is widely perceived as dangerous, and science a Frankenstein's monster lurching out of human control.

A cultural mirror of science's reversal of fortune lies as near as the movie theater. The standard science fiction plot of the 1950s casts scientists as down-to-earth "regular guys" who put their knowledge to practical use as they team up with the military to dispose of invading aliens or monsters.[44] This pattern characterizes such classics as *Invaders from Mars* (1953), *The War of the Worlds* (1953), *This Island Earth* (1955), *Earth Versus the Flying Saucers* (1956), *The Beast from 20,000 Fathoms* (1953), *Them!* (1954), *It Came from Beneath the Sea* (1955), *Tarantula* (1955), and *Godzilla* (1956). Although atomic testing or experiments gone awry might be responsible for rousing the monster in the first place, this background tension between science and society never interferes with the scientist's image as rescuer. At worst the scientist is childish, mistaken, or tragically flawed, as in *The Thing* (1951) or *Forbidden Planet* (1956), but not a villain. By the 1960s the military falls out of sympathy, as in *Five Million Years to Earth* (1967), and technology becomes the enemy, as the computers in *The Forbin Project* (1969) or *2001: A Space Odyssey* (1968), but scientists themselves remain untarnished.

What a change a few years make. From the 1970s onward, science turns bad and becomes the enemy, chasing friendly aliens with heartless intentions in *E.T.* (1982) and *Starman* (1984) or creating monsters as part of some weapons program in *The Blob* remake (1988). Throughout the *Alien* series (1979–98), a greedy corporation seeks the monster to sell on the military market while the audience understands how surely such a "weapon" will backfire. The utopian future turns dystopic in the soulless cityscapes of *Blade Runner* (1982) and the relentless robots from the future arriving to kill present-day humans in the *Terminator* movies (1984, 1991). The *Mad Max* series (1979–85) depicts a world reverted to barbarism after civilization collapses, while a similar fate follows the global warming catastrophe responsible for *Waterworld* (1995) or a scientist's unwise experiments with deadly viruses in *12 Monkeys* (1996). At a minimum, scientists and military authorities conspire to withhold knowledge of alien visitation (*Close Encounters of the Third Kind* [1977], *Stargate* [1994], *Contact* [1997]); at worst, they are aliens in disguise (*The Arrival* [1996]). If the scientist is a hero today, he is a Cassandra warning against tampering with nature or a loner and an outsider to his profession, like Jeff Goldblum in *Jurassic Park* (1993) and *Independence Day* (1996). A mystical quality like the Force replaces human intellect as the dominant power in the *Star Wars* trilogy (1977–83), and while the *Star Trek* movies still celebrate human achievement, science remains largely in the background as a necessary but obscure trapping for the plot. For now the movies typecast scientists as horned and hoofed and reeking of brimstone.

Abandoned or even threatened by official culture, ordinary people have little choice but to seek their own salvation. A hallmark of the times is religious individualism carried to extremes, now that the canopy of wholeness once woven over individuals and society by churches, doctrines, and symbol systems has collapsed in tatters.[45] The search for wholeness and human support has set off a migration to alternative churches and religions, a resort to do-it-yourself creeds. Pentecostalism rewards its practitioners with emotion and joy in worship, the clear-cut struggle between God and Satan, a world reenchanted with miracles and healing, and promises of an imminent Second Coming.[46] Other people turn to the New Age movement for personal and social transformation.[47] The paranormal beliefs long favored in folk culture gain ground against official culture, part of the occult revival that Mircea Eliade describes as "a revolt against the religious establishment . . . seeking personal and collective *renovatio,* a way out of the chaos and meaninglessness of modern life."[48]

These personal quests for fulfillment lead to a chaotic landscape of beliefs. When opinion polls show that 90 percent of the population believes in heaven while only 73 percent believes in hell, or 96 percent in God and 65 percent in the devil, the gap in religious reasoning assumes the dimensions of a canyon; yet these same figures testify perhaps that faith in a good Lord and happy afterlife carry a stronger appeal than recognition of evil and punishment as the necessary other side of the same coin. Even modern theologians who hailed secularism thirty years ago have come around to admit the human value of these contemporary religious experiments.[49]

Reason is too stringent a creed for most people. They want to escape the confines of its discipline, to embrace the magic, mystery, and irrationality that had a rightful place in traditional religion but no standing in a secularized worldview. Enter the UFOs. They reopen the airtight compartments that separate science and religion, matter and spirit, natural and supernatural. They belong with every nut and bolt to a technological age and yet bear a kind of wonder and mystery very much at home in the mythic past. Positioned between the usual firm categories to serve as scientific ghosts and technological angels, UFOs reconcile modern and future realities with age-old human needs. To look for UFOs is to look toward heaven again and rediscover magic in technological guise. For some people UFOs even bring hope that a savior from a better world has arrived to settle the problems of this one. One sociologist who recognized the limitations of secularism predicted that "a rediscovery of the supernatural will be . . . a regaining of openness in our perception of reality,"[50] but as usual the academic was the last to know. The folk got there first and battered down the door.

UFO Religion

With their heavenly connections and richness of meanings, UFOs have attracted the interest of many spiritual seekers and tempted some commentators to see a space-age religion in the making. An essential part of any religion is its conceptual features, the myths or narratives tracing its origin and history as well as doctrines or philosophical reflections expressing the truths of the faith. In these respects UFOs enjoy a widespread and vigorous currency. Yet religion means action as well as thought, engaging both the individual and the collective in experiences and emotions, rituals and practices. Another cardinal dimension of religion is its regulation of personal and social behavior through ethical and legal obligations, organization of the faithful into a church or community, and influence over art, architecture, politics, and economy.[51] Definitions that accent only conceptual or psychological aspects overlook the necessity for religion to exist among people in a society, as sociologist Émile Durkheim recognized: "A religion is a unified system of beliefs and practices relative to sacred things, that is to say, things set apart and forbidden—beliefs and practices which unite into one single moral community called a Church, all those who adhere to them."[52]

All the pieces seemed to be falling together in the 1950s, at a time when the most visible social consequence of flying saucer beliefs was the contactee movement.[53] George Adamski, already a veteran teacher of the occult, created a distinctive flying saucer faith in 1952 when he claimed to have met a saucer occupant in the California desert. Adamski said his alien came from Venus; but the real home of this visitor with long blond hair and a saintly demeanor was the realm of angels. Adamski showed vivid but unconvincing photographs of the Space Brothers' craft and passed along their platitudinous messages of love, peace, and enlightenment, in a mixture of literal spacefarers with caring, spiritual missionaries that proved to be a winning combination just right for its time. Truman Bethurum,

Daniel Fry, George Van Tassel, Orfeo Angelucci, Howard Menger, and other contactees famous or obscure soon followed Adamski's lead. Beginning as rugged individualists with distinctive stories to tell, contactees quickly pulled together a loose confederation with a similar theology and mutually supportive claims, aided by a shared speakers' circuit and Van Tassel's Giant Rock convention as an annual mecca for believers. The messages expressed bland religious and spiritual themes that no one would dispute, but application to key popular concerns of the day such as nuclear testing and the threat of war lent the messages a timely urgency, while an extraterrestrial source sided the authority of higher wisdom with common wishes or common sense.

Public contactees declined in popularity after the 1950s, but private claimants still flock to the annual "contactee conference" that University of Wyoming psychologist Leo Sprinkle has hosted since 1980. Several organizations surrounding a charismatic leader have enjoyed long-term survival, such as Unarius, the Aetherius Society, and the Raelians. Most institutionalized contactee groups are innocuous, open-door clubs, but an exception was the notorious Heaven's Gate, an authoritarian, high-demand cult that underwent several mutations from its beginnings as "Human Individual Metamorphosis" in the mid-1970s. Giving themselves various non-names like "Him and Her," "Bo and Peep," or "The Two," founders Marshall Applewhite and Bonnie Nettles recruited followers around the country in 1975, declaring that a spaceship would rescue believers from a coming catastrophe. The UFO never arrived, but the cult survived this disappointment and the death of Nettles, finally settling in San Diego for several years before Applewhite and thirty-eight members committed mass suicide on 26 March 1997 so that their spirits could ascend to a UFO traveling in the wake of the Hale-Bopp comet.[54] Cultists still find UFOs a draw: according to the *New York Times* of 27 February 1998, a Taiwanese group called the "God Saves the Earth Flying Saucer Association" milked members of their life savings, then descended on Texas to wait for the UFO that will ferry the faithful to Mars.

Time has not borne out the prediction that a major religious movement would arise out of extraterrestrial beliefs. The UFO faith has established a church, in Durkheim's sense of a moral community, only here and there and for small groups at a time, while UFO-based beliefs have never sustained the distinctive rituals, ethics, and creeds characteristic of a full-bodied religion. The typical New Age seeker favors the journey over the destination and takes an interest in many paranormal subjects, with little enduring loyalty to any one of them.[55] A case in point is the millenarian sect described in the 1956 sociological study *When Prophecy Fails*.[56] Mrs. Keech, the leader and chief medium of the group, stitched together a patchwork quilt of occult ideas and added flying saucers as just one more belief out of many to confirm her prophecies of an impending doomsday. For contactees and New Age seekers, UFOs serve as little more than props and aliens as convenient informants to mouth the same lines once spoken by prophets, angels, or spirits from beyond, messages readily traceable to long religious and occult traditions.

The Meaning of Myth

The religious potential of UFOs breaks free in their mythical aspect, when they build worldviews and visions rather than churches. Writers as diverse as Jung and skeptical astronomer Donald H. Menzel have bandied about the notion that something is mythical about UFOs. The meanings these scholars intend are poles apart, but then, *myth* has spent most of its history as a term encrusted with multiple definitions and diverse usages, to the confusion of all. The folklorist defines myth as a sacred narrative explaining the origins of man and the universe,[57] an idea akin to the religious scholar's identification of myth as the narrative, explanatory dimension of religion. An additional meaning often forwarded by anthropologists specifies that myth is true to its believers and false to nonbelievers.[58] For theologian Rudolf Bultmann, myths acknowledge human limitation. They "express the knowledge that man is not master of the world and of his life, that the world . . . is full of riddles and mysteries."[59] Scholars add characteristic slants of many disciplines to these basic generalizations. Psychologists have treated myth as an expression of the unconscious or deep structure of the mind, anthropological functionalists regard myth as a mirror of culture and a charter for beliefs and practices, literary critics see a form of symbolic expression, sociologists the basis for a worldview, and religious scholars a genre that shapes religious communication.[60]

To say that UFOs have a mythical aspect does not mean that the whole phenomenon reduces to myth. An acknowledgment of the mythical face simply recognizes that the human uses of UFOs often obscure the experiential face. Whatever that experience may be, it blends with beliefs, expectations, hopes, fears, even aesthetic patterns to create a cultural image that stands in for the whole phenomenon in many eyes but distorts and misrepresents it in ways both subtle and profound. How human interest mythologizes UFOs appears most clearly when they serve as subjects of controversy, a nucleus for symbolism, a master key for understanding, mirrors of contemporary concerns, carriers of traditional patterns, and harbingers of transformation.

UFOs as Subjects of Controversy

In everyday parlance *myth* is a perjorative term meaning false belief. My beliefs are truths; yours are myths if I disagree with them. Donald H. Menzel titled a skeptical paper "UFOs—The Modern Myth" and classed UFOs together with unicorns, demons, and sea serpents as simply one more mistake among human efforts to understand the unexplained.[61] The notion that UFOs are a belief held in error underlies all skeptical treatments of the subject whether or not the skeptic invokes the name of myth. Of late the term has grown popular enough to appear in the titles of two books of scholarly skepticism, *Watch the Skies! A Chronicle of the Flying Saucer Myth*[62] and *UFO Crash at Roswell: The Genesis of a Modern Myth*,[63] perhaps since the term also suggests a complex and systematic error rather than scattered false beliefs.

Myths, then, are bones of contention, the centerpieces of a conflict. With UFOs these conflicts center less often on the experiential substance of reports than on issues one or more steps removed, notably the philosophical shortcomings of anecdotal evidence. Observation and experience side with the proponents; the impassioned advocacy of witnesses and the cumulative evidence that ufologists have gathered over fifty years back the cause. The opposition asks where is the hard, unbending proof that survives justifiable misgivings about eyewitness testimony and the failure of ufologists to submit a universally persuasive alien artifact. Ufologists say the evidence is overwhelming enough to convince anyone with an open mind; skeptics call the evidence an example of the "bundle of sticks" fallacy—a collection of cases that looks strong when taken together, yet each case snaps in two on close examination until not even one case remains to support the claim. The one indisputable constant is the dispute itself.

A controversy energizes its participants in a way mere curiosity cannot. On their own, UFO beliefs may fascinate or intrigue, may inspire the commitment individuals devote to a hobby, but controversy elevates the subject to the status of a cause. A shared interest unites proponents into a folk group.[64] Linked via newsletters, magazines, and the Internet, versed in a shared gospel of theories and alleged facts through exposure to the UFO literature and mass media, people who seldom or never meet face-to-face maintain a conduit of communication that preserves, shapes, and advocates the corpus of UFO lore.[65] This conduit joins like-minded people loyal to UFOs and holds together a far-flung community, insulating it against hostile challenges and disruption by interlopers such as New Age seekers whose primary commitments lie elsewhere. Skeptics perpetuate their viewpoint through a parallel conduit of self-selected individuals and define themselves in part by their opposition to UFO believers.

UFO proponents regard themselves as defenders of "embattled truths"[66] who fight the good fight against well-defined villains. Ufologists are seldom modest about the importance of their subject; for example, the Mutual UFO Network (MUFON) 1992 International UFO Symposium sported the title "UFOs: The Ultimate Mystery of the Millennia." Skeptics likewise see themselves as warriors in a crusade and adopt equally flamboyant rhetoric. A 1997 fund-raising flyer for the Committee for the Scientific Investigation of Claims of the Paranormal admonished its readers that "CSICOP is one of few bulwarks against a future where young people grow up believing they are surrounded by aliens. . . . With your help we can win many more battles, turning Roswell and similar charades into platforms *for* science rather than against it."

A standoff between truth and error presents the most hackneyed sense of myth, but also a sense with enormous human appeal. Serious business is at stake. Both sides in the controversy find purpose and excitement in the struggle, along with community, loyalty, and a sense of being on the cutting edge of an earthshaking issue. The "ecstasy deficit" of the secular age converts to surplus, and a new identity replaces the one lost by dissolution of old religious ties, as long as the dispute flourishes. The consequences of controversy for the UFO behind the myth are easy to imagine and by no means good. Controversy polarizes the issue by engaging hopes, expectations, and egos until personal concerns outweigh reason. The believers' conduit resists legitimate questions by its rapid dissemination of favorable information and suppression or positive reinterpretation of any negative evidence. This conduit always serves up a sunny image of the state of the controversy and recycles erroneous or distorted information as long as it helps the cause.

UFOs as Symbols

One object is what it is and nothing more. Another suggests additional meanings spreading outward in a widening gyre of relationships from the object itself and in no way apparent from its inherent identity. The actors, objects, and events of myth are at once tangible or visible, yet they stand for a great deal more than their familiar appearance suggests. These elements are symbolic because they absorb enough ideas and associations to represent multiple objects as well as intangible or abstract ideas within the society, becoming living ambiguities, ordinary and extraordinary at the same time and consequently charged with mystery and fascination.[67]

UFOs attracted Jung because they resonate with psychological symbolism. In their roundness he recognized a mandala, or symbol of wholeness expressed in visionary rumors from the collective unconscious throughout history. This psychological symbolism meant that "unconscious contents have projected themselves on these inexplicable heavenly phenomena and given them a significance they in no way deserve," a human meaning related to age-old salvation myths and valid whether the objects themselves were natural or extraterrestrial.[68] Michael Grosso follows Jung to interpret abductions as symbolic evidence for disturbances in the collective unconscious. Visions of unhealthy-looking beings who examine captives and take genetic materials to create a hybrid species mean "*we* are the sick ones, and . . . we, as a species living on planet Earth, are in need of regeneration." The fetal appearance of these beings suggests the child, the continuity of human life, threatened as never before by pollution and neglect. Yet even a sick child symbolizes a new beginning, and these alien "children" perform an operation, an act of healing that may correct the imbalance between the conscious and unconscious in this rationalistic age and bring life to humanity in a New Age. According to Grosso, "The 'new man,' the future of the species, is in great danger—our future is threatened with extinction. . . . If we learn to cooperate with the forces of rebirth, we may yet rise from the 'examination table,' resuscitated from our planetary near-death experience."[69]

One theory of how myths work proposes that they serve as logical templates to reconcile cultural contradictions. Creative minds guarantee that belief clashes with belief in any society, and thoughts contradict observed reality. The result is a cognitive stress that demands relief. Myths show the way. They are a form of language with terms rich in symbolic meanings. The terms are concrete objects, but multiple meanings allow such an object to serve several conceptual roles at once, unlike terms of an abstract logic where meanings are fixed and single. A myth not only tells a story but also establishes a structure of relationships that mediates and resolves logical oppositions among the terms. By trading on the ambiguities of its actors, objects, and events, myth realigns its components according to their alternative symbolic meanings, charting a path by which irreconcilable differences reconcile after all. This mediation establishes its pattern at an unconscious level and feels as "natural" as one's native language, but with the social consequence that seemingly irrational beliefs make deep and satisfying sense.[70]

This structuralist view commits itself to complex and debatable assumptions, but the theory highlights several unmistakable characteristics of the UFO myth. UFOs pose a conundrum of oppositions: hard metal and pure technology in their construction, they flit through the sky as if weightless and turn or vanish like immaterial spirits. Able to register on radar and photographs, UFOs are nevertheless elusive, impossible to capture, bound to the shadowland of rumor. Exemplars of wonder and progress, they also pose the threat of invasion and the vague terror of alienness. Futuristic in design and the product of advanced civilization, they also mirror a bygone past of magic, angels, demons, and supernatural power.

Sleek and silvery by day, luminous and ethereal by night, UFOs break natural laws and even firm categories of being to hover on the margin between a physical and an immaterial state unlike any conventional phenomenon.

UFOs draw so many contradictory meanings within their circle that they constitute a symbol of almost unrivaled richness. Nearly as familiar and potent as the mushroom cloud, the saucer image is even more versatile because it reaches in all directions, toward hope and unknown possibility as well as danger, whereas the bomb permits only a one-way trip to destruction and finality. UFOs embody technology as both mastery of nature and soulless destroyer of life, science as self-salvation and self-exaltation, symbolizing a love-hate dilemma that divides the two throbbing lobes of the modern mind. This versatility plays both sides of an opposition and permits the UFO to mediate between them. The UFO myth unites technology and magic, restores the astronomers' sky as the home of gods, and injects mystery into the certainties of a scientific era, all without rejection of the secular present and with a nod of acceptance toward the future. If humanists admire the symbolic fecundity of UFOs, scientists despair of that same quality. The social, cultural, and psychological meanings that bind the phenomenon into a fabric of myths resist the isolation and separation a scientific study requires.

UFOs as Key to Understanding

Myth builds order out of the chaos of experience. A society constructs an ethos and cosmos out of its mythical symbol system, contriving the motivations, moods, and morality of the community, establishing an intellectual understanding of how the world works and what belongs in it. The system unifies the fragmented pieces that make up a life—aspects individual and social, known and unknown, physical and moral, sacred and profane—into an interconnected, meaningful whole.[71] This worldview enjoys the privileged status of ultimate truth, the expression of what is really real, the final answer to all questions and arbiter of all human actions. Within this scheme a world of uncertainties balances and makes sense.

For many people, UFOs make the world make sense. UFOs fit into the belief system of some Christian fundamentalists as vehicles bringing an invasion of demons, while Billy Graham sets UFOs in a more benign corner of Scripture by hinting they might be angels.[72] Skeptics invoke UFOs to show that all's quiet on the worldview front. The investigative strategy of Donald Menzel, Philip Klass, and Robert Sheaffer conventionalizes UFO sightings into misidentifications of familiar phenomena, while some critics of abductions psychologize them into false memories created in fantasy-prone people through hypnotic confabulation.[73] Finding a conventional explanation reconfirms that official knowledge and ways of knowing are essentially correct.

The most committed takeover of UFOs for worldview revision originates with thinkers under the influence of Jungian psychology. Picking up Jung's implication that UFOs are too important to be just spaceships, these interpreters recast all paranormal phenomena as a glimpse of some larger reality. It may be the juncture where psychic and physical worlds join, a parallel universe, or an imaginal realm, but it is now slipping through the cracks in our everyday continuum, breaking into awareness through altered states of consciousness or gradual weakening of a rational, materialistic worldview. In these speculations UFOs fast-change from physical to mental or spiritual roles and back again. They are deceivers and shape-shifters, tricksters on a mission to violate boundaries and sow confusion. They are agents to rearrange human consciousness, perhaps initiating a new religion, in any case sensitizing people to encounters with a reality beyond the ordinary.[74]

UFOs make finer predators than prey, and the myth has swallowed both past and present history. The ancient-astronaut craze of the 1970s reinterpreted the pillar of fire from Exodus, Ezekiel's wheel, and the star of Bethlehem as spacecraft, saw the pyramids of Egypt, the Nazca Lines of Peru, and the statues of Easter Island as alien handiwork, or reread myths of wars between gods as titanic battles of aliens using spaceships and nuclear weapons.[75] Another long tradition unlocks the present with UFOs as the key. Donald Keyhoe, a writer and leading advocate of alien visitation in the 1950s, was convinced that a conspiracy of silence at the highest levels hid the extraterrestrial origin of flying saucers from the public. The motive may have been benevolent, a desire to prevent another panic such as Orson Welles provoked with his "War of the Worlds" broadcast of 1938, but the concrete result was a shadowy control group that manipulated information and public opinion to contain the secret. The crashed saucer claims associated with Roswell, New Mexico, sprouted ever more florid conspiracy myths during the 1980s, such as MJ-12, a higher-than-top-secret panel of military officers and scientists entrusted with oversight of the crash, and a corollary yarn that lasers, integrated circuits, and all other major technological advances of the past half century derive from captured alien hardware.[76]

Like lost civilizations themselves, the idea of visitation is too romantic to perish. It explains too much too handily to die. For people on both the pro and con sides of the issue, the UFO myth with all its attachments and extensions has become a vital organ in the physiology of their thinking, an integral and irreplaceable part of how they reason about the world. Genuine objectivity about the UFOs themselves and the meanings they bestow becomes major surgery—something few people undertake on themselves and almost everyone postpones seeking from others for as long as possible, if ever. In any case, the prognosis for success is guarded at best.

UFOs as Reflections of Shifting Concerns

Mythology and marble statues belong together when the myths are cold, dead relics of another time and place. Living myths are too busy in everyday affairs to lie down in a storybook, too internalized into thought and action to show themselves for what they are. A myth bound skintight to understanding and human concerns necessarily changes as they change, either conforming to cultural trends already under way or prefiguring them before awareness and behavior catch up.

UFOs have drifted on the cultural tide from machinery to paranormal phenomena and back again, their origin earthly, extraterrestrial, ultraterrestrial, and now alien once more.[77] Flying saucers passed the 1950s as machines endowed with the speed and maneuverability of alien technology. Their program progressed from distant reconnaissance to closer encounters and fed the insecurities of a cold war era. A final resolution of the mystery seemed imminent, and ufologists set physical evidence, reliable photographs, and government confessions as their goals. With the 1964–68 pandemic of sightings, ufologists threw up their hands and declared futile the chase for hard evidence. Respected investigators like John Keel and Jacques Vallee declared the phenomenon elusive by nature and pronounced that UFOs were not just stranger than anyone imagined but stranger than anyone *could* imagine. They disappeared, materialized and dematerialized, shape-shifted, and fraternized with monsters or other paranormal events. The occupants acted more like fairies or spirits than scientific explorers. UFO research came to mean speculation about alternate universes or an impending shift of human consciousness as nuts-and-bolts machines dissolved into a wooly New Age spirituality of the counterculture era.

The road to current interests took a U-turn at Roswell and the dark byways where abductors lurk. In the 1980s Roswell returned hardware to the center of debate and resurrected a government cover-up of vaster proportions than Donald Keyhoe ever imagined. Pursuit of MJ-12 and Roswell witnesses crowded out the airy musings of theorists, and even the UFOs themselves seemed to salute their new military affinities by frequent appearances in the shape of deltas or flying wings rather than the usual disk. Abductions, rife as they are with memory impairment, loss of volition, dreamlike floating, and otherworldly visions, offset this surrealism with a hard physical edge of pain, cold, implants, and cuts, while the aliens pull out no-nonsense machinery to complete purposeful, efficient examinations. Now the wheel turns once more as theorists speculate on a shift of consciousness as the ultimate purpose behind the abduction experience.

Some inner elements of abduction content shift direction in the prevailing cultural breeze. Alien messages to abductees have redirected from the nuclear fears characteristic of the 1950s contactee era to the ecological concerns prevalent over the last two decades.[78] Another cultural influence betrays itself in British reports where the proper look for an alien changes from tall human "Nordics" to short humanoids after the cover of Whitley Strieber's *Communion* becomes well known.[79] A less programmed convergence of cultural traditions arises in the ghostly traits the abductors have acquired. They pass through walls and float in the air and haunt bedrooms at night, but investigator Joe Nyman adds an especially classic motif: "I was told by an individual that at his mother's death in 1937, he and his two sisters were terrified to see a figure descending the stairs. The figure had a face that the man saw again years later—on the dust jacket of *Communion.*"[80]

UFOs as Manifestations of Tradition

The most unmistakable interplay of myth with UFOs lies in the way people perceive, think about, and relate their experiences according to traditional forms. The pieces of UFO stories settle into idealized stations, with stereotypes, formulas, and motifs bending narratives, beliefs, even observation itself, into old and familiar shapes—shapes often far out of line with reality. Folklore scholarship is, famously, the study of ideal patterns in storytelling. A story is not a recounting of facts. Facts are disposable, but traditional form and content persist—in the plot formulas and recurrent motifs of folktales; in the pattern that shapes biographies of heroes as culturally diverse as Heracles, Moses, and King Arthur;[81] in formulaic accounts of final battles like Saul on Mount Gilboa, the three hundred Spartans at Thermopylae, or Custer's last stand.[82] Even ordinary narrations about everyday events assume a rhetorical shape,[83] while narratives about unusual occurrences such as crime victim accounts[84] or near-death experiences[85] assume sharp formulaic outlines.

Bringing order to experience and artistic symmetry to narratives is a human proclivity ingrained to the bone. Even with the best intentions, a narrator often promotes cultural ideals at the expense of dry facts and creates a satisfying story rather than an accurate one. Traditional patterns assist with a ready-made scaffolding to build on, their structure unrecognized and yet always close at hand. These patterns have a knack for turning up again after generations of dormancy. A case in point is *The Awful Disclosures of Maria Monk*, one of a rash of scurrilous anti-Catholic tracts from the 1830s and 1840s describing sex, obscene rituals, and infanticide inside convents. In the 1980s, accusers quite ignorant of the earlier claims leveled almost identical charges of sexual abuse and satanic rituals against day care operators.[86]

Answers for where those ideal patterns originate rely on poly-genesis, an inherent tendency of human minds to think alike and create similar ideas, or dissemination, the transmission and learn-ing of mythical patterns. Polygenetic theories explain that the ste-reotypical hero's life cycle survives as a relic of widespread primitive birth, initiation, and death rituals.[87] If Jung is right, archetypes of the collective unconscious guarantee a universal symbolism in all human creative endeavors, while Claude Lévi-Strauss proposes that the linguistic construction of human thought standardizes myths as inevitable logical solutions to comparable intellectual problems. The physiological phenomena of the dying brain may determine the nature of the near-death experience,[88] or certain congenital malfor-mations may give rise to belief in fairies.[89]

Dissemination theory allows that myths share general themes, but it denies any supposed universality as an illusion and asserts that all narratives owe their form and meaning to cultural influences. The enduring myth wins a "survival of the fittest" contest as a story too good to forget, too perfect to replace, because it has adapted to express the needs and values of its audience. Tragedy as an orga-nizing principle may derive from analogies in human and natural cycles, where the phenomena of autumnal decline correspond to reversal of fortune and death of the hero to reinforce a sense of cos-mic importance.[90] Literary and cinematic patterns are often mere conventions perpetuated in deliberate efforts to recapture the popu-larity of a predecessor. The standard formula for 1950s science fic-tion movies begins with mysterious occurrences traced to an invader or monster by a scientist-hero, who meets doubt at first but then leads the defenders of the world to destroy the enemy.[91] This for-mula may succeed because of deep psychological resonances, but it owes its repetition to immediate reasons like an ability to sell tick-ets and popcorn. Accidents of history may capture collective imagi-nation for the long haul, as perhaps a volcanic catastrophe on the island of Thera about 1450 B.C. has lived on in stories of Atlantis ever after.[92]

Mysterious, symbolic, and open to interpretation, UFOs fall easy prey to the patterning impulse. One of the first rules a ufologist learns is that most sightings are unidentified only to the witness. A conventional solution—planets, stars, aircraft, weather balloons, mirages, hoaxes—accounts for so many reports that truly puzzling unidentifieds constitute no more than 10 to 20 percent of all sightings,[93] perhaps as few as 3 to 5 percent of the total. Expectations make a world of difference, as happened on 3 March 1968 when *Zond IV*, a Soviet moon probe, fell back into the atmosphere and burned up at high altitude over the central United States. Of seventy-eight reports received by the U.S. Air Force, most witnesses described with accuracy a half dozen meteor-like objects shooting across the sky, and some even recognized the incident as a reentry. A minority of witnesses watched the same event but saw something else entirely. Descriptions included a formation of lights, objects in pursuit of one another, a single saucer-shaped object, a cigar-shaped craft with fire at both ends, a craft with lighted windows and riveted plates along the hull. Several people vouched that the object flew at treetop level, made a sound, or frightened the dog.[94] For a few individuals the idea of a spaceship controlled even their basic observations.

The *Zond* case is extreme but hardly unique. An idea of how UFOs ought to look has imposed a false image on fifty years of sightings, most of them in no way remarkable. The reporter who coined the term *flying saucers* on 24 June 1947 misrepresented Kenneth Arnold's description. His objects were heel- or crescent-shaped, at best a saucer with a bite taken out of the back; but no matter. Whatever the several thousand objects reported over the next two weeks really looked like, newspaper accounts rounded off the descriptions into "saucers" or "flying disks" and established an enduring stereotype. A close examination of the reports reveals some diversity of forms, but the cigars, triangles, spheres, and hybrid shapes remained poor relations until the less suggestive term *UFO* loosened the monopoly of the saucer image.[95]

As the UFO story grows in complexity beyond simple sightings, so do the patterns and associations aligning it with traditional forms. Abductions head the complexity list with a recurrent sequence of episodes—capture, examination, conference, then on rare occasions a tour of the ship, journey to an otherworld, and a scene of apparent sacred significance before the captive returns. Several episodes follow sequences of their own, with silence, paralysis, and flotation accompanying capture, a pattern of manual and instrumental procedures comprising examination, and teachings or prophecies the subject of conferences. Conscious memory of the abduction usually fades and leaves the captive with about two hours of lost time. Physical, psychological, and long-term aftereffects follow, such as nosebleed, nightmares, and life changes like development of a more spiritual or humane personality. Most of the beings are short, gray-skinned humanoids with large, hairless heads and huge eyes, while the mouth is a mere slit and all other facial features are vestigial.[96] Why do aliens go to all this trouble? Reports of stolen genetic materials and encounters with hybrid children suggest an interbreeding program to create a part-human, part-alien race.[97]

A minor scholarly industry among ufologists and skeptics associates abduction descriptions with psychological phenomena and cultural antecedents. The shamanic initiation pattern includes loss of consciousness, guiding spirits, an underworld ordeal followed by a meeting with wise beings who impart wisdom to the candidate, who then returns to earth with magical powers and an ability to communicate with the spirit world.[98] Many interpreters cite these parallels as evidence that abduction reports enact an internal formula rather than external events.[99] Another search for resemblances has uncovered analogies with the seventeenth-century witchcraft mania, which evolved consistent claims of a large-scale conspiracy, a "devil's mark" corresponding to the modern implant, and sexual contact with demonic beings.[100] Traditions of the incubus and succubus, demons that visited men and women in the night for sexual liaisons, approximate modern abduction accounts and belong to a larger cycle of stories about supernatural kidnap for sexual purposes. Parallels in these narratives indicate "the existence of a close developmental similarity between what appear to be superficially disparate experiences."[101]

Comparativists struck perhaps the richest vein of parallels in the traditions of fairy lore.[102] Belief in diminutive supernatural beings is worldwide and age-old,[103] but the typical short UFO humanoid fits the functional role of these beings with little obvious difference than a change of address and mode of transportation. The entrance to fairyland is often a hill or an ancient burial mound that rises on luminous pillars during nights of fairy revelry to resemble a landed UFO. Fairyland itself has a luminous but sunless sky similar to the alien otherworld or UFO interior described by abductees. Like their alien counterparts, fairies practice abduction of humans, especially women and children, who seem essential to perpetuation of a fairy race that, like the modern aliens, has lost its reproductive self-sufficiency. Fairies often exchange their elderly for a human baby, and this "changeling" possesses old wisdom despite its infant form—a motif now similar to reports of hybrids and "wise baby" dreams from abductees.[104]

A close encounter with fairies is perilous business. Any human who spends an hour or so in their company may return home to find that fifty or one hundred years have passed—a motif called the "supernatural lapse of time in fairyland,"[105] with hints of the time-lapse phenomenon in abductions. The human risks paralysis or injury as well as capture, and UFO researcher Peter Rogerson emphasizes that the dark and fearful side of fairies reasserts itself in reports of aliens:

> That the fairies were equivalent to the dead was an important strand in the old tradition. See the clues in the new fairy faith: the starved, skeletal entities, with their grey, putty-like skin, their aversion to light and day. They are often described as curiously weak and vulnerable, as being light, hollow, unreal. . . . These are the ghostly, drifting dead of Hades or Sheol, who must snatch the living to steal their blood and sex and life.[106]

In light of comparison, almost every syllable of the modern UFO myth reads as a quote from the past, and UFO reports begin to look like fantasies built from psychological, sociological, and cultural raw materials, not a witness to alien visitation. The similarities are undeniable but the interpretations speculative. The archives of tradition are so rich they contain parallels for everything, especially if the comparativist settles for superficial analogy, abstraction, and pulling clues out of cultural or literary context, selecting favorable findings and discarding the rest of a connected tradition if it fails to bolster the argument. The resulting portrait of cultural parallels bears a false likeness.

How old stories escape dusty tomes to alarm abductees today remains a weak link in psychosocial theory. One answer has been birth trauma and perinatal imagery,[107] with the fetal alien and tunnels inside the UFO representing memories of the unborn self and the birth canal. This explanation draws on universal experience but raises fatal questions like how a fetus can see itself. Jung's archetypes give the odds-on favorite answer for many theorists, but at best these archetypes are vague forms capable of stimulating symbolic images and not scripts for the elaborate experience of a UFO encounter. Moreover, the theorist often treats them as blank checks to fill in as needed, begging the question of where UFO lore originates by equating anything the reports include with promptings from the archetypes.

A better-grounded diffusionist argument traces the origin of UFO ideas to borrowing from past or recent cultural traditions. A convincing example of influence is abductee Barney Hill's alien. When Hill described his captor's eyes under hypnosis, two key qualities were an elongated, "wraparound" appearance and their ability to "speak" to him. These same two distinctive features characterize the alien in an episode of *The Outer Limits* TV series. What makes the case for influence even more compelling is the fact that this "Bellero Shield" episode aired less than two weeks before Barney provided his description, and prior to hypnosis he expressed no specific memory of the alien eyes.[108] Critics have long pilloried the mass media for nurturing uncritical UFO beliefs. An investigation of the French wave of 1954 concluded that it amounted to a farrago of misidentifications and hoaxes trumped up by the press. Interviews with supposed witnesses revealed that they seldom described anything like the sensationalized and distorted impressions conveyed in news reports.[109] The media have glamorized abductions until many people claim them in pursuit of attention and profit, while tabloid and television treatments supply the hoaxer with a blueprint for fabricating a story with all the right details.[110]

An impressive body of scholarship lays to rest any notion that abductions arose out of nowhere as something new under the sun. Two familiar UFO themes of a dying planet and large-headed aliens echo speculations about Mars and principles of evolutionary theory that H. G. Wells blended in *The War of the Worlds*. Antecedents for circular spaceships, alien kidnap, even many descriptive motifs of current abduction reports appear in the pulp magazines of the 1920s and 1930s.[111] Alien invasion movies of the 1950s such as *Invaders from Mars, Earth Versus the Flying Saucers,* and *Killers from Space* presented the audience with vivid images of big-headed aliens, implants, examination, memory loss, a domed interior, and hypnotic eyes. The consistent sequence of events most abductees describe represents nothing more remarkable than a sense of good dramatic structure.

It is pervasive in storytelling and organizes an alien kidnap sequence in the Buck Rogers comic strip from the 1930s along lines repeated in modern abduction reports.[112] A follower of the obscure and tangled paths of UFO literature over the years runs into ideas of "being taken" at every turn and finds the familiar motifs of abduction piling up along the way before they finally crystallize into the current abduction myth.[113]

The UFO myth may also borrow the temper of the times. Does abduction reflect the wrenching issue of abortion? Themes of missing fetuses and fetal aliens have grown apace with the practice of abortion since the early 1970s, suggesting that the clinical experience and emotional pain of abortion have burrowed into the psyche to haunt a guilty society with alienated fantasies of the unborn.[114] Explanations for UFO activity have related its ups and downs to economic stress,[115] social or political crises,[116] and, most successfully, instances of national shame. *Sputnik*, the 1966 Watts riots, and Watergate struck serious blows against national pride; they also correlate with major UFO waves. This association suggests paranoia, a transient or chronic psychological consequence of shame and humiliation.[117] Paranoia abides as a theme of UFO history, manifested in fears of flying saucers as spies and invaders in the 1950s, of UFOs as dangerous sources of radiation and injury in the 1960s, and of aliens as abductors and sexual abusers thereafter. The paranoia has evolved from hypochondria to a preoccupation with conspiracies and ever more insistent themes of world destruction in the last two decades.[118] These views implicate UFOs as symbolic or expressive effects responding to a social cause.

If abduction claimants are innocent of duplicity, critics see investigators as agents for handing down the myth. They bring an agenda and engage in risky techniques, especially hypnosis, with the likelihood that it magnifies the subject's susceptibility to cues and role-playing behavior. Without deliberate intention, investigators lead the subject to tell the story they want to hear. Its consistency from subject to subject reflects the influence of a preexisting UFO myth and confabulation rather than consistency in experiences. The culpability of investigators becomes an issue in the Roswell case as well, since in the critical view they stitch together vague recollections, questionable claims, and likely hoaxes into circumstantial evidence for a UFO crash.

Much of the UFO myth threatens to go up in cultural smoke, but influence raises problems of its own to caution that the skeptics' victory celebration is premature. Science fiction movies and literature describe many types of aliens, but abductees describe few; extraterrestrial kidnap opens up all sorts of possibilities for adventure and romance, yet abductees cleave to a repetitive plot of victimization. Why this narrow return on such a broad investment of imagery and opportunity? A natural affinity for dramatic structure does not explain why the same content fulfills the same plot function in narrative after narrative. This is no way for a respectable fantasy to behave. Variation is so characteristic of folklore that the absence or curtailment of this dynamic should provoke as much interest as the similarities in content.[119]

Some cultural arguments are just plain wrong. Descriptions of standard humanoids by Travis Walton, Betty Andreasson, and others before the 1977 release of *Close Encounters of the Third Kind* refute the claim that short gray aliens originated with Steven Spielberg's popular movie.[120] Investigating the investigators of the 1954 French wave revealed that the skeptics resorted to hearsay, distortion, and trivial cases in their effort to paint the entire wave as a social panic.[121] Failure to separate better reports from hoaxes and low-quality dross is a common shortcoming among cultural arguments and blurs any patterns that might exist. A sense of proportion also gets lost when cultural proponents stress the importance of one deviant report while they ignore a hundred that are similar. Efforts to relate UFOs with crises can hardly go wrong, since a crisis of some sort is always under way. National shame has a sharper definition and surpasses most rivals by coming packaged with a full theory of cause and effect, but even this significant proposal requires testing against not just national waves but also waves of localized and international scope. Even if a psychosocial solution accounts for waves or some other aspects of UFOs, whether it explains UFOs or only human behavior surrounding them still remains in question.

Beyond any quibbles over the relevance of a particular cultural element and how or why it works, there stands the fact that human factors take an active, creative hand in the cultural presentation of UFOs. The patterns and motifs of age-old tradition persist as standing waves amid the shifting currents of human thought, and these fixtures sweep the passing needs and themes of the times into stereotypes of description, conception, even observation itself to create a myth at once up-to-date and antique. When the mythmaking process takes over, UFO reports idealize history. They tell a story the way it ought to happen, not the way it did, and shroud the experience in the preconceptions of the myth.

Alien Horseman of the Apocalypse

UFOs herald the end or a new beginning of the world—so say contactees, abductees, conspiracists, fundamentalists, even ufologists and skeptics alike. In a strict sense, apocalyptic transformation qualifies only as one more cultural influence and another way people make sense of their situation, not as an independent category of the UFO myth. Still, apocalypticism addresses some capital-letter issues of existence—fear of destruction, the fate of mankind, cosmic justice, an end to suffering and evil, hope for personal salvation—and expresses them in the most theatrical manner. Any drama so laden with human interest and able to focus such strong emotions deserves close inspection. It pays off with a showcase example of how an age-old cultural theme, the heartbeat of visionary movements all over the world, grafts itself to a fresh belief and the two grow into one.

Apocalypse refers to a disclosure of things to come. In Christian tradition the term is synonymous with the Book of Revelation, inseparable from the cataclysms of a Second Coming and Last Judgment, equally bound to visions of a blissful millennium when Christ rules on earth and a heavenly kingdom of utter happiness, once "the former things are passed away." Early Christians expected an early return, their medieval and Reformation era successors excited themselves with countless millenarian enthusiasms, upstate New York earned the title of "burned-over district" for its millenarian and utopian movements in the 1830s and 1840s, and the drumbeat to doomsday has only quickened its pace in modern times.[122] Recent interpreters of biblical prophecy clock current events like AIDS, the foundation of Israel, and the cold war and its conclusion as ticks in a countdown to Armageddon. A preoccupation with the end renews itself endlessly: where the Russians of Tolstoy's *War and Peace* identify Napoleon with the Antichrist, the latest apocalypse watchers hang a similar identity on Mikhail Gorbachev and recognize bar codes as the Mark of the Beast.[123]

The Christian apocalypse tradition represents merely the most familiar version of a broader myth. Social movements with expectations of miraculous transformation cross cultural boundaries freely enough to suggest that such hopes lie close to the hearts of all people. The cargo cults of New Guinea, the Ghost Dance religion of the Plains Indians in the 1880s, the Taiping Rebellion in China (1845–64), the Xhosa cattle-killing epidemic of 1856–57 in South Africa, and South American migrations in search of the Land Without Evil represent a few examples of millenarian movements, where prophets inspire widespread expectations of a coming upheaval that will bring abundance, restore the dead to life, and usher in a time free of hardship or oppression.[124]

Millenarian movements spring from the need to revitalize a society shattered by deprivation and despair. When troubles overwhelm traditional assurances of social worth and integrity, the last recourse is radical transformation, a change so revolutionary it sweeps away established customs and reconfigures the world itself. Extreme misery demands extreme solutions, and in their darkest hours people yearn for a supernatural break with the past to create a new heaven and new earth.[125]

A dose of revitalization seems in order for the modern secular condition. Its social fractures and moral chaos echo the situation that precedes numerous outbreaks, and millenarian movements share many phenomena with UFO abductions. An instructive test case is the reform begun around 1800 by Handsome Lake, a Seneca Indian whose visionary experiences became the basis of a new religion and helped reverse the decline of his culture.[126] Compared side by side, the Seneca example and UFO abductions reveal striking parallels:

Seneca Visionary Experiences	*UFO Abductions*
After an era of political strength and sufficiency of traditional culture,	After an era of religious and economic stability,
Warfare, loss of land, famine, and demoralizing contact with European culture	The stress of secularization, social and economic change

Led to alcoholism, domestic violence, and intensified suspicions of witchcraft.

Led to religious drift, distrust of institutions, anger, and fear.

Handsome Lake underwent a series of trance visions, wherein he ascended to the sky, visited heaven and hell, and received messages of apocalyptic warning and spiritual reform from supernatural beings.

Many people report abductions into UFOs, where they undergo examinations, see other worlds, and receive apocalyptic messages from alien beings.

Handsome Lake gave up his own immoral habits and began his career as a prophet, preaching a code of behavior and reform of customs, attracting a large following that adopted a moral, purposeful way of life.

Abductees undergo life changes, becoming more spiritual and feeling a sense of mission.

His movement routinized into a church that continues today.

Any connection between modern stress and abduction must be speculative, but the comparison argues for itself. Substitute current talk of conspiracy for witchcraft, and the litany of today's anxieties sounds like a page straight from the history of Seneca cultural crisis. Handsome Lake's sky journey, tour of heaven and hell, and apocalyptic messages from spiritual beings borrow from Seneca religion and Christian influences, but the parallels with abduction accounts are plain. Prophetic visions typically serve as "personality transformation dreams" and bring radical reform to the life of the visionary,[127] while abductees sometimes report comparable changes. Hereafter the two patterns diverge. Handsome Lake became a prophet and led a movement; no one has assumed the mantle of leadership among abductees. They feel a sense of mission but seldom know what their mission is. UFO beliefs poise at an emergent stage with a tempting package of apocalyptic themes,[128] but UFO-based millenarian activity has not solidified into a movement with a plan and a direction.

The appeal of millenarian apocalypticism escapes religion to pursue an independent secular career. A pessimistic version requiring destruction before improvement is reflected in survivalist expectations that big government and a pluralistic society will lead to social calamity, in Marxist doctrine that inequality increases until revolution abolishes class distinctions and ushers in the millennium of the proletariat, and in ecological apocalypticism that looks for overpopulation and pollution to destroy a corrupt technological civilization, followed by an Arcadian society living in harmony with nature. An optimistic version has underwritten liberal reform and ideas of gradual social progress creating a better life. Perhaps the most conspicuous religious aspect of science is its promise to perfect the future, since as science grows, reason triumphs over ignorance, cooperation over faction, and abundance over want, fulfilling the positivist definition of civilization as "the general improvement of mankind . . . to the end of promoting at once man's goodness, power, and happiness."[129] A more concrete vision of the scientific and technological future, long depicted in science fiction and abetted in no small way by actual scientific achievement, promises leisure, health, material well-being, the capabilities of gods, and miraculous wonders without end, with even immortality, that old mainstay of millennial yearning, held out as a technical problem capable of eventual solution.[130]

Apocalypticism in secular belief and folk religion has blossomed into a significant aspect of the UFO myth. The 1950s contactees hoped that the Space Brothers would inspire peace and disarmament, while some abduction investigators see the experience as an educational process leading to eventual cosmic citizenship,[131] or as an agent of new consciousness to turn aside our materialistic drive toward self-destruction.[132] Apocalyptic imagery soaks deep into abduction accounts, in the barren and lifeless otherworld some abductees report, in the sickly and sunless appearance of the aliens themselves and their occasional statements that they come from a dying planet, damaged by disaster or their own mismanagement until they can reproduce themselves only by stealing genetic materials from earthlings. Otherwise it is the earth that figures into images of destruction or prophetic warnings of disaster. Whitley Strieber saw a vision of the world exploding and his son in the land of the dead.[133] Yet in the course of his experiences, he came to believe—as many abductees do—that these horrific scenes are not fated but mere possibilities, and that mankind forewarned can avert them.

The aliens assume some uncertain role in preventing or ameliorating future catastrophe. Their warnings against nuclear weapons, moral decay, or, most often, pollution and ecological destruction of the earth may serve to motivate change in one abductee at a time.[134] Some abductees believe they will help deflect catastrophe or else aid the injured "when the time is right." On occasion the aliens cross the line into a benign premillennial mode and promise to rescue some earthlings by spaceship before the time of tribulation begins. This sort of promise motivated the Heaven's Gate suicides, but the usual alien Rapture allows the chosen to leave earth in full fleshly attire.

The business of UFO encounters is individual and planetary transformation, say some theorists. Personal changes are apparent in abductees who turn vegetarian, stop smoking, thirst for knowledge, become more creative, take interest in spiritual matters, and desire to help others. Some abductees feel caught in the midst of a transformation, their loyalties divided between this world and another. All their lives these "star children" feel a strong attachment to the stars and a wish to return to them, a sense of being abandoned here and belonging somewhere else. If hypnotized to explore abduction experiences, these people recognize one alien being as familiar from repeated abductions and even from meetings prior to birth.[135] The collective scale remains speculative, but in these views UFOs reunify a divided psyche or condition our thinking or enlarge our consciousness as they lead us toward something old or something new, but away from our present, parlous state toward a better way of living on earth.

For every friendly Klaatu who has visited the movie screens of earth, mass culture has depicted a dozen invasions of body snatchers and wars of the worlds. Ufological speculations have been less one-sided, but doomsday scenarios and negative views of alien intentions have prospered in UFO mythology until anyone who listens for a central theme in UFO history hears a fifty-year-long dirge of paranoia.[136] The watchwords of 1950s ufology were "something is about to happen." This conviction sharpened the excitement of the era for insiders and enveloped the subject in a hothouse unreality from the perspective of onlookers. An end-time urgency riddles the writings of Donald Keyhoe, who lived in expectation that UFO events would "blow the lid off" of government secrecy and spill the greatest secret of all time to the public. If nothing else, the earth's teeming millions "stood on the threshold of something strange and tremendous. . . . How it would happen, when it would come, there was still no way of knowing. But one thing was certain, beyond all doubt. The world would never be the same."[137] At best the UFO visitors promised a final weaning of humanity from its geocentric, anthropocentric pretensions. At worst—and Keyhoe often expected the worst—the visitation would prove unfriendly. A military officer himself, Keyhoe found an ominous pattern in the interest UFOs seemed to take in military installations and nuclear facilities, major cities and defense plants—"It looks as though they're measuring us for a knockout."[138]

The timetable for invasion seemed scheduled to oppositions of Mars in the early 1950s, when near approaches corresponded to major waves of sightings.[139] Ufologists held their breath for the planet's closest approach in 1956, but this time bomb proved a dud. Expectations of a climax revived during the UFO pandemic of the mid-1960s, when the invasion assumed a more subtle, more sinister form. Men in Black, monsters, and Fortean phenomena seemed to join forces with UFOs, themselves now possessed of phantom properties, as all things weird congealed into a shadowy but interrelated whole. A secular demonology was born in the Age of Aquarius, the entities de-deviled in name but not in function, and formidable in their power. They hung up their ray guns to tamper with our thoughts on a large and growing scale, and investigator John Keel anticipated a sinister intent when he asked readers to suppose "the plan is to process millions of people and then . . . trigger all those minds at one time[.] Would we suddenly have a world of saints? Or would we have a world of armed maniacs shooting at one another from bell towers?"[140]

From the 1980s onward, the aliens lent their faces and personalities to an even more extravagant saga of interplanetary threat. Rumors of crashed UFOs mutated into a fantastic yarn about vast tunnel complexes under Dulce, New Mexico, and alien grocery shopping sprees from this base that left mutilated cattle and human disappearances across the country. After a military expedition to drive out the intruders ended in disaster, Ronald Reagan's "Star Wars" defense evolved as a weapon against this danger rather than the Soviets.[141] Abductees feel an ambivalence about alien motives, as some people find the experience stressful but benign, others see themselves as guinea pigs, robbed of choice, volition, even memory by cold, manipulative beings bent on subjecting them to a gruesome examination. As investigators pursue the nature of this program, the picture darkens, with alarming implications. The scale is enormous, involving millions of people and growing all the time. The captors take genetic material to breed a hybrid race, progressively more human in appearance but predominantly alien in mind, for the purpose of an ultimate takeover of the earth. Abductees report an ever more insistent signal that this project is about to culminate in The Change, a time when the hybrids and normal humans coexist in a world of extraordinary beauty. Yet this coexistence will be altogether on alien terms. Their paradise is a soulless alien realm that snuffs out the uniqueness of humanity and leaves little hope that we can avert its coming.[142]

The contours of apocalypticism show like ribs stretching through the flanks of UFO lore. All aspects of the religious tradition have become internalized and integral parts of the UFO myth, from the cleansing of the earth and rescue of the elect to cosmic warfare and transition to paradise. If this likeness is not enough to demonstrate that apocalyptic mythology stays true to itself amid whatever other beliefs it assimilates, a brief excursion into the history of history reveals that apocalypticism restores one of the oldest myths of all. The idea of an unfolding succession of time comes late to human thinking. Archaic man lacks an apocalyptic sense of finality because he has no concept of linear, purposeful history. For him time rolls in a closed cycle, starting with a primordial pattern of right and wrong established by the creator god as a sacred, ideal way to live. Any deviation diminishes this perfection, any change lessens and corrupts the cosmos. Through rituals of purification and symbolic repetition of the creative act, archaic man abolishes the particularities of personal experience to recover the timeless primordial state.[143]

Suffering remains a fact of life, history or no history. Sickness, death, toil, want, malice, evil, accident, and disaster play an inescapable counterpoint to the sacred ideal, and they gain meaning as consequences of witchcraft, sin, or angry gods. The ancient Hebrews went one step farther to recognize the will of God in every good or ill that befell the people. Suffering thereby acquired the deepest of meanings, and unique events like the Exodus became purposeful acts of God in the world. The fixed and eternal model of creation gave way to successive interactions between God and man, a relationship ever changing through historical time.[144]

The discovery of history only exacerbates the corrosion of time. Man still suffers and sins and now measures his shortcomings against a personal, demanding, unpredictable god of history. To find history also means finding the terror of history. Societies manage this terror as long as it keeps its distance, but they face a crisis when history intrudes with such speed and devastation that suffering overwhelms ordinary channels of amelioration. The conflicts arising from migrations and growing populations of the second millennium B.C. threatened lives and ways of life on an unprecedented scale. One response to this emergent situation was the millennial vision of the prophet Zoroaster (ca. 1400 B.C.), who conceived a cosmic drama where the god of goodness struggled against the spirit of evil for both the future of the world and the souls of men. This war had a finite lease. For now each individual fought as a soldier on the side of good or evil through the conduct of his life, but the forces of good would overthrow evil in a great final battle, and the time of "making wonderful" would begin, a time historian Norman Cohn describes in terms already familiar: "What lies ahead, at the end of time, is a state from which every imperfection will have been eliminated; a world where everyone will live forever in a peace that nothing could disturb; an eternity when history will have ceased and nothing more can happen; a changeless realm, over which the supreme god will reign with an authority which will be unchallenged forever more."[145]

This charming promise speaks hope with the roundest phrases of any expression in human imagination, and for good reason arises or spreads throughout the world to shape both sacred and secular futures. Yet the real home of this future is the past. The happy kingdom at the end of time brings back primordial perfection in one final turn of the cycle, then locks the wheel for eternity in unchanging stasis. Many cultures no sooner discover history than they curl it back into cycles, often lengthened from seasonal, annual, or lifetime periods into ages, aeons, or "great years" of many centuries' duration. The Greeks and Romans divided time into declining ages of gold, silver, bronze, and iron, while the Aztecs saw themselves as inhabitants of the fifth world, the other four having ended in cataclysm, and the Norse foresaw that even the gods would perish in Ragnarok. Yet optimistic rivals offset these gloomy notions as Virgil envisioned a new Golden Age, the Aztecs awaited the return of Quetzalcoatl, and the Norse expected the gentle god Baldur to found a better world on the ruins of the old.[146] Apocalypticism is thus a creature of history and yet the enemy of it.

Even scientific progress must grind to a halt before long, once all discoveries are made or human will for outward-directed activity subsides. When the easy science is done and the hard science left to be done will call for more funding than society is willing to provide, the process of discovery will effectively shut down. Science is self-limiting—it has provided (or soon will provide) enough of a good life to fence humanity away from the immediate necessities that once drove the struggle. Now instead of striving outward, we can indulge our stronger inclination toward social and personal preoccupations.[147] The future golden age will exchange intellectual adventure and individuality for the stasis and benign regimentation of a world of lotus-eaters.

Some UFO theorists welcome the prospect of returning to the age of myth. With a UFO-inspired change of consciousness, psychologist Kenneth Ring believes that humanity "would be led *back* to its true home in the realm of the imagination where it would be liberated to live in mythical time and no longer be incarcerated in the doomed prison of historical time."[148] Welcome or not, the eminence of apocalyptic mythology in UFO belief demonstrates how readily spaceships and mystical paradises join together, helped along by the very nature of UFOs that sets them halfway to heaven already. Such ready affinity also cautions that most human interest in UFOs centers on myth rather than science, and the experiential history of UFOs converts with deft and elusive speed into mythical history.

Clearing the Myths

Underlying this discussion is a premise that UFOs as we know them divide into two ontological spheres: on the one hand lie the UFO experience and whatever causes it; on the other hand lie the human construction and uses made of UFOs—in other words, the myth. These two spheres are separate but not readily separable. This chapter has not attempted to address the considerable body of research and vast litany of reports attesting to a phenomenon that is physical enough to produce photographs, radar returns, electromagnetic interference, ground traces, and human physical effects, some of them anomalous enough to resist conventional explanations. The value and nature of these experiential claims are not under the microscope here. What is at stake remains a case not for extraterrestrial visitation or even for an unidentified physical phenomenon but for the basic study of UFO claims. The purpose of this chapter has been to point a finger at why a phenomenon with all the qualifications of UFOs for serious scientific attention remains an outcast and scorned as an enemy of reason. If my argument holds true, the reason is the myth.

For most people it is the cultural rather than the physical reality that counts, and the resulting myth serves far more purposes than the realities. It imposes a full system of thought with its own premises and paths of reasoning, its own accepted truths and criteria of acceptance, enclosing the underlying phenomenon, whatever it may be, with the self-confirming verities, certainties, assumptions, theories, speculations, tales, and rumors that creative human intellect has assembled in its effort to understand and imagine UFOs. Elite thinkers may devalue the myth as a cluttered attic of inconsistent ideas and intolerable logical compromises, but to believers this myth is knowledge tried and true, neither pretty nor elegant, perhaps, but the surest way to make personal and social sense of everything from odd sights in the sky to governmental behavior, ancient history to future prospects. Who would readily surrender such a useful and intriguing idea?

Flying saucers bear a cup that runs over with human significance, but few drops fall in the direction of a scientific search for truth. Small numbers of people have found a new religion in UFOs, but many who feel abandoned by established churches or rootless in a secular world discover a substitute in the excitement, participation, and easy answers of UFO belief. The myth is more insidious than organized religions, since no authority controls it or keeps it orthodox, no theologians systematize its tenets to obey rules of logic. This do-it-yourself faith liberates believers to create a world of their own making, with no limit on imagination—and no tether to reality. Ties to the past remain strong. The myth stays the same for ages while time and fashion pull fresh guises over the underlying framework, so the devil becomes communism or Men in Black, who shift in turn from aliens to government agents and back without revising the basic ideas. Renaming without rethinking makes for quick and easy change. In such a climate the believers' small regard for truth underscores that humans are social animals first and rational animals second—a very distant second. To forget the human appeal of the myth is to underestimate its power and belittle a monster.

The myth also hides the subject from scientific interest. Credulity, emotion, and fantasy surround UFOs; the language of faith, hope, and personal need replaces the language of evidence; and expectations inspired by the mass media crowd out enough clear thinking and even clear seeing to persuade most scholarly passersby that their negative cursory appraisal holds true down to the core. The myth throws up this camouflage, and they seldom see beyond it. Those few exceptions to the rule are instructive—a hard look at the evidence and actual investigation of sightings convinced scientists such as James McDonald, J. Allen Hynek, and members of the French GEPAN organization that a genuine mystery was afoot. The fact that much thinking about UFOs is unscientific hardly means that scientific investigation is predestined to fruitlessness. Creationist literature expresses religious wishes rather than a scientific search for truth without calling into serious question the reality of evolution, but UFOs have not been so lucky. Their unscholarly literature and human commitments have prospered until the subject appears ridiculous and disreputable, a thing to avoid, when in fact this judgment condemns not the subject but its mythical alter ego.

A first step in understanding UFOs must be disentanglement of the myth from the evidence. The small cadre of serious UFO researchers has recognized a distinction all along, not perfectly by any means, and hampered by the limitations of time, funding, equipment, and expertise that often plague their investigations, but still with an ear for the signal beneath the noise. At worst ufologists have cultivated the myth by accepting a claim as a fact before they establish the facticity of the claim. Undocumented accounts of missing fetuses, material fragments unavailable for analysis, and instances of sleep paralysis mistaken for abductions add phantom links to the chain of evidence, while alternative solutions and legitimate criticisms go unheard, thrown out of court in wrongful acts of evidence selection. At best ufologists have recorded, preserved, investigated, and sifted a staggering volume of reports, dismissed most of them as trivial or conventional, and winnowed out a remainder that maintains a deserved grip on curiosity.

Skeptics fly the banner of science but rarely honor its spirit. They often dismiss UFOs, experience and all, on account of the myth alone or their own mythical version of the evidence. Carl Sagan devotes several chapters of *The Demon-Haunted World* to UFOs and abductions—lucid, rational, persuasive arguments that human error, the will to believe, cultural influences, and overzealous hypnotists sum up the mystery, that the nonexistence of physical evidence and the aliens' all too earthly preoccupation with sex and morality seal the case for UFOs belonging to inner rather than outer space.[149] Sagan's reasoning sounds so right, so irrefutable, so scientific, that readers easily overlook its shortcomings. What is missing is any instance where he investigates a case or interviews an abductee. The scientific ideal of an unbiased examination of evidence has twisted into an elegant argument from authority and accepted truths, an airtight system where any empirical novelty dies of suffocation without a hearing.

Skeptics hold "traditions of disbelief" that are as deeply felt as and no better justified than the traditions of belief these skeptics criticize. Folklorist David Hufford points out that "there is one kind of logical error that is the peculiar property of disbelievers; i.e. the *a priori* exclusion of one whole class of hypotheses—the supernatural ones—as unnecessary to consider. 'It can't be so; therefore it isn't.'"[150] He has led a growing realization among folklorists and scholars of religious belief that psychological needs or cultural influences are insufficient to explain the origin and persistence of belief traditions. His field research on supernatural traditions convinced him that "a fundamental reason that spiritual beliefs have been able to resist the enormous social pressures toward secularization is that they are, in part, rationally founded on experience (that is, empirically grounded)."[151]

To admit an experiential basis for belief does not prove any one interpretation of that belief. Ghosts or aliens may or may not be the final answer, and conventional verities may—probably will—win out in the end. What this admission does reveal is a greater depth to these claims than the usual official explanation allows, and reason to resist the comfortable psychologizing and armchair speculation that all too often satisfy the skeptic. Such dogmatism has potentially catastrophic consequences for the integrity and reputation of science. For people who live their intellectual life half under the roof of official knowledge and half in the mythical out-of-doors, the contempt and dismissal of scientific authority only drives them further away and increases their wariness of science as a way of knowing. For anyone steeped well enough in the myth to hold strong suspicions already, authoritative denials achieve a mental alchemy that transmutes lack of UFO proof into proof of UFO conspiracy. The insistence that there is nothing to UFOs only pours fuel on the conspiratorial fire, convincing the believers that the doubters act out of fear, ignorance, or cover-up. In a sense, UFOs bring out the worst in science. Instead of a demonstration of systematic and unbiased inquiry open for all eyes to follow, the public sees arrogance and sophistry, rhetoric and ridicule—a theater of human failings likely to rank science alongside today's self-formulated religions and the self-indulgent tribalism of postmodernist academics in too many eyes.

The occasional meetings between science and UFOs are seldom happy or scientific, and are stained with prejudice. The foremost object lesson in mishandling UFOs is the Condon Committee, an investigation carried out at the University of Colorado under U.S. Air Force sponsorship in 1967–68 and trumpeted as the final scientific word on UFOs. That final word said that UFOs promised to add nothing to scientific knowledge and that further study was not justified. The status quo was satisfied, but a notable discontinuity separated this dismissal from the case studies themselves, where investigators left a third of the reports unidentified and assigned some identifications that raised more questions than they answered, like "almost certainly [a] natural phenomenon, which is so rare that it apparently has never been reported before or since."[152]

A similar standoff followed after a panel of disinterested scientists met with a panel of proponents at the estate of Laurance S. Rockefeller to review some of the best UFO evidence. In the summer of 1998 the scientists issued a cautious conclusion that "anything not explained is something science at some level ought to be interested in,"[153] but even this cool reception, barely one degree above zero, heated one skeptic to decry the panel for legitimizing UFO research, and the writer of a simple news article for *Science* to fill almost half of his one and a half columns with unfavorable commentary. Another accusation that the panel was a promotion by believers[154] seems to confuse the presenters, who were proponents, with the panel itself, whose members were not. No midnight ride to shout that aliens are coming stirred up this fuss, only a spare admission that UFOs could stand a little scientific study.

Another case in point is an incisively written but misinformed book review by Frederick Crews, with its roundhouse punch against all UFO beliefs.[155] Crews assumes that skeptic Philip Klass has successfully knocked down every UFO that J. Allen Hynek and, by extension, every other ufologist regards as a serious contender for unknown status. In a similar vein, spaceships, aliens, and abduction plots owe their similarities to nothing more mysterious than movie and TV influences. Klass and the psychosocial reductionists often sound convincing. Their explanations may well be right, but blanket acceptance is an act of faith, not science. The mere appearance of success does not make an explanation true, and who would tolerate such loose standards if the subject were anything but UFOs? Crews raises the important issue of false memory but bumps up against a genuine scientific finding in this field, the failure of studies to reveal any mental abnormality or fantasy-proneness among abductees. He admits they are "intelligent, articulate, and rational in all respects but one" (p. 17) and lays all the blame on investigators, the "Pied Pipers who induce false belief." The 27 February 1997 episode of *Nova* captures investigators red-handed as they lead their subjects into abduction fantasies, he believes, but he accepts this program at face value without awareness of bias so extreme that the ufological community now pronounces *Nova* as a byword for unfairness and distortion.

Apocalyptic fears of science stamped out by ignorance have a sounder basis than passing anxiety or millennial jitters. People today, from the high echelons of government to children in school, seem ever more inward-turning as they reach for absolutes and plant their feet in stubborn resistance to unwelcome ideas. The myth, with its personal answers and magical solutions, reshapes the world to suit a static human ideal. It is the intellectual equivalent of the primate's inclination to backscratch and delouse rather than venture into the dangerous country beyond familiar tramping grounds. Pseudoscience and rejection of real science ring an alarm that will go unanswered only at the risk of burning modern civilization to the ground. Yet to counterbalance this worry must be a concern that science may die by its own hand, if overconfidence forecloses inquiry and leads to a preference for pontification over learning. Science enjoys no special exemption from the eternal return of mythical thinking. A response to UFOs that favors armchair deduction over actual investigation resorts to just such a backward turn, its basis the authority of the past rather than curiosity about the present and future. This authority may not haul out the rack and thumbscrews of an Inquisition for added persuasion, but the arrangement is one Galileo might recognize. Without curiosity, the heart of science stops beating and leaves a dry husk behind. As an example, consider one skeptic's comment that "calling in all the people who have seen strange things just gets you a roomful of strange people."[156] My (admittedly limited) experience with abductees and other experiencers has been just the opposite—I find a roomful of normal people who have seen strange things. Who's right or wrong is not even the issue at this point. What matters is a difference of perception and therefore a possibility that one of us is wrong. I'm still curious enough to want to know which of us it is.

A call to study UFOs is not a call for science to lower its necessarily high standards of evidence but simply a summons for scientists to do science, scholars to undertake scholarship. Millions of people have puzzled over objects in the sky, and abduction claimants report encounters profoundly disturbing. Right or wrong, these people deserve a fair hearing, and basic curiosity seconds the motion. There are intriguing cases on the books, reports for which Phil Klass's explanations fall short, aspects of abduction that defy facile answers.

A minimal, foot-in-the-door argument for UFO study need not begin with the evidence itself but with a simple recognition that something worth investigating is going on here. So far the impulse to investigate the experience has all too often confused it with the myth and stopped short. As things now stand, the very profusion of solutions betrays the tenuousness of our knowledge, and the noise level of the ongoing controversy reminds us of the disorganized state of current research. Ufologists and skeptics often argue at cross-purposes, uncertain whether they dispute the experience or the myth, evidence or rumor. Investigators must discriminate matter from myth and pursue each half by the appropriate methods—an interdisciplinary task of formidable proportions. Recourse to Occam and other formalisms achieves little when the questions and their objects are so indistinct; the razor slashes through vapors without ever reaching its target. In matters of experiential claims, there is no substitute for hands-on investigation, however difficult and untidy the effort may be.

UFOs will stay lost in their own mythology until a patient, thorough, and evenhanded investigation addresses the experiences rather than hearsay and prejudice based on myth—a trust, if you will, that science done right will change open minds to face the truth, whichever way it falls. The myth will continue to go its merry way, and true believers will keep the faith in spite of any evidence, but only science can answer the scientific question of what is the origin and nature of the UFO experience. Then we can know whether the ufologists or the skeptics have been right all along, whether "real" UFOs will dissipate with the myths or jump out with a roar.

Chapter Seven

The UFO Abduction Controversy in the United States

David M. Jacobs

Controversy has been central to the UFO phenomenon from the start in 1947 when it first came to public consciousness. At that time witnesses claimed to see unusually configured objects in the sky, which appeared to be artificially engineered and intelligently controlled. These reports ignited an emotional, and sometimes fierce, worldwide debate among the scientific community, governments, the media, the public, and lay UFO organizations. After the sightings came the reports of aliens regularly abducting people and forcing them to undergo physical and mental examinations. By the early 1990s, abductions were profoundly changing UFO studies. For researchers who were persuaded that UFOs represented alien intelligence, abductions, rather than sightings, seemed to be the key to understanding alien intentions.

The 1950s: Before the First Abduction Reports

The 1947 reports of unidentified flying objects propelled the U.S. government, using the vehicle of the U.S. Air Force, into undertaking and funding a series of investigative research projects. Once the air force began to release findings, a segment of the public became concerned about the objectivity and adequacy of the research and founded independent civilian UFO research groups.[1]

Dissatisfied with the air force's investigation, civilian UFO researchers focused on establishing whether unidentified flying objects were anomalous, artificial, and/or intelligently controlled. They asked: Are the objects conventional or extraterrestrial? If extraterrestrial, who are they and why are they here? After almost fifty years of research, these remain the central questions. Although some UFO researchers have addressed the "who" and "why" questions, the main battle has been over validation of the phenomenon's existence. Purpose and motivation have been secondary objectives.[2]

Meanwhile, the scientific and academic community kept its distance. Relying on the extremely high probability that UFOs could not represent extraterrestrial intelligence and aware that the subject was ripe for ridicule, the scientific community was more than willing to allow the air force to study the phenomenon. The scientific community's analysis was seemingly bolstered by the lack of "hard" evidence for the existence of the phenomenon.

Furthermore, scientists did not want to be associated with fringe groups such as "the contactees," who claimed ongoing contact with benevolent "Space Brothers" who had come to earth to stop war, cure disease, and help mankind. Led by "Professor" George Adamski, "Dr." Daniel Fry, Truman Bethurum, Orfeo Angelucci, and others in the 1950s and early 1960s, the contactees spun tales of meeting Space Brothers in their backyards or even at lunch counters and going for rides on UFOs and sometimes even visiting other planets.[3] Like the scientists, most UFO researchers wanted to distance themselves from the embarrassing contactees, but it was more difficult for a layperson to do.

The 1960s: The First Abduction Cases

Contactees notwithstanding, early on there were indications that there was more to the UFO phenomenon than sightings of anomalous objects. Witnesses claimed to have seen strange beings near the UFOs or through their windows. They described a wide variety of occupants: some were large and covered in hair, others were human-like; some looked like "monkeys," others were small with large eyes.

They seemed to behave in puzzling ways: they appeared to be study-ing the flora and the fauna, collecting leaves and bark from trees. They seemed to avoid contact and, according to witnesses, immo-bilized humans and then "inspected" them when they accidentally encountered the beings.[4]

Betty and Barney Hill

The Hill case marked the beginning of serious inquiry into ab-ductions. The Hills' story has been told many times. In 1961 Betty and Barney Hill were driving late at night in New Hampshire when they saw an unusual object. They stopped the car and got out to get a better look. Barney Hill said the object was hovering about twelve hundred feet above the ground and that its occupants were peering out at him. Panicked, he and Betty jumped back in the car and sped down the highway. After they inexplicably turned onto a dirt path, their car stalled, and they received a mental impression that they should go limp and close their eyes.

The Hills said that aliens from a nearby landed UFO took them on board and examined them. Placing them in separate "rooms," the aliens took sperm from Barney and injected a needle into Betty's navel, which she believed was some type of "pregnancy" test. She "conversed" with the UFO occupants and then they were released. They drove back onto the highway, promptly forgot what had tran-spired, and arrived home about two hours late.

Soon thereafter the Hills began having unusual dreams, strange memories, and, in Barney's case, depression. By 1964 they sought the help of the renowned psychiatrist and hypnotist Benjamin Simon. It was during these hypnosis sessions that they separately and indepen-dently remembered their abduction events. Simon was at a loss to explain how the two of them would have independently and sepa-rately generated such a bizarre story, but he never believed that they were abducted. In fact, he spent considerable time during hypnosis trying to get them to admit that they had unconsciously generated the event, which they insisted they had not. Simon eventually con-cluded vaguely that the Hills had experienced some sort of shared dream.[5]

The Hill case received widespread media coverage. In 1966 columnist John Fuller wrote a best-selling book about their experiences and received more national attention from the excerpts in the popular *Look* magazine.[6] (An embarrassed Barney had requested that Fuller exclude the "sperm collection" account, and it was not widely known until many years later.)[7] The Hill case quickly became the most prominent in UFO history and has remained extremely important for several reasons: it was the first to gain public recognition; there was little chance of media contamination; a hypnotist with impeccable credentials recovered it; and the Hills were responsible and credible citizens.

The national UFO organizations of the time were split on the Hills. The Aerial Phenomena Research Organization (APRO), which previously had championed a number of "occupant" cases, accepted the case as feasible. The National Investigations Committee on Aerial Phenomena (NICAP) was more conservative. Although it had accepted some occupant cases as potentially authentic, the Hills' story smacked of the hated "contacteeism," and NICAP feared that the Hills were simply new contactees with a different, more credible twist.

The Hill case came to represent a line over which many researchers would not step. After years of struggle to build the scientific legitimacy of the UFO phenomenon, this extreme case threatened to bring down what little UFO researchers had accomplished. In effect, the Hill case became the test to show how tough-minded investigators could be. In order to move into the mainstream, they were keen to demonstrate that they would not automatically accept any claim no matter how credible the witnesses. The case tested that resolve, in image if not in fact.

In spite of UFO researchers' suspicion, the Hills' account and behavior did not contain the normal contactee elements. The Hills did not try to achieve monetary gain from the episode—although they eventually received a percentage of profits from Fuller's book. They never varied from their original account and refused to embellish it. They did not claim, contactee-like, to make trips to other planets, or to have ongoing contact with Space Brothers. Nor did they even speculate on the reasons for the aliens' behavior. However, both assumed that they were being experimented upon or "studied."

The Hills were middle-class, functioning members of society without a background of association with paranormal activities or groups. And, in addition to their story, they presented some non-anecdotal circumstantial evidence for their experience. The tops of Barney's shoes were scuffed, supposedly as a result of the aliens' having dragged him into the object. A semicircle of warts appeared around Barney's groin, presumably matching the placement of the device used to extract his sperm. And Betty's dress contained pink spots that she said were not there before the abduction.[8]

Antonio Villas-Boas

Although receiving the most public notoriety, the Hill case was not the first abduction account that UFO researchers knew about. A year earlier, the story of Antonio Villas-Boas had been published (although it remains virtually unknown to the public). Villas-Boas was a Brazilian law student whose parents owned a ranch. In 1957, while home on vacation, he was plowing at night (when it was cool enough to remain on the tractor for any length of time) when, he reported, a UFO landed near him. He was immediately beset by several small aliens who brought him aboard. The aliens removed his clothes, examined him, drew blood from his chin, and forced him to have sexual intercourse with a strange female who looked only partly human. When the female left the room afterward, she pointed to her belly and then upward toward the sky. Villas-Boas was left with the distinct impression that he was being used like a "stallion to improve their stock."

The account was published in a British UFO periodical in 1965 and then in Coral Lorenzen's 1967 book, *Flying Saucer Occupants*.[9] The publication of this case proved to be enormously embarrassing to the skittish and public relations–minded UFO researchers. They mistakenly thought Villas-Boas was an illiterate farmer who had concocted this sexually lurid story of a UFO kidnapping. It reeked of sensationalism and seemed more suited to pulp magazines than to serious inquiry. Furthermore, South American cases had a reputation of being poorly investigated and/or hoaxes. James E. McDonald, professor of atmospheric physics at the University of Arizona and a UFO researcher, had a typical response: in this "wild tale . . . the guy gets dragged aboard the saucer and is stripped and dipped and in due time they pop a 4'6" slant-eyed, blond, curvaceous 'beauty' whose only blemish is a slit where her bee-stung lips ought to be. Not just once, but twice she seduces our poor hero Antonio. God save our sex-starved souls—what are the Lorenzens thinking of to run such a story?"[10]

Unnoticed at the time, the Hill and Villas-Boas cases contained some surprising similarities. Both involved aliens controlling their human victims and taking them on board a UFO against their wills. Both cases seemed to suggest a study of humans and an interest in reproduction. Both Barney and Antonio gave sperm. In both cases the victims were "solid citizens" (Villas-Boas became an attorney) who never embellished their accounts or claimed ongoing meetings with Space Brothers. The two cases differed in the way in which the participants remembered their alleged experiences; Villas Boas consciously recalled the events, and the Hills remembered them with the help of hypnosis. Together, however, they displayed many of the abduction phenomenon's familiar characteristics.

Only a few other abduction cases came to light in the second half of the 1960s. By the end of the decade, the abduction phenomenon seemed to be an isolated and most likely psychological phenomenon to which the UFO research community gave little attention.

The 1970s: More Abductions

Hickson and Parker in Pascagoula

An intense wave of sightings in 1973 contained incidents that changed the way in which researchers perceived the UFO and abduction phenomena. During this wave, Charles Hickson (age forty-two) and Calvin Parker (age nineteen) reported that they were fishing on the banks of the Pascagoula River in Mississippi when a UFO landed about fifty feet from them and, before they could react, two aliens grabbed them and "floated" them into the UFO. Hickson said he was suspended in midair while a football-shaped device slowly passed around his body. After a short time, the two were released from the object. Hickson and Parker went to the sheriff with their story. The sheriff put them together in a room with a hidden microphone and listened from another room to their private conversation. Rather than laugh about how they were putting one over on the authorities, the shaken men talked about what had happened to them and then kneeled and prayed. A local reporter put the case on the wire services, and it made the national news.

Two prominent scientists investigated the case. One was J. Allen Hynek, who had been the chief civilian scientist in charge of the U.S. Air Force's official UFO investigation unit (Project Blue Book) and was chair of the astronomy department at Northwestern University. The second was James Harder, a professor of engineering at the University of California at Berkeley, a UFO researcher, and an experienced hypnotist. They asked permission to conduct hypnosis as part of their investigation: Hickson consented, but Parker, not wishing to deal with the media, refused to talk about the abduction. During the hypnosis, Hickson became too frightened to continue as he neared the beginning of the event and Harder ended the session, fearing that reliving the trauma would be too risky.[11]

Some in the media attacked the credibility of Hickson and Parker, charging them with trying to make money from the event. The fact that they seemed unsophisticated and lived in a small town in Mississippi suggested to some members of the northern press that these "rubes" could not tell reality from fantasy.[12] More important, researchers noted that the aliens they described did not resemble reports of other UFO occupants. The Pascagoula aliens were large, with elephant-like wrinkled skin, pointed noses, small eyes, and no neck. Most researchers considered this case to be either a hoax or psychologically generated.

Travis Walton

Two years later, in 1975, another abduction case was nationally publicized. In this instance, Travis Walton and six other men who were cutting trees near Snowflake, Arizona, were driving down a mountain when they spotted a UFO hovering above the tree line near their pickup truck. They stopped, and Walton climbed out to get a closer look at the object. A flash of light came out from under it and struck Walton, who fell over, seemingly unconscious. The others, still in the truck, panicked and sped away. After about fifteen minutes, they went back to get Walton, thinking that he might have been hurt. Walton had vanished. Search parties combed the area but did not find him. After five days, he showed up, disoriented and talking about being on board a UFO. He was able to remember only about twenty minutes of the previous five days.[13]

As in the earlier cases, controversy immediately ensued. Critics claimed the Walton case was a hoax, pointing to the fact that he had failed an early lie detector test and alleging that he had been interested in UFOs before the event. Coral Lorenzen and other proponents pointed out that seven witnesses had seen the UFO and that Walton had passed all subsequent polygraph examinations. APRO became Walton's champion, but the case was so controversial that most researchers remained unconvinced of its legitimacy or of the legitimacy of the abduction phenomenon in general.[14]

The Kentucky Case

One of the few early multiple subject abductions that came to researchers' attention occurred in 1976. Three women in Kentucky said they had been driving when they were abducted from their car. With the help of hypnosis from University of Wyoming professor of guidance and counseling Leo Sprinkle, they remembered being on a table and having an examination conducted upon them—one woman remembered a gynecological procedure. A few other people also saw UFOs approaching them, followed by several hours of missing time, physical sequelae, and sometimes-returning memories of lying on a table in a UFO. During the investigation, the three women passed a polygraph examination.[15]

Other Strange Reports

Although the abduction reports were strange enough, other bizarre events were also reported. Witnesses said that a UFO appeared directly in front of them and then "dematerialized." Others reported UFOs swooping down on their cars—sometimes just a few feet from the roof—and chasing them. People reported being "transfixed" or "hypnotized" by a UFO, unable to take their eyes off it. Other witnesses reported a strange "psychic" connection to the UFO; they felt that they were being "watched" by a UFO during a sighting, or that the UFO "knew" everything about them. Witnesses reported seeing only the underside of a UFO. Others reported having the strange feeling that they had floated out the window upon seeing a UFO. Some said they could describe the interior of the UFO even though they only remembered seeing the object hovering above them. Other people reported sighting a UFO and then having "deep communications" with an animal—a cow, deer, raccoon, owl, and so forth. Investigators would record the details of these cases, but they could not fathom their import.

The Debate and the Debaters

The abduction debate quieted in the early 1970s, and abduction claims became an exotic sidelight to the core of UFO research—the investigation of object sighting reports. There was little speculation about abductions. In a 1972 published interview with Betty Hill, psychiatrist Berthold E. Schwartz and UFO researcher Marjorie Fish hypothesized about an alien interest in the reproductive aspects of humans, but they relegated the idea to a footnote.[16] Researchers hoped that rather than focusing on abductions, a comprehensive analysis of sighting reports would result in a methodology to explain the entire phenomenon. The UFO research community had built a substantial knowledge base of UFO sightings and had accumulated an impressive body of physical and anecdotal evidence to support the extraterrestrial hypothesis. Yet as researchers learned more about the UFO phenomenon, they understood less, and the phenomenon grew more, rather than less, mysterious. The sighting reports displayed patterns, but the meaning of these patterns continued to elude investigators.[17]

The 1970s

Although most researchers concentrated on object sightings, some tried to make scientific sense of abduction reports. Alvin Lawson, a professor of English at California State University at

Long Beach, devised an experiment in 1977 to determine if abduction stories were psychologically derived. He recruited sixteen student volunteers, had them hypnotized, and asked them to describe what happened after he told them that they were to imagine that they were abducted by aliens. He prompted them along their imaginary way and later correlated their accounts with those of "real" abductees. He reported that "an average comparison of data from four imaginary and four 'real' abduction narratives showed no substantive differences."[18] Although Lawson carefully enumerated the less-than-substantive differences, his study seemingly strengthened the premise that abductions were psychologically based.

Some researchers who reviewed Lawson's study argued that the data did not support his conclusions, and that the fake accounts not only were different from the "real" accounts but also were different from what abductees routinely reported. Yet because so little was known about the phenomenon, most researchers could not understand the difference between Lawson's prompted accounts and "real" abduction narratives. More important, Lawson's work brought the dangers of memory to the fore. Even if "real" abduction narratives existed, how much of these stories could be trusted? Although UFO researchers criticized Lawson's study, he had correctly identified the risks of believing everything that abductees recalled.

Around the same time, UFO researcher Ray Fowler investigated the Andreasson case (which he later published as *The Andreasson Affair*). In this case a woman and her daughter were abducted while the rest of the family was placed in a form of suspended animation. The abductors seemed to come directly through the wall into the house. The woman recounted a complex set of events, including being immersed in liquid, traveling to an alien location, and having medical procedures administered to her. The woman was quite devout, and religious imagery surfaced in her hypnotically recalled testimony, which suggested a strong psychological component.[19]

In the late 1970s, Budd Hopkins, an internationally renowned artist, began to address the confusing abduction problem in a more systematic way than anyone had done before. Using the services of a clinical psychologist as hypnotist (the first time this had been done), Hopkins investigated seven abduction cases for patterns, similarities, and convergences. He found that inexplicable one- to two-hour gaps of time were more pervasive than he had previously realized.

He discovered seemingly unaccountable bodily scars whose origin was the result of abduction activity. He explained how a person could be an abductee without remembering seeing a UFO, and argued that abduction accounts could be hidden beneath the surface of "screen memories" in which abductees might, for example, falsely remember that they had talked with a "deer" or raccoon or other animals with large black eyes. His data showed that abductees could have recurrent experiences. In 1981 he published the results of his investigations as *Missing Time*.[20]

The 1980s: Into the Deluge

The publication of *Missing Time*, and Hopkins's subsequent radio and television appearances, triggered thousands of letters from possible abductees. The astonishingly large number of people who contacted Hopkins indicated that abductions might be far more widespread than had been imagined. Furthermore, as researchers looked back at older cases, they found missing time and other patterns in the more puzzling accounts that they now recognized as possibly masking abductions.

Even if UFO investigators suspected that there was more to the case than a simple sighting, they did not have an adequate investigative methodology. When hypnotists were called in, they were not experienced enough in abduction research to ask the right questions. They did not know if the subject was confabulating or "filling in" with false information, if the witness had slipped into a dissociative "channeling" mode, or if the subject was relating dream material or "screen" memories. It was exceptionally difficult for researchers to separate fact from fantasy.

Likewise, most UFO researchers did not understand the implications of the abduction data. They had been schooled in the older sighting-analysis techniques and were ill-equipped to study abduction cases. The procedures that UFO researchers had developed for deciphering witness observations did not apply in the troublesome area of recovering memories. Most researchers found it difficult or impossible to make the transition. They had toiled for years tracking down the origin of sightings, calling airports, consulting star charts, questioning witnesses. Abduction research required very different skills. They had to learn not only proper questioning techniques but also the ability to separate out "signal" from "noise." Moreover, sighting researchers found themselves discussing extremely personal and sensitive aspects of peoples' private lives. These UFO investigators had no training in this endeavor and little stomach for it. Without their ability to identify potential abductions, and because of their reluctance to investigate cases indicating potential abductions, the majority of possible abduction cases went uninvestigated.

In spite of the problem of identifying abductees, claimants were generating so many reports by the mid-1980s that researchers could not keep up with them. Following Hopkins's example, more investigators, such as NASA scientist Richard Haines (who developed a unique, three-stage method of questioning abductees),[21] and me, a historian and UFO researcher, began to use hypnosis. The new researchers added a large amount of data from each abduction investigation to the growing abduction database. In 1987 folklorist Thomas E. Bullard published an analysis of 270 abduction cases reported in UFO literature. He showed numerous structural similarities among the narratives, including the fact that basic underlying structures of abduction accounts were present regardless of who the abductee was—or who the researcher was.[22] Bullard also fashioned the first taxonomy of abduction experiences.

In 1987 Hopkins published *Intruders: The Incredible Visitations at Copley Woods*, which posited an extensive intrusion of the UFO phenomenon into peoples' personal lives. Many victims, Hopkins reported, described how aliens performed genetic experiments on them, including the collection of ova and sperm. Abductees reported fetuses being removed from them. They were often required to interact physically with odd-looking babies who were presumably grown, at least in part, from the abductees' eggs and sperm. The abductees called these babies "hybrids." His data also demonstrated that many abductees have family members who are abductees and that the phenomenon might be intergenerational. Hopkins elucidated the victimization that many abductees felt—they seemed to be traumatized individuals whose lives had seemingly been profoundly affected by their abductions. Hopkins reported on the first psychological blind testing of abductees and showed that they did not manifest serious mental disorders that would account for their narratives.[23]

By mid-1987 I had begun to think that the tide in UFO research had turned away from object studies and toward abduction analysis. This, I suspected, signaled a new era had opened. In a paper given to the fortieth anniversary Mutual UFO Network (MUFON) conference in Washington, D.C., I observed that "we are finally able to push past the study of unidentified flying objects" and that "the coming debate will be over the motivations of the intelligence behind the phenomenon."[24]

Debates in the 1990s

In an effort to make research into abductions more systematic and to upgrade its quality, the growing abduction research community began to organize private conferences to share information. The first conference, held at Fairfield University in Connecticut in 1989, was restricted to an invited audience of thirty researchers, twelve of whom made presentations. The second conference, convened in 1991 by Budd Hopkins and me at Temple University in Philadelphia, had over fifty invited researchers. The third, and largest, conference was convened in 1992 by physicist David E. Pritchard at the Massachusetts Institute of Technology (MIT), with over eighty papers and presentations by researchers and abductees. Although the universities did not formally sponsor any of these conferences, they allowed their names and facilities to be associated with the subject, thereby adding a small bit of academic respectability to the research efforts.

At the Temple University conference in 1991, interested Las Vegas businessman Robert Bigelow provided funding for Hopkins and me to conduct a nationwide poll to ascertain the scope of the abduction phenomenon. The resulting survey of nearly six thousand individuals indicated that about 2 percent of the American people had undergone experiences similar to those abductees had undergone before they knew that they were abductees.[25] Both the poll's methodology and its results were hotly debated among abduction researchers.[26] But regardless of the specific numbers, it was obvious that the number of people who might have had abduction experiences was extraordinarily large. Thousands of people had contacted UFOs researchers with their suspicions that they might be involved with the phenomenon.[27]

In 1992 I published *Secret Life: Firsthand Accounts of UFO Abduction*, in which I outlined the typical procedures that abductees report during their abductions. I was able to create a typology of physical, mental, and emotional experiences. Like Hopkins and others, I found the abductee narratives to be convergent in their detail—everyone was saying the same thing regardless of who they were. The confluence in detail, when most of those details had never been published before, strongly militated against media or cultural contamination. My research pointed to the reproductive aspects of abductions, resulting in the birth of "hybrids," as being central to understanding the phenomenon. Even more important for research methodology, I identified physiological activities that the aliens allegedly conducted on abductees that resulted in the victims "seeing" neurologically generated images and mistaking them for objective reality. This made ascertaining the validity of memories even more complicated.[28]

In June 1992, at the MIT conference, physicist David Pritchard recommended that all the participants read *Secret Life*. At the five-day event, two opposing groups quickly emerged. One group (Hopkins, Haines, psychologist Stuart Appelle, psychiatric social worker John Carpenter, hypnotherapist Yvonne Smith, and me) was focused on developing more rigorous and systematic methods to decipher tangled material from hypnosis and conscious memories. These "Realists" stayed within the confines of "normal" reality and took a "hard-edge" view of the subject: beings from somewhere else were coming to earth to fulfill an unknown agenda of which the abduction of humans was central.[29]

The other, more "positively" oriented, group was more inclined to accept a wide range of nontraditional phenomena, which the Realists rejected. The second group argued that if abductions occurred exactly as people described them, then it was necessary to revise the definition of reality. The phenomenon represented a new paradigm—a different reality that could exist alongside normal reality. These researchers interpreted reports of "paranormal" and "supernatural" events as possible indications that abductees were "tapping into" a new reality. Astral travel, past lives, future lives, out-of-body experiences, religious appearances, and messages of spiritual enlightenment—all could be part of a "world" in which the aliens also dwelled. Who was to say, in this new universe, what was "reality" and what was not? Driving these beliefs was the tendency to accept the literal truthfulness of the abductees' narratives with less regard to the problems of memory recovery than the competing Realist group used. Harvard psychiatrist John Mack, psychologist and abductee Richard Boylan, Boston researcher Joseph Nyman, and others at the MIT conference adopted the attitude that abductions were harbingers of the onset of positively transformational aliens who had the best interests of humanity at heart.

The Positive-Realist debate from the MIT conference came to the fore in the mid-1990s. The Realists argued that the data supported the hypothesis that abductions are a reproductively oriented phenomenon in which humans are used to create hybrid children. Hopkins, Karla Turner (a professor of English at North Texas State University and an abductee), and I speculated that the end result of this program could be detrimental for humanity. The Realists thought not only that occult and metaphysical interpretations were unscientific and detrimental to UFO research but also that they obfuscated the possible danger underlying the abduction mystery.

The Positives, led by Mack, Sprinkle, Boylan, and abductee John Hunter Gray (professor of Indian studies at the University of North Dakota) thought the phenomenon was basically benign. The information they developed from their hypnosis sessions and interviews indicated that the aliens were here to stop the damage to our environment that humans had begun. Although the Positives also found most of the medical and neurological procedures that the Realists had uncovered, they downplayed these and argued that occult and metaphysical interpretations represented the best hope of understanding the phenomenon.

In 1994, two significant books in the debate were published. Karla Turner published *Taken: Inside the Alien Abduction Agenda,* in which she attempted a broad and detailed typology of abduction experiences; Turner began to feel that the aliens were ultimately our enemies.[30] The most important book was John Mack's *Abduction: Human Encounters with Aliens,* in which Mack suggested that abductees had tapped into a new reality that was not accessible through normal Western science and that we might not be able to understand alien motivation through conventional avenues of inquiry. Mack's view that, although some abductees suffered at their hands, the aliens' presence would ultimately benefit humankind found willing adherents in New Age and transformational circles.[31]

For the fiftieth anniversary of the surfacing of the UFO phenomenon, Hopkins and I spoke at the annual MUFON conference in 1997. In our papers we insisted that New Age ideas must be separated from the abduction phenomenon or researchers stood the risk of falling into an unscientific and sometimes spiritually cultist abyss.[32]

The Positives' New Age–style message seemed extreme and unbelievable to most researchers, but the Realists had evolved into a similar predicament. After years of research, in 1996 Budd Hopkins published his account of the Linda Cortile case. *Witnessed: The True Story of the Brooklyn Bridge Abductions* created controversy as Hopkins presented a complex case involving many direct and indirect witnesses (including an important world figure) to the abduction. Hopkins found that abductees were being profoundly manipulated even to the extent of aliens choosing abductee children to be friends with each other and, when they got older, sexual partners.

I published *The Threat* in 1998.[33] In it I attacked the Positive position as being based on unproven metaphysical assumptions and incompetent hypnosis. I warned that consciously recalled events could be very inaccurate and that hypnotists with specific New Age agendas could slant hypnotically recalled testimony to the hypnotists' beliefs.

The book went beyond methodology disputes. By the late 1990s I felt that I had learned enough about the abduction phenomenon to suggest reasons for specific alien procedures that abductees commonly described and linked these procedures to human neurological manipulation. I attempted the first anecdotal evidence–driven explanation of the abduction phenomenon, suggesting that, contrary to what had been assumed, the abduction phenomenon was not for the purpose of experimentation or study. Rather, it appeared to be a complex and systematic program of the production of hybrids for an eventual integration into human society. I discussed the hybrid phenomenon, concentrating on the role that adult hybrids play in abduction procedures. The evidence as I researched it had made my conclusions embarrassing to me, but I was nonetheless confident of the data.

Both Hopkins and I found a curious situation: the more we uncovered about the abduction phenomenon, the more it appeared to have a "plot." This "story line" made it seem less "alien" and therefore less bizarre. The less "alien" it became, the more human it appeared to be and, hence, the more science fiction–like. Thus, the uncovering of its alleged inner workings militated against its strangeness and had the effect of making it more difficult to believe both for the public and for other UFO researchers because of its seeming links to popular culture.

As researchers uncovered the outlines of the abduction experience, they also began to realize that "screen memories" that masked alleged abduction activity were more extensive than they had realized. They found that occupant "inspections" of witnesses, "car chases," "dematerializations," being "transfixed" by a UFO, and other types of previously puzzling UFO behavior were artifacts of memory fragments that could be indications of abduction activity. Even saying that they had "pulled over to the side of the road to get a better look" at a UFO might sometimes mask an abduction event. Therefore, the prevalence of abduction activity might be even greater than they had thought. But for many UFO researchers, the large volume of possible abduction activity seemed ridiculous. Thus, while the abduction researchers thought they were unraveling the magnitude of abduction experiences, the net effect of their efforts was to make it even more difficult for others to acknowledge the phenomenon's verisimilitude.

Searching for an Acceptable Methodology

Much of the abduction controversy involved searching for the proper methodology for investigation. From the beginning, researchers found the abduction claims extraordinarily difficult to investigate. Most abductees forgot what happened to them within seconds of the experience. While many abductees could remember bits and pieces of an event, few remembered a substantial amount, and facilitating memory became the goal of the researcher.

Hypnosis emerged as the most appropriate methodology for this task. Yet hypnosis itself presented considerable problems: leading questions, suggestibility and vulnerability of the abductees, and preconceived notions by both researcher and abductee. Furthermore, under hypnosis, abductees reported events that seemed nonsensical, such as passing through closed windows and solid walls into UFOs.

Moreover, there was no systematic training or certification for abduction hypnotists; anyone could be a researcher or hypnotist by simply proclaiming it. There was a tremendous knowledge gap: on the one hand, trained hypnotists did not know enough about the abduction phenomenon to elicit "clean data" from the abductees; on the other hand, UFO and abduction researchers did not know enough about hypnosis to collect reliable information from the abductees.

In 1992, in an effort to provide improved hypnosis in abductions, Hopkins and I published a fairly rigorous guide aimed at the growing number of hypnotists and therapists who were encountering abductees and did not know how to proceed with them. At the same time, John Carpenter refined a questioning technique calculated to ascertain the degree of suggestibility of abductees in hypnosis.[34] Hopkins, Carpenter, and I (and on one occasion John Mack) delivered a series of free workshops to members of the therapeutic community, speaking to over five hundred psychiatrists, psychologists, and social workers nationwide about the proper methodology for abduction hypnosis, unique problems in therapy for abductees, and the history and cultural background of the UFO and abduction phenomenon. This program helped therapists form a loose network of sympathetic researchers to whom abductees could turn when they needed help.[35]

Also in 1992, following the conference at MIT, Stuart Appelle from the psychology department at SUNY-Brockport, private practice physician David Gotlib, Mark Rodeghier of the Center for UFO Studies, and abductee Georgia Flamburis began work on a code of ethics for abduction researchers. Aimed at regularizing the protocols for hypnosis, the ethics code was completed in 1993 and was the first attempt to bring medical ethics to abduction research.[36]

But developing ethical guidelines and protocols was only one of the difficulties that beset abduction researchers. Even under the best and most controlled of circumstances, human memory was often untrustworthy, and recovering memory through hypnosis was suspect. For example, when abductees described communication with occupants, it was almost always accomplished telepathically; they said they received "impressions" that their minds automatically converted to words. How did a researcher separate alien telepathic communication from an abductee's own inner thoughts? It was easy to mistake dissociative "channeled" information, emanating from the abductee's mind, for "authentic" communication from the aliens.

For me, the issue of improper methodology was the most important problem facing abduction research. It had created the Positive-Realist debate. In 1989 Bullard had studied hypnotically retrieved abductee testimony and consciously recalled testimony and found that certain core events were virtually the same no matter how or by whom the memories were retrieved.[37] In *The Threat* I devoted a chapter to hypnosis problems and abuses, criticizing some abduction researchers for employing faulty hypnotic regressions and accepting confabulated and channeled material as indicative of objective reality.[38]

Debunkers and the Backlash

As the abduction phenomenon became more visible in both UFO research and the media, critics became more vocal. The most strident critic was Philip J. Klass, a member of the skeptical Committee for the Scientific Investigation of Claims of the Paranormal and a confirmed debunker who had written three books about the deficiencies of UFO researchers. Klass claimed that abductees were "little people" who wanted to lead glamorous lives and were lying about their experiences to do so. He also sounded a theme that would be taken up by many other critics: researchers were incompetent in the use of hypnosis and led subjects into bogus abduction fantasies.[39]

Debunking theories expanded throughout the 1990s: millenniumism came after false memory syndrome, which supplanted sexual abuse screen memories, which displaced fantasy-prone personalities, which supplanted multiple personality disorder, which existed with myth and folklore, which supplanted celebrity seekers, which supplanted brain disorders, and so forth. The list was long. It included gullibility, lying, hallucination, waking dreams, sleep paralysis, hypnagogic and hypnopompic experiences, birth trauma, the will to believe, charlatans, psychogenic fugue state, popular culture and media influences, and many more. Carl Sagan opted for the myth and folklore explanation. Modern Language Association president Elaine Showalter said abductions were part of "epidemic hysteria," like Gulf War syndrome or chronic fatigue syndrome. Frederick Crews attributed the abduction phenomenon to researchers' desire to make money writing books, the coming millennium, and incompetent hypnosis.[40] These explanations would fade from popularity only to be rekindled by other critics unaware that they had already been debated and found wanting. Researchers were constantly engaged in battling these explanations, but the onslaught was overwhelming.[41]

The general assumption, widely held by debunkers, was that all abduction stories were psychologically generated; it made little difference how one arrived at that conclusion, and finding evidence that demonstrated this obvious and fundamental fact was unnecessary. Thus, engaging with the data on a serious, scholarly level was a waste of time. Instead, they searched for the specific mental states that caused the delusions and fantasies.

Addressing this "assumption" problem, political scientist and cultural analyst Jodi Dean found that the paucity of knowledge about the abduction phenomenon was directly related to the cultural gestalt of the high-tech cyberspace-dominated world in which it was exceptionally difficult to separate signal from noise in an ever-widening menu of incomprehensible events intruding upon daily lives.[42] Her neutral analysis of the cultural effects of abductions and alien icons drew fire from debunkers.[43]

More serious critics, however, hit hard at the problems of hypnosis, researcher and abductee expectations, and the role of culture in determining narratives. The debate between the Positives and the Realists was seen as a product of both sides ignoring evidence that tended to contradict what the researchers wanted to hear. Thus, not only was the abduction narrative psychologically induced through hypnosis or culture, but critics charged that the researchers shaped the nature of that narrative by emphasizing material that they deemed important and discarding material they thought was unimportant.

To counter the critics, researchers maintained that the abductees said what they remembered and the information derived from them was wholly theirs. They also maintained the investigators were not "holding back" material that might either put the lie to the direction in which they wanted the narratives to go or even disconfirm the entire abduction story. In fact, many of the Realists disliked intensely or were very disturbed by the abductees' testimony and published their accounts in spite of their own aversion to the material. Furthermore, they countered that abductees often remembered abductions without hypnosis; the abductions seemed nonidiosyncratic and divorced from the abductees' normal lives, culture, and upbringing; independent witnesses would sometimes confirm their abductions; abductees were physically missing from their normal environments during their alleged abductions; and abductees had been left with physical sequelae from the events. In addition, they said that abductees from around the country had given precise, detailed information about procedures and events during abductions that had never been made public beforehand.

Abductions in the Marketplace

At the same time that Hopkins's *Intruders* was published in 1987, horror writer Whitley Strieber's *Communion* was released. His account of fear and trauma while being abducted by small gray beings propelled his book to the *New York Times* best-seller list, where it stayed for eight months. Strieber also told his story on hundreds of radio and television shows. It soon became evident that the illustration on the cover of his book—an alien head by artist Ted Jacobs—was as unsettling and startling as the account in the book itself. The large head with the now characteristic staring alien eyes, considered by most abductees to be anatomically incorrect, triggered memories that impelled thousands of people who thought they might be abductees to seek advice and help from abduction researchers.

Strieber's book on his personal, and often unique, experiences established him as a media icon for the abduction phenomenon. In 1987 he and Hopkins appeared on a great number of local and national television and radio programs in connection with the publication of their two books. By the end of the year, the abduction phenomenon had become a "media darling." Researchers and abductees made the rounds of the talk and tabloid news magazine shows. Abductions and UFO themes were featured on scores of television shows from *The X-Files* to *The Simpsons.* Some programs tried a mixture of fiction and authenticity like the 1994 CBS miniseries *Intruders,* which was roughly based on Hopkins's book. But for most, reality was not a high priority. In 1998 the UPN network presented a pseudo-documentary about a family beset by menacing aliens; the program gave the false impression of being a record of actual events. A nationally televised film purporting to depict an alien's autopsy caused embarrassment to serious abduction researchers who were forced to spend time and effort combating what they considered to be a clever hoax.

Corporate America also discovered UFOs and abductions. In a barrage of advertisements in the 1990s, UFOs and abductions were used to sell scores of products from automobiles to guitar picks. Their entrance into the mainstream advertising and popular culture suggested that the media—not science—were their natural arena. Media co-optation of the abduction phenomenon had the effect of "commoditizing" it and thus further marginalizing it from the mainstream scientific and academic communities. It was in danger of being seen as just another sensation that competed with other media fads of the period, thereby further reducing its claim to scientific legitimacy.[44]

Century's End: Pressures and Solutions

By century's end, researchers had uncovered an enormous amount of consistent information about abductions and abductees. UFO organizations around the world began to turn their attention to the abduction phenomenon in their own countries. They, as had their American counterparts, found a bizarre phenomenon not amenable to easy explanations. The abduction phenomenon contained an internal integrity and depth of complexity that stubbornly defied attempts to redefine it as something other than what abductees and their researchers suggested it was, although debates about its meaning, purposes, and very existence still continued.

By 2000, abduction research was in a state of both increasing clarity and increasing confusion. Proponents felt that significant progress had been made in deciphering the UFO phenomenon, and yet the entire phenomenon had become more difficult to accept. Moreover, the pressure to develop better data and more "proof" was intense, as was the need to find a reliable and standard methodology for memory retrieval. Separating fact from fiction in the narratives was still a serious and difficult problem.

The abduction phenomenon seemed on its face to be ridiculous, impossible, and a violation of scientific laws. It had taken researchers to areas within the realm of the fantastic where they did not want to go. Significantly, however, at century's end the debate within the abduction research community had been largely reframed beyond methodology. No longer were the central questions "Are they here?" or "Are they abducting people?" The questions now being asked were "What are they doing, and why are they doing it?" This placed the UFO phenomenon in an entirely different context, one that researchers hoped would finally supply answers, for better or for worse.

Chapter Eight

Hypnosis and the Investigation of UFO Abduction Accounts

Budd Hopkins

Hypnosis is a relaxation process perhaps as old as "temple sleep," an ancient rite of healing, and it can be defined most simply as an altered state of consciousness.[1] The psychiatrist Milton Erickson, perhaps its best-known American practitioner, wrote that "hypnosis . . . is a loss of the multiplicity of the foci of attention. It is a lack of response to irrelevant external stimuli."[2]

However, since the time of Mesmer, hypnosis has been presented as everything from a therapeutic panacea, to a virtually flawless method of recovering memory, to a meaningless, indefinable construct. Common sense tells us that hypnosis is none of these, but because of its many hyperbolic proponents and detractors, it has come to be viewed by the scientific community with a great deal of uncomfortable suspicion. And as if that were not enough, this "suspicious" technique has been employed frequently since 1964 by UFO abduction researchers who have found it extremely useful in their investigations. It should not be surprising, then, that conservative scientists and UFO skeptics have recently seized upon hypnosis as a bludgeon with which to attack the validity of any, if not all, abduction reports, whether or not hypnosis had been used in the first place.[3]

A brief recounting of the history of the UFO phenomenon is necessary to place UFO abduction accounts in context. In the twentieth century, unidentified flying objects were first reported with consistency and frequency, particularly during the last two years of World War II, by Allied airmen who described odd lights or circular, metallic craft accompanying their planes. The pilots' fears that these phenomena were enemy secret weapons eventually began to dissipate because the objects failed to carry out any aggressive action. Also, captured German pilots reported the same curious phenomena near their aircraft and assumed that they were Allied.

After the war, objects that were nicknamed "ghost rockets" were sighted frequently over Scandinavian countries. These objects, which apparently never crashed, were thought to be of Russian origin, perhaps test vehicles built by captured German rocket scientists.[4]

In 1947 the first great UFO wave occurred in the United States: accounts of metallic-appearing disks by daylight and erratically moving lights by night. A Gallup poll, published in August 1947, asked respondents what they thought lay behind the hundreds of recent "flying saucer" sightings that had been widely reported in the press.[5] The results are extremely important: 33 percent either said they did not know or gave no answer; 29 percent cited imagination, optical illusion, mirage, and so on; 15 percent believed UFOs were American secret weapons; 10 percent ascribed them to hoaxes; 3 percent cited weather forecasting devices; and 1 percent cited Russian secret weapons. According to Gallup, the idea that "flying saucers" might be of extraterrestrial origin did not register measurably among the responses.

The significance of this early history of the UFO phenomenon establishes beyond any doubt that the sightings themselves—the consistent reports of odd visible phenomena—*precede* any theory about their possible extraterrestrial origin. No exotic psychosocial mechanism was involved. "Flying saucers" arrived in our skies, not our imaginations.

In later years, as civilian organizations such as the National Investigations Committee on Aerial Phenomena (NICAP) began looking into UFO sightings, the leading investigators continued to hold an extremely narrow view of these craft. Though they accepted the extraterrestrial hypothesis as likely, they routinely rejected—at first—any case material that included reports of UFO *occupants*.

These reports, they believed, must be the result of hysteria, confabulation, and deliberate hoaxes.[6] Thus, for nearly two decades after the first 1947 wave, any report of a UFO *abduction* would have been completely beyond the pale, even among those who took the UFO phenomenon seriously.

It is outside the scope of this chapter to recount the case reports and subsequent investigations that led researchers to rethink their earlier proscriptions against UFO occupant accounts and, later, the abduction phenomenon.[7] It is sufficient to point out that the evidence presented by the results of the 1947 Gallup poll, the view of Allied pilots during World War II, and the narrow view of the phenomenon held by those who took the sighting reports seriously all support one conclusion: the UFO phenomenon originated as a series of mysterious, highly consistent sightings *unconnected* with the extraterrestrial hypothesis, occupant reports, and later abduction accounts. Thus, any of the various psychosocial explanations of the origin of the UFO phenomenon as a purely imaginary "archetypal image," a modern version of older myths, or a replacement for outmoded traditional religions must be rejected on historical grounds.[8]

The Betty and Barney Hill encounter, the first abduction report to come to national attention, took place in 1961 but was not made public until 1966.[9] This case is also important in that it marked the first use of hypnosis in an abduction investigation. The psychiatrist who conducted the hypnosis sessions, Benjamin Simon, was exploring the Hills' memories primarily to treat what would now be called symptoms of post-traumatic stress disorder (PTSD) in both witnesses. Although his goal was therapeutic rather than investigative, he was also aware that there was a potentially significant period of time at the center of the Hills' UFO sighting experience that they could not consciously recall. Ultimately, Simon was struck by the Hills' similarly detailed, hypnotically retrieved accounts of their "missing time" experiences—in which they vividly recalled being taken into a landed UFO and examined by alien beings—and by the emotional force of their abreactions during hypnosis.[10]

History has assigned the Hill case a range of important functions, one of which is that of a control in weighing the validity of subsequent hypotheses regarding the etiology of abduction accounts. For example, the Hill case bears upon one popular theory that has been widely but uncritically accepted by many skeptics: the idea that such accounts have been implanted under hypnosis, consciously or unconsciously, by manipulative practitioners who "believe in" the reality of such events. Simon, who hypnotized the Hills, was avowedly *skeptical* about the reality of the Hills' abduction recollections.[11] Yet the Hills stubbornly held to their interlocking, hypnotically recovered accounts despite Simon's suggestions at the end of treatment that their memories could not be literally true. It can therefore be concluded that the bias of the hypnotist had nothing to do with the content of their hypnotic recall.

During my first seven years of investigation of abduction reports, before I began using hypnosis myself, a number of therapists carried out hypnotic regressions upon those individuals whose abduction accounts I was looking into. All of these therapists—Dr. Robert Naiman, Dr. Aphrodite Clamar, and Dr. Girard Franklin, among others—were initially very skeptical about the reality of the abduction phenomenon and assumed, like Dr. Simon, that such bizarre recollections must have psychological etiologies. But again, as with Dr. Simon, their skeptical biases had virtually no effect upon the abduction memories and their surprising consistencies that emerged under hypnosis.[12]

"The most appropriate conclusion that can be drawn from the available evidence is that hypnosis *does not* reliably produce more false memories than are produced in a variety of nonhypnotic situations in which misleading information is conveyed to participants."[13] This statement by Steven Lynn and Irving Kirsch— undoubtedly surprising to those who see hypnosis as a fount of false memories—is supported by the conclusions of a great many recent experiments.[14]

Many abduction accounts—from 25 to 30 percent—are remembered without the use of hypnosis, and in virtually all the other documented cases are at least partially accessible through normal recall.[15] Thus, in light óf the experimental results quoted previously, one might be tempted to suggest that the hypnotically retrieved abduction accounts—70 to 75 percent of the total—are *more* reliable than the smaller number that are recalled without hypnosis.

These experimental findings about the lack of reliability of hypnosis to produce false memories do not, of course, validate the "truthfulness" of hypnotically recollected UFO abduction memories. They do, however, undermine theories about the ease with which hypnotists can inculcate false memories in their subjects. After these laboratory experiments, the Simon precedent in the Hill case, and the later, similar experience of many other hypnotherapists, skeptics have nothing to present in support of the "hypnotist implantation" theory other than their indefensible belief that it *must* be true.[16]

After decades of research and controversy, several things can now be said with relative certainty, both about the abduction phenomenon and about the process of hypnosis:

1. There exist *two* clearly opposed literatures on the efficacy of hypnosis: the experimental and the clinical. The experimental literature is produced by academic psychologists in neutral—usually university—settings and largely discounts the usefulness of hypnosis. Although there are a few exceptions, so far the results of this experimentally controlled work on hypnosis and memory contradict the idea that when hypnosis is utilized, more—and more accurate—information can be retrieved than through normal recall.[17] This finding is often cited by critics of the use of hypnosis in abduction research.

2. Most of these experiments about the accuracy of hypnotic recall involve the memorization of sequences of words, numbers, names, images, and so on,* and thus have little or nothing to do with the hypnotic retrieval of strongly emotional or even traumatic personal memories such as UFO abduction accounts.[18]

3. A second, quite different literature has been produced by practicing clinicians, police officers, and other investigators. This extensive case material demonstrates, through anecdotal accounts involving emotionally involved or traumatized subjects, the usefulness of hypnosis in certain clinical and forensic settings.[19] Traumatized crime vic-

---

*Ethical concerns naturally prevent the use of experiments in the accuracy of hypnotic recall in which a subject might be forced to endure a (staged) traumatic incident—for example, an attempted mugging by an actor wielding a pistol that "misfires." If such an experiment were possible, however, one could measure the accuracy of the subjects' recollections under hypnosis, findings that would then—truly—bear on the use of hypnosis in UFO research.

tims have, under hypnosis, successfully remembered previously repressed details such as a license plate number or a mugger's clothing.

In the *Journal of Clinical and Experimental Hypnosis*, Kroger and Douce conclude that "hypnosis was of value in providing investigative direction, and, in the [twenty-three] cases described, has led to the solution of major crimes."[20] Jane E. Brody, in a *New York Times* article of 4 October 1980, reminds us of one famous case: "The rescue of twenty-six schoolchildren kidnapped at gunpoint from a school bus in Chowchilla, California, in 1976 was facilitated by hypnosis of the bus driver, who then recalled enough of a license plate number to enable police to find the getaway van."

4. Several prominent UFO investigators who use hypnosis competently to aid in the subject's recall routinely employ the tactic of the "false lead" as a test of the subject's suggestibility or desire to confabulate.* In these researchers' experience, the "abductee" population forcefully resists such attempts, insisting upon the accuracy of their recall, despite the hypnotists' deliberate suggestions.[21]

As an example of a false lead, if a hypnotized subject is describing the "examination room" during an alleged abduction, the hypnotist can ask a disarmingly innocent question such as: "From where you are standing, are you able to see the legs of the examination table?" Although this fact is generally unknown outside of the research community, there are virtually no reports of UFO examination tables with legs; they are described as being either pedestal tables, solid blocks, or floating flat surfaces. Although I have used it many times along with scores of other false leads, I have never yet had a subject confabulate about seeing the legs on the examination table. Thus this seemingly innocuous question about seeing table legs is effective at discerning suggestibility.

With regard to the UFO abduction phenomenon itself, a number of recent findings also merit general agreement.

1. As I have pointed out previously, because of the conscious recollection of many abduction experiences, UFO abduction reports

---

*This same "false lead" tactic routinely employed during hypnosis by UFO investigators was also used by Richard Ofshe to expose the psychodynamics of false memory and confabulation in the well-known case of Paul Ingram of Olympia, Washington (R. Ofshe and E. Watters, *Making Monsters: False Memories, Psychotherapy, and Sexual Hysteria* (New York: Scribner, 1994).

stand independent of the use of hypnosis. For example, the second abduction case to become widely known in the United States involved two men, Charles Hickson and Calvin Parker, in Pascagoula, Mississippi, in 1973, and was recalled prior to hypnosis.[22]

2. In the experience of veteran abduction investigators, most individuals reporting UFO abductions accept the reality of their own recollections only reluctantly and with no sense of personal gratification.[23] This is neither a club to which its members want to belong nor a passionately held, doubt-free belief system.

3. Further, fewer than 5 percent of those who recall such experiences are willing to come forward and publicly discuss their recollections with representatives of the media. Thus, for more than 95 percent of this population, the quest for publicity or monetary gain cannot be shown to be a factor in the etiology of their abduction accounts.[24]

In summary:

- The UFO abduction phenomenon is not an artifact of hypnosis.
- Contrary to popular skeptical belief, experimental evidence demonstrates that hypnosis is *less* effective than non-hypnotic methods in planting false memories.
- Through the device of the "false lead," UFO investigators have demonstrated that subjects reporting abduction experiences virtually always strongly resist such attempts.
- There is no clinical evidence suggesting that hypnosis is ineffective in the recollection of previously repressed *traumatic* or *emotionally laden* memories, and much experimental evidence supporting its efficacy in such cases.
- Individuals who recall UFO abduction experiences—with or without significant use of hypnosis—consistently show neither a subsequent sense of gratification nor a desire for further publicity. Thus these two alleged motives for confabulation and/ or deliberate invention cannot be considered relevant to any but a tiny minority of abduction reports.

One of the most characteristic logical and procedural errors that skeptical writers commit with regard to UFO abduction accounts has to do with their habit of focusing on the content of *hypnotic* recall rather than on the subjects' *conscious* recollections prior to any hypnosis.* As I have pointed out in our control example, what brought Betty and Barney Hill to Benjamin Simon was the undeniable presence of disturbing, PTSD-like symptoms that emerged only after their UFO sighting, and a period of "missing time" at the center of their UFO encounter. Neither Betty nor Barney Hill was able to recall what happened between their observation of the hovering windowed craft in the woods and their next moment of conscious recollection, when they found themselves in their moving automobile about thirty-five miles down the main highway. For everyone involved in the case, including Simon, there was an apparently inexplicable gap in their recall.

Subsequently, in later cases, UFO investigators have used hypnosis because of circumstances similar to those Simon faced in the Hill case: the endeavor to alleviate symptoms such as anxiety, sleep disturbance, and PTSD-like symptoms and the attempt to discover what may have transpired during the troubling "missing time" periods. Without presenting symptoms and/or "missing time" periods similar to those of the Hills, most reputable UFO investigators do not employ hypnosis.

A few examples from my files will demonstrate the kinds of circumstances that eventually led me to employ hypnosis:

1. In October 1971 several members of a family of six, along with a friend, sight a hovering circular craft outside their home during the late afternoon. At the beginning of this incident, two family members are watching TV. The next thing the seven people know is that several of them are now in different locations within the house, at least two are in a state of hysterical fear, the hovering craft has disappeared, and several hours have passed, as a later program on TV immediately demonstrates. One young woman inexplicably finds herself hiding at the back of a bedroom closet, and shortly thereafter another family member begins sleeping with a baseball bat next to his bed. Several other family members also exhibit symptoms of PTSD.

2. In a similar case in New Jersey, three men and two women had gathered at one couple's house for a relaxed social evening in

---

*Possibly this is a tactical decision based on the perceived vulnerability of hypnosis as opposed to the greater challenge represented by the somewhat less bizarre *consciously recalled* material, and the fact that these recollections are often supported by independent witnesses and physical evidence.

March 1993. Again an unidentified craft is sighted, a degree of extreme confusion results, followed by a period of missing time. All five participants regain conscious awareness in odd locations: one man finds himself lying on the floor in the basement. Two of the witnesses remember being physically paralyzed while sitting at the dinner table, and both remember the presence of small, gray alien beings within their home. All are thoroughly frightened, and one of the men, a physician, is distraught for weeks afterward, with symptoms of PTSD.

3. In December 1990 a young man, his fiancée, and a female friend are driving at night from the Epcot Center to Boca Raton, Florida, a roughly three-hour drive. When they enter the Florida Turnpike, they place their toll ticket, along with the few dollars that will be due at the Boca Raton exit, conveniently on the top of the dashboard. At some point they suddenly feel disoriented and lost, and the young man suffers from waves of nausea. To their shock, they realize they are now on the outskirts of Boca Raton, no longer on the turnpike—furthermore, their ticket and cash are still on the dashboard. They understand that there is no way they could have exited the turnpike without remembering doing so, surrendering their ticket, and handing over the toll money for the trip. Other disturbing memories subsequently surface, leading the young man to suspect a UFO had been involved in the mystery.

I cite these accounts to show how the consciously recalled, anomalous circumstances of their shared experiences remain untouched by skeptical attacks on the process of hypnosis. In all three of these cases there is, as in the Hill case, the conscious recollection of a UFO, the awareness of a period of missing time with disturbing, fragmentary memories, and subsequent PTSD symptoms. The three cases involve a total of fifteen people who remember the same initial circumstances and "missing time" period and who exhibit the same unusual behavior for days, or even weeks or months, afterward. I was able to extensively interview thirteen of these fifteen witnesses.

If I were to say that under hypnosis a number of these individuals recall being taken into a landed or hovering UFO where they were then undressed and examined by alien crew members, hard-line skeptics would reply that those recollections are not valid because hypnosis is not reliable; ergo, there is no evidence that they were actually abducted. But let us move the discussion away from the hypnosis controversy and back to the beginning, and ask what *did* happen to cause such drastic, measurable, and lasting confusion in the lives of these fifteen people? What conventional explanations can comfortably account for such consciously recalled, mutually corroborated, but logically "impossible" details as the observation of UFOs and/or alien beings? What caused the sudden appearance of acute anxiety symptoms in so many lives?

Since these mysteries, in all their drama and complexity, *precede* any use of hypnosis, the issue of its validity is irrelevant.

Critics are fond of remarking that there should be corroborating outside evidence to support material that is recovered hypnotically. I agree and will go even further: there should be corroborating evidence to support nonhypnotic testimony, too, whether we are dealing with police work, clinical hypnotherapy, or UFO abduction accounts. I will therefore present several categories of evidence that support the physical reality of specific abduction cases. Familiarity with at least some of these complex cases is essential to an understanding of the reasons many UFO investigators regard abductions as actual, rather than "imaginal," events.

Eyewitness Testimony

Although this kind of confirmation is quite rare, as a result of an extensive, years-long investigation of the 1989 Linda Cortile abduction case, I obtained testimony from four eyewitnesses who, at two different locations, saw Cortile and three small alien figures float out of a twelfth-floor apartment window and then rise up into a hovering UFO.[25] Two other witnesses at separate locations saw the circular craft, though not the small floating figures. Another witness, at yet another location, saw the courtyard of Cortile's apartment building lit by an unusual light shining down from above at a time consistent with the other reports.

In the 1975 Travis Walton abduction case, six tree cutters, moments before driving away from the scene in panic, saw a blue bolt of light from a hovering UFO hit Walton and lift him a few feet above the ground.[26] When they returned minutes later to search for their companion, he had disappeared. Five days later he reappeared, dehydrated and disoriented, consciously recalling a UFO abduction. The results of a series of polygraph tests showed that none of the witnesses revealed any signs of deception. Nevertheless, certain debunkers, insisting that Walton and at least seven other people must have perpetrated an elaborate hoax, presented a mélange of theories and imagined motives but absolutely no evidence to support their hypothesis.[27] Another round of polygraph tests administered twenty years after the original event again found that Walton and the original witnesses showed no signs of deception.

Physical Marks on Abductees' Bodies

UFO investigators have encountered many kinds of scars, fresh lesions, bruises, and other anomalous marks on the persons of those reporting UFO abductions. The most common type—a "scoop mark" —is a small round or oval depression that looks as if it might be the result of the removal of a flesh sample. Scoop marks range from roughly one to two centimeters in diameter and from two to five millimeters in depth, and they generally appear on the subject's leg or arm. Over the years I have seen dozens of such strikingly similar marks and have photographed many of them.

The second type of lesion is a straight-line cut, from one to nine centimeters in length, and is also often found on the subject's arm or leg. As with scoop marks, one can only speculate about the purpose of such incisions. I have also seen scores of these marks, some of which can be quite disfiguring.

There are many compelling reasons why investigators often associate such injuries with abduction experiences. First, the subject usually does not consciously remember what caused the wound— only its sudden appearance after a partially recalled UFO encounter of some kind. As an example, on 17 April 1989 a North Carolina woman left her bed to get a drink of water and, after a period of "missing time," found herself coming to conscious awareness on the floor of her kitchen.[28] She remembered "hands" pressing her down. Frightened and confused, she returned to bed, and in the morning her guest noticed a fresh 3.5-inch incision near the woman's right shoulder blade. The cut was surrounded with a wide bruise. There was no trace of blood on her skin, her nightgown, the sheets or pillowcases, nor upon the floor. Two days later her physician pronounced the wound a "surgical incision" and could not believe that she had not recalled receiving it. (Predictably, a debunker later theorized that it must have been self-inflicted, even though stabbing oneself in the back probably requires more dexterity than this individual possesses.)

Physical Traces on the Ground

In my book *Intruders* I published photographs and a laboratory analysis of an eight-foot-diameter circle of dead grass and pale, desiccated soil that Kathie Davis believed was the result of a UFO landing in the abduction experience she recalled.[29] Extending outward from this affected area was a three-foot-wide, forty-nine-foot-long straight swath of similarly desiccated soil that ended in an almost geometrically perfect arc. The unaffected surrounding area was quite dark and moist from recent rainstorms. Over the next several years the grass slowly grew from the perimeter inward, gradually breaking down the apparently heat-altered, rocklike soil. In the winter the snow melted more quickly over the dehydrated, hardened material than over the surrounding unaffected areas.

In the 1971 Delphos, Kansas, case, a similar alleged UFO landing area—a doughnut-shaped hollow ring—was described by newspaper reporter Thaddia Smith as follows: "The circle was still very distinct . . . the soil was dry and crusted. The circle or ring was approximately eight feet across, the [unaffected] center and outside area were still muddy from recent rains. The area of the ring that was dry was . . . very light in color. The object had crushed a dead tree to the ground . . . and from its appearance had broken a limb of a live tree when it landed."[30]

Investigator Ted Phillips has compiled over two thousand such reports of the apparent physical effects of landed UFOs upon the immediate environment.[31] The famous 1981 Trans-en-Provence UFO landing report was investigated thoroughly by GEPAN, a scientific subcommittee of the French version of NASA.[32] In a closely reasoned, sixty-six-page report, the group found that something extraordinary, possibly technological, had interacted with the soil and plants.

Photographic Evidence

Over the decades, scores of photographs, videotapes, and film seg-
ments showing unknown objects in the sky—flying or standing
still—have been studied by scientists and trained photo analysts
such as optical physicist Bruce Maccabee. Although in this area
there admittedly are many hoaxes, there also are many photographs, films, and videotapes consistent with witness descriptions
of the large, unknown craft they claim to have seen, photographed,
and deemed authentic after thorough examination by scientists and
photo analysts.[33]

To summarize, hundreds upon hundreds of alleged UFO abduction recollections are supported by corroborating and confluent
evidence of various kinds: eyewitness testimony; a repeated pattern of physical scars and lesions that suddenly appear upon the
bodies of subjects reporting abductions; similar effects on the soil
and vegetation at the site of alleged UFO landings associated with
abduction accounts; and photographs, videotapes, and films of
UFOs that establish the physical reality of the alleged abduction
vehicles.

One of the most frustrating obstacles to the intelligent discussion of
the UFO abduction phenomenon—one that precedes any talk of
hypnosis—is the fact that most experimental and many clinical psychologists show a nearly complete lack of knowledge of the subject.
For example, psychologists Michael Ross and Ian Newby make the
following assertion: "There is no physical evidence that the abduction episodes occurred; the lack of films, pictures or telltale marks
on individuals or the landscape obviates the possibility of an external reality check."[34] This is not a casual, offhand remark, where its
naïveté might be excusable; rather, it appears in their contribution
to *Psychological Inquiry*. Although Ross and Newby—along with two
dozen other academics and clinicians—were making what they believed to be an intelligent contribution to this special abduction issue
of *Psychological Inquiry*, their ill-informed comment about the lack
of corroborating evidence is sadly representative of most of their
colleagues. The reference list at the end of the article is one of three
in the journal that does not include a single book or article present-

ing abduction case material. Believing that the UFO abduction phenomenon is, on its face, "impossible," these authors seem to feel no need either to interview subjects claiming abduction experiences or to familiarize themselves with the abduction literature. Had they bothered to do either, they would not have made such an egregious factual error. Thus, with little or no information about the physical evidence supporting the reality of UFO abductions, they were apparently content merely to cite various comfortable psychosocial etiologies in order to believe they have solved the mystery.

Further, it should always be remembered that any evidence that supports the physical reality of large, maneuvering, intelligently controlled craft of unknown origin—the UFOs themselves—opens the door to the *possibility* of the UFO abduction phenomenon. If such UFOs exist, one cannot reject the possibility of UFO abductions.

Unfortunately, the limitations of this chapter preclude the discussion of the vast body of evidence supporting the physical reality of UFOs (in addition to the evidence previously cited in support of UFO abductions) beyond mentioning the hundreds of cases in which UFOs are seen visually and simultaneously on radar; the sighting reports by highly trained astronauts like Gordon Cooper, James McDivitt, and Deke Slayton; by astronomers such as Clyde Tombaugh, the discoverer of Pluto; and by hundreds of airline pilots and air traffic controllers over the past fifty years.[35] Any psychosocial explanation of the abduction phenomenon must also consider this basic material.

Against this background, we must now ask if there is any evidence that specifically supports the validity of *hypnotic recall* in UFO abduction cases. The answer is a very firm yes, and that evidence appears in several areas.

Congruence of Details from Account to Account

Because of the publication of books and articles and the broadcast of TV documentaries on the phenomenon, some basic details from UFO abduction accounts may be widely known by the public. This was not always so, however. For decades UFO investigators were struck by the similarity of highly specific details that emerged from the hypnotically recalled accounts of individuals who had never met and who were ignorant of the specific details of the abduction scenario.[36]

As an example of such material, I have gathered from subjects recalling abduction experiences a collection of forty samples of what seem to be an "alien" notational system. Thirty of these sets were elicited from people under hypnosis while ten were recalled normally; there are no measurable differences between the two sets.

I have shown one or two of these "notational" sets to three different individuals immediately after they made their own drawings of the symbols they recalled. So strong is the resemblance of these sets, and so shocked have been the subjects by what they perceived as a highly unwelcome confirmation of their experiences, that in all three cases they burst into tears.

It should be mentioned that none of this material has ever been published. It is far too valuable an aid in checking the veracity of an individual's account to lose through reproduction in a book or article.*

As a counterpart to the large number of similarities from various individuals reporting UFO abduction experiences, there is a second pattern of significant details that are *never* reported. These are details that one might expect to hear if abduction accounts are influenced by popular culture: *The X-Files*, films like the *Star Wars* trilogy, *Independence Day*, and so on. Despite the laser weapons and ray guns and similar ubiquitous military staples of cinema science fiction, no "abductee" with whom I have ever worked has described such armaments as part of the alien presence. Abductees also do not describe UFOs as having lounge areas, kitchen facilities, toilets, or a variety of furniture other than consoles, examination tables, and seats. They never describe UFO occupants as ingesting food or water,

---

*A psychologist at an eastern university with whom I have shared this material has devised and will soon implement an experiment in which students are asked to invent a series of "extraterrestrial symbols." This experiment will act as a control to discover what a random sample of individuals might invent, and how close their symbols are to those retrieved from subjects reporting abduction experiences.

and in my extensive experience, every attempt to lead a subject under hypnosis into confabulating such features has failed.

One familiar staple of earthly physical examinations involves the monitoring of the cardiovascular system. Stethoscopes, blood pressure gauges, and electrocardiogram machines are familiar to most of us, and yet in my experience *no abductee has ever described alien interest in the human heart* during the onboard physical examination. In contrast to this apparent lack of concern about the human heart, there is a remarkable consistency in the reports of alien interest in the reproductive system, the nervous system, the head, and certain other areas of the body. These highly consistent reports of alien curiosity about—and disinterest in—specific parts of the human anatomy argue strongly against fantasy and confabulation. If "alien physical examinations" were the product of the human imagination, we would expect to find an enormous range of quasi-medical procedures involving virtually every part of the body, including, of course, the human heart.

Similar Testimony from
Multiple-Participant Abductions

Many mutually corroborative, hypnotically retrieved abduction accounts have been received from different individuals involved in the same incident, and their accounts match—even in very small details.[37] In his 1996 paper on the subject of multiple-participant abductions, John Carpenter presents at some length five cases in which the participants, hypnotized separately, closely corroborate one another's accounts. He states that his files contain a total of sixteen such multiple-participant cases, and that "in all of these sixteen cases, whatever was reported and believed to have occurred was verified accurately by *all* witnesses—*all of the time*. . . . These similar reports obtained separately [under hypnosis] describe not only matching physical details, but correlations regarding the sequence of events, emotional reactions, confusing physics, and observations of each other."[38]

Carpenter cites one example that is particularly interesting because two different hypnotists were involved, with neither having prior awareness of the other's findings. One evening in 1969, a young couple, Karen and Richard, were walking in Springfield, Missouri, when they sighted a round, Saturn-shaped object, orange lights circling its perimeter, hovering quietly above the treetops. Although Karen was frightened, Richard, fascinated, approached it. Some sixty to ninety minutes later, they "came to awareness" feeling disoriented and walking down a different street. Neither could recall what had occurred during the period of missing time, or how the craft departed. Nevertheless, as often happens with such confusing experiences, they did not talk much about it afterward.

Twenty-one years later—and ten years after Karen and Richard had last seen one another—Karen began to feel a compulsion to settle the strange matter of the UFO sighting and the ensuing period of missing time. She approached John Carpenter, asking to be hypnotized so as to unlock the amnesia and prove, in her words, "that nothing weird had ever happened."

What emerged through hypnosis was a classic abduction account, involving both Karen and Richard. Shocked and refusing to believe her own recollections, Karen decided to test her memory of that night. She located her friend Richard, now living in eastern Pennsylvania, and told him only that she had "learned more about that strange evening" and that she wanted him to "contact Dr. David Jacobs [a colleague of Carpenter's] in Philadelphia for hypnotherapy." Richard agreed, apparently also curious about that strange evening.

Carpenter did not speak either to Richard or to David Jacobs before the hypnosis. Karen awaited the results, assuming that they might show she had imagined the entire incident. However, Richard's hypnosis confirmed her account, detail by detail. At the outset, each had been floated up into the craft from underneath and installed on examination *chairs* while some kind of special apparatus was placed on each of their heads. Karen had recalled that when an alien touched Richard's hand he floated off the floor and turned toward a "window" of some kind. Richard also described the touch of the alien's hand and the subsequent floating, and his depiction of what he saw "through the window" tallied exactly with hers.

In yet another example, the veteran investigator Raymond Fowler presents a case in which four men reported a 1976 UFO sighting and a subsequent period of missing time during a camping trip along the Allagash River in Maine.[39] Under separate hypnosis, the recollections of each of the four men corroborated the others' accounts in extraordinary detail.

There are similar cases in my files, too, and in one instance I made a videotape record of the emotional reactions of two subjects as they discovered the similarity of what each had independently recalled under hypnosis about their shared period of "missing time."[40] In my experience, if a witness feels that some type of outside evidence, such as virtually identical recollections by another participant, confirms the reality of a UFO event, that realization is a cause for depression and shock rather than elation or relief.

Hypnosis as a Means of Discovering Previously Unknown Lesions

I will present one example of a situation I have encountered at least four times in my work with individuals reporting UFO abduction experiences.[41] A middle-aged man, "Ed," recalled under hypnosis a childhood abduction in which one detail concerned his having been cut on the back of his lower calf. After the session ended, when I asked him if there was any sign of such a cut, he said, "I don't have any marks or scars on me that I don't know about." I asked him if he would, nevertheless, let me look at his calf, and he agreed. Ed is quite hirsute, and as I parted the curly black hairs at the back of his calf, I discovered a two-inch-long, vertical, hairline scar, perfectly straight and regular, a mark that neither he nor his wife had ever noticed. He was astonished when I pointed it out to him.

The efficacy of hypnosis in UFO abduction research is illustrated by Ed's recollection of a previously unknown scar, and by the three similar cases in my files in which other individuals, through hypnosis, also discovered abduction-connected lesions.

In recent years the issue of false memory formation, particularly with regard to recollections of incest and "satanic ritual abuse," has received a great deal of attention both in the press and in the psychological literature. It was therefore inevitable that skeptics would associate the recovered memories in UFO abduction cases with these other troubling areas, particularly since hypnosis has often been employed in all three cases. In order to demonstrate their similarities and differences—a complex undertaking—it will be necessary to generalize. Much of what follows is based on my own files and on material in the valuable book *Making Monsters* (1994) by Richard Ofshe and Ethan Watters.[42]

The formation of false incest memories, inadvertently demonstrated by a number of hypnotherapists, follows the ensuing general pattern: a female patient (unlike those reporting UFO abductions, the vast majority of these patients are women) seeks therapy for problems of low self-esteem, depression, or similar issues. The therapist—usually another female—is ideologically predisposed to assume incest as a possible or even probable cause of such common presenting symptoms, *even though the client has not suspected such a thing*. Nevertheless, the therapist—often very early in treatment—informs her client of her incest diagnosis.

In a typical example of the forcing of incest memories upon a client who recalled no such experiences, Ofshe quotes a dialogue between a therapist, Charlotte Krause Prozan, and the client.[43] After telling her therapist about a dream of being bitten on the hand by three dogs, the client asks, "But why did I dream about hands?" The therapist, assuming the dogs represent her "forgotten" sexual abuser, answers, "Your hand may have been held back so you could stroke his penis."[44] At another point Prozan claims that her great skill at interpreting dreams allowed her to interpret her client's nightmare of a Volkswagen bus crashing into a house as an indication that the suspected molestation likely consisted of anal sex.[45]

If hypnosis is ultimately employed by practitioners with such beliefs, previously implanted incest memories could, in some cases, be strengthened by the therapist. Such coercive behavior on the part of ideologically motivated hypnotists is to be deplored. It is also counter to the practice of serious, competent UFO investigators.

With regard to the abduction phenomenon, the reason people seek out a UFO investigator is because they remember all or parts of a UFO abduction experience, causing them to suspect they might be abductees. Without what seem to them compelling recollections, they would never have initiated the contact. This is the reverse of the false incest memory formation I have presented here, in which the suspicion of incest originates with the therapist, not the client.

Ofshe and Watters clearly demonstrate, through many quotations from "recovered incest memory" transcripts, the way previously imposed incest recollections can be deliberately strengthened through hypnosis. In the trance state, clients are asked, in what can only be called "fishing expeditions," to travel back through the mists of time to an "event or experience that is important for you to know about." Such a vague direction, delivered by an authoritative therapist who has been trying for months to convince the client that she is a victim of completely "unremembered" incest, offers the client an open invitation to please her therapist by confabulating an incest account.

It goes without saying that sexual problems of one sort or another often occur within an individual's development. Also, we inevitably resent certain aspects of the behavior of members of our family. Therefore, depending on the degree of the client's sexual problems, her anger toward family members, her imaginative powers, and her obedience to the therapist's authority, a persuasive hypnotist may be able to gradually persuade her client to "remember" the childhood incest experiences that she has been told are the cause of her current problems, whatever they may be.

Most UFO researchers, however, will use hypnosis only if the subject recalls a *recent* specific incident or situation that the subject and the investigator feel is possibly a partially remembered abduction experience. To make the contrast of approach as clear as possible, an incest-focused therapist might begin hypnosis because the client dimly remembers, under aggressive questioning, her father standing near her bed when she was three or four years old. She may recall nothing more specific than that, she may have no "suggestive" memories from later times, and she may currently be enjoying a good relationship with her father. Still, the therapist might initiate hypnosis in the hope of validating her incest theory.

By contrast, if someone came to me saying he dimly remembers one time when he thought shadowy, frightening figures stood near his bed when he was three or four years old, *but remembers nothing since* and has been generally free of excessive anxiety, I would not proceed. Unless the client recalls one or more *recent* specific episodes (see the examples described earlier), presents at least some symptoms similar to those of PTSD, and demonstrates through an extensive interview a sufficiently stable life situation, his case will not be accepted for further investigation—and certainly not for hypnosis.

Attempts by debunkers or ill-informed therapists to connect reports of "satanic ritual abuse" with UFO abduction accounts face even more difficulties. No one doubts the existence of incest within society, but there is an almost total lack of evidence supporting the reality of a widespread satanic sect in the United States—theoretically a violent and supersecret cult given to torture, murder, rape, and so on.[46] As the authors state in *Making Monsters*, although there is almost never any kind of physical evidence to support such lurid accounts, there should be. For example, when a young woman accused her father and others of impregnating her "many times" and then ritually murdering the babies, a gynecologist's examination showed she had never given birth.[47] Claims of a body scarred as a result of torture evaporated when no scars could be found.[48] By contrast, as I demonstrated previously, there is an abundance of physical evidence—scars, ground traces, broken tree branches, and so on—as well as eyewitness testimony to corroborate the recollections of those reporting UFO abductions.

Personal experience has taught me how strongly proponents of a ubiquitous satanic cult conspiracy hold to their belief despite the lack of corroborating evidence. In one memorable conversation, a psychiatrist began telling me about the pervasive nature of secret satanic cults. I countered by saying that I knew of no evidence supporting her conviction. "If these cults were so all-pervasive," I said, "cult members would have to be constantly trying to recruit new people, and I've never read about anyone going to the authorities to report a recruiting attempt.

"In every cult or secret group I've ever heard of," I went on, "there are always defections. People have left the Rev. Moon's Unification Church, Heaven's Gate, Scientology, the Branch Davidians, the Mafia, and so on. If the satanic cults are even more widespread, why don't we ever hear of someone defecting and telling us how these organizations work?"

I continued with a final question: "And considering television and the print media, why hasn't at least one enterprising reporter made his reputation by infiltrating a satanic cult—as has happened with the Ku Klux Klan and so many other groups—and produced an exposé of their violence and abuse?"

The psychiatrist had a ready explanation for my last question. "You know why the press hasn't done anything, don't you? They haven't published anything because the media is completely controlled by satanists."

I gasped and replied: "Well, I've always thought Barbara Walters was a satanist." Humor is my instinctive defense against hokum.

Skeptics may argue that the UFO abduction phenomenon displays at least some features similar to those of satanic ritual abuse. For example, proponents of the reality of UFO abductions note that these incidents—like the purported crimes of the rampant satanic cults—are quite widespread, though rarely witnessed by outsiders.[49] According to the logic of this skeptical pairing, since the facts of everyday life decree that neither phenomenon could be simultaneously "invisible" and widespread, both are fictional.

In fact, the comparison is specious. If satanic cults exist as described, their activities would be subject to the same limitations of technology, skill, and human psychology as those of nonsatanic Americans. Knowing what we know about our fellow humans, any nationwide secret organization given to murder, rape, and human sacrifice on an enormous scale and continuing over decades would sooner or later be found out.

However, if UFOs and their occupants exist as described, no such limitations can logically be placed upon them. Their reported ability to operate both widely and nearly "invisibly" is therefore as fully possible as any other aspect of their extraordinary behavior and technology.[50] Skeptics such as Richard Ofshe and Frederick Crews also insist that there is no psychological mechanism that can account for the huge number of cases of previously "unremembered" incest and satanic abuse recollections that recovered memory therapists allegedly find in their clients.[51]

UFO researchers, using hypnosis, have also uncovered thousands of previously unremembered, but now highly detailed, abduction accounts. Therefore, the argument goes, since no known mechanism of repression can be established, *neither* group of recollections can be true.[52] There are three objections to this seemingly logical conclusion. First, UFO researchers have posited, from their careful study of the case material, an "alien" ability to impress a state of highly selective amnesia upon those whom they abduct. Without going into the extensive evidence for this position—which depends on the existence of UFOs and their occupants as previously described—it is enough to point out that the mechanism of repression described by recovered memory therapists has little or no bearing on the abduction phenomenon.

Second, since recovered memory therapists generally elicit recollections of abuse from their clients *before* hypnosis is employed, hypnosis is not implicated as central even in these cases.[53] And since many UFO abduction memories are *retained from the time of the incident* without hypnosis, no mechanism of repression is necessarily involved in them, either.[54]

Third, substantial evidence exists to support the idea that in some cases traumatic material can be repressed, even though the mechanisms of repression are not exactly understood.[55] That these verifiable cases of repression are far rarer than most recovered memory therapists believe is irrelevant; if *any* such cases exist, this extremely dogmatic aspect of the skeptical argument against recovered memories is untenable.

The protocols followed by UFO investigators and therapists who work with "abductees" differ greatly from those followed by recovered memory therapists working with "incest survivors" and "satanic ritual abuse victims." Since most recovered memory therapists focus on issues of sexual abuse, their treatment usually entails identifying the previously unremembered abuser—most often a family member or members.[56] It is here that the most unfortunate results of such therapy manifest themselves. Families can be virtually destroyed when the incest victim names her "abuser," often a close but innocent relative. Ofshe and Watters recount more than a few such horror stories, most of which have been culled from the writings of recovered memory therapists themselves.

Over the past few years, the media have reported cases in which therapists have been successfully sued by family members who argue that false charges of sexual abuse, systematically inculcated during treatment, have virtually destroyed the integrity of their lives and families.[57] It is significant that not once in thirty years of active abduction research have I heard of such a lawsuit against an investigator/hypnotist. The reason lies in the nature of the two investigations and the differences between abduction investigators' methods and protocols and those of many recovered memory therapists.

Once again, it should be pointed out that the vast majority of recovered memory therapists carry out no independent study of the charges they inculcate in their clients. The amassing of evidence—the allegedly recovered abuse memories—takes place entirely within the confines of the therapist's office. Thus the guilt of the demonized "abuser" is ultimately presented as a fait accompli rather than as an open issue deserving factual investigation.[58]

Herein lies another pair of major differences with the protocols followed by UFO investigators/hypnotists. First, as I have stated previously, the abduction researcher seeks outside evidence, interviews family members and other potential witnesses, and seeks to verify whatever abduction recollections arise through hypnosis or office interviews.[59] As an example, in the complex Linda Cortile case I documented in *Witnessed*, I interviewed perhaps forty individuals; submitted physical samples to two different laboratories for testing; made inquiries at the New York office of the Secret Service, the New York City Police Department, the United Nations Secretariat, the Russian and British missions to the UN, and the United States Department of State, among other sources.[60] My work also included the analysis of several audio and video tapes, as well as handwriting and typing samples, medical examinations, research in the archives of the *New York Times*, and official weather reports—all in the search for evidence to either corroborate or contradict the various eyewitness accounts and the testimony elicited during hypnosis.

A second major difference between the work of abduction researchers and that of the recovered memory therapists has to do with attitudes toward the clients' social and familial relations. Rather than deliberately fomenting enmity between clients and members of their families, abduction hypnotist/investigators work to strengthen the preexisting bonds that their clients feel with their friends and families. They see the existence of a social and familial safety net as a necessary condition before hypnosis is undertaken.[61]

My confidence in the methods and protocols observed by my colleagues and myself is such that I have frequently invited interested therapists, journalists, and academics to observe hypnosis sessions. Theoretical psychologist Nicholas Humphrey, who has held teaching posts at both Oxford and Cambridge Universities, and psychiatrist Donald F. Klein, director of research at the New York State Psychiatric Institute and professor of psychiatry at the College of Physicians and Surgeons, Columbia University, are but two of those who have observed my work firsthand. None of these visitors—all presumably skeptical about the abduction phenomenon—have reported anything that suggested I was attempting to lead the subjects. As French journalist Marie-Therese de Brosses remarked, "I have been able to observe several of [Budd Hopkins's] regressions, and I remember being favorably impressed by the extreme prudence with which he conducts them so as not to influence his subjects."[62]

Another invited observer, Greg Sandow, a contributor to the *Wall Street Journal* and many other publications, completed a long article generally supporting the reality of UFO abductions and based largely on his close study of my work and the work of Dr. David Jacobs.[63]

C. D. B. Bryan, journalist and author of *Close Encounters of the Fourth Kind: Alien Abduction, UFOs, and the Conference at MIT*, originally came to this subject with the idea of writing a somewhat humorous piece for the *New Yorker*. His subsequent investigation of abduction accounts by two highly credible women led him to write, instead of a short, dismissive piece, a full-length, thoroughly researched study in which he took the subject seriously.[64] During his lengthy investigation, Bryan attended a number of hypnotic sessions I conducted with the two women, and he wrote approvingly of my work.

Bryan, Sandow, and de Brosses are skilled observers and refreshingly fair-minded journalists; each spent a great deal of time looking into the practice of UFO abduction researchers. However, they are, in my experience, quite rare. I have found that journalists, scientists, and academics fall into two basic groups with respect to the UFO abduction phenomenon. The first, as exemplified by those I have mentioned here, along with scores of others, are initially skeptical but open-minded, even curious about the abduction accounts. They recognize that if we are actually being visited by another, non-human intelligence, then nothing could be more important, and they have therefore taken steps to educate themselves.[65]

The second, much larger group is made up of those (usually skeptical) individuals who are woefully uninformed about the phenomenon. Many, exercising a kind of intellectual snobbery, hold the subject beneath contempt because of its admittedly bizarre nature.[66] Others are more innocent in their ignorance, having never bothered to pay these consistent reports any attention—though they often feel qualified to discount them, nevertheless. As an example, a year ago I appeared on a Canadian TV program to discuss several UFO abduction reports. To represent the skeptical position, the program's host had secured a young astronomer who explained why, theoretically, UFOs cannot exist: distances in space are too great, "you can't get here from there," and so forth.

During our dialogue, I asked him about his view of the famous Trans-en-Provence case, which had been thoroughly investigated by a subcommittee of the French version of NASA.[67] He had never heard of it. I mentioned several other extremely well-known cases, but he had not heard of them either. Finally, I asked what books he had read on UFO phenomena, what case material he was familiar with, and he replied somewhat sheepishly that he had read virtually nothing about the subject. I asked how, then, the two of us could be expected to have a dialogue.

Preparing this chapter on the use of hypnosis in UFO abduction research has been somewhat disheartening because, in perusing the psychological literature on the subject, I was so often reminded of my television experience with the designated skeptic. Far too many otherwise informed writers—both clinical and experimental psychologists, but especially the latter—seemed as woefully ignorant of the UFO abduction research literature, and the investigator's use of hypnosis, as that young astronomer. Unfortunately, Schopenhauer's remark is all too true: every man takes the limits of his own field of vision for the limits of the world.

To summarize, hundreds of powerful, detailed, coherent abduction accounts exist in which hypnosis was never used. Thus the abduction phenomenon cannot be seen as an artifact of hypnosis. In many cases in which hypnosis is used, extensive physical evidence and independent corroborative witness accounts support the event-level reality of the experiences thus elicited. Finally, based on recent experimental evidence, hypnosis does not reliably produce more false memories than can be produced in nonhypnotic situations.

Chapter Nine

How the Alien Abduction Phenomenon Challenges the Boundaries of Our Reality

John E. Mack

Overview

Speaking about the alien abduction phenomenon in 1994, Credo Mutwa, a renowned Zulu shaman, urged me to "ask the Americans to stop arguing about this. The reality of extraterrestrial intelligences should not be made the plaything of skeptics. This thing is too vital for the existence of the human race."[1] But the argument does continue here and in other Western countries about whether the phenomenon is "real," and the skeptics, often with little more to support them than their a priori certainty that such things are not possible, continue to dominate the opinions on this subject held by most of our leading intellects, institutions, and public officials. This phenomenon, however, is not so easily dismissed. Whatever its source, it now seems clear that it cannot be explained psychiatrically or, evidently, by any other conventional theory. I will show why this is so and also address why that may be so difficult for the Western mind, especially among mainstream elites, to accept.

My own experience when I was introduced to this subject may be instructive. Even though for several years I had been using nonordinary states of consciousness,[2] such as various meditative and breathing approaches, to explore unseen realities, the idea that many people of sound mind could be experiencing being taken by humanoid beings into some sort of spacecraft and subjected to various intrusive procedures seemed preposterous. After all, my education in the scientific paradigm had taught me, there was no evidence for any kind of life in the universe outside of the earth, despite the efforts of Carl Sagan and others to detect the signals of extraterrestrial intelligence through various electronic devices.

Yet, in 1990 I began to meet and interview individuals of diverse socioeconomic and ethnic backgrounds from all over the United States who were reporting just that. They told me (and many other people) that strange beings—most often the short, thin ones with great black eyes that are now a familiar image in popular culture but were unknown to me at that time—were abducting them into some sort of enclosure and subjecting them to highly invasive examinations and various other procedures. Furthermore, these people, when I examined them, appeared to be of sound mind, had appropriate emotional responses and self-doubt with regard to what they were relating, had no apparent motive for concocting such stories, were not in contact with each other, and, at least in the first years, were providing details that had never, as well as one could ascertain, been reported in the media. Finally, the accounts were eerily similar from one person to another, allowing for differences of personality style in talking about the experiences.

In short, these individuals were talking the way people talk about something that has actually happened to them in the "real world." I detected none of the imaginative strangeness and inconsistency of dreams, the idiosyncratic quality of personal fantasy, or the accompanying distortions of thinking or functional impairment that accompany various psychoses. Finally, allowing for the way small children talk about their experiences, I also heard accounts of what sounded like abductions from two- and three-year-olds. The dilemma I faced was this: while from a clinical standpoint these reports sounded like occurrences in the "real world," my worldview at the time simply discounted the existence of such things. The choice, then, was to persist in trying to find a conventional explanation for the phenomenon,[3] forcing it into molds that it seemed not to fit, or to consider the possibility that my worldview was incomplete.

After two years of doing this work, I had seen more than fifty people whose stories of abduction reflected a consistent pattern of events: being taken, usually against the person's will, by strange

humanoid beings into an enclosure with rounded walls and subjected to examinations or other intrusive procedures. In 1994 I also
began to discover and explore cases from several other cultures. In
no case has a careful exploration yielded an explanation other than
the apparent one—that is, I perceived no form of mental illness,
mimicking of an account seen or read in the mass media, or another
sort of trauma. The now familiar phenomenology of abductions does
seem to support the assertion that something very real has happened
to these individuals who, nevertheless, themselves find such asser-
tions extraordinarily hard to comprehend, much less accept.

Worldviews and Resistances to Knowledge

Before describing the basic elements of the abduction phenomenon
and how we study it, I will consider why the reports of these experiences have been met in our culture—this has not been true among
the indigenous peoples with whom I have met—with such incredu-
lity, anxious ridicule, and outright anger. These remarks of *Boston
Globe* music critic (!) Milo Miles in a review of the first edition of my
book *Abduction* are not atypical of how, at least until recently, work
that credited the phenomenon has been greeted in the mainstream
media: "The secular world and the spirit world should be kept as
separate as church and state. . . . Mack should beware that if rationality and objective truth are thrown out the door no one can predict what will rush in through the opening."[4]

In a similar vein, *Boston Globe* science writer Chet Raymo, reporting on the 1992 study conference on abductions at the Massachusetts Institute of Technology (MIT), likened the phenomenon and
our interest in it to the European fear of witchcraft and Victorian
apprehensions of incubi and succubi.[5] Admittedly, my own reaction was initially equally dismissive—that is, it must be a new sort
of psychosis—until I had had a chance to examine the abduction
experiencers themselves. To better understand such reactions, it
is necessary first to identify our culture's predominant worldview
and the basic assumptions about the nature of reality and our ways
of knowing that are embedded within it; second, to consider how
the alien abduction phenomenon so radically challenges this worldview; third, to understand how our worldview (or perhaps any

worldview) functions from a psychosocial standpoint; and finally, in the light of these observations, to appreciate why the reactions to abduction reports have been so intense.

The Miles and Raymo responses give indications of what characterizes our dominant worldview. It has been variously called scientific materialism, positivism, rational empiricism, anthropocentric humanism,[6] the Newtonian/Cartesian paradigm, or simply the Western mind. What this worldview basically asserts is that the predominant cosmic reality is the one that we can observe and objectify with our senses and understand by rational analysis.[7] If there is another realm or realms, it is the stuff of psychology, literature, anthropology, and religion, to be known by intuition or other subjective means if it is to be studied at all. Like the academicians of the eighteenth-century Enlightenment this worldview underscores the triumph of scientific rationalism as the preeminent epistemology for the human future.[8]

This worldview also posits a near-absolute barrier between the material world and the world beyond, sometimes relegated to the domain of spirit. Nothing can "cross over" materially from that world into our reality, and evidence for such traffic tends to be dismissed a priori.[9] The scientific method of hypothesis building, testing, replication, and analysis is the principal way of knowing about the universe. Within the framework of this worldview, reports of human experience that cannot be verified empirically are referred to as anecdotal or merely "stories," or, if they are particularly powerful, are credited as having validity as "narrative" or "narrative truth."[10]

The incentive for the development of the materialist worldview is not difficult to understand. It has overcome—or seemed to—some of our helplessness in the face of storms, diseases, threatening creatures, and other forces of nature; has improved living standards for many people; and has vastly advanced travel, communication, and weaponry. The achievements of Western science hardly need to be summarized here. But, at the same time, in its extreme form the Western worldview appears to have virtually voided the cosmos of all intelligence that is not a projection of the brains of advanced animals (our own in particular). The consequence of this ideology, what Tulane philosopher Michael Zimmerman calls *anthropocentric humanism*,[11] has proved to be the loss of a sense of the divine or the sacred and a kind of species arrogance that leaves humankind at liberty to treat the earth as its own property and other people or peoples as without intrinsic value. As a result, the planet is fast becoming uninhabitable, and we are in danger of obliterating much of its life with weapons of mass destruction.

There are, however, many phenomena now being studied by qualified researchers that challenge the preceding worldview. These include near-death experiences;[12] the findings of parapsychology;[13] Marian apparitions;[14] mass free energy;[15] nonlocality;[16] healing at a distance;[17] research on past life experiences;[18] and, of course, the UFO and alien abduction phenomena. Far from being welcomed as advancing our knowledge of ourselves and the cosmos, such work is frequently rejected out of hand in mainstream science and critically reviewed in prestigious media in language that conveys a kind of hysteria, as dangerous assaults on rationality and science itself. Science writer James Gleick, for example, with nothing to go on but his own opinion, called the "abduction mythology" a "leading case of the anti-rational, anti-science cults that are flourishing with dismaying vigor in the United States."[19]

The alien abduction phenomenon, if taken seriously, seems to challenge many, if not all, of the basic assumptions of the Western worldview. First, it indicates that there are other intelligent beings in the cosmos (a fact never doubted by most of the peoples of the earth throughout history), whatever their precise ontological status and however eccentric their style of contact and communication may seem. Second, these entities appear to possess advanced psychological and physical technologies that make our own seem quite primitive, if not in some ways foolish. Apparently, there is no military defense against these beings and their craft should they turn out to be hostile invaders, which does not seem to be the case. Third, the beings violate a central tenet of the Western worldview, namely, that entities from the "other world" cannot cross over into ours (one may recall the eighteenth-century debate about meteorites, the assumption until that time being that rocks could not fall onto earth from the sky).[20] Above all, the phenomenon shatters any illusions we may have had that through scientific rationalism we can conquer nature and achieve the dominance and safety in the universe that knowledge derived from its methods was meant to provide.

The abduction phenomenon also challenges the adequacy or completeness of the scientific method itself as a way of learning about the universe, at least its emphasis on replicable measurement.[21] The point is not that empirical studies cannot help to document those aspects of the abduction phenomenon that appear to manifest in the physical world. Such studies are being done and should continue.[22] The problem is that the physical findings, though real, are not, by and large, sufficiently robust to satisfy the requirements of the natural and medical sciences. The information about alien abductions is preponderantly experiential (i.e., reports from the experiencers themselves). Although these accounts are quite consistent among abductees, for the most part they cannot be verified by the methods of the physical sciences. Rather than dismiss these data because of the limits of their accessibility by traditional scientific approaches, we should remain open-minded and further explore their potential for helping us extend and refine our understanding of ourselves and the universe we occupy.[23]

The intensity of some of the responses to my efforts to have people take the alien abduction phenomenon seriously has made me think more deeply about how a worldview functions and what it means to threaten it. Language traditionally applied to political betrayal and religious heresy—one colleague lamented my "defection" from scientific responsibility; another accused me of deviating from the consensus by crediting "irrational beliefs" not shared by the "compact majority" (which, presumably, decides for us what is real)—has sometimes greeted my writings, suggesting that something more than scientific discourse is taking place. These reactions have of course been mild compared with the fate of Renaissance figures whose observations challenged the prevailing authority of their time, but their seeming emotionality has made me appreciate that the way we construct reality is politically as well as scientifically determined.[24]

We seem less willing to die or kill others to defend a cosmology than in earlier times, but it is clear to me that the breaking down of a worldview can be a personally shattering experience. It is as if the boundaries we place on reality help to orient us in the world; restricting the possibilities or mysteries of the infinite seems to hold the psyche together. The psyche and its worldviews seem almost to be one entity. Thus, a challenge to a worldview or cosmology threatens the disintegration of the psyche itself, inasmuch as a worldview defines who we are in the deepest sense. And it seems not to be just a matter of survival of the individual person; the larger self, its values and integrity, appears to be at risk. But there is more. Inasmuch as our well-being in the world depends on the feeling of belonging and acceptance in society, the collapse of a worldview can cause us to feel adrift, alienated, without connection to the authority of social consensus. A shared worldview allows us to feel one with our families, community, and professional institutions. Conversely, to depart from the ontological consensus brings to mind images of ostracism and the catastrophe of excommunication.

I have taken pains to spell out how a worldview seems to function, for I have found that it is difficult for people to even consider the data that constitute the UFO abduction phenomenon unless the extent to which it radically challenges the dominant ontological paradigm is appreciated. The worldview of scientific materialism as described here has functioned as a kind of guiding secular religion for many of us in the West, but it is gradually being eroded by the increasing number of anomalies that challenge its primacy, the abduction phenomenon being one of the clearest examples. Certainly, the acceptance or rejection of the reality of the phenomenon will depend on the power of its presence and the quality of the observations through which it is documented. But by providing the background discussed here, I hope to show what might be in the way of greater openness to the consideration of its basic phenomenology and potential implications.

How We Work with Abductees

Abduction researchers vary considerably in their methods of examination and analysis, which may account for the different findings and interpretations of the phenomenon among people who work in this field. The population that comes to us at the Program for Extraordinary Experience Research (PEER) is certainly self-selected.[25] People who choose to contact us know that I do not consider abductees to be victims, although naturally I try to be empathic in relation to the pain and trauma they have undergone. But, rather, I have come to view experiencers as participants in a compelling mystery. For the deeper one looks into this intriguing subject, the more uncertainties and questions arise.

Psychiatric social worker Roberta Colasanti, who is present during most of the meetings with experiencers, helps to select the individuals with whom we will meet. We can see only a small fraction of those who contact us, but we use no fixed criteria in choosing people. Generally, we look for people who seem quite clearly to have had anomalous experiences as suggested by apparent contact during waking hours with an unexplained "presence" (interpreted sometimes as angels, ghosts, spirit guides, or other entities known within the belief structure of a particular culture), nonhuman entities, close encounters with UFOs, strange, unexplained bright lights, periods of missing time, and odd small lesions noticed on the body that seem to have appeared in conjunction with the preceding indicators.

Individuals contact us primarily by letter or phone. Roberta, in her role as the clinical director of PEER, screens individuals with the use of a structured phone interview. The intention of this screening tool is to help rule out gross mental illness, substance abuse, and suicidality. Once the individual has been appropriately screened, he or she is asked to write a brief letter specifying his or her reason for contacting us, as well as to gather basic personal and medical information. The individual is offered an initial interview to determine the extent to which such interaction might benefit both the "experiencer" and the researcher. Sometimes the perceived risks outweigh potential benefits. There are occasions, after meeting with an individual, in which we decide that he or she is not an experiencer or that even if the person is experiencing anomalous events, it is not in his or her best interest to pursue further investigations at that time.

The initial interview usually takes two hours, for we must establish trust, take a full personal history, examine the individual for possible psychiatric symptoms that may or may not relate to the presenting reason for coming, and, of course, review in detail the story of possible abduction encounters or other anomalous experiences. Sometimes there is a relative or other individual present, who may serve as a support person or corroborating witness.

A modified hypnosis or relaxation exercise (which involves asking the individual to lean back or lie down, breathe more deeply, and let go of tension) may be used to help focus the person's attention on his or her inner experience and memories. In this slightly altered state of mind it is easier for these individuals to recall more fully their experiences, which are generally not deeply repressed, and to begin to discharge the intense energies that seem to be held as if in the very tissues of their bodies. We try to be careful not to lead individuals, or to encourage them to "produce" an abduction story, using neutral, encouraging comments and questions. But we must enter deeply into the experiencers' worlds in order to create trust, help them tell their disquieting stories in a safe environment, and "hold" the power of the experiences as they are relived. Sometimes the recall appears so emotionally intense that it seems as if the experience is being relived in the present moment.

Needless to say, the researcher must conduct such interviews with great care. Psychiatrist C. Brooks Brenneis has framed well the dilemma clinicians face in doing any sort of exploration that seeks to recover memories. "Leaning in the direction of doubt," he writes, "threatens betrayal," while "leaning in the direction of belief" promotes fabrication. "If one does not believe, no memory can be tolerated; and if one does believe, whatever memory appears is suspect."[26] Our clients will return as often as seems to be needed to integrate their experiences emotionally, and also to help them live in a society that does not even recognize, at least among its elite, the vast realms of being to which they have been opened. Needless to say, this integration is never altogether satisfactory.

Working with abduction experiencers requires something more or different than anything I have known about in working with other patients, clients, or research populations. This is difficult to express clearly, but it involves the capacity to let go more fully of one's ego boundaries in order to follow the experiencers into whatever "energy field" or nonordinary state of consciousness they may take us, as they remember or relive their encounters. At the same time, one must provide a holding container for the intense emotions and energies that come forth (experiencers may sweat, sob, shake, or scream during these sessions), while retaining an observing, mindful presence that maintains appropriate control of the process.

And there are other challenges. For what we hear may seem so bizarre or impossible from the standpoint of the worldview in which we are enmeshed that our minds rebel and want to intervene with the reality-testing confrontations that psychiatrists know so well. But to do so will abort communication and destroy trust. We are, of course, aided in this curious "suspension of disbelief" by the fact that we are concerned only with the authenticity and honesty of the client's report, and the presence or absence of psychopathology or another biographical experience that might account for it. There is no injunction to establish the literal or material actuality of the reported experiences.

Our conviction of the truthfulness of what has been witnessed and recalled comes from the sheer intensity of feeling and its appropriateness to what is being reported; the consistency of the narrative with what has become familiar from work with other clients; the absence of apparent secondary gain or other motive; and, finally, a judgment, which can be quite subtle and might not always be correct, that the individual is being as truthful as he or she is able to be. Surely, researchers in this line of work must be prepared, as the poet Rilke wrote, "for the most strange, the most singular and most inexplicable that we may encounter."[27]

Phenomenology

Unlike many syndromes in medicine or psychiatry, it is difficult to enumerate the basic features of the abduction phenomenon in a straightforward, linear fashion. There are several reasons for this. For example, the experiences seem to change over time for particular abductees, depending on the approach that the facilitator uses and the changes of consciousness that take place for a particular experiencer. Furthermore, the shape or evolution of the experience, and even what may be considered the basic elements of the phenomenon itself, will be affected by the clinical background or consciousness of the facilitator and/or by what he or she can accept or tolerate within his or her own psyche or worldview. My own list of the important features of the phenomenon has expanded as I have explored it more deeply. While most investigators might agree on the first item on my list, there might be less concurrence in regard to the five that follow. That points to one of the more frustrating aspects of this kind of research—the fact that researchers have attained only a limited degree of consensus regarding the contours, scope, and meanings associated with this strange phenomenon.

Since this chapter is concerned with possible explanations of the abduction phenomenon, it seems to me worthwhile to set forth its complex dimensions in sufficient detail (even then, many important elements will have to be left out because of space limitations) to provide a caution to anyone who might wish to offer a theory, for an explanation to be taken seriously must account for *all* of the basic elements. There is a tendency in this field for critics to pick out one or two elements from the cluster of features that constitute the abduction phenomenon and then make up a theory based on only those few elements. Because the phenomenon often occurs at night and the experiencer may not be able to move, for example, sleep paralysis has been offered as an explanation,[28] even though some abductees insist they are wide awake and abductions can occur in the course of daytime waking life. Because UFOs seem to contain rounded enclosures, the possibility that we are dealing with womb or pregnancy fantasies has been put forth.[29] Or because sudden shifts of consciousness occur during abductions and these can be brought about by temporal lobe stimulation, some sort of temporal lobe activation might be behind it all (as Michael Persinger suggests elsewhere in this volume). One psychiatrist even suggested at a conference that we might be dealing with a variation on an eating problem, since a client whose case I presented had had a period of anorexia, and eating disorders were this psychiatrist's specialty.

Intrusive, Medical/Surgical-like Procedures

Abduction experiences appear to concentrate in families, sometimes over several generations. They seem curiously "democratic," as no distinction by race, gender, socioeconomic status, or age has been discovered. Although experiencers may ask to be seen in order to explore a particularly well-remembered event, it may turn out that they have had many such experiences during their lifetime. Memory behaves oddly in relation to abductions, which makes poll-taking a hazardous adventure, for what is "forgotten" one day may be remembered the next. Something more than ordinary repression seems to be at work here, for understandable psychological motives for remembering or forgetting can be difficult to identify.

Characteristically, abductees are in their bedroom or some other room at night, driving a car, or, in the case of children, playing outside when the experience begins. They may or may not see a UFO close by. They then may sense a "presence," or that "they" (unidentified beings) are nearby. They may hear an audible humming sound or, more frequently, see an intense, bright light that fills the room, or experience some other sort of vibratory or "electrical" energy.[30] One or more small beings may be seen close by, who, "real" or not, possess features that have become firmly embedded in popular culture and contemporary lore. They are characteristically three to four feet tall, with disproportionately large, bald heads that protrude in the back, grayish tan facial skin that is variously wrinkled, huge oval pupil-less black eyes, rudimentary noses with nostril holes, small slitlike mouths, thin bodies, spindly legs and arms, hands with three or four long fingers, and a one-piece tuniclike garment for clothing. These so-called gray beings move, float, or glide about easily, their movements sometimes being described as robotic. Their communication is always telepathic or mind to mind. In addition, other reptilian, luminous, insectlike, or even more human-appearing beings have also been identified inside or outside of what appear to be spacecraft.

Experiencing great fear—at least until the reality is confronted or the beings do something to calm them (touching with a hand or rod, reassuring the experiencer that he or she will be all right)—the abductees find themselves unable to move. In this paralyzed state the experiencers are "floated"—the word they virtually always use—out of the room, down a hall, and right through the window, door, or ceiling of the house, usually accompanied by the beings, with a beam of light that emanates from some outside source providing the energy that moves them. They may see their house or neighborhood recede below them as they are moved up and into a waiting spacecraft—either a small podlike vessel that takes them to the "mother ship" or directly into a large craft. Curiously, the experiencers do not feel cold as they travel upward, and they may sense that this is because they are protected by some sort of tube or tunnel of light or other form of energy that surrounds them. Witnesses to this event are rare,[31] but the experiences are so intensely physical that abductees feel quite certain that some, though not all, of the time their physical form, as opposed to their astral or other forms of the subtle body, are taken.

Once inside the craft, the experiencer may see more beings moving about purposefully in cool rooms with curved walls that may contain a musty or other unpleasant smell. Around the walls, which have no apparent corners, complex computer-like equipment may be seen, and various sorts of recessed or mobile lighting are visible. The experiencer, who has usually had most, if not all, of his or her clothes taken along the way, is usually next placed on a table, although abductees may be shown about the ship and often see other abductees like themselves there. The activities seem to be under the direction of a leader figure, who usually is described as a little taller than the other alien "drones."

On the table the abductee is stared at, sometimes close up, by one or more of the beings with their large black eyes and is subjected to a variety of medical/surgical-like procedures with instruments with which we are not generally familiar. These include probing of various orifices of the body through the eyes, nose, ears, navel, and rectum. The abductees may feel or be told that they are being checked up on, their health monitored or even in some way healed. Sometimes they experience an "implant" has been inserted in their bodies, a kind of tag, which allows the aliens, they believe, to follow or find them in the future. Various tiny objects, which the abductees have identified as implants, have been removed from under the skin. The results of the analysis of these objects have been controversial, with some researchers[32] failing to find any convincing evidence that they are of extraterrestrial or other unusual origin, while others[33] are convinced that they are truly unusual.

Hopkins,[34] Jacobs,[35] and other investigators (including myself) have documented that some sort of complex, reproductive-like process or "project" appears to be a central feature of the UFO abduction phenomenon, beginning sometimes with sperm being taken from men by forced ejaculation and eggs from women via the vagina. After a sequence of abduction experiences, strange fetuses that become babies and then small children seem to be created. These are seen in the ships by the abductees on subsequent abductions, and they are encouraged to nourish these odd hybrid creatures, who do appear as a kind of cross between human and alien beings. One of the most convincing aspects of the phenomenon is the intense maternal distress of women who recall with certainty that they have been presented with their own hybrid offspring but have no say about when they will be able to see these creatures again. After the procedures are completed, the abductee is returned to, or close to, the place from which he or she was taken. Odd, even humorous, mistakes seem to occur—the person being returned, for example, to the bed the wrong way around or with clothes on backward, or a child may be tucked too tightly into its bed.

Energetic Elements

Even a brief acquaintance with the UFO/abduction field will show that there are extraordinary energies involved.[36] These range from the propulsion system of UFOs themselves to the experience of cellular change that abductees feel they have undergone during their experiences. Some sort of intense, high-frequency vibrations seem to be present in the room when the alien beings arrive. Brilliant light emanates from the craft and may flood the area where the abduction begins. The abductees report being moved mysteriously on a beam of light or by some other energy or force out of their rooms or cars and into the craft. Strange, rapid healing processes have been observed,[37] which seem to be brought about by some sort of energy that the experiencers feel certain of but cannot explain.

When they are taken or floated through the wall, ceiling, or window of their homes or through the door of a car, the abductees feel as if an intense energy is separating every cell, or even every molecule, of their bodies. So powerful is this feeling that experiencers often find it remarkable that they "come back together" whole on the other side of the wall. After their experiences, abductees characteristically feel that powerful residual energies are left in their bodies, as if stored in the cells themselves. Interestingly, in an EEG study Don and Moura showed that abductees reveal a hyperarousal state comparable only to those of advanced meditators or yogis when they are encouraged to relive their experiences imaginatively.[38] Nothing else in my clinical experience has ever quite reached the dramatic intensity of the release of these energies during the relaxation sessions in which the abduction experiences are relived. The abductees speak of powerful vibratory sensations in their arms, legs, and other parts of their bodies. It feels to them as if every cell in their bodies is vibrating, and their bodies may literally shake or "vibrate" on the couch as the experience is recalled or relived. Bloodcurdling screams or loud sobbing may help to relieve the tension they feel.[39]

Knowledge: Protecting the Earth

Many abductees feel that through the probing or by contact with the large black eyes that the beings are studying or "download-ing" information from their minds and brains. At the same time the experiencers frequently feel that knowledge has been *given* to them through the eyes, telepathically, in scenes and symbols shown to them on the ships on television-like monitors, or even through "libraries" that may appear to hold books or to be contained in balls of light. From this information the abductees may feel that they have acquired understanding of subjects they have not otherwise studied, or have gained special insights or psychic abilities. Credo Mutwa, for example, feels certain that his abilities as an artist and his knowledge of science and technology came to him from the Mantindane, the Zulu word he uses for beings that seem quite like the grays described in Western reports.[40]

Often the information that abductees take in concerns the earth, its jeopardy, and human responsibility for the future of the planet's life. Sometimes the "lessons" are conveyed through apocalyptic images of destruction of the earth's life or even of the earth itself. These may be juxtaposed with other scenes of transcendent beauty, which may leave the experiencers emotionally shaken. In one ab-duction experience Jim Sparks, formerly a real estate developer, was shown scene after scene of magnificent earth landscapes, followed by images of the same areas now devastated by pollution and ero-sion. Several of the children at the Ariel School in Zimbabwe, who witnessed the landing of several UFOs in September 1994, reported that the beings conveyed through their eyes that we were not tak-ing "proper care" of the planet.[41]

The impact of this information about the state of the planet may affect abductees profoundly. They may feel a visceral identification with the earth itself, which becomes for them a kind of living organism, and may feel a sense of despair. Some experiencers will devote their lives to protecting the earth and become active, directly or indirectly, in ecologically related efforts. Abduction researchers and abductees themselves disagree about the possible motives behind such experiences. Some are convinced these entities love the planet and wish to protect it, while others cynically conclude that the beings are trying to protect the planet for their own agendas, or even that they are simply testing our reactions as part of a human study program. It often seems that, in this and other instances, the attribution of motive or intention to the beings, since we cannot really know what they are trying to do, reflects more the psyche and outlook of the witness than anything else.[42]

Symbols and Shamans

Abduction researchers have frequently observed that the alien beings, especially the typical grays, sometimes appear initially to the experiencers as familiar animals. Owls, eagles, raccoons, and deer are a few of the animal forms in which the beings have been initially perceived. Less well appreciated is the fact that these animal representations are not simply forms of disguise but may have symbolic meaning or may have some connection with the psyche of the experiencer. Brazilian shaman Bernardo Peixoto told me that the Ikuyas (the word that his tribe uses for entities that seem to resemble our gray beings) will represent themselves to abduction experiencers in a form that connects with the animal spirit or spirits associated with a particular individual.[43]

As I have explored abduction experiences over the past decade and analyzed the language of abduction reports, it has become apparent to me that there is a rich symbology to be explored in relation to this phenomenon. It is as if the energies associated with abductions press the abductees into a kind of primal consciousness (what Freud called *primary process thinking*), psychic states that are rich with symbolism and metaphoric meaning. Egyptian, Greek, Hindu, and Native American symbols have been perceived or shown to abductees I have worked with during their encounters, as well as universal symbols (archetypes) of birth, death, and rebirth. Even creation myths have been communicated to abductees, which seem to connect to possible spiritual, if not the biological, origins of the human race.

Abductees are sometimes drawn to the worlds of shamans, for even without a background in ethnographic studies they seem to understand the realms of symbolism and spirit guidance to which shamans are connected. I do not mean to imply that the rich symbolism that accompanies abduction experiences can explain them, or explain them away. On the contrary, what this suggests is that the experiences draw the abductees psychologically, and perhaps physically, into deeper, more meaningful realities that are not so readily available to us in ordinary waking consciousness. This subject is explored more fully in *Passport to the Cosmos*, which includes the encounter stories of three native medicine men from the United States, Brazil, and South Africa.[44]

Trauma and Transformation: Returning to the Source

Needless to say, many abduction experiences are traumatic. To be paralyzed, taken against one's will to a strange place, and subjected to a variety of intrusive procedures can be enormously disturbing and overwhelming. In addition, experiencers may feel quite isolated, having no one, at least initially, to whom they can tell what has occurred without fear of ridicule or suspicion of being mentally ill. The fact that psychological studies have failed to find significant psychopathology among experiencers does not help them in the immediate circumstance.[45] Furthermore, most abductees, as they confront the fact of their experiences, seem to undergo something like what I have called "ontological shock," that is, their view of reality has been shattered by the experiences. Finally, the abduction experience further erodes many individuals' sense of stability and well-being because of its frequent but unpredictable recurrence and because many experiencers who are parents feel utterly powerless to protect their children from also being abducted. It may be this latter anxiety that finally prompts some individuals to approach me.

It has been reported that there may be a higher incidence of sexual abuse among abductees than in the general population.[46] This is difficult to assess, since the definition of sexual abuse varies, and the establishment of its incidence depends on the accuracy of recalled memory,[47] which is uncertain at best and treacherous in the case of sexual trauma. Furthermore, abductees, by virtue of the opening of consciousness associated with their encounter history and its exploration, may be more than usually able to recall other sorts of trauma, and may even assume, since the abduction experiences may have sexual elements, that they have been sexually abused.

Interestingly, when abductees begin to explore their personal histories, they seem quite readily able to distinguish experiences with "aliens" from encounters with human beings. In my own experience there has not been a case where a suspected abduction case turned out to mask a story of sexual abuse. But the reverse has occurred—that is, exploration of a presumed history of sexual abuse has led inadvertently to the discovery of an abduction experience. In any event, it is clear that sexual abuse cannot be a very frequent explanation, since many cases seem to provide no suggestion of a history of sexual molestation or abuse.[48]

When I am able to help abductees confront their fear as they relive the experiences, and bear with them the great distress and energies they have been holding in their bodies, the experiences seem to transform. Although fear and resentment can persist, the abductees may come to accept their experiences as something to which they have in some way agreed. Women who have been used as "breeders" in the bearing of what they perceive to be hybrid babies or children sometimes feel that they are contributing to a life-creating project. I know that this is controversial, and that other investigators do not see these expressions of acceptance as I do. It has been suggested, for example, that the abductees have been deceived by the beings or, like hostages, they are engaged in a kind of identification with their captors.

I have become persuaded of the genuineness of abduction-related personal transformation on the part of the abductees by the other examples of personal growth and spiritual awakening that they undergo. Part of the confusion around this issue has to do, I believe, with a misunderstanding of the role of trauma, which is thought of primarily as a destructive or harmful experience rather than as one that contains the possibility of spiritual growth or transformation. Whether such change is a "purpose" of the experiences or a by-product of it cannot be answered without knowing the "intention" of the intelligence that lies behind the whole abduction phenomenon.

As abductees look more deeply into themselves and their experiences, the quality and meaning of the encounters tend to shift and the relationship with the beings sometimes changes. Such abductees come to see them not as aliens or tormentors but as spirit guides or guardians with whom they have had a long relationship and who come to them as emissaries of the divine, or what they usually call Home or Source, a place beyond or outside of space and time that is pure light or creative possibility itself—words will fail them when they try to talk about this. Our work with experiencers sometimes becomes a kind of vehicle for the reconnecting of the experiencers with Source, from which, they come to realize, they feel and have felt an agonizing separation. This consciousness or spiritual expansion and awakening seems to have little relationship to the abductees' religious background, although in a few instances I have seen them bring a new vitality to, or even transform, an earlier faith that had lost its relevance for their lives.

Relationships

Although they may remember the beings as friendly playmates in childhood, many of the adolescent or adult abductees I have interviewed tend to describe the alien beings initially as cold, indifferent to their well-being, and businesslike, as they go about the tasks of bringing them to the ships and working on their bodies and psyches. But here, too, change occurs over time as the experiences are explored more deeply. The abductees sometimes report that they feel intense bonds with one or more of the alien beings, and even that they have a beloved alien mate "on the other side," with whom they are parenting hybrid offspring. They also describe ecstatic contact or a kind of physical merger, which has an erotic quality but is more total or spiritual and less genitally focused than human sexual love.

Abduction experiencers may feel that these relationships provide models that transcend the antagonisms and jealousies that characterize human relationships. Abductees may also feel that they have a dual human-alien identity, and it is a challenge to sort out in our discussions of human-alien connection in which persona the human being finds him- or herself during particular encounters. The intensity of the human-alien bond can create problems of jealousy in families, and some of the counseling that Roberta and I must do involves working with couples around how the relationships "on the other side" affect their marriages. This could be comical were it not emotionally so poignantly real.

Finally, it must be noted that it is through contact with the aliens' huge black eyes, sometimes spoken of as like looking into a vast, all-knowing or engulfing void, that the most powerful feeling of connection occurs. The beings' eyes seem to provide a kind of intimation of the infinite, appearing to contain or evoke the sense of ancient, unfathomable depths.

Summary and Conclusions

The descriptions provided here give only a sketchy summary of some of the principal features of the abduction phenomenon. Researchers do differ with regard to some of the details, or what should be emphasized, and certainly do not agree on the possible meanings and implications of the phenomenon, which lie beyond the scope of this chapter. But even this brief overview should suggest that no psychiatric condition or obvious other psychophysiological or sociocultural explanation can account for all, or even most, of the vast range of elements that constitute the phenomenon, only a fraction of which have been described here.

It is my view that we would not even search so hard for alternative, "conventional" (conventional in terms of our culture's definitions of reality) explanations were it not for the fact that the abduction phenomenon as reported so violates the prevailing worldview of scientific materialism or anthropocentric humanism. Indeed, none of the scores of explanations proposed, from sleep paralysis to media contamination to mass delusion, accounts, even potentially, for more than a small fraction of the many elements that make up the full picture. The search for alternative explanations will, and perhaps must, continue if for no other reason than that this is part of the process by which inadequate ontologies weaken and lose their hold on the human mind.

Perhaps now it will not be long before we, as a society, may let go of resistance and fear of the unknown, and appreciate that the abduction phenomenon, near-death experiences, the experiments of parapsychology, and other well-documented anomalies that challenge the Western worldview are forcing us to change our thinking about who we are and the nature of the cosmos in which we exist. We may then be able to accept the UFO/abduction phenomenon for what it seems to be, namely, the penetration into our minds and worlds of physical objects and strange beings brought into our reality by a mysterious intelligence whose purposes or intention we can only surmise. Such acceptance might allow us to encounter and explore the phenomenon in its own right, including its more disturbing aspects, and get on with the exciting project of learning more deeply about its nature and meaning for our current lives and future possibilities.

Chapter Ten

The UFO Experience: A Normal Correlate of Human Brain Function

Michael A. Persinger

All of your experiences are generated within your brain. They emerge
from complex, subtle electromagnetic patterns created within the
intricate, minute interactions that represent your cerebral space. These
experiences, which define who you are, range from the immediate
impressions of normal stimuli that directly affect your senses to the
reconstruction of representations that compose the temporal record
of your personal past. Even the conviction that an experience is either a real memory, a wish, or the remnants of dream is due to activations in specific regions of your brain.

The structural organization of the human brain allows you to
be only aware of the activity (or states) of your brain cells. You do
not directly respond to the stimulation of your eyes, ears, or other
senses. Instead, the information within the stimuli that impact upon
your sensors is transformed into the language of the brain. This brain
language is a series of digital and analog signals that are continuously produced within your brain for every millisecond of every day
as long as you live. When you are aware of images, emotions, or their
memories, you are experiencing these transformed patterns of brain
signals and *not* the actual events that produced them.

This fundamental organization of human experience means that
any stimulus that can induce specific patterns of activity within
groups of brain cells can generate experiences that are equally as real

and as compelling. If the same pattern of brain activity that is induced by the observation of a human being is reproduced within your brain by *direct* stimulation of those cells, without the input from the eyes, you would experience that specific observation of the same human being even though there was no person present.

For thousands of years and within every known human culture, normal individuals have reported brief and often repeated "visitations" by humanoid phenomena whose presence produced permanent changes within the psychological organization of the experient.[1] When these phenomena were labeled as deities, the "messages" were employed to initiate religious movements that changed the social fabric of the society. When these phenomena were labeled as personal guides, the "messages" were interpreted as cosmic insights for the understanding of the purpose of an individual's existence.

The main theme of this chapter is to explore visitation experiences, now attributed by many people to UFO and implicitly "extraterrestrial" phenomena, from the perspective of modern neuroscience. Our approach has not emphasized the veridicality or truth of the experiences. From an operational perspective, the average visitation experience attributed to an alien entity is indiscriminable from the average mystical or religious experience attributed to gods and to spirits. Instead, we have been attempting to isolate those areas of the brain and those electromagnetic patterns within the brain that are involved with the generation of visitation phenomena.

We realize that if all experiences are due to brain activity, and the experience of "an entity" is associated with a specific pattern or algorithm of electromagnetic sequences within the brain, then there may be stimuli, as yet not identified, that can evoke these sequences and produce these experiences. Science is, after all, the pursuit of the unknown. To dismiss a phenomenon as untrue simply because it is not compatible with the contemporary belief of reality reflects the behavior of scientists but not the theme of science.

Within the universe there may be phenomena whose existence we can only infer but at present cannot measure because our tools are too crude or too insensitive. The inference of the existence of bacteria was discussed a century before the microscope revealed their presence. The inference of DNA, the chemical structure of the genetic code, was considered for decades before the X-ray diffraction required to discern this structure was perfected. As long as the phenomenon in question is *not* defined as nonphysical, and hence never testable or verifiable, its measurement is always potentially possible.

A Brief Description of the Human Brain

If the primary tool of measurement for all human experience is the human brain, then understanding its fundamental structure and function is important. At the cellular level, the brain is composed of an estimated hundreds of billions of two major classes of cells, neurons and glia, that constantly transform the digital and analog electromagnetic information into chemical codes that transmit these data across time and space to functionally associated neurons. The presence of these chemical codes is the primary reason that drugs, such as hallucinogens, can change the shape of normal perceptions or even induce subjective fabrications.

Drawings of different perspectives of the human brain are shown in Figures 10.1 and 10.2. The brain can be conceived as a four-dimensional structure that exists in three-dimensional space and over time. The first conspicuous physical feature is the two hemispheres, the left and right side of the brain. Even though they appear identical, there is very little exact similarity in the surface microstructure between the two sides of the brain. Because structure dictates function, this means that the two sides of the brain will have slightly different functional capacities for detecting stimuli and for organizing them into the patterns of experience.

The left hemisphere is more involved with the experience and expression of the meaning of language and word images within serial time. Language processes are also associated with the sense of self, the experience of who and what you are. The right hemisphere engages more in simultaneous processing of the visuospatial, novel, and emotional dimensions of perception. The different textures of experiences associated with the average activity within the left and right hemispheres are analogous to the differences between the waking state and the dream state. Under normal conditions the two hemispheres are constantly interacting within the time frame of milliseconds. Your sense of consciousness is the interaction between them

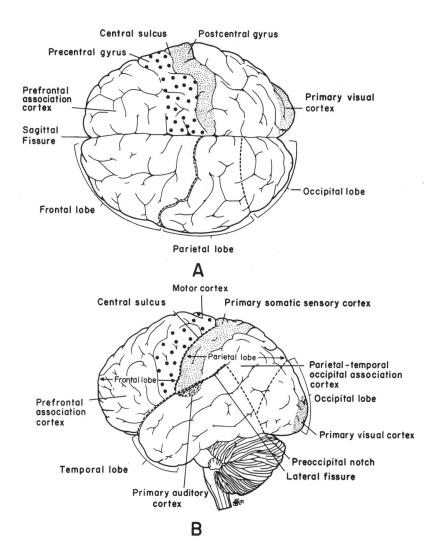

Figure 10.1. (A) A view of the human brain from the top, showing the left and right hemispheres. The major lobes, visible from this perspective, are shown. The region between the central sulcus and the primary visual cortex is the parietal lobes. (B) Lateral (side) view of the human brain showing the major lobes of the left hemisphere.

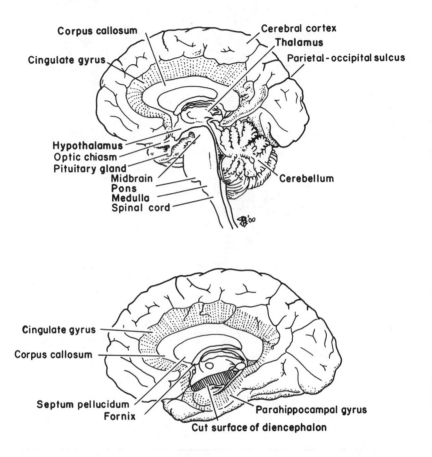

Corpus callosum

Cerebral cortex
Thalamus

Cingulate gyrus

Parietal - occipital sulcus

Hypothalamus
Optic chiasm
Pituitary gland
Midbrain
Pons
Medulla
Spinal cord

Cerebellum

Cingulate gyrus

Corpus callosum

Septum pellucidum
Fornix

Parahippocampal gyrus

Cut surface of diencephalon

Figure 10.2. Medial sagittal section of the human brain. The hidden space between the hemispheres can be seen. Relevant structures are the corpus callosum and the cingulate gyrus.

and the deeper portions of the cerebrum that mediate meaning and memory.

The second obvious feature of the cerebrum is its organization into larger regions or lobes.[2] In general, sensory information or input into the brain, from both inside and outside of the body, is received by the posterior portions of the cerebrum. After coding into language equivalents, this information is propagated by neurons to the massive prefrontal regions. Within the prefrontal regions of the brain, information is discriminated, organized, planned, and given attributions (for cause) before one acts upon the environment.

Beliefs are peoples' experiences of how they organize, predict, and explain the myriad of random stimuli that impinge upon them. Without the structure-making properties of beliefs and a functional prefrontal region, normal people experience incessant anxiety, panic, or feelings of impending doom. Without shared beliefs that there is a tomorrow, the complexities of cultural order and social conduct would deteriorate within days. When the majority of people within a culture share a belief about why they exist and what will happen to them in the future, the belief is considered normal. If a belief is not shared by the majority, it is labeled as delusional. The label does not reveal the source of the belief, nor does it help elucidate its origin.

The loss of a few neurons, particularly those that inhibit other neurons from activity, is a surprisingly common event in the normal brain as a result of aging, stress, minor changes in blood flow within the brain, and environmental chemical toxins. When slight hypofunction in the posterior regions of the cerebrum occurs, the person may hear a sentence but not be able to recognize or know what it means. When above-average stimulation occurs in the same area, the person may listen to nonsense syllables and yet have the experience that he understands the cosmic and personal significance of their meaning. However, when the prefrontal area is functioning below average, the person may not be able to organize his behavior or to discriminate between wishes, dreams, and experiences. When this area is slightly stimulated, the person may organize his or her perceptual world into an elaborate connection of personal, meaningful, and inflexible cognitions that will dictate every aspect of his or her life. All experience, no matter how mundane, becomes connected to a belief.

The third feature of the human brain is that many areas are associated with general functions.[3] The occipital cortices are associated with seeing and recognizing what one sees. Loss of neurons in this region can cause blindness, while overstimulation can evoke sensations that range from bright, rotating colorful spheres to detailed landscapes. The parietal cortices are integral to experiencing the body and its image. The major input for the body image is derived from the movement of muscles and stimulation to the skin after birth. When the normal interactions between the two parietal lobes are disrupted, the person may feel as if he or she has two selves or there is another "self" present just outside of the peripheral vision.

Two less well known areas of the human brain are the insulae and the "limbic lobes."[4] The insulae are two massive islands of neurons hidden below the surface of the cerebrum. Their neurons are associated with the experience of taste and the modulation of the internal organs of the body. Specific patterns of electrical stimulation within the insula affect heart rate. Changes in the state of the uterus for the female specifically and the abdominal and anal regions for men and women in general are represented within the insula.

The "limbic lobe" is located along the bottom surface of the cerebrum and extends deep within its middle portions, the cingulate gyrus. Normal activity of neurons within the right limbic lobe is associated with a sense of a familiarity, while normal activity within the left limbic lobe is associated with the sense of personal meaning.[5] Hyperstimulation of the neurons within the right limbic lobe, even for a few minutes, can be associated with intense panic and anxiety. The anterior portions of the cingulate mediate the awareness of this emotional experience. This area also contributes significantly to the feelings of love, bonding, and the requirement to be near loved ones.

The temporal lobes are associated with experiences of hearing and the sensation of movement. For example, if you listen to music, without lyrics, neurons within the right temporal lobe are more activated because this region is involved with the representation of sound patterns in time. If you listen to a person speaking, then neurons within the left temporal lobe are more activated because this region of the brain is involved with understanding spoken language.

However, the reverse process can also occur. If neurons within your right temporal lobe are *appropriately* stimulated by electrical sequences, you would experience music that could appear as real and as rich as that generated by an orchestra. If neurons within your left temporal lobe were stimulated, you would hear an internal voice call your name and even engage in a conversation with your sense of self. This experience would be normal and would *not* necessarily indicate the presence of any psychosis or mental illness.

Although the specific details of the music you would hear or the verbal message you would "receive" would reflect your history and the culture with which you are associated, the auditory theme would remain the same. In some areas, particularly those associated with vision, fundamental perceptions, or "wholes," require the normal function of groups of neurons. The ability to perceive and to recognize a human face or a human hand requires the integrity of neurons within the limbic region of the ventral portions of the temporal lobes. If this area is stimulated, vivid human faces or shapes of hands can be perceived.

Given the representations of all the volume of the body within the brain and the brain's control of every cell of the body, the fact that subtle changes within the brain can stop the heart, produce local anomalies on the skin of the feet or legs, and even alter the perception of the world would not be surprising. Thinking, manifested as beliefs or repeated experiences, is also a feature of brain activity. Consequently, what one believes has happened or expects will happen can influence the entire body.

Which Areas Are More Stimulated During the Visitation Experience?

Neuroscientists have known for centuries that individuals with electrically overactive brains, most of whom have been diagnosed with partial complex epilepsy with the area of electrical sensitivity within the temporal or limbic lobes, report intense experiences. Virtually every basic element of mystical, religious, and the UFO visitor experiences has been associated with spontaneous electrical seizures that are not necessarily associated with convulsions or obvious changes in behavior. The characteristics of the experiences reflect the function of the regions within the cerebrum where the electrically active neurons reside. The most common themes are fear, the smell of odd substances, amnesia, vestibular effects, rising sensations through the viscera, sexual stimulation, feelings of familiarity or reminiscence, the doubling of consciousness (as if another "awareness" was present), dreamlike states, and very complex hallucinatory experiences that are integrated into the person's ongoing cognitions.[6]

The experiences can range from the peak of ecstasy to the mundane. For example, the Russian novelist Dostoyevsky, who exhibited complex partial epileptic seizures, reported that "the air was filled with a big noise and I thought that it had engulfed me. I have really touched God. He came into me, myself; yes, God exists . . . such instances were characterized by a fulguration of the consciousness and by a supreme exaltation of emotional subjectivity."[7]

However, the experiences are not always cosmic. One young epileptic woman was about to enter her car when she discovered she was being followed by a very tiny man dressed in a frock coat and striped trousers. With the exception of his diminutive size, the man had a normal appearance. He entered the car, accompanied the woman to her friend's apartment, and followed her to the door of the apartment, where he disappeared. On several occasions, she saw the little man again, but never as clearly.[8]

Similar experiences, unique to the person, have been evoked by *directly* stimulating the person's brain with electric currents that were below the intensity required to produce convulsions. Although the shape of the electric currents was very crude, usually square wave pulses that contained minimal information, the experiences elicited by the stimulation were often identical to those produced by spontaneous hyperactivity (electrical seizures) of the neurons. The consensual, and most parsimonious, explanation is that these crude current shapes were simply activating the same or similar aggregate of neurons that were always near the threshold for activation and whose activation *was* the experience. Even the representations or memories of emotionally intense events from childhood can become integrated consistently into the details of the experience.

Nearly every basic element of mystical, religious, and visitor experiences has been evoked with direct electrical stimulation. For example, one patient, when directly stimulated within the deep regions of the right temporal lobe, felt "fear and the feeling of someone being nearby." She then distinctly saw a "person who seemed to be standing in the sun." Another man, who was stimulated in the same hemisphere, reported, "It feels like a dream. Some people are talking behind me. I can hear their voices, but I don't understand what they say." Another patient reported, "I feel as if I was detached from my body, floating above it, everything looked familiar and I had the feeling I could tell what was going to happen. . . . I was being forced into another time and place."[9] Still another patient reported, "I see an angel."

However, not every region, when stimulated electrically, has resulted in experiences that are perceived by the waking experient. The creation of experience by direct surgical stimulation of the brain requires the involvement of two critical structures: the hippocampus, the gateway to memory, and the amygdala. The location of these structures deep within the left and right temporal lobes is shown in Figure 10.3. These two structures have the lowest threshold (most easily stimulated) for electrical excitability within the brain. They are intimately involved with the normal consolidation of memory and the pairing of reward or aversion (pleasure or pain) to every experience as it is being encoded.[10]

Mild enhancement of hippocampal activity is associated with hypermnesia, an increase in memory capacity, that is evident within populations of highly suggestible or very creative individuals. Mild interference within hippocampal activity produces distortions in subjective time or no memory (amnesia) because the fragile electrical representations of experience (those complex codes of digital sequences) become masked or expunged by the excessive activity.[11] Even normal overarousal such as a stressful event or intense anger can result in the person reporting an incomplete memory of the event or the experience as if there were "blanks" in subjective time.

The two amygdala, which are primarily anterior to the hippocampus in the deep portions of the temporal lobes, are the mediators of affect. Depending on the pattern and place of stimulation within the amygdala, the experiences range from sexual orgasm to existential terror.[12] For example, during electrical discharges within the vicinity of the right amygdala (but including other areas), one woman repeatedly experienced a feeling of familiarity, flashes of light moving in the upper left peripheral field, an experience of falling, an unpleasant metallic taste, olfactory sensations, and pleasurable sensations in her sexual organs, occasionally feeling as if someone touched the sensuous areas of her body. Another woman,

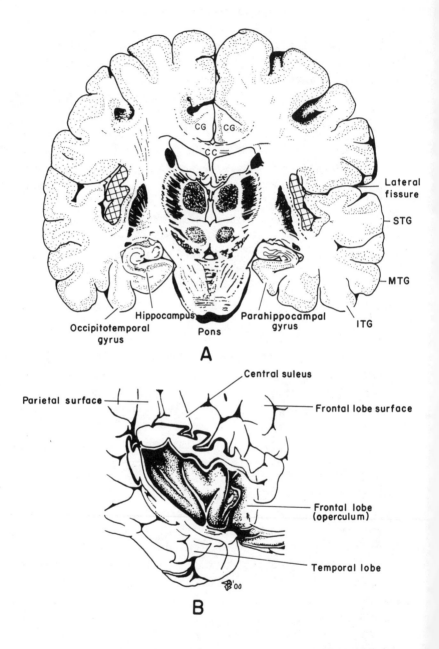

A

Labels in figure A:
CG | CG
CC
Lateral fissure
STG
MTG
ITG
Hippocampus
Occipitotemporal gyrus
Pons
Parahippocampal gyrus

B

Labels in figure B:
Central suleus
Parietal surface
Frontal lobe surface
Frontal lobe (operculum)
Temporal lobe

Figure 10.3. (A) Coronal section of the brain. The major gyri of the temporal lobes are indicated. Note the position of the two hippocampal formations deep within the temporal lobes. The amygdala would be anterior to the hippocampus in each hemisphere. The hatched areas are the insulae. (B) The presentation of the insula after the overlaying temporal lobe and frontal lobe has been removed.

a childless physician, would experience strange sensations of rising from the stomach to the throat followed by a pleasant sensation of anal and vaginal contraction approaching sexual orgasm.[13]

If you were reading a mundane sequence such as "Jack and Jill went up the hill . . ." and your amygdala was stimulated appropriately at that moment, your experience might be so profound and meaningful that these words would appear to contain the cosmic clue to the universe. If you visualized, due to direct observation or following instruction by a therapist, a simple geometric structure when this area was being stimulated, you might feel as if the current experience is the repetition of something already lived and the actions about to happen can be predicted. These episodes of reminiscence or déjà vu accompany great personal significance. However, because of the structure of the amygdala and the propensity for most hyperstimulations to be above the narrow band required to evoke the more subtle emotions, the most typical correlate of frank amygdaloid activity is fear.

The "realness" of the experiences evoked by direct electrical stimulation of the brain is not because they are always "memories" of what actually occurred. For example, an epileptic patient reported he saw four German soldiers walk down a U.S. city street, turn, and fire at him; the bullets suddenly appeared to stop and fall immediately in front of him. Electrical stimulation appears to enhance *the ongoing cognitive* process.[14] If the person is perceiving at the time of the stimulation, the perception is more real. If the person is thinking with visual imagery at the time of the stimulation, the imagery may be so intense that it appears to be due to the actual presence of the object, person, or place. Direct electrical stimulation evokes activity in other neurons as well as those associated with the experience. As the numbers of neurons activated increases, the correlative experiences become "more real."

Subtle and Long-Term Consequences of Overactivity in the Temporal Lobes

Brief periods of optimal electrical stimulation within the temporal and limbic lobes alter the microstructural connections between neurons.[15] Since all memory is consolidated as complex patterns of connections between neurons, repeated, brief periods of electrical stimulation within the overactive brain often encourage the production of different functions and behaviors. One of the most frequent observations of people (or rodents) who display overactivity within the limbic and temporal lobes is the insidious changes in behavior and the manner in which they respond to the world. The organism slowly becomes, behaviorally at least, a different individual.[16]

Three phases of change can be distinguished when this type of occasional stimulation occurs within the temporal-limbic lobes. The immediate effects include intense dreamlike experiences, sensations of déjà-vu, depersonalization (the feeling as if one is not real or the situation is not real), and vertigo. There are often prominent vestibular sensations of floating, flying, or spinning. Auditory experiences are described as "knowing" without hearing. These phenomena are always punctuated by intense meaningfulness.

The second phase, which can last for days to weeks, includes confusion and disorientation. The person may experience periods of amnesia, which is the psychological experience for the disruption of the transient electromagnetic patterns within the hippocampus. Because of the normal processes of memory consolidation, information that is told to the person after the experience can be incorporated into the amnesic interval. Even the imagery of the words employed to label the possible source of the dysmnesia can affect memory. The person would begin to experience "recollections" or "new memories" concomitant with the feeling of "regaining the memory" as this postepisodic information is integrated into the repeated reconstructions of "what" actually happened.

The third phase may continue for years and is associated with a change in the experient's "personality." The most common features of these slow alterations in behavior are (1) bouts of automatic behavior (and amnesia) followed by auditory instructions from a voice or a strong intuition about where or when to find objects that were misplaced during the period of automatic behaviors; (2) a sense of the personal, when novel odd or unexpected events are interpreted as signs specific to and intended exclusively for the person; and (3) enhanced interest in mystical or religious concepts (more than religious institutions) with focus upon nascent themes such as who are we? what is the nature of the universe? and where do we go when we die?

Because of the involvement of the amygdala, these experiences are considered so important and meaningful that the person feels compelled to record every one of them. Consequently, diaries and personal memoirs become the written records of the person's change in behavior. Most individuals feel so unique they are convinced they have been "selected" for a purpose. With such affective compulsion, they soon develop the conviction to proselytize, to "spread the word." All these experiences and behaviors are integrated within a person who has normal intelligence, normal social skills, and no psychiatric disorder. Because the person's beliefs and interests change, he or she usually shifts from an old vocation and develops friendships with people who share a history of similar experiences.

The Typically Active Brain

The relationship between the numbers of neurons that are activated and the intensity of the experience is not specific to patients whose brains are directly stimulated. New technologies—functional magnetic resonance imaging (fMRI) and positron emission tomography (PET)—have demonstrated this relationship in normal people who respond to verbal instructions or who perceive ordinary objects. Both procedures allow relatively precise (to the nearest millimeter) measurement of the metabolic activity of the neurons within increments of seconds in response to environmental stimuli. Unfortunately, the resolution of these procedures is not sufficient to discern the activity between neurons or to detect the interactions of the complex electromagnetic fields.

For example, people who are particularly creative and can experience vivid imagery and physiological changes (when they are "absorbed" while reading a novel) show greater general activation in the right temporal lobe relative to the left hemisphere. People who do not display this characteristic for vivid imagery do not display this permanent level of brain activation.[17] Individuals who hallucinate sounds to an instruction when told to do so (these people are convinced the sound was "real") show specific and marked activation, at the time of memory of the "sound" (which never actually occurred), in areas of the brain involved with attention and emotional bonding (anterior cingulate) to other human beings. When an experience is intense enough, it can be labeled as an ongoing perception or as a memory.

The new technologies have also verified what psychologists have suspected for centuries: there are different classes of memories whose activations involve different regions of the brain. The request to recall memory about facts, such as who is the president of the United States or the prime minister of Canada, involves different regions of the cerebrum than the request for you to remember what happened to yourself last year. This class of memory, autobiographical memory,[18] is associated with more specific activation of the frontal lobe in the right hemisphere.[19] As a result, the details of the types of "memories" one recalls will be affected by who asks the question, how many times the question is asked, and the experient's level of depression and anxiety.

The UFO Visitor Experience

When the explanation and contemporary beliefs of the culture are accommodated, the UFO experience is very similar thematically to other visitor experiences such as incubi, succubi, angels, and fairies. They have occurred in temporal clusters or epidemics congruent with gradual changes in the complex expectancies about the future. Like all experiences, the UFO visitor experience has common antecedent, concurrent, and consequent commonalities.

The most typical antecedent conditions for the visitation experience are periods when the person has been either personally distressed, due to a loss of a significant person or vocation, or has sustained a recent (within the previous year) mild to moderate brain trauma that may not have been associated with a period of unconsciousness. Another common antecedent for these experiences is the anticipation of a permanent change in lifestyle. The latter ranges from the normal progression through the stages of life (aging) to the anticipation of the end of the world. Prone individuals are usually the more intuitive, creative members of a society who are proficient as poets, artists, and musicians. They usually have had histories of a sensed presence before the experience that is attributed to the "UFO visitation/abduction."

The most typical condition at the time of the experiences is an altered state (usually during early morning hours between 2:00 and 4:00 A.M.) or in contexts, such as a protracted period of driving, when right hemispheric activity and interruptions of consciousness are encouraged. If the person is asleep, he or she usually awakens suddenly and feels a presence or multiple presences and perceives a humanoid being (or beings) nearby. There are also vestibular sensations (vibrations or floating). If the sensation of detachment and movement up or through an aperture occurs, the person may feel as if he or she is in another space (location) or time.

Depending on the presence of the entities primarily to the left or right of the person (assuming the normal left-hemispheric dominance), the person may experience intense fear or apprehension (particularly for a left-sided presence) or the sounds of speech or a message (particularly for a right-sided presence). Sensations of stimulation of feet and lower legs and genitals, usually the uterine region for women and the anal area for men, are often secondary. All these themes and specific experiences have been evoked by stimulation of the temporal lobes, their ventral surfaces (the limbic lobes), and the indirect connections through the insulae.

The post hoc interpretation of these experiences and their attribution (the explanation for their cause) depends on the person's cultural expectations and his or her reinforcement history. If the experience is negative and aversive, it is more likely to be attributed to negative symbols and explanations such as a devil, incubus, or evil alien. If the experience is positive, a less frequent event because pleasant experiences are evoked by a narrow range of hyperactivity, the presence may be attributed to positive symbols such as gods, angels, or good aliens. Once this label has been applied, which requires less than two hundred milliseconds (about one-fifth of a second), the time required for the experience of "now," all the other imagery supplied by the person's memory and delivered through the culture will affect the reconstruction of the details of the experiences.

The experiences of UFO visitor profiles are really not that uncommon, if the professional remains open to the patient's explanations. Most people who report these experiences display average to above average intelligence, are not "crazy," and are very aware of the social and personal consequences of their experiences upon their families, friends, and vocational opportunities. The details may not be shared with others. One thirty-five-year-old woman reported to me the presence of multiple, elongated alien humanoids, in shimmering gray-silver clothes, that would surround her bed for a few nights every few months. The "things" would move very quickly, "like a movie in fast speed." She experienced probing and manipulation of her abdomen and inner vagina, which resulted in "embarrassing" lubrication and discharges. Sometimes there were small cuts on her left ankle, and the heels of her feet were sensitive. The experiences were terrifying, and she wished them terminated but was reluctant to tell her physician because he might think she was "crazy."

The experiences disappeared when she began a low-dose regime of the antiepileptic compound carbamazepine (Tegretol). This case does not indicate that all people who report visitor experiences associated with UFOs are undiagnosed epileptics or that the phenomena will cease with this particular medication. Instead, it indicates that well-formed and meaningful experiences, attributed to alien sources and sufficient in magnitude to disrupt the person's sense of self and adaptability, can be associated with periods of electrical activity that can be affected by treatments not typically associated with these types of experiences.

Although descriptions of the quintessential or "prototypical" visitor experience are useful for discussion, they should not be considered as proofs of a rigid similarity of the experiences. There are great individual differences in anomalous subjective experiences that are largely and falsely homogenized by the requirements to communicate the concept.

For example, most readers probably assume that the near-death experience always involves movement through a tunnel, a bright light, spiritual contact with dead relatives, and return. Such stereotypy does not reflect the data. The tunnel experience can range from moving through a cave to being driven in a white car down a narrow road. The spiritual contact can range from experiencing a god to contacting an extraterrestrial entity, and from seeing shining palaces with golden streets to surrealistic cities surrounded by odd flying "ships." Most important, not all near-death experiences are positive. Some of them, between 5 and 10 percent, are intensely aversive and terrifying experiences.

Prevalence of Reported Experiences Relevant to the Visitor/Abduction Phenomena

About twenty years ago, Kate Makarec and I developed a 140-item, true-false questionnaire designed to help understand the multivariate relationships between temporal lobe–like experiences within the normal population and the proportions of religious beliefs and exotic beliefs. The questionnaire was called the Personal Philosophy Inventory in order to minimize response bias.[20] Quantitative analyses indicated that clusters of items shared similar sources of variance, or factors, and these items were representative of the classes of experiences reported by people with epileptic foci within the limbic or temporal lobes. A similar interrelation of these experiences was also reported by Richard Roberts and his colleagues, employing different measurement scales and assumptions.[21] They called these experiences the *epileptic spectrum disorder*.

The results of the Personal Philosophy Inventory indicated that the experiences of normal people were distributed along this *continuum* of temporal lobe sensitivity. However, unlike epileptic patients with electrical foci within the temporal or limbic lobes, or individuals who had sustained mild to moderate brain trauma, the experiences were not as frequent or pervasive within the normal population. Although there was a moderate correlation between the numbers of these experiences and temporal lobe electrical activity, the latter was associated with variability of alpha rhythms (an easily recognized electroencephalographic pattern between 8 and 13 Hz) and not with paroxysmal discharges.[22]

During the last two decades, the Personal Philosophy Inventory has been administered during the first day of class to students in a first-year psychology course. Approximately seventeen hundred participants, with an average age of twenty-four, have been involved. The prevalence of a few of the experiences that constitute the temporal lobe continuum[23] of sensitivity are shown in the table below. During these two decades there have been no statistically significant increases or decreases in the prevalence of the proportion of the reports of these experiences.

Proportion of respondents (about 1,700) over a twenty-year period who reported yes to the item from the Personal Philosophy Inventory

Q 18. At least once in the last ten years, I have fallen asleep and then awakened the next morning in another room. 24%

Q 27. About once a year, I will awaken during sleep and not be able to move. 20%

Q 29. While sitting quietly, I have had uplifting sensations as if I were driving over a rolling road. 24%

Q 38. At least once in my life very late at night, I have felt the presence of another Being. 39%

Q 63. Sometimes, in the early morning hours between midnight and 4:00 A.M., my experiences are very meaningful. 31%

Q 71. My soul sometimes leaves my body. 5%

Q 76. I have heard an inner voice call my name. 14%

Q 82. At least once a month, I experience intense smells that do not have an obvious source. 16%

Q 96. As a child I played with an imaginary friend. 27%

Q 110. I have dreams of floating or flying through the air at least once per year. 40%

Q 115. Alien intelligence is probably responsible for UFOs. 36%

Q 113. I have had an epileptic seizure. 2%

Q 133. I have been visited by a Spiritual Being. 7%

When the items in the above table were factor analyzed in order to reveal which experiences were related to the same source (of numerical variance), the sensed presence (Q 38) item was loaded on the same factor as experiences of presleep amnesia (Q 18), sleep paralyses (Q 27), uplifting vestibular sensations (Q 29), early morning meaningful experiences (Q 63), odd smells (Q 82), dreams of flying (Q 110), and beliefs that alien intelligence is responsible for UFOs (Q 115). A second factor, which was more strongly loaded by the visitor experience, also contained shared variance with hearing an inner voice call the person's name (Q 76), visitation by a Spiritual Being (Q 133), and sleep paralyses (Q 27). The incidence of frank epilepsy was not correlated significantly within either of these two factors. The composition of the two factors strongly suggested that there was intrinsic organization or experience within normal people that was associated with acknowledgment of the experience of a visitation. One was associated with beliefs in alien intelligence, while the other displayed a more religious connotation.

Simulation of the UFO Visitor/Abduction Experience

Reports of the visitor experience, regardless of the details, the sincerity of the experient, or the eloquence of the philosophical argument by popular writers, are only correlations for which the actual sources are not always clear. The primary tool by which science attempts to isolate the causes and characteristics of any phenomena is the experiment, which allows the researcher to manipulate and control the possible events that cause a phenomenon. For the last decade, members of the Laurentian University Neuroscience Research Group have been pursuing the technology for re-creating the characteristics of the "alien visitation" component of the UFO experience within the laboratory.

Our pursuit of the physical bases to the luminous displays, which are in large part unusual balls of light that display odd colors (with occasional metallic sheen) and movements, has resulted in the development of the tectonic strain hypothesis by John Derr and myself.[24] The mechanisms are clearly within the domain of geophysics and geology, as shown by the recent field data from Paul Devereaux's research group.[25] Occasionally a person will approach a bright ball of light, and the consequences will elicit the visitor experience. In these instances the two pursuits, the understanding of luminous displays and the visitor experience, interconnect. However, most visitor experiences do not involve direct contact with intense luminous displays.

Five factors have been isolated that determine a person's experiences and the memories of those experiences in both natural and laboratory settings. These five factors are remarkably similar to those that affect the themes and contents of experiences evoked from the brains of individuals who display complex partial electrical anomalies within the limbic or temporal lobes. The primary difference between the epileptic studies and our research is that all of our subjects are *normal* individuals. Their temporal lobe activity, as inferred by electroencephalographic and psychometric testing, is within the above-average range. In addition, except for clinical trials, we do not expose individuals who have verified histories of epilepsy.

The first factor that affects the details of the experience is the person's beliefs or expectations, which reflect the idiosyncratic reinforcement history. The second factor, which appears to largely determine why some people are more prone to the visitor experience, is the lability or sensitivity of the person's temporal lobes and limbic regions. We have been developing paper-and-pencil tests in order to extract the profile of subjective experiences that would discern these normal people more easily.

Individuals with enhanced temporal lobe sensitivity can associate vivid imagery with their internal states (a history of meditation facilitates this process) and suffuse ordinary sensory input with personal meaning. These people are very sensitive to subtle changes in physical and social environment. Quite remarkably, many of these normal individuals can reliably respond to the presence of weak, complex magnetic fields that other individuals either cannot detect or label accurately.

These individuals are the more creative of the population and usually endorse exotic beliefs rather than traditional religious beliefs. Exotic beliefs are inferred from the subjects' positive endorsement of items such as "UFOs are due to alien intelligence," "There is the possibility of life on other planets," and "I think I may have lived a previous life." The personality structure of these people is similar to but less intense than those associated with patients who have histories of extreme temporal lobe lability (epilepsy). The incidence of psychosis within the population who report an alien-like experience is not any different from those who do not.

The third factor is the demand characteristic of the setting. We have found that subtle context and stimuli affect the details of the experiences. In one experiment we exposed volunteers to one of two subtle conditions before the lights were extinguished and they were asked to engage in spontaneous narrative. For one group, a cross had been hung in the setting, and music of Gregorian chants had been played for about a minute. For a second group, a picture of the earth taken from a satellite had been hung where the cross had been, and about one minute of music from *Close Encounters of the Third Kind* was played in the background. This single manipulation, which was not mentioned by the experimenters because the experiment was involved with "relaxation," was sufficient to change subjective experiences from emphasis on themes of religion (and death) to space and extraterrestrial (usually movies) references. This influence occurred even *without* direct stimulation of brain areas.

The fourth factor that affects the theme and some of the details of the experiences in the laboratory is the complexity of the electromagnetic field applied through the brain and the hemisphere over which the field is most focused. The fifth factor that affects the memory of these fleeting experiences is the label that is given to the person at the end of the stimulation. We usually administer a specific exit questionnaire that asks the person to rate the relative incidence of experiences such as "dizziness," "leaving the body," and the feeling that the experiences did not come from the person's own mind. Because each subject has a baseline capacity to generate imagery, the effects of specific patterns of electromagnetic stimulation are discerned by contrast. Specific patterns of electromagnetic sequences evoke specific experiences disproportionately within the person's profile of imagery.

The history of science has shown that the most optimal manner to re-create a natural phenomenon is to simulate its temporal and spatial characteristics in the laboratory and then to modify one variable in a given experiment. Our attempts to synthesize the antecedent, concurrent, and consequent conditions of the visitor experience have been limited by the fact that we may not have isolated all of the variables of spontaneous or "natural" visitor experiences and we are bound by strong ethical constraints not to cause harm, psychologically or physically, to volunteers. The normal activation of the human brain and the stimuli that produce it are not inhibited by such restraints.

The Typical Laboratory Experiment

In order to minimize expectancies, normal university students or special volunteers are recruited for relaxation studies. Each person sits in a comfortable chair within an acoustic chamber. During the experiment, the subject wears opaque goggles. The purpose of this technique is to remove all visual and auditory input, which effectively imitates the nocturnal or sleeping context, and to allow those millions of neurons typically involved in visual and auditory surveillance to be recruited into the ongoing activity induced by the applied complex magnetic fields. One analogy would be a neural net with two major inputs. If one eliminated the input and increased the gain, the output would more likely reflect the ongoing "internal wiring" of the neural net or the noise within the system.

To activate the deep regions of the temporal lobes, we have developed complex sequences of magnetic field patterns that imitate some of the fundamental patterns found within populations of normal neurons and hyperactive neurons. The actual shapes of these patterns have been collected from neurons of people who have been in particular states or have been generated synthetically according to our theories of brain function. The sequence is essentially a code of between five hundred and ten thousand lines. Each line contains a number between 0 and 255, which is converted into voltage. If one imagines the sequential order of each of the ten thousand lines along the horizontal axis and the voltage along the vertical axis, then one can appreciate the complexity of patterns that can be generated. We have employed frequency-modulated patterns as well as those that imitate burst firing of neurons during the release of opiates and the consolidation of memory.[26]

The fields have been applied through solenoids that are embedded within helmets or movable containers. Pairs of solenoids are placed on each side of the head, at the level of the temporal lobes such that when the solenoids are activated, the flux lines penetrate the brain. The usual strength of the fields near the scalp is in the order of five to ten microtesla, or fifty to one hundred milligauss, within the areas of the skull to about one microtesla within the cerebral volume. The latter intensities would be similar to those generated by a computer or its screen. However, the difference between the latter and our experimental fields is that they contain information and are generated repeatedly to induce "entrainment" or recruitment of neurons whose pattern of firing is resonant with the applied fields.[27] We are expecting that specific applied patterns should evoke specific intrinsic algorithms and generate specific experiences.[28]

The primary differences between our protocol and protocols associated with surgical stimulation of brain tissue are important. First, although the magnetic fields from our equipment are emphasized over one region of the brain, they still penetrate through the brain because of the nature of these forces and our application geometry. This condition more closely approximates the natural activity of the brain. Surgical stimulation requires the physiological extremes of removing portions of the skull and direct insertions of electrodes. Second, we have been attempting to engage the basic patterns or algorithms that are associated with specific classes of experiences rather than to evoke paroxysmal activity per se. We have replaced the concentration on current or focal field intensity with field complexity.

From our perspective, increasing the strength of the magnetic field is neither prudent nor required. Recent research in contemporary neuroscience has indicated that resonance interaction between complex magnetic fields and the neural nets that compose consciousness lies within a narrow band of intensities. Although intense fields with crude temporal shapes may more easily evoke simple responses that are easily seen in a single measure, such forced or coerced distortions within neural aggregates remove the complexity required for conscious experiences. Intense, highly homogeneous magnetic fields are very important for measuring the characteristics of the density of the structure neuronal tissue (such as magnetic resonance imaging); however, they are not very effective for inducing the temporal patterns to simulate natural biological effects.

A metaphoric example of this methodological issue would be the following. If you and I were listening to a repeated sine wave of sound at one thousand cycles per second, we would probably not attend to it until the amplitude became painful at ninety decibels. At that point this sound would interfere with our conversation, and we would engage in a simple response: escape from the situation. However, if I whispered, around thirty decibels, a complex sound wave in the form "please help me," you would respond with great impact even though the amplitude was about a million times less intense.

Once the equipment has been applied outside the scalp, the subject is then exposed to an anisotropic hemispheric field. For about fifteen minutes the subject is first exposed to a pattern whose strength is higher by about a factor of two to five over the right hemisphere compared with the left. Usually the frequency-modulated patterns, developed by Alex Thomas, are employed because they enhance arousal and epileptiform activity. During the subsequent fifteen minutes, another field pattern, known to produce mild opiate-like effects, is applied equally across both hemispheres. Our explanation, although clearly not totally substantiated as yet, is that the initial activation of the right hemisphere followed by the subsequent activation of both hemispheres allows the neuroelectromagnetic representations of phenomena within the right hemisphere to enter into left hemispheric awareness.

This procedure simulates the activity of the normal brain during dream sleep (when regions within the right hemisphere tend to be slightly more active), personal distress, and maintained vigilance during the early morning hours. The procedure also simulates the condition that would exist for many individuals during periods of enhanced geomagnetic activity. We have shown geomagnetic intensity–dependent increases in the incidence of experiences that reflect a factor containing internal vibrations and the sensed presence. They increase, when pulsed fields are applied, if the amplitude of the geomagnetic variations had exceeded twenty to thirty nanotesla during the previous night and was still above this threshold at the time of the experiment.

The Sensed Presence in the Laboratory:
The Prototype of the Entity Experience

About 80 percent of the people exposed to the right hemisphere–bipolar hemisphere pattern have reported a sensed presence within the chamber during the exposures to the experimental magnetic fields for forty minutes (twenty minutes of right hemispheric stimulation, twenty minutes of bipolar stimulation). In comparison, only about 27 percent of the subjects exposed during similar periods to only bipolar stimulation by one of a variety of complex magnetic field patterns have reported this experience during the experimental periods. Because the latter proportion represents a pooled average of ten different experiments (involving more than 150 subjects) involving hypotheses that ranged from consolidation of memory to out-of-body experiences, optimal parameters for the production of the sensed presence were not always generated experimentally.

As noted in the earlier table, the lifetime prevalence of a generic sensed presence is 39 percent in the population from which the subjects were sampled for our experiments, whereas the prevalence of these experiences for subjects exposed only forty minutes to the more optimal field parameters was 80 percent. To discern if the experimental fields were simply evoking the person's experiential profile, quantitative analysis was completed between those who had or had not experienced a sensed presence sometime in their life with those who had or had not experienced a sensed presence during the exposure to the complex magnetic fields.

The concordance was marginally significant statistically and was equivalent to a correlation coefficient of about .14. If the correlation had been much stronger (those people who were prone before the experiment were the ones who always reported the sensed presence in the laboratory), then the experiences reported during the applied magnetic fields might be considered reiterations of "a memory" or related to the person's history of attributions for odd experiences. The results supported our assumption that the sensed presence within the laboratory was more specific to the experimental procedures.

The most common experiences accompanying the sensed presence during the electromagnetic stimulation employed in our studies have been fear, dizziness, floating, odd tastes, vivid images from a dream, and the experience that the thoughts were not from the experient's own mind. Quantitative analyses have indicated two sources of variance for the experiences of sensed presences. The first type is also associated with vivid images, pleasant vibrations moving through the body, the feeling of being detached or leaving the body, and the experience of "being in another place." One would expect that an experience dominated by the latter theme (another place) would be more likely to be remembered, described, and attributed to an "abduction" if it occurred in an ambiguous, nonexperimental setting.

The second type of sensed presence has been associated with a strong sense of fear, thoughts from childhood, and "forced thinking." The subject reports that the same idea kept occurring again and again. As expected, visual images during the negative presence have been reported more along the left peripheral field. If traditional neurofunction is in operation, this left-side lateralization would imply relatively greater input from right hemispheric sources. On the other hand, the more pleasant sensed presences have been associated with the reports of visual images along the right peripheral visual fields. When they are particularly intense, the experient feels as if the self is moving or has been moved into another space.

Specific experiments have shown that when a person is instructed to press a button in the left hand or a button in the right hand when a presence is felt along the left or right side, respectively, only specific patterns of complex magnetic fields evoke these experiences. In addition, the delay between the change in the occurrence of these fields and the response is in the order of thirty to sixty seconds, which is within the range of the anticipated propagation times between the limbic structures, such as the hippocampal formations through the dorsal hippocampal commissure, from one hemisphere to another.[29]

The sensed presence can range from diffuse spatial feelings, as if the experimenter or someone is standing beside the percipient in the chamber, to a detailed description of an entity with spatial density. For example, a twenty-three-year-old female subject reported she could experience a presence along the right side. It was a very pleasant experience, human in characteristic; she felt immediately at peace. When she attempted to "mentally focus" on the presence by shifting her attention in its direction, the "presence" moved to the other side of the chair in which she was sitting. Every time she attempted to "mentally focus" in the direction of the "entity," it moved around her back to the other side.

The coupling between the ongoing brain activity and the applied field could be considered a dynamic interaction between the person's sense of self and the subtle representations of the complex applied magnetic field within the cerebrum. This example would be consistent with our hypothesis that when the person "intends" or engages volition, such as an attempt to perceive the entity or to "focus" upon the entity, the resulting change in the person's own brain activity alters the patterns induced by the field within this new pattern. As a result, the "experience" seems to move in phenomenological space. Considering the egocentric nature of reality, one could appreciate how a normal person might conclude that the "entity" was responding to her thoughts.

When the field was stopped and the presence disappeared, this volunteer felt very sad and began to cry. She felt as if she had lost something very important to her. When she was exposed to a sham field on a separate occasion, without her knowledge, the sensed presence did not occur. She was disappointed because she had returned to the project in order to "experience the presence again and to feel that sense of tranquility."

However, the presence may not always be pleasant. In fact, most are not, particularly ones that are experienced along the left side. Many subjects who experience the presence along the left side also report fear or apprehension, as well as odd sensations within the legs and bottoms of the feet. The tingling sensations or experiences of heat within the body are attributed to the left side. The most powerful negative experiences occur during the first half of the protocol when the field is applied to the right side of the brain, while the more pleasant experiences, especially associated with difficulties in articulation, occur during the second half of the protocol when the fields are applied bilaterally.

The more common complex visual imageries include long, colorless faces, skulls, or humanoid bodies along the left side of phenomenological space. One subject, a professional writer in his late forties, reported a rush of intense fear and then began to perceive an apparition slowly forming along his left side. He was terrified, even within the experimental setting, but requested the experiment to be continued. During the peak of this experience, rapid paroxysmal electrical changes, similar to epileptic patterns, emerged over his temporal lobes and were measurable by conventional electroencephalographic recordings. Both his heart rate and the artifacts from muscle contractions strongly indicated his experiences were very real to him.

What Is the Sensed Presence?

We consider the neuroelectrical substrate to the sense of self as one of the last major enigmas of human existence. The questions about our place in the center of the universe and our biological heritage were answered by Copernicus and Darwin. If we understand the true composition of the sense of self, the philosophical questions that have perturbed our species could be examined in their entirety. The sense of self, which depends strongly on autobiographical memory, may be unique to just a few species on this planet.

The human being is one of these species. One of the properties of this process that results in the sense of being an individual with consciousness and purpose is the ability to engage in mental time travel. Effectively, your sense of self can move in time through your representation of experience. When these portions of the brain are activated, you feel as if those memories are yours and yours alone.

One general explanation for the emergence of the sense of self in the human being is that it occurred as an emergent property from the utilization of linguistic processes. From this perspective, the sense of self is intimately associated with one's language and its major conservator-human culture. Sociologists have implied, and psychologists have shown, that many people undergo a crisis in the sense of self when they move to a new culture and must communicate with a different language. One adaptive strategy, to minimize this change in the sense of self, has been to establish microcommunities within the new land or to maintain some type of communication with the past.

We have reasoned that if left hemispheric processes (which may not involve the left hemisphere per se in all people) are associated with the sense of self, then there must be a similar phenomenon associated with right hemispheric activity.[30] This similar phenomenon would be dominated by intense emotion, vague linguistic features, and visuospatial detail: the functional characteristics of the right hemisphere. Because the right hemispheric activities would be coded somewhat differently from left hemispheric patterns, this homologue of the self would not be identical. Consequently, any direct access to this experience would be perceived as real but "not self" or "ego-alien."

During most waking-state activity, the interaction between left and right hemispheric processes that converge into awareness is most affected by left hemispheric function and strongly structured by normal activity within the prefrontal regions of the brain. However, during twilight states, when the normal interaction is changed for a few seconds to kiloseconds (about fifteen minutes), the self can become more directly aware of the right hemispheric activity not filtered or translated by left hemispheric sequences. We have suggested that during these transient intercalations, you become aware of the right hemispheric homologue of the left hemispheric sense of self, and you experience the presence. The presence is effectively your right hemispheric representation of your self.

These periods of intercalation do not occur constantly. They are more likely to occur, with modulation by the left hemisphere, during normal dreams. A frequent experience during dreams is perceiving from within your body yet at the same time being aware from outside of your body while it engages in some behavior. These periods are more likely during the early morning hours, between 2:00 and 4:00 A.M., particularly if you would normally be asleep during this period. Because apprehension, periods of personal distress, and the psychological depressions associated with changes in emotional bonding to others affect the timing of dream sleep and deep sleep, the visitor experience often accompanies these conditions.

We have been pursuing the working model that the intrusion of right hemispheric processes into left hemispheric awareness during this time should be associated with a presence. Musicians, artists, and writers, in particular, because of the involvement of the left hemisphere with language, have frequently reported a sensed presence during these periods. Some cultures, such as that of the ancient Greeks, attributed the human creativity of these periods to those presences—they were called the Muses.

The most parsimonious explanation for the neuroelectrical source of the visitor experience at this time in human history is that it is a normal phenomenon whose prototype is the "sensed presence." From this perspective the visitor experience is a necessary and expected general theme because of the subtle differences in structural and dynamic organization between the left and right hemispheres.

Subjective Comparisons

One partial test of the similarity or the identity of an experimental stimulus to a suspected stimulus in the environment is to compare the experiences evoked by both. We have found that some of the complex patterns generated by computer (especially ones that imitate opiate-like responses) are experienced by people who have consumed hallucinogens (particularly those that affect the serotonin system such as lysergic acid diethylamide [LSD]) as similar to the states induced by those drugs. People who have experienced the kundalini phenomena also report a marked approximation between certain field patterns and the sensations associated with original kundalini experience.

To date we have tested only five individuals who reported a strong presence that was attributed to a UFO experience. In all situations, the experience of the sensed presence was evoked and the person attributed it to the entity. Interestingly, when the presence occurred within the experimental setting and the subject knew we were applying the complex fields, the interpretation was still the presence of "that entity."

Problems of Post Hoc Retrieval

A person's autobiographical memory is totally dependent on how the experience was encoded, consolidated, and retrieved. Without direct video or tape recordings, there is no absolute collaboration for the veridicality of a person's autobiographical memory. If an experience has been labeled by the brain as an autobiographical memory, it will be experienced as that memory. Polygraphic measurements or hypnotic regressions do not reveal if an event occurred. The data obtained from these measurements only indicate if the person believes the experiences were true. A memory can be believed to be true without being correct or accurate.

Although statements of groups of people that report the "same memory" are strong evidence of reliability, the validity of the details is not proved. Groups of human brains are no less impervious to the normal mechanisms of memory than are individual brains. This limitation is particularly evident for unusual and infrequent events whose occurrence or existence is not congruent with the person's beliefs about the world and the future.

Many of the researchers who have interviewed experients of UFO phenomena, particularly the visitor experience, must rely on the experient's verbal reports. When people are depressed psychologically or are experiencing the anxiety associated with a fragmentation of their worldview, then *any* structure-making context can affect the details of *autobiographical* memory while other classes of memories, for facts and normal events, remain unchanged.

In our experimental studies, we have shown that one subtle reference to a verbal label with strong emotional connotations is sufficient to introduce illusory memories. In one study, normal university students between the ages of twenty and twenty-four years volunteered for a "relaxation study." They were randomly selected from a first-year university class. This procedure is important because people with specific beliefs will volunteer for experiments that emphasize their interests. Similarly, patients will choose therapists, psychologists, and psychiatrists who agree with their perspective. Patients anticipate, based upon reputation or advertisements about the therapist, what to expect about their experiences within the clinical setting.

In the experimental study, the students were asked to listen to a five-minute narrative called "The Billy Story." While each subject sat singly in an acoustic chamber listening to the story, burst-firing magnetic fields were applied through the entire brain, with emphasis over the right temporal lobe. The stimulation was also continued for twenty minutes after the termination of the story in order to enhance the emotive component. The right hemisphere was emphasized because its activation is often associated with hypnosis and results in an increased suggestibility as defined by hypnotic induction profiles.

The story was about a young boy and his family. One night the boy goes to bed, awakens in the middle of the night, feels a presence and a smothering weight on his chest, senses an odd smell and movements through his body, and perceives sexual stimulation. He awakens to find red marks on his body. Although the sequence actually represented the subjective experiences associated with a complex partial epileptic seizure (temporal lobe epilepsy was called "nocturnal epilepsy" during the last century), no attribution was given to the source.

After the twenty-minute period had elapsed, the subjects were given a distracter task (twenty minutes) and then read a brief descriptor about the prevalence of phenomena that are sociologically relevant. One-third of the students, randomly selected, heard the descriptor that UFO abduction phenomena might exist, while another one-third were read the same descriptor, but the term *childhood sexual abuse* was substituted for UFO *abduction phenomena*. The remaining students were told nothing. The students were asked to return to the setting one week later for further testing. They were not told they would be required to reconstruct the story.

One week later, each subject was asked to reconstruct the Billy Story. As expected, these normal subjects remembered only about 20 percent of all the basic ideas within the five-minute story. More details from the beginning and the end of the story were reconstructed than from the middle of the story. However, there were marked differences between the primacy and recency effect. Information from the beginning of the story was more likely to be rote memory (identical reproductions of the original word sequences), while the details from the last part of the story were primarily inferences and contained the personal signatures of the interpretation. To the sentence "The boy had not eaten, and his eyes were in the direction of the window," an inferential reconstruction might be "The little boy was sick and couldn't eat and was staring out the window." Although the theme is similar, the attribution of cause is quite different between the rote and inferential reconstruction of the sentence.

We also found that illusory memories, that is, references to experiences that did not actually occur, constituted about 5 percent of the ideas within the reconstructions of the story for the two groups that had been asked the question about the prevalence of sociologically relevant phenomena. The two groups who had been asked about the prevalence of UFO abductions or sexual abuse, even though this question was *never* directly linked to the story heard forty minutes earlier, reported fabrications that were consistent with the question. About half of the subjects who had been asked the UFO question attributed the boy's experiences to an abduction, while those who received the question about sexual abuse attributed the boy's experience to molestation by the father.

The primary results of this study indicated that the questions asked after a condition that mildly enhances the vividness of the visual imagery associated with verbal input can affect the details of the memory of the experience. However, not all of the memory was changed. Instead, the illusory memories were integrated with the other more veridical components of the memory of the story.

The effects of the postepisodic conversation became a component of the experience that was attributed to the person's memory of the Billy Story.

This experimental example is likely to be a conservative representation of what occurs in actual UFO visitation experiences. This experiment involved semantic memory, which is more resistant to postepisodic modification than autobiographical memory. Recent positron emission tomography (PET) experiments indicate that recalling autobiographical memory about oneself activates different areas of the brain than recalling biographical memories about other people.[31] There is a preponderant right hemispheric increase in blood flow during these periods, particularly within the right temporal lobe (including the amygdala), right anterior insula, right posterior cingulate (involved with imagery), and especially the right prefrontal cortices.

Second, these experiences occurred within the context of a laboratory where subjects realized they could have left any time they wished, and they knew they would be exposed to no harm. What would be the experience, postexperience attribution, and ultimate integration of these memories into the person's record of the self if they had occurred unexpectedly in the middle of the night in the bedroom or along a deserted road?

Is There a Visitor Pattern Within the Brain?

The experiences of humanoids can be reported as "small little men" who sit upon the chest and inhibit breathing or the "Old Hag" who leers over the helpless sleeper. During the last century, the experiences often were described as fairies or elfs. People then, like the UFO abductees today, reported missing time, sexual probings, strange marks on the body, and the sudden cessation of pregnancies. The primary perceptual features of the entities were their large heads, conspicuous eyes, and unusual shapes. These entities would pester the experient with the persistence of harpies.

The similarity of themes for the visitation/abduction experience suggests that there is a statistical sequence of activity during twilight states. We suggest that the experiences of movement, a dreamlike atmosphere, the inability to move, sensed stimulation of the anal or genital regions, feelings of "probing," and the intrusion of humanoid perceptions are experiences of a synthesis. The synthesis is due to the electrical coherence that occurs between regions of the brain that are partitioned or maintained functionally isolated during the normal waking state.[32]

However, during dream sleep or periods of personal stress, the functional correlates from these areas within the hippocampus, amygdala, insula, and ventral limbic region are integrated, due to shifts of the steady potentials that define the context within which groups of neurons are activated, into a specific sequence of experiences. Information from the person's neurological past, including the representations (but not memories) of the shape of the body during fetal development, might also be accessible. The occurrence of hippocampal electrical activity that emerges in the fetus about four months before birth would be consistent with this possibility.

During these twilight states, when perception focuses within the processes that generate consciousness rather than on the external world, the smaller tract systems whose functions are masked by the massive activities of vision and hearing contribute their components to generate the experiences of these altered dimensions. Like a kaleidoscopic field whose shape and intrinsic organization change with each reconfiguration, a different perception emerges.

Candidate systems would include the vestigial components of the hippocampal formation, such as the tracts of Lancisi and the indusium griseum.[33] Activity within this thin band of cells would allow state-dependent representations, present from early ontogeny, to be blended into the ongoing experiences. During these twilight states, stimulation of the right hippocampus might be communicated through the dorsal hippocampal commissure into the left hippocampus.

Like the specific neurons that respond for hours after the organism leaves a specific space, the left hippocampal neurons would continue to represent this signature. Whatever match of linguistic images exists within the left hippocampus for the patterns received from the right hippocampus might later emerge as "sudden images of memories." Because human brains are more similar than they are different, the themes of these experiences have been and remain remarkably similar across space and time. The details are simply punctuations from the person's culture.

Possible Stimuli That Evoke the Experience:
Speculations to Be Tested

The aggregate of neurons, distributed over large areas of brain space, whose activation *is* the UFO experience is expected to be stimulated by more than one stimulus. A sneeze, which involves a much simpler neuronal circuitry, can be elicited by pepper, an allergen, or a bright light. To isolate one stimulus to a sneeze and consequently dismiss all other possible stimuli that could also cause the sneeze would be erroneous. A similar argument could be applied to the UFO visitor experience.

Because all people do not have UFO experiences constantly, the stimulus sequence that evokes the experiences must not always be present or, if it is present, is not effective. Because even the people who are prone to these experiences do not experience UFO phenomena continuously, there must be a phasic property to these stimuli. We suggest that this property is a combination of variables, which when presented in the appropriate sequence and translated into brain language, unlocks and evokes the visitor experience by stimulating a *pattern* of activity within those aggregates of neurons.

We do not assume there is only one pattern. The sequences of electromagnetic information that could elicit visitation experiences are most likely to constitute a class of signals that would involve basic commonalities with a moderate degree of stimulus substitution. This temporal sequence would be analogous to the spatial sequence of the dozens of amino acids that compose the neuropeptides that can evoke specific behaviors. Although the display of these specific behaviors is maximally evoked by injecting an optimal neuropeptide that was fifteen amino acids in length into the brain, a limited number of substitutions of the amino acids in this sequence with other amino acids could also elicit the behavior. However, its strength was diminished.

We suggest five factors, each associated with a cluster of variables, that may evoke the experience, and each of which might interact to facilitate the experience. The first factor is the occurrence of complex electromagnetic fields within the environment that are similar to those we have generated experimentally. The prevalence of complex magnetic fields within the biosphere can be considered the definition of late-twentieth-century Western civilization.

Because of the escalating number of signals generated continuously within the environment by modern communication systems, from satellite links to cellular telephones, a synthetic electromagnetic matrix has been formed. It is generated by the beats and combinations of the simpler transmissions that carry the telecommunications. The frequency shifts that carry radio and television data are too fast to be deciphered by the brain. However, the mixtures of these fields, their subharmonics, are within the one- to three-millisecond pixel duration that resonates within cerebral space.

One would expect, in a manner analogous to the millions of monkeys typing randomly, the occasional sequence containing meaningful information to the vulnerable brain. If the sequence is resonant with the aggregates of neurons that is the visitor experience, it is elicited. One would also expect the occasional creation of these pulses by local combinations of variables, which result in local "epidemics."[34]

The second source is from the earth itself. All human beings are immersed within the static component of the earth's magnetic field. One can conceive each of the approximately six billion members of the human species as organic semiconductors immersed within this common integrating force. Small, complex ripples of activity within the geomagnetic field have been shown by different researchers to be associated with increased electrical lability within the temporal lobes of sensitive brains.

These small changes in the intensity of the earth's magnetic field are only about 1 percent of the amplitude of the static field. At present these changes are measured only as shifts in magnitude or intensity per three-hour increments per day or as twenty-four-hour arrays. The time frame necessary to understand their possible effect on brain activity would require measurements on the order of every minute.

However, the changes in amplitude do not reflect temporal patterns that contain the actual information that affects the sensitive brain. Until the temporal composition of these changes in amplitude over second-to-second and minute-to-minute time is obtained, the critical variables will remain more hidden. Without the temporal decoding, the measurements are analogous to recording only the loudness of someone speaking without understanding the conversation.

A similar problem would exist for the interpretation of normal brain activity if electroencephalographers measured only amplitude of cerebral output. If the frequency patterns generated by the brain could not be measured directly and one could see only "intensity variations," a normal person's passage through states of conscious-' ness would be difficult to detect. The complex and revealing information of spectral analyses could not be obtained. Instead, there would be a period of consistent moderate intensity (waking), an interval of increased amplitude and variability (alpha rhythms), a period of low-intensity output (alpha dropout), and then an epoch of slowly escalating amplitude (deeper stages of sleep).

One hypothesis, of moderate probability, is that there are and have been intrinsic patterns of activity generated by the geomagnetic field that can evoke the visitor experience during specific states of consciousness. This factor could explain the pervasiveness of visitor and abduction experiences throughout human history. This factor might also explain their propensity to occur as epidemics or in temporal clusters whose intervals follow the most prominent geophysical periods of ten to eleven years and twenty to twenty-two years.

The third factor involves luminous phenomena (that can be measured by instruments other than the human brain), which in large part appear to be associated with tectonic strain within the earth. Direct stimulation of the brain by close proximity of the experient to these luminous phenomena could evoke experiences that range from dreamlike states to the sensed presence. If the induction was too extreme, automatic behaviors and amnesia for hours to a few days after the insult could result. During this time, if the person survived, the label placed upon these experiences and the attributions for the fragmented amnesia would affect the details of these experiences forever. If the current intensities were sufficient to produce amnesia, they would also be sufficient to begin the slow changes in brain microstructure that result in insidious alterations in personality.

We suspect that the observation of very energetic luminous displays are only one manifestation of the phenomena associated with the very local (a few meters), very transient (a few decaseconds) manifestations of tectonic strain. Like most physical phenomena, there is very likely to be a continuum of intensities. These smaller intensities would not be associated with bright balls of light but would be suffi-cient to affect the brain of the vulnerable percipient. The effectiveness of these transient forces would be greatest where a person sleeps be-cause he or she would be within the same space for several hours. When people are ambulatory, they can move through or away from these fields before the critical periods required for significant reso-nance with cerebral activity have occurred.

The fourth factor is the generation of the electromagnetic se-quence by combinations of activities, from social and personal stimuli, within the brain of the experient. This factor would require no external electromagnetic sources. Instead, if the person with the creative brain[35] was experiencing personal stress, a loss of personal purpose, and apprehension about the future of the world, then those combinations of neuronal activities would create the sequence that would access the visitor experience.

The fifth factor may be that the experience actually represents what was perceived. From this perspective, the experiences reported by the thousands of normal people who have reported visitation phenomena—from the Virgin Mary to the most repugnant alien—are primarily veridical. The similarity of the experiences would be due to the similarity of the actual stimuli that produce them rather than to a mundane stimulus that simply activates an intrinsic pat-tern of complex neuronal activity. In the pursuit of the Unknown, all possibilities must be considered.

Why Pursue This Model of the
Visitation/Abduction Experience?

Although we have evoked many of the experiences associated with the UFO visitor experience, in my opinion we have not reproduced its complete sequence in detail. Until we can systematically evoke the sensed presence with the analytical overlay of the UFO details in *every* person who displays a particular profile of temporal lobe lability by our experimental methods, there are still missing variables.

There are two extreme explanations for this fact. The first is that we are pursuing a parallel model that is only spuriously related to the nonlaboratory experiences. The second is that we have not ac-cessed the specific pattern of neuronal activities that elicit the experience. Considering the importance of context, belief, expectancy, and the limitations of ethical guidelines when treating human subjects, we may never be able to imitate the exact conditions that result in the UFO experience. At most we may only obtain successive approximations.

Fragments of the UFO experience are relatively frequent within the normal population. Quantitative analyses indicated that the experience of a visitation by another entity was associated with the same factor as experiences of vibrations, floating, and disruptions in autobiographical memory. When these experiences occur, particularly during the night or during transient physiological states, they are perceived as meaningful but anomalous. Their interpretation is strongly dependent on the belief system of the perceiver.

Are the UFO experiences absolutely real or absolutely fictitious? If these experiences are like any other cluster of experiences, such a dichotomous question cannot have a discrete answer. What our experiments have suggested is that very meaningful experiences can be evoked experimentally and their characteristics are very similar to those people experience and report as visitations or abductions. The results of the experiments also imply that literal interpretations of these experiences with respect to their causes or the information contained in them must be considered cautiously.

The human brain can be conceived as an organic camera. Suppose one takes a picture of an apple. If, when the film is developed, you see an apple, then you are comforted by this independent verification of your perception. However, suppose you take a picture of empty space. If, when the film is developed, the picture of the apple is still present, then there is another explanation. The picture of the apple reflects some intrinsic process, some internal mechanism within the camera itself. The results would profoundly affect your definition of reality.

The methodology of science is difficult but not impossible to acquire or to pursue. It requires time, patience, and a dispassionate perspective that must be maintained long after fads and epidemics of belief have passed. The history of science has shown that through this method the Unknown has become the Known, and these new discoveries have opened unimagined perspectives of powers within the environment and within ourselves. Almost all of these discoveries were ultimately explained by processes whose characteristics shared minimal concordance with the hypotheses and beliefs of those who pursued them. Perhaps the systematic collection of data obtained from the examination of the UFO experience within experimental settings may reveal important information about the genetic past, contemporary organization, and the future development of the human brain.

Chapter Eleven

Research Directions

David M. Jacobs

Studying the UFO and abduction phenomenon is no easy task. Rather than having a readily accessible body of agreed-upon data, the inquiring researcher must sort through a bewildering array of information, of which only a small portion is worthy of scholarly attention. And there are few guideposts to help the researcher with the daunting task of "separating the wheat from the chaff" in a large body of literature.

Even if a researcher can make sense out of the information, the would-be scholar is left with a suggestive body of evidence that other researchers are still hotly debating. The present volume displays some of the deep divisions in UFO and abduction research. Yet virtually all researchers, including the contributors to this book, agree on the basic underlying premise of the existence of a potentially important phenomenon: people around the world have been reporting UFOs and abduction events for the majority of the twentieth century.

All would agree that the reporting phenomenon has had significant impact upon both the public policy of the United States and its popular culture. As early as 1949, "flying saucers" was one of the most recognizable topics that the Gallup organization had ever measured and already a publicly debated phenomenon. UFO-related images have pervaded the culture and society of the United States ever since, and in recent years these images have increased in their cultural visibility.

All would agree that UFO and abduction reporting is truly a global phenomenon. People in diverse political, economic, intellectual, geographic, ethnic, religious, technological, and educational areas have all reported strikingly similar events.

All would agree that abductees have recounted narratives (whatever their origin) that are extraordinarily detailed and often dovetail precisely with other accounts. The accounts have described specific instruments, procedures, and other aspects of abduction accounts.

All would agree that if the phenomenon suggests some socio-cultural-psychological-neurological impulse that primarily takes the form of UFOs and abductions in the twentieth century, then the academic community has been presented with an area of study that might yield important information about the human condition. The benefits accruing from models of human thought and behavior that could account for the UFO and abduction evidence could be great.

All would agree that if this is an objective, physical, anomalous phenomenon, it might have enormously surpassing importance. Indeed, this is the assumption that drives most UFO researchers in the United States today.

Finally, virtually all participants in the debate would agree that the intellectual community has inadequately confronted this phenomenon, not because of the paucity of evidence but because of entrenched political and cultural bias. Rarely has a logical viewpoint toward a legitimate topic of scholarship been greeted with such steadfast opposition. In the 1960s, Allen Hynek liked to characterize the air force's stance toward the existence of UFOs as "It can't be; therefore, it isn't." Hynek could have easily expanded his characterization to include nearly the entire scholarly community.

The intellectual resistance to studying UFOs and abductions is made even more puzzling by the tenets of the phenomenon itself. It is, as Hynek also stated, "persistent and consistent." It seems to have little regard for societal events in general, or for predictions of its eminent demise. Although many have felt that the phenomenon's origin is in some way linked to societal events and would therefore soon disappear, as have other fads, in fact the opposite has proved to be true. Reports and accounts are so commonplace now that most people do not bother to report them (although only 10 percent of the public reported them in the 1950s). Through the years, the UFO phenomenon's persistence has enabled UFO researchers to develop protocols and methods to study it. They have amassed the breadth of the evidence for its physicality. In addition to recorded images of the phenomenon, researchers have studied reports of objects on the ground that have led to traces of their existence. Researchers have cataloged objects' effects on the environment, automobiles, plants, animals, and humans. They have gathered together thousands of abductee narratives and physical evidence in support of these narratives.

The societal reaction to the phenomenon has been very different than would be indicated by its persistence as a cultural artifact. Rather than the society fashioning UFOs and abductions into new directions as the culture evolves over the years, the phenomenon stays the same (although knowledge of its tenets is growing), and the society changes its reactions to it. The UFO and abduction phenomenon remains stubbornly what it is. As such, it appears to have an internal integrity devoid of cultural determinants. As General John A. Samford stated in 1952 during a press conference about UFO sightings over Washington, D.C., witnesses were "credible observers of relatively incredible things."[1] Change the word *observers* to *experiencers*, and the abduction phenomenon fits in as well.

Although many scholars think that people who relate abduction stories must be victims of serious mental illness, psychological studies of abductees indicate a distinct lack of pathology. Occasionally mental health researchers will slice off a piece of the event and then issue an explanation for it, which they expand to account for the entire phenomenon. This is seen in a variety of explanations such as sleep paralysis, popular culture osmosis, sexual abuse repression, hypnosis problems, and so on. In spite of this, no psychological or psychiatric model has ever been presented that takes into account the totality of the phenomenon, assuming that a single causative factor accounts for the abduction phenomenon. Having multiple factors would pose difficult problems. If the abduction phenomenon is the product of a variety of unrelated causative factors, then we are presented with an interesting problem: How can a variety of societally induced factors create coherent, cohesive, and detailed narratives about a single, especially bizarre, subject? Can the pieces be replicated in a laboratory and then used in concert to create the narrative? Can, then, an examination of one's life and circumstances lead to predictability of abduction stories?

There are, of course, some people who at first think that they have been abducted and then come to realize that they are not abductees. This is bound to happen in a widespread phenomenon. Surprisingly, however, even with the nonprofessional quality of research in this area, no community of "recanters" has emerged dedicated to setting the record straight. Abductees have not sued investigators for having them remember their abduction accounts. Legal complaints have not been lodged against the UFO research organizations. Some abduction researchers have used hypnosis for many years without a single serious complaint. Oddly, abductees seem to be satisfied with their bizarre knowledge, even though most of them wish it were not true.

Rather than psychosocial factors, abductees tend to concentrate on physical evidence of their experiences. They claim to see each other being abducted. They say they are physically missing from their normal environment. They claim to have come back with scars, marks, bruises, and other indications of physical trauma on their bodies as a result of alleged abductions. They sometimes present artifacts, such as "implants," or rust-colored or fluorescent pink stains on their clothes, in support of their narratives. The events they describe have often happened as recently as the day before the recounting and are consciously remembered, eliminating the therapist-driven false memory syndrome.

Obviously, this is a phenomenon that demands intellectual engagement. A few academic studies of the phenomenon have been mounted; but, by and large, it has been ignored. This book has shown that there are a variety of perspectives from which scholars can become productively involved with the subject apart from proving or disproving its origin. As in most academic disciplines, the variety of topics and fields within it spans virtually all aspects of the fields that make up modern intellectual discourse.

The social sciences, the humanities, and the sciences in general all have methods and approaches that could illuminate the phenomenon. This volume provides ample indication that productive work can be accomplished using different methodologies from these different areas. There are also many more directions that research can take.

Historians have shown that important work can be done in the history of the society's confrontation with UFOs. Archival research about the government's and the society's encounters with UFOs is just beginning. Enough documents already exist (and more are continually uncovered) to allow historians to gather a different interpretation of the early years of the government's confrontation with UFOs. The development of popular attitudes toward the subject, the media's influence on it, motion picture and television portrayals of it, the scientific community's relation to it, and so on—all are important research areas for historians. Even the intellectual neglect that it has endured constitutes a fruitful area of research for historians of science that could reveal insights about the politics of academic research.

Of course, members of the psychological community can find an extensive number of areas to research. Researchers who could develop a model to explain the abduction phenomenon's unique combination of mental and physical states might uncover knowledge about the relationship between cognition and physicality that could be revolutionary.

Psychological studies of witnesses and abductees are important to learn what psychological determinates, if any, cause these narratives to appear. People living with the idea that they are being abducted on a regular basis by extraterrestrial beings (whether or not this is happening) are in a unique psychological state that requires counsel and study. Indeed, the entire phenomenon requires a complete psychological theory that would account for the data. To date no such theory has been developed. Research into the exact number of people who claim abduction experiences and who have also experienced sexual, physical, and emotional abuse has not been conducted. Similarly, there has been no investigation into how many abductee claimants have temporal lobe epilepsy or lability or other neurologically based abnormalities.

Future abduction research could reveal how memory is organized and memories are recovered. Psychologists could shed light on whether people can be convinced that a falsely implanted, complicated event actually happened to them the day (or hours) before. Indeed, constructing a much more complete and reliable model for memory appears to be critical for advancing our comprehension of the abduction phenomenon and many types of UFO sightings. Such a model will also inevitably improve our understanding of the limits and potential of hypnosis.

Anthropological studies and content analysis of the abduction narrative, real or not, could help delineate the type of society portrayed in these accounts, which seem to paint a consistent and detailed picture of an alien society engaged in task-oriented activities. Among other things, what does this collective society construct tell us about human cognition?

Sociologists must confront the extraordinary phenomenon of large groups of people across national boundaries coming forward with surprisingly similar reports and narratives. Although Robert Hall and others have strongly argued against mass hysteria, if these accounts are psychologically based, then some unknown form of mass activity must be taking place that would be appropriate for study and analysis.[2]

In recent years, a growing number of abductees have themselves published books describing what they think has happened to them. These sincere individuals have carved out a unique niche in autobiography that could have antecedents in Indian abduction narratives of the eighteenth and early nineteenth centuries. By the end of the twentieth century, over twenty abductee personal experience books have appeared, and more are being published. Studying them as autobiography, as literature, or as psychologically based self-referential narratives could reveal important evidence of the abduction phenomenon's origin.

Philosophers, folklorists, and religious scholars will all find in UFO and abduction lore a field ripe for investigation. They certainly could help expand our knowledge of how belief, religion, and spirituality influence human confrontations with this phenomenon. Similarly, exploring the differences and similarities between "channeling" and abduction narratives might prove to be much more than an esoteric exercise.

For scholars in philosophy, jurisprudence, and forensics, the nature of evidence strikes at the heart of any anomalous phenomenon. The epistemology of UFO research is surely an issue that requires attention. Can hypnosis, for example, be used as evidence? How can we discern if a person is relating an accurate account of objective reality if that account with hypnosis differs from the person's conscious memories of the event?

Physicists could follow the lead of optical physicist Bruce Maccabee, who has devoted his energies to analyzing photographic evidence presented for the existence of UFOs. The tremendous number of videotapes and other images presented as evidence constitute a wealth of scientific data that cries out for systematic analysis and categorization. Studies of the movements and color changes of UFOs might also yield important information about their energy source and therefore their origin.

Furthermore, as new astronomical discoveries refine our theories of the cosmos, the possibility of life existing outside of our solar system seems ever more likely. That should, in turn, encourage astronomers, astrophysicists, and other members of the scientific community searching for extraterrestrial intelligence to look seriously at the UFO phenomenon. They might ultimately reject the extraterrestrial hypothesis, but at least that rejection would emerge from a position of knowledge. And, of course, it is possible they might come to realize that searching for extraterrestrial life is a lot easier than they thought.

Biomedical researchers also have an important role to play in studying the phenomenon. Abductees often say that they have organic and metallic "implants" in their bodies. Few serious studies have ever been mounted to examine such claims, and implants have not been investigated with the full resources of the radiological community.

The nature of memory and cognition—the province of neurologists and neurobiologists—are natural areas of inquiry. Such scientists could help determine if abduction memories are accessed from different anatomical sites in the brain than "normal" memories. Can the memory loss alleged by abductees be duplicated in a laboratory situation? Can complex abduction memories from people who know little about the subject be duplicated in a laboratory situation? These are some of the questions they might explore.

Similarly, abductees have consistently described having anomalous bruises, "puncture" wounds, and scars. To date, no studies of these marks have been attempted. Some researchers theorize that abductees suffer from an increased incidence of chronic fatigue syndrome and fibromyalgia. Whether or not this is true has yet to be determined.

The very disturbing phenomenon of "missing fetuses" that many abductees describe requires very careful study and analysis not only to verify the existence of the phenomenon but also, if the claims are legitimate, to understand the fetus's physiological processes. Such investigation might provide insight into the poorly understood process of fetal absorption. How many abductees have undergone the little-known process of fetal absorption and in what gestational period? It is as yet unknown how many abductees have had pseudocyesis, or whether abductees have a greater number of miscarriages than the nonabductee population, or whether the nature of the spontaneous abortion is different than in the nonabductee population. Gynecologists are needed to ascertain whether abductees have a greater incidence of anomalous gynecological scarring than the general population.

This list of possible research directions only skims the surface. But it should be readily apparent that the study of UFOs and abductions can easily encompass the entire breadth of intellectual inquiry. It is long past time for the intellectual community to engage with the data, especially given a subject that could be of surpassing importance on a number of levels. Entering into this field requires the ability to look forthrightly and with "fresh eyes" into a field of discourse long held to be illegitimate. We must place UFO studies within the confines of normal intellectual pursuit and embark upon a journey of understanding. That journey might take us to surprising destinations.

Notes

Introduction

1. James E. McDonald, "Science in Default: Twenty Years of UFO Sightings," in *UFOs: A Scientific Debate*, ed. Carl Sagan and Thornton Page (Ithaca, N.Y.: Cornell University Press, 1969).

2. See David M. Jacobs, *The UFO Controversy in America* (Bloomington: Indiana University Press, 1975).

3. Peter Sturrock, *Report on a Survey of the Membership of the American Astronomical Society Concerning the UFO Problem* (Stanford, Calif.: Institute for Plasma Research, Stanford University, 1977).

4. Charles Emmons, *At the Threshold: UFOs, Science, and the New Age* (Mill Spring, N.C.: Wild Flower Press, 1997).

5. See, for example, Mark Rodeghier, *UFO Reports Involving Vehicle Interference: A Catalogue of Data Analysis* (Evanston, Ill.: Center for UFO Studies, 1981); and Ted Phillips, *Physical Traces Associated with UFO Cases: A Preliminary Catalog* (Northfield, Ill.: Center for UFO Studies, 1975).

1. Ufology and Academia: The UFO Phenomenon as a Scholarly Discipline

1. Jon Cohen, "Scientists Who Fund Themselves," *Science* 279 (1998): 178–81.

2. Daryl Chubin, "The Conceptualization of Scientific Specialties," *Sociological Quarterly* 17 (1976): 448–76.

3. Diana Crane and Henry Small, "American Sociology Since the Seventies: The Emerging Identity Crisis in the Discipline," in *Sociology and Its Publics: The Forms and Fates of Disciplinary Organization*, ed. Terence Halliday and Morris Janowitz (Chicago: University of Chicago Press, 1992).

4. David M. Jacobs, *The UFO Controversy in America* (Bloomington: Indiana University Press, 1975), p. xvi.

5. Julie Thompson Klein, *Crossing Boundaries: Knowledge, Disciplinarities, and Interdisciplinarities* (Charlottesville: University Press of Virginia, 1996), p. 4.

6. Burton R. Clark, *The Higher Education System: Academic Organization in Cross-National Perspective* (Berkeley: University of California Press, 1983).

7. Klein, *Crossing Boundaries*.

8. Boyer Commission on Educating Undergraduates in the Research University, *Reinventing Undergraduate Education: A Blueprint for America's Universities* (Stony Brook: State University of New York at Stony Brook, 1998).

9. Beth Azar, "Federal Agencies Encourage More Cross-Disciplinary Work," *APA Monitor*, May 1998, p. 18.

10. Edward O. Wilson, "Scientists, Scholars, Knaves, and Fools," *American Scientist* 86 (1998): 6–7.

11. Ibid., p. 6.

12. Timothy Ferris, "The Risks and Rewards of Popularizing Science," *Chronicle of Higher Education*, 4 April 1997, p. B6.

13. Carl Sagan and Thornton Page, eds., *UFOs: A Scientific Debate* (Ithaca, N.Y.: Cornell University Press, 1972), p. xi; italics added.

14. Stuart Appelle, "The Abduction Experience: A Critical Evaluation of Theory and Evidence," *Journal of UFO Studies* 6 (1995–96): 29–79.

15. Allen Hynek, *The UFO Experience: A Scientific Inquiry* (Chicago: Henry Regnery, 1972), p. 143.

16. Ibid., p. 166.

17. Jerome Clark, *The UFO Encyclopedia*, vol. 2, *The Emergence of a Phenomenon: UFOs from the Beginning Through 1959* (Detroit: Omnigraphics, 1992).

18. Edward U. Condon, ed., *Scientific Study of Unidentified Flying Objects* (New York: Bantam Books, 1969).

19. William Hartmann, "Direct Physical Evidence," in Condon, ed., *Scientific Study of Unidentified Flying Objects*, p. 86.

20. Roy Craig, "Indirect Physical Evidence," in Condon, ed., *Scientific Study of Unidentified Flying Objects*, p. 115.

21. Franklin E. Roach, "Visual Observations Made by Astronauts," in Condon, ed., *Scientific Study of Unidentified Flying Objects*, p. 208.

22. Condon, *Scientific Study of Unidentified Flying Objects*, p. 1.

23. For example, Michael D. Swords, "The University of Colorado UFO Project: The Scientific Study of UFOs," *Journal of UFO Studies* 6 (1995–96): 149–84.

24. For example, David R. Saunders and Roger Harkins, *UFOs? Yes!* (New York: World Publishing, 1969).

25. Sagan and Page, *UFOs: A Scientific Debate*, p. xiv.

26. Ibid., p. xii.

27. Ibid., p. 11.

28. Hynek, *The UFO Experience*, pp. 50–51.

29. James E. McDonald, "Science in Default: Twenty-two Years of Inadequate Investigations" in Sagan and Page, eds., *UFOs: A Scientific Debate*, pp. 52–53.

30. Ibid., p. 121.

31. Carl Sagan, "UFOs: The Extraterrestrial and Other Hypotheses," in Sagan and Page, eds., *UFOs: A Scientific Debate*, p. 274.

32. Robert M. L. Baker, "Motion Pictures of UFOs," in Sagan and Page, eds., *UFOs: A Scientific Debate*, pp. 190, 210.

33. Robert L. Hall, "Sociological Perspectives on UFO Reports," in Sagan and Page, eds., *UFOs: A Scientific Debate*, p. 222.

34. Andrea Pritchard, David E. Pritchard, John E. Mack, Pam Kasey, and Claudia Yapp, eds., *Alien Discussions: Proceedings of the Abduction Study Conference Held at MIT* (Cambridge, Mass.: North Cambridge Press, 1994).

35. For example, C. D. B. Bryan, *Close Encounters of the Third Kind: Alien Abductions, UFOs, and the Conference at MIT* (New York: Knopf, 1995).

36. See David Gotlib, Stuart Appelle, Mark Rodeghier, and Georgia Flamburis, "Ethics Code for Investigation and Treatment of the Abduction Experience," *Journal of UFO Studies* 5 (1994): 55–82.

37. V. Eshleman, T. Holzer, R. Jokipii, F. Louange, H. J. Melosh, J. J. Papike, G. Reitz, C. Tolbert, and B. Veyret, "Summary Report of the Scientific Review Panel," in P. A. Sturrock, ed., "Physical Evidence Related to UFO Reports: The Proceedings of a Workshop Held at the Pocantico Conference Center, Tarrytown, New York, September 29–October 4, 1997," *Journal of Scientific Exploration* 12 (1998): 179–229.

38. For example, Carl Sagan, *The Demon-Haunted World: Science as a Candle in the Dark* (New York: Random House, 1996).

39. Peter A. Sturrock, "Report on a Survey of the Membership of the American Astronomical Society Concerning the UFO Problem: Part 1," *Journal of Scientific Exploration* 8 (1994): 4.

40. Michel C. L. Bounias, "Biochemical Traumatology as a Potent Tool for Identifying Actual Stresses Elicited by Unidentified Source: Evidence for Plant Metabolic Disorders in Correlation with a UFO Landing," *Journal of Scientific Exploration* 4 (1990): 1–18.

41. Ibid., p. 17.

42. Ibid., p. 1.

43. Edward J. Zeller and Gisela Dreschoff, "Geophysical Parameters and UFO Sighting Frequencies," *Journal of UFO Studies* 7 (2000): 1–10.

44. David E. Pritchard, "Physical Evidence and Abductions," in Pritchard et al., eds., *Alien Discussions*, 286.

45. Charles B. Moore, "The Early New York University Balloon Flights," in *UFO Crash at Roswell: The Genesis of a Modern Myth*, ed. Benson Saler, Charles A. Ziegler, and Charles B. Moore (Washington, D.C.: Smithsonian Institution Press, 1997), pp. 74–114.

46. Jack Kasher, "Anomalous Images on Videotape from Space Shuttle Flight STS-48: Examination of the Ice-Particle Explanation," *Journal of UFO Studies* 6 (1995/1996): 80–148.

47. Martin P. Kress, letter from the assistant administrator for legislative affairs, NASA, in response to an inquiry from the Honorable Helen Delich Bentley, House of Representatives, dated 22 November 1991.

48. Charles A. Ziegler and Benson Saler, "Three Images of Roswell," in Saler, Ziegler, and Moore, eds., *UFO Crash at Roswell*, pp. 150–68.

49. Thomas E. Bullard, "Mysteries in the Eye of the Beholder: UFOs and Their Correlations as a Folkloric Theme Past and Present" (Ph.D. diss., Indiana University, 1981), p. 48.

50. Michael A. Persinger, "The Tectonic Stress Theory as an Explanation of the UFO Phenomenon: A Non-technical Review of the Research, 1970–1990," *Journal of UFO Studies* 2 (1990): 105–37.

51. Nicholas Spanos, Patricia A. Cross, Kirby Dickson, and Susan C. Dubreuil, "Close Encounters: An Examination of UFO Experiences," *Journal of Abnormal Psychology* 102 (1994): 628–29.

52. Robert A. Baker, *They Call It Hypnosis* (Buffalo, N.Y.: Prometheus Books, 1990).

53. Kenneth Ring, *The Omega Project: Near-Death Experiences, UFO Encounters, and Mind at Large* (New York: William Morrow, 1992).

54. Appelle, "The Abduction Experience," p. 29.

55. John Mack, *Abduction: Human Encounters with Aliens* (New York: Scribner, 1994); David Gotlib, "Psychotherapy for the UFO Abduction Experience," *Journal of UFO Studies* 6 (1995–96): 1–23.

56. Carl Jung, *Flying Saucers* (New York: Signet, 1959).

57. Charles F. Emmons, *At the Threshold: UFOs, Science, and the New Age* (Mill Spring, N.C.: Wild Flower Press, 1997).

58. Robert E. Bartholomew and George S. Howard, *UFOs and Alien Contact: Two Centuries of Mystery* (Amherst, N.Y.: Prometheus Books, 1998).

59. Budd Hopkins, David M. Jacobs, and Ron Westrum, *Unusual Personal Experiences: An Analysis of the Data from Three National Surveys Conducted by the Roper Organization* (Las Vegas: Bigelow Holding Corporation, 1992).

60. Robert L. Hall, Mark Rodeghier, and Donald A. Johnson, "The Prevalence of Abductions: A Critical Look," *Journal of UFO Studies* 4 (1992): 131–35.

61. Jacobs, *The UFO Controversy in America*.

62. David M. Jacobs, *Secret Life: Firsthand Accounts of UFO Abductions* (New York: Simon and Schuster, 1992); Jacobs, *The Threat* (New York: Simon and Schuster, 1998).

63. Michael D. Swords, "Donald E. Keyhoe and the Pentagon: The Rise of Interest in the UFO Phenomenon and What the Government Really Knew," *Journal of UFO Studies* 6 (1995–96): 195–212.

64. Michael E. Zimmerman, "The 'Alien Abduction' Phenomenon: Forbidden Knowledge of Hidden Events," *Philosophy Today* 41 (1997): 235.

65. Ibid., p. 251.

66. John C. Hickman, E. Dale McConkey, and Matthew A. Barrett, "Fewer Sightings in the National Press: A Content Analysis of UFO News Coverage in the *New York Times*, 1947–1995," *Journal of UFO Studies* 6 (1995–96): 224.

67. Ibid.

68. Jodi Dean, *Aliens in America: Conspiracy Cultures from Outerspace to Cyberspace* (Ithaca, N.Y.: Cornell University Press, 1998), p. 6.

69. Ibid., p. 7.

2. Limited Access: Six Natural Scientists and the UFO Phenomenon

1. Hidetaka Nishiyama and Richard C. Brown, *Karate: The Art of Empty Hand Fighting* (Rutland, Vt.: Charles E. Tuttle, 1960), p. 20.

2. Bruno Latour, *Science in Action* (Milton Keynes, England: Open University, 1987); James D. Watson, *The Double Helix: A Personal Account of the Discovery and Structure of DNA* (New York: Signet, 1969).

3. Susan West, "Dinosaur Head Hunt," *Science News* 116, no. 18 (November 1979): 314–15.

4. Ian Mitroff, *The Subject Side of Science: A Philosophical Inquiry into the Psychology of the Apollo Moon Scientists* (New York: Elsevier, 1974).

5. Thomas S. Kuhn, *The Structure of Scientific Revolutions*, 2d ed. (Chicago: University of Chicago Press, 1970).

6. Ron Westrum, "Social Intelligence About Anomalies: The Case of UFOs," *Social Studies of Science* 7 (1977): 271–302; Westrum, "Science and Social Intelligence About Anomalies: The Case of Meteorites," *Social Studies of Science* 8 (1978): 461–93.

7. Stephen Toulmin, *Human Understanding*, vol. 1 (Princeton, N.J.: Princeton University Press, 1972).

8. J. Allen Hynek, "Conferences with Astronomers on UFOs," in *Project Blue Book*, ed. Brad Steiger (New York: Ballantine, 1976).

9. Jacques Vallee, *Anatomy of a Phenomenon: Unidentified Flying Objects in Space—A Scientific Appraisal* (Chicago: Henry Regnery, 1965); Jacques Vallee and Janine Vallee, *Challenge to Science: The UFO Enigma* (Chicago: Henry Regnery, 1966).

10. J. Allen Hynek, *The UFO Experience: A Scientific Inquiry* (Chicago: Henry Regnery, 1972).

11. Ron Westrum, "Social Intelligence About Hidden Events: Its Significance for Scientific Discovery and Social Policy," *Knowledge: Creation, Diffusion, Utilization* 3 (1982): 381–400.

12. Donald Menzel, *Flying Saucers* (Cambridge, Mass.: Harvard University Press, 1952); Donald Menzel and Lyle G. Boyd, *The World of Flying Saucers* (New York: Doubleday, 1963); Donald Menzel and Ernest H. Taves, *The Truth About Flying Saucers* (1977).

13. Jerome Clark, "Donald Howard Menzel," in *The UFO Encyclopedia: The Phenomenon from the Beginning* (Detroit: Omnigraphics, 1998).

14. Jacques Vallee, *Forbidden Science, Journals: 1957–1959* (Berkeley, Calif.: North Atlantic Books, 1992), p. 247.

15. Clark, "Donald Howard Menzel."

16. Ibid.

17. Henry S. F. Cooper, "Profiles: Resonance with Something Alive," *New Yorker*, 21 June and 28 June 1976.

18. Vallee, *Forbidden Science*, p. 86.

19. William Dicke, "Carl Sagan, Author and a Popularizer of Space, Dies at 62," *New York Times*, 21 December 1996, pp. 1, 12.

20. Armand Mauss, *Social Problems as Social Movements* (1965).

21. Carl Sagan and Thornton Page, eds., *UFOs: A Scientific Debate* (Ithaca, N.Y.: Cornell University Press, 1972).

22. Ibid.

23. Ron Westrum, David Swift, and David Stupple, "Extraterrestrial Intelligence: The Sociology of an Idea," in *People in Space*, ed. James Katz (New Brunswick, N.J.: Transaction Books, 1986), pp. 189–92.

24. McDonald (1968).

25. Richard Muller, "Innovation and Scientific Funding," *Science* 209 (August 1980): 880–83.

26. Paul McCarthy, "Politicking and Paradigm-Shifting: James McDonald and the UFO Case Study" (Ph.D. diss., University of Hawaii, 1975).

27. *New York Times*, 1971.

28. J. Allen Hynek, personal interview, 27 April 1973.

29. Valerie Vaughn, ed., *UFOs and Science: The Collected Writings of James E. McDonald* (Mount Rainier, Md.: Fund for UFO Research, 1995), p. 52.

30. Hynek, personal interview, 27 April 1973.

31. John C. Sherwood, *Flying Saucers Are Watching You: The Incident at Dexter and the Incredible Michigan Flap* (Clarksburg, W.Va.: Saucerian Publications, 1967), pp. 34–35.

32. David M. Jacobs, *The UFO Controversy in America* (New York: Signet, 1976), p. 178.

33. Hynek, personal interview, 27 April 1973.

34. Jacques Vallee, telephone interview, 12 July 1979.

35. Vallee, *Anatomy of a Phenomenon;* Vallee and Vallee, *Challenge to Science.*

36. Jacques Vallee, *The Network Revolution: Confessions of a Computer Scientist* (Berkeley, Calif.: And/Or Press, 1982).

37. Hynek, personal interview, 27 April 1973.

38. Daniel S. Gillmor, ed., *Scientific Study of Unidentified Flying Objects* (New York: Bantam Books, 1969).

39. Richard Greenwell, personal communication.

40. David R. Saunders and Roger Harkin, *UFOs, Yes! Where the Condon Report Went Wrong* (New York: World Publishing, 1969).

41. Michael D. Swords, "The University of Colorado UFO Project: The 'Scientific Study of Unidentified Flying Objects,'" *Journal of UFO Studies,* n.s., 6 (1995–96): 168.

42. Clark, "Donald Howard Menzel."

43. For example, Jacques Vallee, "Estimates of Optical Power Output in Six Cases of Unexplained Aerial Objects with Defined Luminosity Characteristics," *Journal of Scientific Exploration* 12 (autumn 1968): 345–58.

44. Budd Hopkins, *Intruders: The Incredible Visitations at Kitley Woods* (New York: Random House, 1987); David M. Jacobs, *Secret Life: Firsthand Accounts of UFO Abductions* (New York: Simon and Schuster, 1992).

45. Peter A. Sturrock et al., "Physical Evidence Related to UFO Reports," *Journal of Scientific Exploration* 12 (summer 1998): 179–230.

46. Rodeghier (1981).

47. Ted Phillips, *Physical Traces Associated with UFO Sightings* (Chicago: Center for UFO Studies, 1975).

48. Schuessler (1996).

49. Westrum, "Science and Social Intelligence About Anomalies."

50. Hynek, *The UFO Experience.*

51. Ursula Marvin, *Continental Drift: The Evolution of a Concept* (Washington, D.C.: Smithsonian Institution Press, 1973).

52. Westrum, "Science and Social Intelligence About Anomalies."

53. Richard Hall, ed., *The UFO Evidence* (Washington, D.C.: National Investigations Committee on Aerial Phenomena, 1964).

54. Frank B. Salisbury, *The Utah UFO Display: A Biologist's Report* (Old Greenwich, Conn.: Devin-Adair, 1974); Harley D. Rutledge, *Project Identification: The First Scientific Field Study of UFO Phenomena* (Englewood Cliffs, N.J.: Prentice-Hall, 1981).

55. For example, Ray Fowler, *The Allagash Abductions* (Tigard, Ore.: Wild Flower Press, 1993); Hopkins, *Intruders;* Walter N. Webb, *Encounter at Buff Ledge: A UFO Case History* (Chicago: J. Allen Hynek Center for UFO Studies, 1994).

56. Allan Hendry, *The UFO Handbook* (Garden City, N.Y.: Doubleday, 1979).

57. For example, Roy Craig, *UFOs: An Insider's View of the Official Quest for Evidence* (Denton: University of North Texas Press, 1995).

58. Hynek, personal interview, 27 April 1973; J. Allen Hynek (1977), pp. 25–26.

59. Jacobs, *The UFO Controversy in America*, p. 184.

60. Peter A. Sturrock, *Report on a Survey of the Membership of the American Astronomical Society Concerning the UFO Problem* (Stanford, Calif.: Institute for Plasma Research, Stanford University, 1977).

61. Hynek, "Conferences with Astronomers on UFOs."

62. For example, Vallee, "Estimates of Optical Power Output."

63. See Hansen (1992).

64. For example, Hendry, *The UFO Handbook*, p. 87.

65. Battelle Memorial Institute, *Project Blue Book Special Report No. 14: Analysis of Reports of Unidentified Aerial Objects* (Dayton, Ohio: Wright-Patterson Air Force Base, Air Technical Intelligence Center, 5 May 1955), p. 24.

66. For example, Sturrock et al., "Physical Evidence Related to UFO Reports."

3. Science, Law, and War: Alternative Frameworks for the UFO Evidence

1. J. Allen Hynek, *The UFO Experience: A Scientific Inquiry* (Chicago: Henry Regnery, 1972); Allan Hendry, *The UFO Handbook* (New York: Doubleday, 1979); Budd Hopkins, *Missing Time: A Documented Study of UFO Abductions* (New York: Marek, 1981); Hopkins, *Witnessed: The True Story of the Brooklyn Bridge UFO Abductions* (New York: Pocket Books, 1996); Don Berliner, *Unidentified Flying Objects Briefing Document: The Best Available Evidence* (Mount Rainier, Md.: UFO Research Coalition, 1995).

2. Donald H. Menzel, *Flying Saucers* (Cambridge, Mass.: Harvard University Press, 1953); Philip J. Klass, *UFOs—Identified* (New York: Random House, 1968); Carl Sagan, "UFOs: The Extraterrestrial and Other Hypotheses," in *UFOs: A Scientific Debate*, ed. Carl Sagan and Thornton Page (Ithaca, N.Y.: Cornell University Press, 1972), pp. 265–75.

3. Thomas S. Kuhn, *The Structure of Scientific Revolutions*, 2d ed., enlarged (Chicago: University of Chicago Press, 1970).

4. Abraham Pais, *Subtle Is the Lord: The Science and Life of Albert Einstein* (New York: Oxford University Press, 1982).

5. Kuhn, *Structure of Scientific Revolutions*, p. 79.

6. Ibid., pp. 78–79.

7. David M. Jacobs, *The UFO Controversy in America* (Bloomington: Indiana University Press, 1975), pp. 299–300.

8. Menzel, *Flying Saucers*, pp. 205–24; Michael A. Persinger, "The Tectonic Strain Theory as an Explanation for UFO Phenomena: A Non-technical Review of the Research, 1970–1990," *Journal of UFO Studies*, n.s., 2 (1990): 105–37.

9. Thomas E. Bullard, "Folkloric Dimensions of the UFO Phenomenon," *Journal of UFO Studies*, n.s., 3 (1991): 1–58.

10. Kuhn, *Structure of Scientific Revolutions*, p. 77.

11. Karl R. Popper, *The Logic of Scientific Discovery* (New York: Harper and Row, 1968).

12. Charles Mackay, *Extraordinary Popular Delusions and the Madness of Crowds* (Boston: L. C. Page, 1932), pp. 462–564.

13. Ron Westrum, "Thinking by Groups, Organizations, and Networks: A Sociologist's View of the Social Psychology of Science and Technology," in *The Social Psychology of Science*, ed. W. R. Shadish and S. Fuller (New York: Guilford Press, 1994), pp. 329–42.

14. See, for example, M. A. Conway, ed., *Recovered Memories and False Memories* (Oxford: Oxford University Press, 1997); J. G. Hull, "When Explanations Fail: Science and Pseudoscience in Psychology," *Psychological Inquiry* 7 (1996): 149–55.

15. Elizabeth Loftus, *Eyewitness Testimony* (Cambridge, Mass.: Harvard University Press, 1979); Alvin H. Lawson, "A Touchstone for Fallacious Abductions: Birth Trauma Imagery in CE III Narratives," in *The Spectrum of UFO Research*, ed. Mimi Hynek (Chicago: J. Allen Hynek Center for UFO Studies, 1988), pp. 71–98; Leonard S. Newman and Roy F. Baumeister, "Toward an Explanation of the UFO Abduction Phenomenon: Hypnotic Elaboration, Extraterrestrial Sadomasochism, and Spurious Memories," *Psychological Inquiry* 7 (1996): 99–126; Robert E. Bartholomew, Keith Basterfield, and G. S. Howard, "UFO Abductees and Contactees: Psychopathology or Fantasy-Proneness?" *Professional Psychology: Research and Practice* 2 (1991): 215–22; Persinger, "Tectonic Strain Theory."

16. Persinger, "Tectonic Strain Theory."

17. Elizabeth Loftus, *The Myth of Repressed Memory: False Memories and Allegations of Sexual Abuse* (New York: St. Martin's Press, 1994).

18. Lawson, "Touchstone for Fallacious Abductions."

19. N. P. Spanos, P. A. Cross, K. Dickson, and S. DuBreuil, "Close Encounters: An Examination of UFO Experiences," *Journal of Abnormal Psychology* 102 (1993): 624–32.

20. Newman and Baumeister, "Toward an Explanation of the UFO Abduction Phenomenon."

21. C. C. McLeod, B. Corbisier, and J. Mack, "A More Parsimonious Explanation for UFO Abduction," *Psychological Inquiry* 7 (1996): 156–67; and R. L. Hall, "Escaping the Self or Escaping the Anomaly?" *Psychological Inquiry* 7 (1996): 143–48.

22. S. Freud, "The History of the Psychoanalytic Movement," in *The Basic Writings of Sigmund Freud*, ed. A. A. Brill (New York: Modern Library, 1938), pp. 938–40.

23. George Orwell, *Nineteen Eighty-Four* (New York: Harcourt, Brace, 1949); Arthur Koestler, *Darkness at Noon* (London: Jonathan Cape, 1940).

24. S. Freud, "The Interpretation of Dreams," in *The Basic Writings of Sigmund Freud*, p. 534.

25. Ernest R. Hilgard, *Divided Consciousness: Multiple Controls in Human Thought and Action* (New York: Wiley, 1977), pp. 5–12.

26. Ibid., pp. 155–84.

27. English Bagby, *The Psychology of Personality: An Analysis of Common Emotional Disorders* (New York: Henry Holt, 1928), pp. 43–46.

28. Joseph Wolpe, *Psychotherapy by Reciprocal Inhibition* (Stanford, Calif.: Stanford University Press, 1958), pp. 94–95.

29. J. W. Schooler, M. Bendiksen, and S. Ambadar, "Taking the Middle Line: Can We Accommodate Both Fabricated and Recovered Memories of Sexual Abuse?" in *Recovered Memories and False Memories*, ed. M. A. Conway (Oxford: Oxford University Press, 1997), pp. 251–92.

30. John G. Fuller, *The Interrupted Journey* (New York: Dial Press, 1966); John S. Carpenter, "Double Abduction Case: Correlation of Hypnosis Data," *Journal of UFO Studies*, n.s., 3 (1991): 91–114; Hopkins, *Witnessed*.

31. Andrea Pritchard, David E. Pritchard, John E. Mack, Pam Kasey, and Claudia Yapp, eds., *Alien Abductions: Proceedings of the Abduction Study Conference* (Cambridge, Mass.: North Cambridge Press, 1994); Carpenter, "Double Abduction Case"; D. M. Jacobs and Budd Hopkins, "Suggested Techniques for Hypnosis and Therapy of Abductees," *Journal of UFO Studies*, n.s., 4 (1992): 138–50; B. Hopkins, "Investigating Abduction Cases," in *The Spectrum of UFO Research*, ed. Mimi Hynek (Chicago: J. Allen Hynek Center for UFO Studies, 1988), pp. 169–74.

32. "Appendix A: Statistical Approaches, Probability Interpretations and the Quantification of Standards of Proof," in *The Evolving Role of Statistical Assessments as Evidence in the Courts*, ed. Stephen E. Feinberg (New York: Springer-Verlag, 1996), pp. 191–210.

33. Ronald J. Delisle, *Evidence: Principles and Problems*, 3d ed. (Toronto: Carswell, 1996), pp. 10–30.

34. J. S. Mill, "Chapter VIII: Of the Four Methods of Experimental Inquiry," in *A System of Logic* (New York: Longmans, 1884).

35. D. C. Donderi, unpublished manuscript.

36. Ibid.

37. W. Hoville and D. C. Donderi, "R.R. 2 au Lac Baskatong," *UFO-Québec* 16 (1978): 8–18; and Jacques Lavoie, "Rapport sur l'Evenement du 11 mars 1978," *UFO-Québec* 16 (1978): 18–22.

38. E. J. Ruppelt, *The Report on Unidentified Flying Objects* (New York: Ace Books, 1956), pp. 275–96; and D. S. Gillmor, ed., *Scientific Study of Unidentified Flying Objects* (New York: Bantam Books, 1969), pp. 517–25, 905–19.

39. R. V. Jones, "The Natural Philosophy of Flying Saucers," in *Scientific Study of Unidentified Flying Objects*, ed. D. S. Gillmor (New York: Bantam Books, 1969), appendix V, pp. 922–33.

40. R. V. Jones, *Most Secret War: British Scientific Intelligence, 1939–1945* (New York: Coronet Books, 1979).

41. Ibid., p. 426.

42. Ibid., p. 564.

43. Ibid., p. 472.

44. Ibid., p. 478.

45. Menzel, *Flying Saucers*, pp. 49–62; Klass, *UFOs*.

46. Kuhn, *Structure of Scientific Revolutions*, p. 79.

47. Donald H. Menzel, "UFO: Fact or Fiction?" Committee on Science and Astronautics, U.S. House of Representatives, 90th Cong., 2d sess., 29 July 1968 (Washington, D.C.: Government Printing Office, 1968), pp. 199–205.

48. James E. McDonald, "Science in Default: Twenty-two Years of Inadequate UFO Investigations," in *UFOs: A Scientific Debate*, ed. Carl Sagan and Thornton Page (Ithaca, N.Y.: Cornell University Press, 1972), pp. 52–122.

49. *Federal Rules of Evidence, 1974*, R. 401, cited in Delisle, *Evidence*, p. 23.

50. William Manchester, *The Last Lion: Winston Spencer Churchill, Alone 1932–1940* (Boston: Little, Brown, 1988), p. 207; see also Jones, *Most Secret War*, p. 577.

51. Philip Morrison, "The Nature of Scientific Evidence: A Summary," in *UFOs: A Scientific Debate*, ed. Carl Sagan and Thornton Page (Ithaca, N.Y.:

Cornell University Press, 1972), pp. 276–90; Carl Sagan, "The Extraterrestrial and Other Hypotheses," in Sagan and Page, pp. 265–75.

4. UFOs, the Military, and the Early Cold War Era

1. Project RAND, James Lipp et al., *Preliminary Design of an Experimental World-Circling Spaceship*, RAND report no. SM 11827, 2 May 1946.
2. R. Cargill Hall, "Early U.S. Satellite Proposals," *Technology and Culture* 4 (fall 1963): 410–34.
3. P. Hagen, "The Viking and the Vanguard," *Technology and Culture* 4 (fall 1963): 435–51; G. A. Tokaty, "Soviet Rocket Technology," *Technology and Culture* 4 (fall 1963): 515–28; R. W. Bussard and R. D. Delauer, *Fundamentals of Nuclear Flight* (New York: McGraw-Hill, 1965); James Lipp, *Status of Satellite Study*, RAND report no. RA 15006, 1 September 1946.
4. Tokaty, "Soviet Rocket Technology," p. 523.
5. Loren Gross, *UFOs: A History: 1946: The Ghost Rockets* (Fremont, Calif.: the author, 1988); "Ghost Rocket Committee," Letter to the Commander in Chief of the Swedish Defense Staff, 23 December 1946, quoted in Jerome Clark, "Ghost Rockets," in *The UFO Encyclopedia*, vol. 2, *The Emergence of a Phenomenon: UFOs from the Beginning through 1959* (Detroit: Omnigraphics, 1992).
6. Department of State, Office of European Affairs (Stockholm) to Secretary of State, telegram, 11 July 1946 (Center for UFO Studies [hereafter CUFOS]).
7. George C. McDonald, Secret Memorandum for Commanding General, Army Air Forces, subject: Reports of "Rocket" Sightings over the Scandinavian Countries, 19 July 1946 (CUFOS).
8. E. G. Fitch to D. M. Ladd, memorandum, 19 August 1947 (CUFOS).
9. Anders Liljegren and Clas Svahn, "The Ghost Rockets," in *UFOs: 1947–1987*, ed. H. Evans and J. Spencer (London: Fortean Tomes, 1987); Anders Liljegren, "General Doolittle and the Ghost Rockets," *AFU Newsletter* 36 (1991): 14–19.
10. *New York Times*, 14 August 1946, p. 11; R. V. Jones, "The Natural Philosophy of Flying Saucers," in *Scientific Study of Unidentified Flying Objects*, ed. Daniel Gillmor, appendix V (New York: Bantam Books, 1969); *Newsweek*, 26 August 1946, p. 32; William H. Stringer, "The Great Swedish Rocket Mystery," *Christian Science Monitor*, 16 August 1946.
11. Ossian Goulding, "Ghost Rockets over Scandinavia," *London Daily Telegraph*, 27 August 1946.
12. *Intelligence Review* 47 (9 January 1947): 17–20.
13. David S. McLellan, "Cold War," in *Software Toolworks Illustrated Encyclopedia* (Novato, Calif.: Grolier, 1990).
14. R. W. Bussard and R. D. DeLauer, *Fundamentals of Nuclear Flight* (New York: McGraw-Hill, 1965); Welman Shrader, *Fifty Years of Flight* (Cleveland: Eaton, 1953); Jack Manno, *Arming the Heavens* (New York: Dodd-Mead, 1984); Alfred C. Loedding, "Low Aspect Ratio Aircraft," U.S. Patent Office patent no. 2619302, application 25 August 1948; Tokaty, "Soviet Rocket Technology."
15. Jerome Clark, "Kenneth Arnold Sighting," in *The UFO Encyclopedia*, vol. 2, pp. 216–18.
16. United States Air Force, Project Blue Book microfilms, rolls 1 and 2. These microfilms are of the USAF UFO files from the variously named projects Sign, Grudge, and Blue Book, plus some earlier records. National Archives, Washington, D.C. (hereafter Blue Book).

17. Loren Gross, *UFOs: A History*, vol. 1, *1947* (Stone Mountain, Ga.: Arcturus, 1990).

18. N. LeBlanc, *German Flying Wings Designed by Horten Brothers*, Technical Intelligence summary report number F-SU-1110-ND, 5 July 1946 (Wright Field, Dayton, Ohio: HQ Air Matériel Command); Col. Howard M. McCoy to Gen. George McDonald, chief of Intelligence, USAF Pentagon, "Flying Disk" letter, 24 September 1947 (CUFOS).

19. E. G. Fitch to D. M. Ladd, "Flying Disks" office memorandum with annotations by J. Edgar Hoover, 10 July 1947 (CUFOS).

20. FBI, "Flying Disc, Information concerning," teletype messages from FBI Dallas (TX) office to Director and SAC, Cincinnati, 8 July 1947 (CUFOS). The alleged crashed disk at Roswell has become, in the 1980s and 1990s, one of the signature stories of UFO literature. This story was largely overlooked at the time and did not emerge until the late 1970s, when the air base's intelligence officer, Major Jesse Marcel, went public with details of the claimed crash.

21. "Sky Disc Hunted by Coast Planes," *New York Times*, 7 July 1947, pp. 1, 3.

22. Blue Book, Harmon Field, Newfoundland, file.

23. Edward Ruppelt, *The Report on Unidentified Flying Objects* (Garden City, N.Y.: Doubleday, 1956).

24. E. G. Fitch to D. M. Ladd, "Flying Disks" office memorandum, 19 August 1947 (CUFOS).

25. "AFBIR-CO" (Lt. Col. George Garrett), "Flying Discs," an analysis of sixteen flying disc cases, 30 July 1947 (CUFOS).

26. N. F. Twining to Brig. Gen. George Schulgen, "AMC Opinion Concerning Flying Discs" letter, 23 September 1947 (CUFOS); Douglas Eiseman to T-2 (Col. Howard McCoy), "Reported Sightings of Flying Discs" letter, 11 September 1947 (CUFOS).

27. United States Air Force, Memorandum from Headquarters European Command to Counter Intelligence regions, 20–28 October 1947 (CUFOS).

28. Gross, *UFOs: A History*, p. 61.

29. Ruppelt, *Report on Unidentified Flying Objects*, p. 28.

30. Walter Millis, *The Forrestal Diaries* (New York: Viking, 1951).

31. Richard K. Smith, "Balloon," in *Software Toolworks Illustrated Encyclopedia* (Novato, Calif.: Grolier, 1990); Tokaty, "Soviet Rocket Technology."

32. Shrader, *Fifty Years of Flight;* Manno, *Arming the Heavens;* Hall, *Satellite Proposals*.

33. Blue Book, rolls 1 and 2, passim.

34. Ibid., Godman AFB, Mantell incident file.

35. Ibid., Norcatur, Kansas, file; Chiles-Whitted (Montgomery, Alabama) file; and Col. Howard M. McCoy to CS, USAF, letter of 8 November 1948 (CUFOS); Phoenix, Arizona, Rhodes photo file; and Holloman AFB file.

36. J. Allen Hynek, *Final Report, Project 364* (Columbus: Ohio State University Research Foundation, 1949); Hynek, *The Hynek UFO Report* (New York: Dell, 1977). He was later appalled to find out how eagerly USAF officers used these improbable explanations in the post-Sign era as if they were solid reasons to dismiss a case.

37. Blue Book, Chiles-Whitted (Montgomery, Alabama) file; C. S. Chiles to J. E. McDonald, phone call, 6 January 1968, notes and audiotape, Archives, University of Arizona, Tucson.

38. Donald E. Keyhoe, *The Flying Saucers Are Real* (New York: Fawcett, 1950); Ruppelt, *Report on Unidentified Flying Objects;* Michael D. Swords, "Donald Keyhoe and the Pentagon," *Journal of UFO Studies* 6 (1996): 195–211.

39. Michael D. Swords, "Astronomers, the Extraterrestrial Hypothesis, and the United States Air Force at the Beginning of the Modern UFO Phenomenon," *Journal of UFO Studies* 4 (1992): 79–130.

40. Irving Langmuir, *Pathological Science,* transcript of one version of his talks on this subject, ed. R. N. Hall, 18 December 1953 (CUFOS); and Horace Kallen, "Shapley, Velikovsky and the Scientific Spirit," *Pensée* 2, no. 2 (1972): 36–40.

41. Ruppelt, *Report on Unidentified Flying Objects,* pp. 41, 45.

42. Brooke Allen to Chief Air Intelligence Division, memorandum, 11 October 1948, and related documents (CUFOS); Swords, "Donald Keyhoe and the Pentagon."

43. Edward J. Ruppelt, notes on the early UFO Project and Personnel (CUFOS) (hereafter Ruppelt Notes).

44. United States Air Force Directorate of Intelligence and Office of Naval Intelligence, "Analysis of Flying Object Incidents in the U.S.," Air Intelligence Report 100-203-79, 10 December 1948.

45. Blue Book, Moscow, USSR, and Hamel, Minnesota, files.

46. United States Air Force Directorate of Intelligence, "Flying Object Incidents."

47. Blue Book, Fukuoka, Japan, file.

48. Blue Book, Fargo, South Dakota, file; C. P. Cabell to CG, AMC, letter, 3 November 1948 (CUFOS); H. M. McCoy to CS, USAF, letter, 8 November 1948 (CUFOS); H. M. McCoy to CS, USAF, letter, 2 December 1948 and related documents (CUFOS); Ruppelt, *Report on Unidentified Flying Objects,* p. 59.

49. H. W. Smith and G. W. Towles, "Unidentified Flying Objects: Project Grudge" (Dayton, Ohio: Air Matériel Command, August 1949).

50. United States Air Force Europe, memorandum, top secret USAF 14, 4 November 1948 (CUFOS).

51. Sidney Shalett, "What You Can Believe About Flying Saucers," *Saturday Evening Post,* 30 April 1949, 7 May 1949.

52. C. P. Cabell to James Forrestal, memorandum concerning publicity on flying saucer incidents, 30 November 1948, and related documents (CUFOS).

53. E. Moore, memorandum concerning proposed magazine article by Sidney Shalett, 2 March 1949, and related documents (CUFOS).

54. C. P. Cabell to CS, USAF, comment on Walter Winchell's 3 April 1949 broadcast, 6 April 1949 (CUFOS).

55. A. J. Boggs, memorandum regarding General Cabell's response to Dr. Theodore von Karman, 18 February 1949 (CUFOS).

56. Stephen Leo, memorandum: Flying Saucer Story, April 1948 [*sic*], and related documents (CUFOS); A. J. Boggs, memorandum regarding Flying Saucer Story release, 25 April 1949 (CUFOS).

57. United States Air Force, *Project Saucer* (Washington, D.C.: National Military Establishment, 27 April 1949).

58. Keyhoe, *The Flying Saucers Are Real,* pp. 18–22; Donald E. Keyhoe, "Flying Saucers Are Real," *True,* January 1950, pp. 11–13, 83–87; Jerome Clark, "Keyhoe, Donald Edward," in *The UFO Encyclopedia,* vol. 2, pp. 219–22.

59. Ruppelt, *Report on Unidentified Flying Objects,* p. 60; C. P. Cabell, cover sheet regarding Report of Aerial Phenomena, 20 July 1949 (CUFOS).

60. Edward R. Murrow, "The Case of the Flying Saucers," CBS radio, summer 1950; David Levy, *The Man Who Sold the Milky Way* (Tucson: University of Arizona Press, 1993).

61. Psychological Warfare Division (Lt. Colonel Hoffman), Routing and Record Sheet regarding Project Grudge, 3 April 1950 (CUFOS).

62. Walter R. Agee, letter draft regarding flying saucer reports, 7 April 1950 (CUFOS); L. S. Harns, memorandum regarding phone call to Watson as to General Moore's instructions, 12 October 1950 (CUFOS).

63. Ruppelt Notes.

64. Douglas Larsen, "U.S. Air Force Has Flying Disc Debunker," *Dallas Daily Times Herald*, 4 April 1950.

65. Swords, "Donald Keyhoe and the Pentagon"; Keyhoe, *The Flying Saucers Are Real*; Gerald Heard, *The Riddle of the Flying Saucers* (London: Carroll and Nicolson, 1950); Frank Scully, *Behind the Flying Saucers* (New York: Henry Holt, 1950).

66. Blue Book, White Sands, New Mexico, file; John Schweizer, memorandum for the Security Review Branch, 21 December 1949 (CUFOS); Robert B. McLaughlin, "How Scientists Tracked a Flying Saucer," *True*, March 1950, pp. 25–27, 96–99.

67. Congressional Quarterly, *Congress and the Nation, 1945–1964* (Washington, D.C.: Congressional Quarterly Service, 1965).

68. R. C. Brixner, Record of Basic Correspondence, re: Unidentified Flying Object, 12 April 1950, and related correspondence (CUFOS); H. J. Kieling to Commanding General, Far East Air Forces, letter, 31 July 1950, and related documents (CUFOS).

69. C. J. Stattler, Record of Basic Correspondence, re: Unidentified Flying Objects, 29 August 1950, and related documents (CUFOS); Colonel Barber, memorandum for Col. H. E. Watson, AMC, 7 July 1950 (CUFOS); C. P. Cabell to Art Lundahl, annotation by James McDonald from a conversation with Lundahl and Richard Hall, 17 May 1970; Marginalia in copy of Ruppelt's *Report on Unidentified Flying Objects* owned by McDonald, Archives, University of Arizona, Tucson; Ruppelt Notes; United States Air Force Headquarters, letter, re: destruction of Air Intelligence Report 100-203-79, 25 September 1950 (CUFOS).

70. Jerome Clark, "Aerial Phenomena Research Organization," "Civilian Saucer Investigation," and articles on specific contactees in *The UFO Encyclopedia*. passim.

71. Paul Fitts, "Psychoanalyzing the Flying Saucers," *Air Force*, February 1950, pp. 15–19; Arthur C. Clarke, "Flying Saucers," *Journal of the British Interplanetary Society* 12, no. 3 (1953): 97–100. In addition, Walter Orr Roberts wrote a series of general education–type articles on the theme of flying saucers during the summer 1947 wave for the *Denver Post*.

72. David M. Jacobs, *The UFO Controversy in America* (Bloomington: Indiana University Press, 1975).

73. Donald K. Slayton to J. Allen Hynek, letter, 1 February 1973 (CUFOS); Blue Book, Lubbock, Texas, file; R. S. Underwood to ATIC, letter, 1 June 1952, found in Project Blue Book "extra" letter and news clippings and microfilms (copy in CUFOS file).

74. Ruppelt Notes.

75. Ruppelt, *Report on Unidentified Flying Objects*, p. 87.

76. Ruppelt Notes.

77. Ibid.; William A. Adams to Col. E. S. Leland, memorandum, 19 October 1951 (CUFOS).

78. Ruppelt Notes.

79. Ruppelt, *Report on Unidentified Flying Objects*, p. 94; Harold Watson to Director of Intelligence, letter, 23 April 1951 (CUFOS).

80. C. P. Cabell to Chief, ATIC, letter, 22 October 1951 (CUFOS); William Adams memorandum; Bruce S. Maccabee, *Historical Introduction to Project Blue Book Special Report #14* (with report attached) (Evanston, Ill.: CUFOS, 1979); W. M. Garland to Chief, ATIC, memorandum, 16 January 1952 (CUFOS).

81. W. M. Garland for General Samford, memorandum, 3 January 1952 (CUFOS).

82. Memorandum for the Record, 29 April 1952 (CUFOS).

83. Ruppelt Notes; Stephan Possony, "Microwaves and Mind Control," *Second Look II*, no. 1 (1979): 18–20; and Dewey Fournet, Memorandum for Record, 12 September 1952 (CUFOS).

84. William A. Adams for the Office of Public Information, memorandum, 17 April 1952 (CUFOS).

85. J. Allen Hynek, Special Report on Conferences with Astronomers on Unidentified Flying Objects, 6 August 1952 (CUFOS).

86. Hynek, *The Hynek UFO Report*; and personal communication, ca. 1986; Idabel Epperson, correspondence to NICAP, 1965, 1966 (CUFOS) passim; Ruppelt, *Report on Unidentified Flying Objects*, pp. 131, 204–5; Clark, "Civilian Saucer Investigation."

87. Blue Book. The files for the summer 1952 era show a several-page handwritten plan, probably by Col. John O'Mara, listing the names of a dozen or so elite candidate advisers.

88. Blue Book, Tremonton, Utah, file; also see Ruppelt, *Report on Unidentified Flying Objects*, chap. 12 and pp. 219–23; Donald E. Keyhoe, *Flying Saucers from Outer Space* (New York: Henry Holt, 1953), chap. 9.

89. Blue Book, Washington, D.C., file; Robert B. Landry, oral history interview, Harry S. Truman Library, 28 February 1974; Ruppelt Notes; Department of Defense, minutes of press conference held by Maj. Gen. John A. Samford, 29 July 1952 (CUFOS); and Ruppelt, *Report on Unidentified Flying Objects*, pp. 168–69.

90. Keyhoe, *Flying Saucers from Outer Space.*

91. Blue Book, Great Falls, Montana, file; Ruppelt, *Report on Unidentified Flying Objects*, first draft copy (CUFOS).

92. Gerald K. Haines, "The CIA's Role in the Study of UFOs, 1947–90," *Studies in Intelligence* 1 (1997): 67–84.

93. Ralph L. Clark to Robert Amory, memorandum, 29 July 1952; CIA released documents on UFOs, 1952–53, (CUFOS) passim; Haines, "The CIA's Role in the Study of UFOs"; and Minutes of Branch Chief's Meeting, 11 August 1952 (CUFOS).

94. Edward Tauss to Deputy Assistant Director/SI, memorandum, 1 August 1952 (CUFOS); Dewey Fournet, "Interview with Antonio Huneeus," *UFO Universe*, November 1988, pp. 14–17.

95. A. Ray Gordon, memorandum on the Air Force stand on "Flying Saucers," ca. 22 August 1952 (CUFOS); Walter B. Smith to Director, Psychological Strategy Board, memorandum, undated, ca. late August 1952 (CUFOS).

96. George Carey for Deputy Director (Intelligence), memorandum, 22 August 1952 (CUFOS).

97. Marshall Chadwell for Director of Central Intelligence, memoranda, 17 September 1952 and 2 October 1952 (CUFOS).

98. Edward J. Ruppelt with an addendum by Michael D. Swords, "Are There Men on Mars? Or Other Worlds?" *International UFO Reporter* 23, no. 1 (1998): 10–12, 31.

99. Chadwell, memorandum, 17 September 1952.

100. Blue Book, handwritten plan, probably by Col. John O'Mara.

101. James Reber for Deputy Director (Intelligence), memorandum, 13 October 1952 (CUFOS).

102. Marshall Chadwell for Director of Central Intelligence, memorandum, 2 December 1952 (CUFOS).

103. Richard D. Drain, Minutes of Intelligence Advisory Committee meeting, 4 December 1952 (CUFOS).

104. Philip Strong, Memorandum for Record, 3 December 1952 (CUFOS).

105. Frederick Durant, Memorandum for Record, 9 December 1952 (CUFOS); Thornton Page to H. P. Robertson, letter, 12 December 1952 (CUFOS); and Daniel Lang, "A Reporter at Large: Something in the Sky," *New Yorker*, 6 September 1952, pp. 64–89.

106. Donald Menzel to Lyle Boyd, letter, 13 June 1961 (APL).

107. Ruppelt, *Report on Unidentified Flying Objects*, draft; Frederick Durant, Report of Meetings of Scientific Advisory Panel on Unidentified Flying Objects convened by Office of Scientific Intelligence, CIA, 14–18 January 1953, n.d. (hereafter Robertson Panel Report); letter exchanges between Robertson, Chadwell, Durant, John Wheeler in late December 1952 and early January 1953, Archives, California Institute of Technology and CUFOS; Ruppelt Notes.

108. J. Allen Hynek, audiotape reminiscences about the Robertson Panel, ca. 1970s (CUFOS); Robertson Panel Report; Michael D. Swords, "Dr. Robertson Requests the Honor of Your Attendance," *International UFO Reporter* 20, no. 4 (1995): 16–20.

109. Robertson Panel Report.

110. Ibid.

111. Ibid.; Chief, Contact Division, FBI, to Assistant for Operations, OSI (CIA), memorandum, 9 February 1953 (CUFOS); H. P. Robertson to Marshall Chadwell, letter, late January 1953, Archives, California Institute of Technology.

112. Haines, "The CIA's Role in the Study of UFOs."

113. Ruppelt, *Report on Unidentified Flying Objects*, chap. 16 and pp. 228–29.

114. Keyhoe, *Flying Saucers from Outer Space*, pp. 219–21, 242–45.

115. Capt. J. Cybulski, "Unidentified Flying Objects," portion of the memorandum of the 3d Commander's Conference, HQ 4602d AISS, Ent AFB, Colorado, n.d. (ca. December 1954), and other 4602d documents of the same general time frame (CUFOS); conference took place 13–16 January 1954.

116. Ruppelt Notes.

117. Ibid.; Donald Menzel and Lyle Boyd, *The World of Flying Saucers* (Garden City, N.Y.: Doubleday, 1963).

118. Hynek quote incorporated in Cybulski, "Unidentified Flying Objects."

119. Project Blue Book memorandum, Agenda for UFO Policy Meeting, n.d. (ca. November–December 1958) (CUFOS); Hynek, *The Hynek UFO Report*; and J. Allen Hynek, *The UFO Experience* (Chicago: Henry Regnery, 1972).

120. Ruppelt, *Report on Unidentified Flying Objects*, pp. 79–82.

121. David R. Saunders and R. Roger Harkins, *UFOs? Yes! Where the Condon Committee Went Wrong* (New York: World, 1968), pp. 113–16.

122. Richard E. O'Keefe, "UFOs Serious Business," briefing from the Office of the Inspector General for all Operations and Training Commands, 24 December 1959, reported in *The UFO Investigator* 1, no. 9 (March 1960): 1, 3.

123. Coral Lorenzen, *The Great Flying Saucer Hoax* (New York: William-Frederick, 1962), pp. 62–63 and chap. 7, passim.

124. Ruppelt, *Report on Unidentified Flying Objects,* chap. 15; and Civilian Saucer Investigation, *Quarterly Review* 1, no. 1 (September 1952); *Quarterly Review* 1, no. 2 (winter 1953).

125. Clark, "Civilian Saucer Intelligence of New York"; "Bloecher, Ted"; "Davis, Isabel," in *The UFO Encyclopedia.*

126. Civilian Saucer Intelligence of New York, J. Allen Hynek file, notes and letters (CUFOS).

127. Clark, "Keyhoe, Donald" and "National Investigations Committee on Aerial Phenomena"; NICAP, *UFO Investigator,* passim.

128. Richard Hall, personal communication.

129. Philip G. Evans, memorandum: "Unidentified Aerial Phenomena," 27 December 1960 (CUFOS).

130. Julian Hennessey to Alvarez, Goudsmit, etc., various letters in NICAP files; also letters by Leon Davidson to same; William Daniel to Lloyd Berkner, audiotape of phone conversation (CUFOS); H. P. Robertson to Gen. Millard Lewis, letter, 26 August 1957, Archives, California Institute of Technology; H. P. Robertson to Maj. James F. Byrne, letter, 7 October 1957, Archives, California Institute of Technology.

131. CBS television documentary, "UFOs: Friend, Foe, or Fantasy," narrated by Walter Cronkite, 1966.

132. Thornton Page to Fred Durant, letter, 8 September 1966, Archives, Smithsonian Institution.

133. Michael Swords, "The University of Colorado UFO Project: The 'Scientific Study of UFOs,'" *Journal of UFO Studies,* n.s. 6 (1995): 149–84.

5. The Extraterrestrial Hypothesis in the Early UFO Age

1. Thomas E. Bullard, "Anomalous Aerial Phenomena Before 1800," in Jerome Clark, *The UFO Encyclopedia, 2nd Edition: The Phenomenon from the Beginning* (Detroit: Omnigraphics, 1998), pp. 121–38.

2. Charles Fort, *The Books of Charles Fort* (New York: Henry Holt, 1941); Thomas E. Bullard, ed., *The Airship File* (Bloomington, Ind.: the author, 1982); Gordon I. R. Lore Jr. and Harold H. Deneault Jr., *Mysteries of the Skies: UFOs in Perspective* (Englewood Cliffs, N.J.: Prentice-Hall, 1968); Robert E. Bartholomew and George S. Howard, *UFOs and Alien Contact: Two Centuries of Mystery* (Amherst, N.Y.: Prometheus Books, 1998).

3. Jerome Clark, "Spaceship and Saltshaker," *International UFO Reporter* 11, no. 6 (November/December 1986): 12, 21.

4. Bullard, *Airship File;* Wallace O. Chariton, *The Great Texas Airship Mystery* (Plano, Tex.: Wordware Publishing, 1991); Daniel Cohen, *The Great Airship Mystery: A UFO of the 1890s* (New York: Dodd, Mead, 1981).

5. Bullard, *Airship File;* Bartholomew and Howard, *UFOs and Alien Contact;* Lucius Farish and Dale M. Titler, "When What to My Wondering Eyes

Should Appear," *Yankee* 37 (December 1973): 98–101; Nigel Watson, "The Scareship Mystery," parts 1 and 2, *Strange Magazine* 12 (fall/winter 1993): 18–21, 54–57; 13 (spring 1994): 26–27, 56–57.

6. Fort, *Books of Charles Fort*.

7. Loren E. Gross, *Charles Fort, the Fortean Society, and Unidentified Flying Objects* (Fremont, Calif.: the author, 1976); and Damon Knight, *Charles Fort: Prophet of the Unexplained* (Garden City, N.Y.: Doubleday, 1970).

8. Gross, *Charles Fort*; Knight, *Charles Fort*.

9. Vincent H. Gaddis, *Invisible Horizons: True Mysteries of the Sea* (Philadelphia: Chilton Books, 1965).

10. David W. Stupple, "Historical Links Between the Occult and Flying Saucers," *Journal of UFO Studies*, n.s., 5 (1994): 93–108.

11. Michael J. Crowe, *The Extraterrestrial Life Debate: The Idea of a Plurality of Worlds from Kant to Lowell* (New York: Cambridge University Press, 1986).

12. Theodore Flournoy, *From India to the Planet Mars: A Study of a Case of Somnambulism with Glossolalia* (New Hyde Park, N.Y.: University Books, 1963).

13. James H. Hyslop, *Psychical Research and the Resurrection* (London: Fisher Unwin, 1908).

14. J. Gordon Melton, "The Contactees: A Survey," in *The Gods Have Landed: New Religions from Other Worlds*, ed. James R. Lewis (Albany: State University of New York Press, 1995), pp. 1–13.

15. Stupple, "Historical Links."

16. Melton, "The Contactees."

17. N. Meade Layne, "Mark Layne, Baffling San Diego Medium," *Fate* 2, no. 1 (May 1949): 16–21.

18. "Parapsychologist Impatiently Repeats, 'Twas Space Ship in Sky," *San Diego Union*, 18 October 1946; N. Meade Layne, "Welcome? Kareeta!" *Round Robin* 2, no. 10 (October 1946): 3–7.

19. N. Meade Layne, *The Ether Ship and Its Solution* (Vista, Calif.: Borderland Sciences Research Associates, 1950).

20. "Visitors from the Void," *Amazing Stories* 21, no. 6 (June 1947): 159–61.

21. Fort expressed the same sentiment in a letter published in the *New York Times*, 5 September 1926: "If it is not the conventional or respectable thing upon this earth to believe in visitors from other worlds, most of us would watch them a week and declare that they were something else, and likely enough make things disagreeable for anybody who thought otherwise."

22. Kenneth Arnold and Ray Palmer, *The Coming of the Saucers: A Documentary Report on Sky Objects That Have Mystified the World* (Boise, Idaho, and Amherst, Wis.: the authors, 1952).

23. Bruce Maccabee, "The Arnold Phenomenon: Part Three," *International UFO Reporter* 20, no. 3 (May/June 1995): 6–7.

24. Ted Bloecher, *Report on the UFO Wave of 1947* (Washington, D.C.: the author, 1967).

25. "Strange 'Planes' Sighted Shooting Across Heavens," *Vancouver* [Washington] *Sun*, 26 June 1947.

26. Bill Bequette, "Experts Reach Deep into Bag to Explain 'Flying Discs,'" *Pendleton East Oregonian*, 28 June 1947.

27. J. Campbell Bruce, "The Sneide Letter," *San Francisco Chronicle*, 8 July 1947.

28. "Signals from Mars?" *Rockford* [Illinois] *Register Republic*, 5 July 1947.

29. "Rare Book Deals of Freak Discs in Sky Long Ago," *Albuquerque Journal*, 8 July 1947.

30. Claire Cox, "Authority on Spots Before Eyes Discusses Flying Disk Mystery," *Rockford Register Republic*, 7 July 1947.

31. "Three Explanations Given for Those Flying Disks," *San Francisco News*, 8 July 1947.

32. "The Great Moon Hoax," in *Encyclopedia of Hoaxes*, ed. Gordon Stein (Detroit: Gale Research, 1993), pp. 252–53.

33. Bloecher, *Report on the UFO Wave of 1947*.

34. Ibid.

35. George H. Gallup, *The Gallup Poll: Public Opinion, 1935–1948* (New York: Random House, 1972).

36. "What Were the Flying Saucers?" *Popular Science* 159 (August 1951): 74–75, 228.

37. Edward J. Ruppelt, *The Report on Unidentified Flying Objects* (Garden City, N.Y.: Doubleday, 1956); Michael D. Swords, "The Lost Words of Edward Ruppelt," *International UFO Reporter* 20, no. 2 (March/April 1995): 14–15.

38. Michael D. Swords, "The McCoy Letter," *International UFO Reporter* 22, no. 1 (spring 1997): 12–17, 27.

39. Ruppelt, *Report on Unidentified Flying Objects*.

40. Lawrence J. Tacker, *Flying Saucers and the U.S. Air Force* (Princeton, N.J.: Van Nostrand, 1960). Lt. Col. Tacker, a Pentagon UFO spokesman, stated flatly that "there has never been an official Aerospace Technical Intelligence Center estimate of the situation which stated that so-called flying saucers were interplanetary spaceships" (p. 83), even though the air force had earlier cleared for publication Ruppelt's book, which reported the opposite.

41. Ruppelt, *Report on Unidentified Flying Objects*.

42. *Air Force to Terminate Project "Blue Book"* (Washington, D.C.: Office of Assistant Secretary of Defense [Public Affairs], 17 December 1969); David R. Carlson, "UFOs: The Air Force and the UFO," *Aerospace Historian* 22, no. 4 (winter 1974): 11, 30–32; J. Allen Hynek, *The UFO Experience: A Scientific Inquiry* (Chicago: Henry Regnery, 1972).

43. Sidney Shallett, "What You Can Believe About Flying Saucers," parts 1 and 2, *Saturday Evening Post*, 30 April 1949, pp. 20–21, 39; 7 May 1949, pp. 36, 184–86.

44. David M. Jacobs, *The UFO Controversy in America* (Bloomington: Indiana University Press, 1975).

45. Donald E. Keyhoe, "The Flying Saucers Are Real," *True*, January 1950, pp. 11–13, 83–87.

46. Donald E. Keyhoe, *The Flying Saucers Are Real* (New York: Fawcett, 1950).

47. Gerald Heard, *The Riddle of the Flying Saucers: Is Another World Watching?* (London: Carroll and Nicholson, 1950).

48. "Professor's Idea—Saucer Pilots Could Be Smart Bugs or Plants," *Los Angeles Times*, 14 March 1950.

49. Frank Scully, *Behind the Flying Saucers* (New York: Henry Holt, 1950).

50. George M. Eberhart, ed., *The Roswell Report: A Historical Perspective* (Chicago: J. Allen Hynek Center for UFO Studies, 1991); Kevin D. Randle and Donald R. Schmitt, *UFO Crash at Roswell* (New York: Avon Books, 1991).

51. J. P. Cahn, "The Flying Saucers and the Mysterious Little Men," *True*, September 1952, pp. 17–19, 102–12.

52. Ed Sullivan, "To the Man with the Pickle Jar," *Civilian Saucer Investigation Quarterly Bulletin* 1, no. 1 (September 1952): 5.

53. Hynek, *The UFO Experience*.

54. Hal McCune, "Man Sticks to His Report," *Pendleton East Oregonian*, 24 June 1987.

55. Michael D. Swords, "Donald E. Keyhoe and the Pentagon: The Rise of Interest in the UFO Phenomenon and What the Government Really Knew," *Journal of UFO Studies*, n.s., 6 (1995/1996): 195–211.

56. Maurice Weekley and George Adamski, "Flying Saucers as Astronomers See Them," *Fate* 4, no. 5 (September 1950): 56–59; George Adamski, "I Photographed Space Ships," *Fate* 4, no. 5 (July 1951): 64–74.

57. Desmond Leslie and George Adamski, *Flying Saucers Have Landed* (New York: British Book Centre, 1953).

58. George Adamski, *Inside the Space Ships* (New York: Abelard-Schuman, 1955).

59. Pat Rimmington, "The Legend of Giant Rock," *Hi-Desert Magazine*, summer 1991, pp. 37–41; Gregory Bishop, "Calling Occupants," *Fortean Times* 118 (January 1999): 28–29, 31. See also "Giant Rock Interplanetary Spacecraft Convention," *The UFO Encyclopedia, 2nd Edition*, 447–49.

60. Daniel Fry, *The White Sands Incident* (Los Angeles: New Age Publishing Company, 1954).

61. Truman Bethurum, *Aboard a Flying Saucer* (Los Angeles: DeVorss and Company, 1954).

62. Leon Festinger, Henry W. Riecken, and Stanley Schachter, *When Prophecy Fails* (Minneapolis: University of Minnesota Press, 1956); "The End of the World," *The Saucerian* 3, no. 2 (spring 1955): 4–7, 55–60; Jerome Clark, "When Prophecy Failed," *Fortean Times* 117 (December 1998): 47.

63. James W. Moseley, ed., Special Adamski Exposé Issue, *Saucer News* 27 (October 1957); "Adamski's Latest Claim Blasted by NICAP Affiliate," *The U.F.O. Investigator* 1, no. 8 (June 1959): 1, 3–4.

64. The English writer Harold T. Wilkins (*Flying Saucers on the Attack* [New York: Citadel Press, 1954]) and the American ufologist Leonard H. Stringfield, editor of *C.R.I.F.O. Orbit* and author of *Inside Saucer Post . . . 3-0 Blue* (Cincinnati, Ohio: the author, 1957), held that UFOs had hostile intentions, as did the prominent Brazilian investigator Olavo T. Fontes in a series of articles for the Tucson-based Aerial Phenomena Research Organization (see, for example, his "Orthoteny in Brazil, Part III," *A.P.R.O. Bulletin*, November/December 1960, pp. 5–7). To the extent that they speculated about the extraterrestrials' intentions, most early ufologists seemed to think UFOs, neither friendly nor unfriendly, were engaged in exploration and scientific research.

65. As late as the mid-1960s, NICAP declared that "objective investigation" of such cases was "nearly impossible" and, by implication, barely worth consideration. These remarks appear in a brief discussion toward the end of a thick book titled *The UFO Evidence* (Washington, D.C.: NICAP). By 1969, however, NICAP treated some CE IIIs sympathetically in the monograph *Strange Effects from UFOs*. Nonetheless, in a book published four years later, Keyhoe, by now retired from NICAP, stated that no credible reports of UFO occupants existed (*Aliens from Space: The Real Story of Unidentified Flying Objects* [Garden City, N.Y.: Doubleday, 1973]). By then Keyhoe was in all likelihood the last UFO proponent holding that view.

66. "Contactee Letters," *Confidential Bulletin to NICAP Members* (6 September 1957).

67. Jacobs, *UFO Controversy in America.*

68. Isabel L. Davis, "Meet the Extraterrestrial," *Fantastic Universe* 8, no. 5 (November 1957): 31–59.

69. See, for example, "State Department Checking Apparent Hoax," *Confidential NICAP Bulletin*, 4 April 1958; "A New 'Contact' Claimant: Howard Menger, the Jersey Adamski," *CSI News Letter* 6 (15 December 1956): 9–12; and James W. Moseley and Michael G. Mann, "Screwing the Lid Down on 'Doctor' Williamson," *Saucer News* 6, no. 2 (February/March 1959): 3–5.

70. Davis, "Meet the Extraterrestrial."

71. Joe Simonton, *The Story of the Flying Saucer as It Was Seen by Joe Simonton* (Eagle River, Wis.: the author, 1961). An analysis of one of the pancakes conducted by the Food and Drug Administration for Project Blue Book determined that it contained "fat, starch, buckwheat hulls, wheat bran, and soybean hulls. The material appears to be a portion of an ordinary pancake made predominantly of buckwheat."

72. "New 'Contactee' Claim," *The U.F.O. Investigator* 1, no. 12 (April/May 1961): 8; "Facts Behind the 'Pancake' Story," *The U.F.O. Investigator* 2, no. 1 (July/August 1961): 8.

73. Waveney Girvan, "Claimants, Ridicule and a Piece of Cake: A Plea for an Open Mind," *Flying Saucer Review* 7, no. 5 (September/October 1961): 12–14.

74. "Editorial," *Saucer News* 8, no. 2 (June 1961): 2.

75. Lloyd Mallan, "UFO Hoaxes and Hallucinations," part 1, *Science and Mechanics* 38, no. 3 (March 1967): 48–52, 82–85.

76. "Wave of Close-Range Sightings Reported," *The U.F.O. Investigator* 2, no. 11 (July/August 1964): 1, 3.

77. Berthold E. Schwarz, "Gary Wilcox and the Ufonauts," in ed. Charles Bowen *UFO Percipients: Flying Saucer Review Special Issue No. 3*, September 1969, pp. 20–27.

78. Reid A. Ochs, "Martian 'Visit' Stirs Tioga," *Binghamton* [New York] *Press*, 7 May 1964.

79. Keith George, "'I Know What I Saw'; Egg-Shaped Craft," *Binghamton Sunday Press*, 24 October 1965.

80. Peter Kor (pseudonym of Thomas A. Comella), "The Solution to the Flying Saucer Mystery," *Flying Saucers*, September 1962, pp. 68–70, 72, 74.

81. John A. Keel, *UFOs: Operation Trojan Horse* (New York: Putnam, 1970); Keel, *The Mothman Prophecies* (New York: Saturday Review Press/Dutton, 1975).

82. For an extended discussion, see "Paranormal and Occult Theories About UFOs," in *The UFO Encyclopedia, 2nd Edition*, pp. 696–713.

83. "Psychosocial Hypothesis," in *The UFO Encyclopedia, 2nd Edition*, pp. 749–59.

84. Vallee, who possessed advanced degrees in astronomy and computer science, had begun as an extraterrestrial theorist (and author of two well-reviewed books on the subject), but by 1969—with *Passport to Magonia: From Folklore to Flying Saucers* (Chicago: Henry Regnery)—had turned to occult and conspiratorial approaches.

85. Andrea Pritchard, David E. Pritchard, John E. Mack, Pam Kasey, and Claudia Yapp, eds., *Alien Discussions: Proceedings of the Abduction Study Confer-*

ence Held at MIT (Cambridge, Mass.: North Cambridge Press, 1994); C. D. B. Bryant, *Close Encounters of the Fourth Kind: Alien Abduction, UFOs, and the Conference at M.I.T.* (New York: Knopf, 1995).

86. P. A. Sturrock et al., "Physical Evidence Related to UFO Reports: The Proceedings of a Workshop Held at the Pocantico Conference Center, Tarrytown, New York, September 29–October 4, 1997," *Journal of Scientific Exploration* 12 (1998): 179–229. "Scientific Panel Concludes Some UFO Evidence Worthy of Study" (Stanford University Press Release, 29 June 1998).

87. Kathy Sawyer, "Study of UFO-Related Phenomena Urged," *Washington Post*, 29 June 1998; Michelle Levander, "Science Panel Says It's Worth Evaluating UFO Reports," *San Jose Mercury News*, 29 June 1998.

6. UFOs: Lost in the Myths

1. For a tour through the personal and human response to UFOs by people around the country, see Douglas Curran, *In Advance of the Landing: Folk Concepts of Outer Space* (New York: Abbeville Press, 1985). A gallery of UFOs in popular culture—movies, pulp magazines, and toys—can be found in Eric Nesheim and Leif Nesheim, *Saucer Attack! Pop Culture in the Golden Age of Flying Saucers* (Los Angeles: Kitchen Sink Press, 1997). George Eberhart reveals the scope of the vast, often obscure and ephemeral UFO literature in his massive bibliography, *UFOs and the Extraterrestrial Contact Movement*, 2 vols. (Metuchen, N.J.: Scarecrow Press, 1986).

2. George A. Gallup, *Gallup Poll: Public Opinion, 1972–1977* (Wilmington, Del.: Scholarly Resources, 1978), pp. 213, 1197.

3. Edward B. Tylor, *Primitive Culture*, vol. 1 (New York: Brentano's, 1924), p. 424.

4. Mircea Eliade, *The Sacred and the Profane* (New York: Harcourt, Brace and World, 1959), p. 11.

5. Rudolph Otto, *The Idea of the Holy* (New York: Oxford University Press, 1969), pp. 1–40.

6. John G. Fuller, *Incident at Exeter* (New York: Putnam, 1966), p. 30.

7. J. Allen Hynek, Philip J. Imbrogno, and Bob Pratt, *Night Siege: The Hudson Valley UFO Sightings* (New York: Ballantine Books, 1987), p. 10.

8. Bill Chalker, "Tully Saucer Nests of 1966—Part Two," *International UFO Reporter* 23, no. 1 (spring): 16.

9. Speculations about ancient visitations were a standard part of many early UFO books, including Desmond Leslie and George Adamski, *The Flying Saucers Have Landed* (New York: British Book Centre, 1953); M. K. Jessup, *The Case for the UFO* (New York: Citadel Press, 1955); Jessup, *UFO and the Bible* (New York: Citadel Press, 1956); Jessup, *The Expanding Case for the UFO* (New York: Citadel Press, 1957); and Brinsley Le Poer Trench, *The Sky People* (London: Neville Spearman, 1960).

10. I. S. Shklovskii and Carl Sagan, *Intelligent Life in the Universe* (San Francisco: Holden-Day, 1966), pp. 455–61.

11. Jacques Vallee, *Passport to Magonia* (Chicago: Henry Regnery, 1969).

12. Jacques Vallee, *The Invisible College* (New York: Dutton, 1975), pp. 196–205; John A. Keel, *The Eighth Tower* (New York: Saturday Review Press, 1975), pp. 211–18.

13. Jerome Clark and Loren Coleman, *The Unidentified: Notes Toward Solving the UFO Mystery* (New York: Warner Paperback Library, 1975).

14. Hilary Evans, *Visions, Apparitions, Alien Visitors* (Wellingborough, Northhamptonshire: Aquarian Press, 1984), pp. 299–309.

15. James R. Lewis, ed., *The Gods Have Landed: New Religions from Other Worlds* (Albany: State University of New York Press, 1995).

16. John A. Saliba, "Religious Dimensions of UFO Phenomena," in *The Gods Have Landed*, ed. James R. Lewis (Albany: State University of New York Press, 1995), pp. 41–51.

17. John Whitmore, "Religious Dimensions of the UFO Abductee Experience," in *The Gods Have Landed*, ed. James R. Lewis (Albany: State University of New York Press, 1995), pp. 65–84.

18. Spencer R. Weart, *Nuclear Fear: A History of Images* (Cambridge, Mass.: Harvard University Press, 1988), pp. 398–401.

19. Howard E. McCurdy, *Space and the American Imagination* (Washington, D.C.: Smithsonian Institution Press, 1997), pp. 72–74.

20. Daniel Wojcik, *The End of the World as We Know It: Faith, Fatalism and Apocalypse in America* (New York: New York University Press, 1997), pp. 175–208.

21. Elaine Showalter, *Hysteries: Hysterical Epidemics and Modern Media* (New York: Columbia University Press, 1997), pp. 189–201.

22. Thomas E. Bullard, "Anomalous Aerial Phenomena Before 1800," in Jerome Clark, *The UFO Encyclopedia* (Detroit: Omnigraphics, 1998), p. 121.

23. Jerome Clark, "The Fall and Rise of the Extraterrestrial Hypothesis," in *MUFON 1988 International UFO Symposium Proceedings*, ed. Walter H. Andrus Jr. and Richard H. Hall (Seguin, Tex.: Mutual UFO Network, 1988), pp. 58–72.

24. H. L. Mencken, *Treatise on the Gods* (Baltimore: Johns Hopkins University Press, 1997), p. 246.

25. Rudolf Bultmann, *Jesus Christ and Mythology* (New York: Scribner, 1958), p. 17.

26. Peter L. Berger, *A Rumor of Angels: Modern Society and the Rediscovery of the Supernatural* (New York: Anchor Books, 1990 [1969]), p. 6.

27. Harvey Cox, *The Secular City* (New York: Macmillan, 1966), p. 15.

28. Berger, *Rumor of Angels*, p. 180.

29. For example, ibid., p. 27.

30. Harvey Cox, *Fire from Heaven* (Reading, Mass.: Addison-Wesley, 1995), pp. xv, 73.

31. Leslie McAneny, "It Was a Very Bad Year: Belief in Hell and the Devil on the Rise," *Gallup Poll Monthly*, January 1995, pp. 14–17; David W. Moore, "Most Americans Say Religion Is Important to Them," *Gallup Poll Monthly*, February 1995, pp. 16–21.

32. Cox, *Fire from Heaven*, pp. 281–87.

33. Debbie Nathan and Michael Snedeker, *Satan's Silence: Ritual Abuse and the Making of a Modern American Witch Hunt* (New York: Basic Books, 1995), pp. 1–7; Richard Ofshe and Ethan Watters, *Making Monsters: False Memory, Psychotherapy, and Sexual Hysteria* (New York: Scribner, 1994), pp. 1–3, 6–8.

34. Lawrence Wright, *Remembering Satan* (New York: Vintage Books, 1994).

35. Jeffrey S. Victor, *Satanic Panic: The Creation of a Contemporary Legend* (Chicago: Open Court, 1993), pp. 27–36.

36. Martin E. Marty, "Religion in America Since Mid-Century," in *Religion and America: Spirituality in a Secular Age*, ed. Mary Douglas and Steven M. Tipton (Boston: Beacon Press, 1983), pp. 283–84.

37. Robert Redfield, *Peasant Society and Culture* (Chicago: University of Chicago Press, 1956), p. 70.

38. Richard M. Dorson, "Folklore in the Modern World," in *Folklore and Fakelore* (Cambridge, Mass.: Harvard University Press, 1976), p. 43.

39. Don Yoder, "Toward a Definition of Folk Religion," *Western Folklore* 33 (1974): 14; Peter W. Williams, *Popular Religion in America* (Englewood Cliffs, N.J.: Prentice-Hall, 1980), p. 5.

40. David Hume, "The Origin of Religion," in *Sociology and Religion*, ed. Norman Birnbaum and Gertrud Lenzer (Englewood Cliffs, N.J.: Prentice-Hall, 1969), pp. 21–22.

41. Bronislaw Malinowski, *Magic, Science and Religion* (Garden City, N.Y.: Doubleday Anchor Books, 1954), p. 29.

42. Cox, *Fire from Heaven*, p. 86.

43. Paul R. Gross and Norman Levitt, *Higher Superstition: The Academic Left and Its Quarrels with Science* (Baltimore: Johns Hopkins University Press, 1994); Theodore Schick Jr., "The End of Science?" *Skeptical Inquirer* 21, no. 2 (1997): 36–39.

44. Robert Lambourne, Michael Shallis, and Michael Shortland, *Close Encounters? Science and Science Fiction* (Bristol: Adam Hilger, 1990), pp. 95–112.

45. Robert N. Bellah, "Religious Evolution," in *Sociology and Religion*, ed. Norman Birnbaum and Gertrud Lenzer (Englewood Cliffs, N.J.: Prentice-Hall, 1969), pp. 78–82.

46. Cox, *Fire from Heaven*, p. 82.

47. J. Gordon Melton, *The New Age Encyclopedia* (Detroit: Gale Research, 1990), p. xiii.

48. Mircea Eliade, *Occultism, Witchcraft, and Cultural Fashions* (Chicago: University of Chicago Press, 1976), pp. 63–64.

49. For example, Cox, *Fire from Heaven*, pp. 300–318.

50. Berger, *Rumor of Angels*, p. 180.

51. Ninian Smart, *Dimensions of the Sacred: An Anatomy of the World's Beliefs* (Berkeley: University of California Press, 1996), pp. 10–11.

52. Émile Durkheim, *Elementary Forms of the Religious Life* (New York: Free Press, 1995), p. 44.

53. Jerome Clark, *The UFO Encyclopedia: The Phenomenon from the Beginning* (Detroit: Omnigraphics, 1998), pp. 243–54; Robert S. Ellwood, "UFO Religious Movements," in *America's Alternative Religions*, ed. Timothy Miller (Albany: State University of New York Press, 1995), pp. 393–99; J. Gordon Melton, "The Contactees: A Survey," in *The Gods Have Landed*, ed. James R. Lewis (Albany: State University of New York Press, 1995), pp. 1–13; David Stupple, "Mahatmas and Space Brothers: The Ideologies of Alleged Contact with Extraterrestrials," *Journal of American Culture* 7 (1984): 131–39.

54. Coverage of the Heaven's Gate cult dates back to 1976, when Hayden Hewes and Brad Steiger profiled "The Two" in *UFO Missionaries Extraordinary* (New York: Pocket Books, 1976), while the staff of the *New York Post*, in *Heaven's Gate: Cult Suicide in San Diego* (New York: Harper Paperbacks, 1997), and William Henry's book *The Keepers of Heaven's Gate: The Millennial Madness* (Anchorage, Alaska: Earthpulse Press, 1997) have treated the suicides. The primary

chronicler is sociologist Robert W. Balch, who followed the cult through two decades of transformations and recorded them in a series of papers. See his notes and bibliography in "Waiting for the Ships: Disillusionment and the Revitalization of Faith in Bo and Peep's UFO Cult," in *The Gods Have Landed*, ed. James R. Lewis (Albany: State University of New York Press, 1995), pp. 137–66.

55. H. Taylor Buckner, "The Flying Saucerians: An Open Door Cult," in *Sociology and Everyday Life*, ed. Marcello Truzzi (Englewood Cliffs, N.J.: Prentice-Hall, 1968), p. 226.

56. Leon Festinger, Henry W. Riecken, and Stanley Schachter, *When Prophecy Fails* (Minneapolis: University of Minnesota Press, 1956).

57. Alan Dundes, "Introduction" to *Sacred Narrative* (Berkeley: University of California Press, 1984), p. 1.

58. William Bascom, "The Forms of Folklore: Prose Narratives," in *Sacred Narrative*, ed. Alan Dundes (Berkeley: University of California Press, 1984), p. 9.

59. Bultmann, *Jesus Christ and Mythology*, p. 19.

60. Lauri Honko, "The Problem of Defining Myth," in *Sacred Narrative*, ed. Alan Dundes (Berkeley: University of California Press, 1984), pp. 47–48.

61. Donald H. Menzel, "UFOs: The Modern Myth," in *UFOs: A Scientific Debate*, ed. Carl Sagan and Thornton Page (Ithaca, N.Y.: Cornell University Press, 1972), p. 123.

62. Curtis Peebles, *Watch the Skies! A Chronicle of the Flying Saucer Myth* (Washington, D.C.: Smithsonian Institution Press, 1994).

63. Benson Saler, Charles A. Ziegler, and Charles B. Moore, *UFO Crash at Roswell: The Genesis of a Modern Myth* (Washington, D.C.: Smithsonian Institution Press, 1997).

64. Alan Dundes, "What Is Folklore?" in *The Study of Folklore*, ed. Alan Dundes (Englewood Cliffs, N.J.: Prentice-Hall, 1965), p. 2.

65. See Linda Degh and Andrew Vazsonyi, "The Hypothesis of Multi-conduit Transmission in Folklore," in *Narratives in Society: A Performer-Centered Study of Narration*, Folklore Fellows Communication no. 255 (Helsinki: Suomalainen Tiedeakatemia, 1995), pp. 173–212.

66. Saler, Ziegler, and Moore, *UFO Crash at Roswell*, pp. 160–61.

67. Clifford Geertz, "Religion as a Cultural System," in *The Interpretation of Cultures* (New York: Basic Books, 1973), pp. 91–92.

68. C. G. Jung, *Flying Saucers: A Modern Myth of Things Seen in the Sky* (New York: Harcourt, Brace, 1959), pp. 18, 152.

69. Michael Grosso, "UFOs and the Myth of the New Age," *ReVision* 11 (winter 1989): 12–13.

70. See Claude Lévi-Strauss, "The Structural Study of Myth," in *Myth: A Symposium*, ed. Thomas A. Sebeok (Bloomington: Indiana University Press, 1971), pp. 81–106.

71. Geertz, "Religion as a Cultural System," pp. 94–123.

72. Representative examples of the demonic invasion school include Frank Allnut, *Infinite Encounters: The Real Force Behind the UFO Phenomenon* (Old Tappan, N.J.: Spire Books, 1978); Basil Tyson, *UFOs: Satanic Terror* (Beaverlodge, Alberta: Horizon House, 1977); John Weldon and Zola Levitt, *UFOs: What on Earth Is Happening?* (Irvine, Calif.: Harvest House Publishers, 1975); and Clifford Wilson and John Weldon, *Close Encounters: A Better Explanation* (San Diego: Master Books, 1975). See also Billy Graham, *Angels: God's Secret Agents* (New York: Pocket Books, 1975), pp. 21–24.

73. Robert A. Baker and Joe Nickell, *Missing Pieces* (Buffalo, N.Y.: Prometheus Books, 1992), pp. 216–26.

74. Peter M. Rojcewicz, "The Folklore of the 'Men in Black': A Challenge to the Prevailing Paradigm," *ReVision* 11 (spring 1989): 10–12; Keith Thompson, *Angels and Aliens* (New York: Fawcett Columbine, 1991), pp. 15–20, 89–98; Jacques Vallee, *Dimensions: A Casebook of Alien Contact* (Chicago: Contemporary Books, 1988), pp. 271–81; Kenneth Ring, *The Omega Project* (New York: William Morrow, 1992), pp. 218–22, 239–40.

75. Thomas E. Bullard, "Ancient Astronauts," in *The Encyclopedia of the Paranormal*, ed. Gordon Stein (Buffalo, N.Y.: Prometheus Books, 1996), pp. 25–32; Jerome Clark, "Ancient Astronauts in the UFO Literature," in *The UFO Encyclopedia*, pp. 75–86.

76. Philip J. Corso, *The Day After Roswell* (New York: Pocket Books, 1997), p. 115.

77. Hilary Evans, "A Twentieth-Century Myth," in *UFO 1947–1997*, ed. Hilary Evans and Dennis Stacy (London: John Brown Publishing, 1997), pp. 257–66.

78. Thomas E. Bullard, *The Sympathetic Ear: Investigators as Variables in UFO Abduction Reports* (Mount Rainier, Md.: Fund for UFO Research, 1995), pp. 67, 101.

79. Jenny Randles, "An Analysis of British Abduction Cases," in *Alien Discussions: Proceedings of the Abduction Study Conference Held at MIT*, ed. Andrea Pritchard, David E. Pritchard, John E. Mack, Pam Kasey, and Claudia Yapp (Cambridge, Mass.: North Cambridge Press, 1994), p. 175.

80. Joseph Nyman, "Familiar Entity and Dual Reference in the Latent Encounter," *MUFON UFO Journal*, no. 251 (March 1989): 10.

81. Lord Raglan, "The Hero of Tradition," in *The Study of Folklore*, ed. Alan Dundes (Englewood Cliffs, N.J.: Prentice-Hall, 1965), p. 145.

82. Bruce A. Rosenberg, *Custer and the Epic of Defeat* (University Park: Pennsylvania State University Press, 1974), pp. 1–2, 155–74.

83. William Labov, *Language in the Inner City* (Philadelphia: University of Pennsylvania Press, 1972), pp. 362–70.

84. Eleanor Wachs, *Crime-Victim Stories* (Bloomington: Indiana University Press, 1988), pp. 51–52.

85. Ring, *The Omega Project*, p. 94.

86. Philip Jenkins and Daniel Maier-Katkin, "Occult Survivors: The Making of a Myth," in *The Satanism Scare*, ed. James T. Richardson, Joel Best, and David G. Bromley (Hawthorne, N.Y.: Aldine De Gruyter, 1991), p. 129.

87. Raglan, "The Hero of Tradition," pp. 150–51.

88. Susan Blackmore, *Dying to Live: Near-Death Experiences* (Buffalo, N.Y.: Prometheus Books, 1993), pp. 3–6.

89. Susan Schoon Eberly, "Fairies and the Folklore of Disability: Changelings, Hybrids, and the Solitary Fairy," in *The Good People: New Fairylore Essays*, ed. Peter Narvaez (New York: Garland, 1991), pp. 227–50.

90. Northrop Frye, *Anatomy of Criticism* (Princeton, N.J.: Princeton University Press, 1957), pp. 158–60.

91. Patrick Lucanio, *Them or Us: Archetypal Interpretations of Fifties Alien Invasion Films* (Bloomington: Indiana University Press, 1987), pp. 25–26.

92. Dorothy Vitaliano, *Legends of the Earth* (Bloomington: Indiana University Press, 1973).

93. Allan Hendry, *The UFO Handbook* (Garden City, N.Y.: Doubleday, 1979), p. 4.

94. William K. Hartmann, "Process of Perception, Conception, and Reporting," in Edward U. Condon, director, *Scientific Study of Unidentified Flying Objects* (New York: Bantam Books, 1969), pp. 571–77; Menzel, "UFOs: The Modern Myth," pp. 155–61.

95. Jan L. Aldrich, *Project 1947: A Preliminary Report* (UFO Research Coalition, 1997).

96. Thomas E. Bullard, *UFO Abductions: The Measure of a Mystery* (Mount Rainier, Md.: Fund for UFO Research, 1987), vol. 1, pp. 48, 189–90, 281–83.

97. David M. Jacobs, *The Threat* (New York: Simon and Schuster, 1998), p. 251.

98. Mircea Eliade, *Shamanism* (Princeton, N.J.: Princeton University Press, 1964), pp. 34–58.

99. Dennis Stillings, "Missing Time, Missing Links," *Magonia*, no. 28 (1988): 3–6; Keith Thompson, "The Stages of UFO Initiation," *Magical Blend*, no. 18 (1988): 9–16; Kenneth Ring, "Near-Death and UFO Encounters as Shamanic Initiations: Some Conceptual and Evolutionary Implications," *ReVision* 11 (winter 1989): 14–22; Whitmore, "Religious Dimensions of the UFO Abduction Experience," p. 71.

100. Robert Sheaffer, "A Skeptical Perspective on UFO Abductions," in *Alien Discussions: Proceedings of the Abduction Study Conference Held at MIT*, ed. Andrea Pritchard, David E. Pritchard, John E. Mack, Pam Kasey, and Claudia Yapp (Cambridge, Mass.: North Cambridge Press, 1994), pp. 384–85.

101. James Pontolillo, *Demons, Doctors, and Aliens*, Occasional Paper no. 2 (Arlington, Va.: International Fortean Organization, 1993), p. 10.

102. Vallee, *Passport to Magonia*; Clark and Coleman, *The Unidentified*; Peter L. Rojcewicz, "Between One Eye Blink and the Next: Fairies, UFOs, and the Problems of Knowledge," in *The Good People: New Fairylore Essays*, ed. Peter Narvaez (New York: Garland, 1991), pp. 479–514; John S. Carpenter, "Encounters: Now and Then," in *MUFON 1997 International UFO Symposium Proceedings*, ed. Walter H. Andrus Jr. and Irena Scott (Seguin, Tex.: Mutual UFO Network, 1997), pp. 216–18.

103. Belief in fairylike beings is worldwide—for the multiple fairy species of Ireland and Britain, see Thomas Keightley, *The Fairy Mythology* (Detroit: Gale, 1975 [1870]); and Katharine Briggs, *An Encyclopedia of Fairies* (New York: Pantheon, 1976); for the elves of Scandinavia, see William A. Craigie, *Scandinavian Folk-Lore* (Detroit: Singing Tree Press, 1970 [1896]); for the dwarfs of Germany, see George Hans Heide, "Dwarfs in German Folk Legends" (Ph.D. diss., University of California at Los Angeles). Other traditions include the Japanese *kappa* (Ishida Eiichiro, "The *Kappa* Legend," *Folklore Studies* [Tokyo] 9 [1950]: 1–152); Hawaiian Menehune (Katherine Luomala, *The Menehune of Polynesia and Other Mythical Little People of Oceania*, Bulletin 203 [Honolulu: Bernice P. Bishop Museum, 1951]); and Ghanian Mmoetia (Gabriel Bannerman-Richter, *Mmoetia: The Mysterious Little People* [Gabari Publishing Company, 1987]). A survey of North and South American Indian folklore finds stories of small, fairylike beings almost universal (John E. Roth, *American Elves* [Jefferson, N.C.: McFarland, 1997]).

104. Budd Hopkins, *Intruders* (New York: Random House, 1987), p. 166.

105. Edwin Sidney Hartland, *The Science of Fairy Tales* (London: Walter Scott, 1891), pp. 161–95.

106. Peter Rogerson, "On a Summer's Day . . . ," *Magonia*, no. 37 (October 1990): 2.

107. Alvin H. Lawson, "Birth Trauma Imagery in CE-III Narratives," in *International UPIAR Colloquium on Human Sciences and UFO Phenomena*, ed. Roberto Farabone (Milan: UPIAR, 1982), pp. 65–117.

108. Martin Kottmeyer, "Entirely Unpredisposed," *Magonia*, no. 35 (January 1990): 10; Kottmeyer, "The Eyes Still Speak," *REALL News* 6, no. 5 (1998): 1, 6–9.

109. Gerard Barthel and Jacques Brucker, *La Grande Peur Martienne* (Paris: Nouvelles Editions Rationnalistes, 1979).

110. Philip J. Klass, *UFO Abductions: A Dangerous Game* (Buffalo, N.Y.: Prometheus Books, 1988), pp. 174, 179, 186–91.

111. Bertrand Meheust, *Science-Fiction et Soucoupes Volantes* (Paris: Mercure de France, 1978).

112. Kottmeyer, "Entirely Unpredisposed."

113. Peter Rogerson, "Fairyland's Hunters," *Magonia*, no. 46 (June 1993): 3–7; no. 47 (October 1993): 4–8; "Sex, Science, and Salvation," *Magonia*, no. 49 (June 1994): 13–17; "Recovering the Forgotten Records," *Magonia*, no. 50 (September 1994): 10–13.

114. Dennis Stacy, "Alien Abortions, Avenging Angels," *Magonia*, no. 44 (October 1992): 12–17.

115. Pierre Vieroudy, "Vagues d'OVNI et Esprit Humain," *Lumieres dans la Nuit*, no. 154 (April 1976): 4–10.

116. Otto Billig, *Flying Saucers: Magic in the Skies* (Cambridge, Mass.: Schenkman, 1982), pp. 81–89.

117. Martin Kottmeyer, "UFO Flaps," *The Anomalist*, no. 3 (winter 1995–96): 78–86.

118. Martin Kottmeyer, "What's Up, Doc?" *Magonia*, no. 44 (October 1992): 3–7; "Swinging Through the Sixties," *Magonia*, no. 45 (March 1993): 7–12, 19; "Shams and Shepherds," *Magonia*, no. 46 (June 1993): 8–12.

119. Thomas E. Bullard, "Folkloric Dimensions of the UFO Phenomenon," *Journal of UFO Studies*, n.s., 3 (1991): 19–28.

120. Peebles, *Watch the Skies!* p. 236.

121. Pier Luigi Sani, "The 'Great Martian Scare' . . . of Two French Ufologists Who 'Now Think Better' and Have Changed Their Minds!" *Flying Saucer Review* 34, no. 3 (1989): 15–22.

122. See Norman Cohn, *Pursuit of the Millennium* (New York: Oxford University Press, 1970), for medieval movements, and Michael Barkun, *Crucible of the Millennium* (Syracuse, N.Y.: Syracuse University Press, 1986), for American antebellum activity.

123. See Paul Boyer, *When Time Shall Be No More: Prophecy Belief in Modern American Culture* (Cambridge, Mass.: Harvard University Press, 1992); and Wojcik, *The End of the World as We Know It*.

124. For a survey of worldwide millenarian movements, see Vittorio Lanternari, *Religions of the Oppressed* (New York: Knopf, 1963); and Anthony F. C. Wallace, "Revitalization Movements," *American Anthropologist* 58 (1956): 264–81. See Peter Worsley, *The Trumpet Shall Sound* (New York: Schocken Books, 1968), for Melanesian cargo cults; James Mooney, *The Ghost-Dance Religion and the Sioux Outbreak of 1890* (Chicago: University of Chicago Press, 1970), for the ghost dance; Franz Michael, *The Taiping Rebellion* (Seattle: University of Washington Press, 1966), and Jonathan D. Spence, *God's Chinese Son* (New York:

Norton, 1996), for the Taiping Rebellion; J. B. Peires, *The Dead Will Arise* (Bloomington: Indiana University Press, 1987), for the Xhosa cattle-killing movement; and Helene Clastres, *The Land-Without-Evil: Tupi-Guarani Prophetism* (Urbana: University of Illinois Press, 1995), for South American millenarian migrations.

125. Kenelm Burridge, *New Heaven, New Earth: A Study of Millenarian Activities* (Oxford: Basil Blackwell, 1969), pp. 165–69.

126. Anthony F. C. Wallace, *The Death and Rebirth of the Seneca* (New York: Knopf, 1970), pp. 194–202, 239–54.

127. Wallace, "Revitalization Movements," p. 272.

128. Wojcik, *The End of the World as We Know It*, p. 208.

129. Tylor, *Primitive Culture*, 1:27.

130. Arthur C. Clarke, *Profiles of the Future* (London: Pan Books, 1983), pp. 224–27.

131. R. Leo Sprinkle, "UFO Contactees: Captive Collaborators or Cosmic Citizens?" in *1980 MUFON UFO Symposium Proceedings*, ed. Walter H. Andrus Jr. and Dennis W. Stacy (Seguin, Tex.: Mutual UFO Network, 1980), pp. 54–75.

132. John Mack, *Abduction* (New York: Scribner, 1994), p. 422.

133. Whitley Strieber, *Communion* (New York: Beech Tree Books, 1987), pp. 64–65, 69–70.

134. Mack, *Abduction*, p. 395.

135. Joseph Nyman, "Familiar Entity and Dual Reference in the Latent Encounter," *MUFON UFO Journal*, no. 251 (March 1989): 10–12; Jenny Randles, *Star Children* (London: Robert Hale, 1994).

136. Martin Kottmeyer, "A Universe of Spies," *Magonia*, no. 39 (April 1991): 8–14; "Eye in the Sky," *Magonia*, no. 40 (August 1991): 3–8; "Eye-yi-yi," *Magonia*, no. 41 (November 1991): 5–9. See also note 118.

137. Donald E. Keyhoe, *Flying Saucers—Top Secret* (New York: Putnam, 1960), p. 283.

138. Donald E. Keyhoe, *Flying Saucers from Outer Space* (New York: Henry Holt, 1953), p. 209.

139. Thomas E. Bullard, "Waves," in Jerome Clark, *The UFO Encyclopedia* (Detroit: Omnigraphics, 1998), p. 1013.

140. John A. Keel, *UFOs: Operation Trojan Horse* (New York: Putnam, 1970), p. 290.

141. Peebles, *Watch the Skies!* pp. 257–58.

142. David M. Jacobs, *The Threat* (New York: Simon and Schuster, 1998), pp. 226–53.

143. Mircea Eliade, *Cosmos and History: The Myth of the Eternal Return* (New York: Harper and Row, 1959), pp. 51–92.

144. Ibid., pp. 95–112.

145. Norman Cohn, "How Time Acquired a Consummation," in *Apocalypse Theory and the Ends of the World*, ed. Malcolm Bull (Oxford: Blackwell, 1995), pp. 29–30.

146. Boyer, *When Time Shall Be No More*, p. 21; Jean Delumeau, *History of Paradise* (New York: Continuum, 1995), p. 7; Burr Cartwright Brundage, *The Fifth Sun* (Austin: University of Texas Press, 1979), pp. 27–29, 118; Brian Branston, *Gods of the North* (New York: Thames and Hudson, 1980), pp. 277–91.

147. Gunther S. Stent, *The Coming of the Golden Age: A View of the End of Progress* (Garden City, N.Y.: Natural History Press, 1969), pp. 77–95.

148. Ring, *The Omega Project*, p. 240.

149. Carl Sagan, *The Demon-Haunted World: Science as a Candle in the Dark* (New York: Random House, 1995).

150. David J. Hufford, "Traditions of Disbelief," *New York Folklore* 8 (1982): 53.

151. David J. Hufford, "Beings Without Bodies: An Experience-Centered Theory of the Belief in Spirits," in *Out of the Ordinary: Folklore and the Supernatural*, ed. Barbara Walker (Logan: Utah State University Press, 1995), p. 18.

152. Edward U. Condon, director, *Scientific Study of Unidentified Flying Objects* (New York: Bantam Books, 1969), p. 140.

153. David Kestenbaum, "Panel Says Some UFO Reports Worthy of Study," *Science* 281 (3 July 1998): 21.

154. Robert Sheaffer, "Massive Uncritical Publicity for Supposed 'Independent UFO Investigation' Demonstrates Media Gullibility Once Again," *Skeptical Inquirer* 22, no. 5 (September–October 1998): 5–7.

155. Frederick Crews, "The Mindsnatchers," *New York Review of Books*, 25 June 1998, pp. 14–19.

156. Kestenbaum, "Panel Says Some UFOs Worthy of Study," p. 21.

7. The UFO Abduction Controversy in the United States

1. See David M. Jacobs, *The UFO Controversy in America* (Bloomington: Indiana University Press, 1975).

2. The literature about the motivations and purposes for UFO visitations is vast. For a short synopsis of some of the main currents in it, see David M. Jacobs, *The Threat* (New York: Simon and Schuster, 1998).

3. See George Adamski and Desmond Leslie, *Flying Saucers Have Landed* (New York: British Book Centre, 1953); George Adamski, *Inside the Space Ships* (New York: Abelard-Shulman, 1955); Adamski, *Flying Saucers Farewell* (New York: Abelard-Shulman, 1961); Truman Bethurum, *Aboard a Flying Saucer* (Los Angeles: DeVorss, 1954); Daniel Fry, *The White Sands Incident* (Los Angeles: New Age Publishing Company, 1954).

4. See cases in Coral Lorenzen and Jim Lorenzen, *Flying Saucer Occupants* (New York: Signet, 1967); and Charles Bowen, ed., *The Humanoids* (London: Futura Publications, 1974).

5. John Fuller, *Interrupted Journey* (New York: Dial Press, 1966).

6. John Fuller, "Aboard a Flying Saucer," *Look*, 4 October 1966, pp. 44–48, 53–56; 18 October 1966, pp. 111–21.

7. Betty Hill, interview with the author, November 1976.

8. Mrs. Hill never had the spots analyzed.

9. Gordon Creighton, "The Most Amazing Case of All, Part 1," *Flying Saucer Review*, January/February 1965, pp. 13–17; Creighton, "The Most Amazing Case of All, Part 2," *Flying Saucer Review*, July/August 1965, pp. 5–8; Lorenzen and Lorenzen, *Flying Saucer Occupants*.

10. James E. McDonald, letter to Richard Hall, 21 October 1966.

11. Jerome Clark, "Interview with James Harder," *UFO Report*, December 1977.

12. Joe Eszterhas, "Clawmen from the Outer Space," *Rolling Stone*, 17 January 1974, pp. 26–27, 38, 40, 42, 44, 46–47.

13. Travis Walton, *Fire in the Sky: The Walton Experience* (New York: Marlowe, 1996).

14. In a private conversation in 1976, Jacobs told Hynek that the Walton and Pascagoula cases were probably hoaxes.

15. Coral Lorenzen and Jim Lorenzen, *Abducted! Confrontations with Beings from Outer Space* (New York: Berkley Books, 1977), pp. 114–31.

16. Berthold E. Schwartz, "Talks with Betty Hill: I—Aftermath of Encounter," *Flying Saucer Review* 23, no. 2 (1977): 19 n.

17. David M. Jacobs, "UFOs and the Search for Scientific Legitimacy," in *The Occult in America: New Historical Perspectives*, ed. Howard Kerr and Charles L. Crow (Urbana: University of Illinois Press, 1983).

18. Alvin H. Lawson, "Hypnosis of Imaginary UFO 'Abductees,'" in *Proceedings of the First International UFO Congress*, ed. Curtis G. Fuller (New York: Warner Books, 1980), p. 195.

19. Raymond E. Fowler, *The Andreasson Affair* (Englewood Cliffs, N.J.: Prentice-Hall, 1979).

20. Budd Hopkins, *Missing Time* (New York: Marek, 1981).

21. Richard Haines, "A 'Three Stage Technique' (TST) to Help Reduce Biasing Effects During Hypnotic Regression," *Journal of UFO Studies*, n.s., 1 (1989): 163–67.

22. Thomas E. Bullard, *UFO Abductions: The Measure of a Mystery* (Mount Rainier, Md.: Fund for UFO Research, 1987). Bullard's taxonomy was expanded with new data from 1995 in his "Abduction Phenomenon," in Jerome Clark, *The UFO Encyclopedia, 2nd Edition, vol. 1: A–K* (Detroit: Omnigraphics, 1998).

23. Budd Hopkins, *Intruders: The Incredible Visitations at Copley Woods* (New York: Random House, 1987); Ted Bloecher, Aphrodite Clamar, and Budd Hopkins, *Final Report on the Psychological Testing of "UFO Abductees"* (Mount Rainier, Md.: Fund for UFO Research, 1985).

24. "From Arnold to Hynek," *MUFON 1987 UFO Proceedings*, p. 129.

25. Budd Hopkins, David M. Jacobs, and Ronald Westrum, *Unusual Personal Experiences: An Analysis of Data from the Three National Surveys* (Las Vegas: Bigelow Holding Corporation, 1992).

26. See, for example, Robert Hall, Mark Rodeghier, and Donald A. Johnson, "The Prevalence of Abductions: A Critical Look," *Journal of UFO Studies*, n.s., 4 (1992): 131–35.

27. By 1995, approximately fifteen thousand people had contacted Hopkins and Jacobs.

28. David M. Jacobs, *Secret Life: Firsthand Accounts of UFO Abductions* (New York: Simon and Schuster, 1992).

29. The symposium proceedings and participant discussions are in Andrea Pritchard, David E. Pritchard, John E. Mack, Pam Kasey, and Claudia Yapp, eds., *Alien Discussions: Proceedings of the Abduction Study Conference Held at MIT* (Cambridge, Mass.: North Cambridge Press, 1994).

30. Karla Turner, *Taken: Inside the Alien Abduction Agenda* (Roland, Ark.: Kelt Works, 1994). See also Turner, "Alien Abductions in the Gingerbread House," *UFO Universe* 3, no. 1 (spring 1993), available on the internet.

31. John E. Mack, *Abduction: Human Encounters with Aliens* (New York: Scribner, 1994).

32. David M. Jacobs, "UFOs at Fifty: Some Personal Observations," in

MUFON International UFO Symposium Proceedings, ed. Walter H. Andrus Jr. and Irena Scott (Seguin, Tex.: Mutual UFO Network, 1997), pp. 16–30; Budd Hopkins, "The UFO Phenomenon and the Suicide Cults: An Ideological Study," in *MUFON International UFO Symposium Proceedings*, ed. Walter H. Andrus Jr. and Irena Scott (Seguin, Tex.: Mutual UFO Network, 1997), pp. 247–57.

33. David M. Jacobs, *The Threat* (New York: Simon and Schuster, 1998).

34. David M. Jacobs and Budd Hopkins, "Suggested Techniques for Hypnosis and Therapy of Abductees," *Journal of UFO Studies*, n.s., 4 (1992): 138–50; John Carpenter, "Abduction Notes," *MUFON UFO Journal*, October 1993, pp. 14–16. See also Victoria Alexander, "New Protocol for Abduction Research," *MUFON UFO Journal*, November 1993, pp. 7–10.

35. These conferences were funded by philanthropist Robert Bigelow.

36. David Gotlib, Stuart Appelle, Georgia Flamburis, and Mark Rodeghier, "Ethics Code for Abduction Experience Investigation and Treatment," *Journal of UFO Studies*, n.s., 6 (1994): 55–81.

37. Thomas E. Bullard, "Hypnosis and UFO Abductions: A Troubled Relationship," *Journal of UFO Studies*, n.s., 1 (1989): 3–40. See also Bullard, *The Influence of Investigators in UFO Abduction Reports: Results of a Survey* (Bloomington, Ind.: the author, 1994).

38. Jacobs, *The Threat*, pp. 30–60.

39. Philip J. Klass, *UFO Abductions: A Dangerous Game* (Buffalo, N.Y.: Prometheus Books, 1988).

40. David Hufford, "Awakening Paralyzed in the Presence of a Strange 'Visitor,'" in Andrea Pritchard et al., eds., *Alien Discussions*, pp. 348–54; Alvin Lawson, "A Testable Hypothesis for Fallacious Abductions: Birth Trauma Imagery in CEIII Narratives," in *The Spectrum of UFO Research: The Proceedings of the Second CUFOS Conference, Held September 25–27, 1981, in Chicago, Illinois*, ed. Mimi Hynek (Chicago: J. Allen Hynek Center for UFO Studies, 1988), pp. 71–98; Elaine Showalter, *Hystories* (New York: Columbia University Press, 1997); Mark Kingwell, *Dreams of Millennium* (Boston: Faber and Faber, 1996); Carl Sagan, *Demon-Haunted World* (New York: Random House, 1995); Frederick Crews, "The Mindsnatchers," *New York Review of Books*, 25 June 1998, pp. 14–19; "When Words Collide: An Exchange," *New York Review of Books*, 8 October 1998, pp. 53–56.

41. For example, a discussion of the "fantasy-prone personality" idea appears in Mark Rodeghier, Jeff Goodpaster, and Sandra Blatterbauer, "Psychological Characteristics of Abductees: Results from the CUFOS Abduction Project," *Journal of UFO Studies*, n.s., 3 (1991): 55–90. Pathology as a causative factor in sightings or abduction accounts is found wanting in Nicholas Spanos, Patricia Cross, Kirby Dickson, and Susan C. DuBreuil, "Close Encounters: An Examination of UFO Experiences," *Journal of Abnormal Psychology* 102 (1993): 624–32. See also Ted Bloecher, Aphrodite Clamar, and Budd Hopkins, *Final Report on the Psychological Testing of "UFO Abductees"* (Mount Rainier, Md.: Fund for UFO Research, 1985).

42. Jodi Dean, *Aliens in America* (Ithaca, N.Y.: Cornell University Press, 1998).

43. Frederick Crews, "The Mindsnatchers," *New York Review of Books*, 25 June 1998, pp. 14–19.

44. See Dean, *Aliens in America*.

8. Hypnosis and the Investigation of UFO Abduction Accounts

1. Harold B. Crasilnech and James A. Hall, *Clinical Hypnosis: Principles and Applications* (New York: Grune and Stratton, 1975), p. 1.
2. E. Erickson and E. Rossi, eds., *The Collected Papers of Milton Erickson* (New York: Irvington Publishers, 1981), p. 1.
3. R. A. Baker, "The Aliens Among Us: Hypnotic Regression Revisited," *Skeptical Inquirer* 12 (1987): 147–62; P. Klass, *UFO Abductions: A Dangerous Game* (Buffalo, N.Y.: Prometheus Books, 1988).
4. Jerome Clark, *The UFO Encyclopedia*, 2 vols. (Detroit: Omnigraphics, 1998).
5. Jerome Clark, "The Salvation Myth," *International UFO Reporter* 21, no. 2 (1996): 3–4.
6. Clark, *The UFO Encyclopedia*.
7. See David M. Jacobs, *The UFO Controversy in America* (Bloomington: Indiana University Press, 1975); Clark, *The UFO Encyclopedia*.
8. Carl Jung, *Flying Saucers: A Modern Myth of Things Seen in the Sky* (New York: Harcourt, Brace, 1959); H. Evans, *Gods, Spirits, Cosmic Guardians: A Comparative Study of the Encounter Experience* (Wellingsborough, England: Aquarian Press, 1987); Jacques Vallee, *Passport to Magonia: From Folklore to Flying Saucers* (Chicago: Henry Regnery, 1969); Clark, *The UFO Encyclopedia*.
9. J. Fuller, *The Interrupted Journey: Two Lost Hours* (New York: Dial Press, 1966).
10. Ibid.
11. Clark, *The UFO Encyclopedia*.
12. B. Hopkins, *Missing Time* (New York: Marek, 1981).
13. Steven Lynn and Irving Kirsch, "Alleged Alien Abductions: False Memories, Hypnosis, and Fantasy Proneness," *Psychological Inquiry* 7 (1996): 151; emphasis added.
14. J. Yuille and N. McEwan, "The Use of Hypnosis as an Aid to Eyewitness Memory," *Journal of Applied Psychology* 70 (1985): 136–400; D. Dinges, W. Whitehouse, E. Orne, J. Powell, M. Orne, and M. Erdeyli, "Evaluating Hypnotic Memory Enhancement (Hypermnesia and Reminiscence) Using Multitrial Forced Recall," *Journal of Experimental Psychology: Learning, Memory, and Cognition* 18 (1992): 1139–47; N. Spanos, M. Gwynn, S. Comer, W. Baltruweit, and M. deGroh, "Are Hypnotically Induced Pseudomemories Resistant to Cross-Examination?" *Law and Human Behavior* 13 (1989): 271–89; W. Whitehouse, D. Dinges, E. Orne, and M. Orne, "Hypnotic Hypermnesia: Enhanced Memory Accessibility or Report Bias?" *Journal of Abnormal Psychology* 97 (1988): 289–95.
15. T. Bullard, *On Stolen Time: A Summary of a Comparative Study of the UFO Abduction Mystery* (Bloomington, Ind.: privately printed, 1987); D. Webb, "The Use of Hypnosis in Abduction Cases," in *Alien Discussions: Proceedings of the Abduction Study Conference Held at MIT*, ed. Andrea Pritchard, David E. Pritchard, John E. Mack, Pam Kasey, and Claudia Yapp (Cambridge, Mass.: North Cambridge Press, 1994), pp. 198–202.
16. Klass, *UFO Abductions*; R. A. Baker, "The Aliens Among Us: Hypnotic Regression Revisited," *Skeptical Inquirer* 12 (1987): 147–62.
17. G. Farthing, *The Psychology of Consciousness* (Englewood Cliffs, N.J.:

Prentice-Hall, 1992); M. Smith, "Hypnotic Memory Enhancement of Witnesses: Does It Work?" *Psychological Bulletin* 94 (1983): 387–407.

18. S. Appelle, "Hypnosis and the Accuracy of Abduction Memory," in Pritchard et al., eds., *Alien Discussions.*

19. Kroger and Douce (1979); Crasilnech and Hall, *Clinical Hypnosis;* Erickson (1970); Brody (1980); Hopkins, *Missing Time;* J. Mack, *Abduction: Human Encounters with Aliens* (New York: Scribner, 1994).

20. Kroger and Douce, (1979).

21. J. Carpenter, "Deliberate Suggestions and Paradoxical Tricks," in Pritchard et al., eds., *Alien Discussions;* Hopkins, Jacobs, personal correspondence.

22. C. Hickson and W. Mendez, *UFO Contact at Pascagoula* (Gautier, Mich.: privately printed, 1983); Clark, *The UFO Encyclopedia.*

23. Hopkins, *Missing Time;* B. Hopkins, *Intruders: The Incredible Visitations at Copley Woods* (New York: Random House, 1987); Hopkins, *Witnessed: The True Story of the Brooklyn Bridge Abductions* (New York: Pocket Books, 1996); D. Jacobs, *Secret Life: Firsthand Accounts of UFO Abductions* (New York: Simon and Schuster, 1992); Jacobs, *The Threat* (New York: Simon and Schuster, 1995); Mack, *Abduction;* Carpenter, correspondence.

24. Smith, Jacobs, Mack, Hopkins, Carpenter.

25. Hopkins, *Witnessed.*

26. Clark, *The UFO Encyclopedia.*

27. Klass, *UFO Abductions.*

28. Hopkins, case files.

29. Hopkins, *Intruders.*

30. T. Phillips, "Landing Report from Delphos," *FSR Case Histories* 9 (February 1972): 4–10.

31. T. Phillips, "Physical Trace Landing Reports: The Case for UFOs," in *MUFON 1985 UFO Symposium Proceedings,* ed. W. Andrus and R. Hall (Seguin, Tex.: Mutual UFO Network, 1985).

32. J.-J. Velasco, "Report on the Analysis of Anomalous Physical Traces: The 1981 Trans-en-Provence UFO Case," *Journal of Scientific Exploration* 4, no. 1 (1990): 27–48.

33. O. Fontes, "The UAO Sightings at the Island of Trindade, Pt. 1," *APRO Bulletin* (January 1960): 5–9; "Pt. 2" (March 1960): 5–8; "Pt. 3" (May 1960): 4–8; B. Macabbee, "The McMinnville Photos," in *The Spectrum of UFO Research: The Proceedings of the Second CUFOS Conference, Held September 25–27, 1981, in Chicago, Illinois,* ed. M. Hynek (Chicago: J. Allen Hynek Center for UFO Studies, 1988), pp. 13–57.

34. Michael Ross and Ian Newby, "Target Article: Toward an Explanation of the UFO Abduction Phenomenon," *Psychological Inquiry* 7 (1994): 175.

35. D. Berliner, M. Galbraith, and A. Huneeus, *Unidentified Flying Objects: Briefing Document: The Best Available Evidence* (Washington, D.C.: CUFOS, FUFOR, MUFON, 1995); R. Hall, *The UFO Evidence* (New York: Barnes and Noble, 1997).

36. Hopkins, *Missing Time;* Bullard, *On Stolen Time;* Jacobs, *Secret Life;* R. Fowler, *The Allagash Abductions: Undeniable Evidence of Alien Intervention* (Tigard, Ore.: Wild Flower Press, 1993).

37. J. Carpenter, "The Significance of Multiple Participant Abductions," in *MUFON 1996 International UFO Symposium Proceedings* (Seguin, Tex.: Mutual UFO Network, 1996), pp. 119–37; Hopkins, *Intruders;* Hopkins, *Witnessed;* Jacobs, *Secret Life;* Fowler, *The Allagash Abductions.*

38. Carpenter, "The Significance of Multiple Participant Abductions," p. 125.

39. Fowler, *The Allagash Abductions*.

40. Hopkins, *Witnessed*.

41. Hopkins, *Intruders*.

42. Richard Ofshe and Ethan Watters, *Making Monsters: False Memory, Satanic Cult Abuse, and Sexual Hysteria* (New York: Scribner, 1994).

43. Ibid., p. 95.

44. Ibid., p. 96.

45. Ibid., p. 95.

46. Ibid.

47. L. Wright, "Remembering Satan," *New Yorker*, 17 May 1993 and 27 May 1993.

48. Ofshe and Watters, *Making Monsters*; Wright, "Remembering Satan."

49. B. Hopkins, D. Jacobs, and R. Westrum, *Unusual Personal Experiences: An Analysis of the Data from Three National Surveys* (Las Vegas: Bigelow Holding Company, 1992); Hopkins, *Witnessed*.

50. B. Hopkins, "Invisibility and the UFO Phenomenon," in *MUFON 1993 International UFO Symposium Proceedings* (Seguin, Tex.: Mutual UFO Network, 1993).

51. Ofshe and Watters, *Making Monsters*; Frederick Crews, "Three Book Reviews," *New York Review of Books*, 25 June 1998.

52. Crews, "Three Book Reviews."

53. Ofshe and Watters, *Making Monsters*.

54. Bullard, *On Stolen Time*; Hopkins, *Witnessed*; Clark, *The UFO Encyclopedia*.

55. L. Terr, *Unchained Memories: True Stories of Traumatic Memories, Lost and Found* (New York: Basic Books, 1994); G. Vaillant, ed., *Ego Mechanisms of Defense: A Guide for Clinicians and Researchers* (Washington, D.C.: American Psychiatric Press, 1992); A. Kasniak, P. Nussbaum, M. Berren, and J. Santiago, "Amnesia as a Consequence of Male Rape: A Case Report," *Journal of Abnormal Psychology* 97 (1988): 100–104.

56. Ofshe and Watters, *Making Monsters*.

57. Ibid.

58. Ibid.

59. Hopkins, *Missing Time*; Hopkins, *Intruders*; Hopkins, *Witnessed*; R. Fowler, *The Andreasson Affair* (Englewood Cliffs, N.J.: Prentice-Hall, 1979); Fowler, *The Allagash Abductions*; J. Hynek, *The UFO Experience: A Scientific Enquiry* (Chicago: Henry Regnery, 1972).

60. Hopkins, *Witnessed*.

61. B. Hopkins, *UFO Abduction Experiences: An Information Kit* (privately printed, 1989).

62. de Brosses (1995).

63. G. Sandow, "The Abduction Conundrum" (manuscript, 1998).

64. C. Bryan, *Close Encounters of the Fourth Kind: Alien Abduction, UFOs, and the Conference at MIT* (New York: Knopf, 1995).

65. Jodi Dean, *Aliens in America* (Ithaca, N.Y.: Cornell University Press, 1998).

66. Crews, "Three Book Reviews."

67. Velasco, "Report on the Analysis of Anomalous Physical Traces."

9. How the Alien Abduction Phenomenon Challenges the
Boundaries of Our Reality

1. See John Mack, *Passport to the Cosmos* (New York: Crown, 1999), chap. 5.

2. Anthropologist Charles Laughlin, noting the ethnocentricity of our use of the term *nonordinary states of consciousness*, remarked at a multidisciplinary conference to study anomalous experiences held at Harvard University on 10–11 April 1999, "What we call altered states of consciousness other folks call reality."

3. See, for example, Michael Persinger, "Geophysical Variables and Behavior: LV, Predicting the Details of Visitor Experiences and the Personality of Experients: The Temporal Lobe Factor," *Perceptual and Motor Skills* 68 (1989): 55–65.

4. Milo Miles, "Aliens Land at Harvard!" *Boston Globe*, 24 April 1994, pp. B15, B17.

5. Chet Raymo, op. ed. *The Boston Globe*, June 1, 1992.

6. Michael Zimmerman, "The Alien Abduction Phenomenon: Forbidden Knowledge of Hidden Events," *Philosophy Today*, summer 1997, pp. 235–54.

7. Ken Wilber, *The Marriage of Sense and Soul: Integrating Science and Religion* (New York: Random House, 1998).

8. Richard Tarnas, *Passions of the Western Mind* (New York: Ballantine, 1991).

9. Dean Radin, *The Conscious Universe: The Scientific Truth of Psychic Phenomena* (New York: HarperCollins, 1997).

10. Donald Spence, *Narrative Truth and Ahistorical Truth: Meaning and Interpretation in Psychoanalysis* (New York: Norton, 1990).

11. Zimmerman, "Alien Abduction Phenomenon."

12. Bruce Greyson and Charles Flynn, *Near-Death Experience* (Springfield, Ill.: Charles Thomas, 1984); Raymond Moody, *Life After Life* (Covington, Ga.: Mockingbird Books, 1975); Kenneth Ring, *Life at Death* (New York: Coward, McCann, 1980); Ring, *Heading Toward Omega: In Search of the Meaning of the Near-Death Experience* (New York: William Morrow, 1984); Kenneth Ring and Evelyn Valarino, *Lessons from the Light: What We Can Learn from the Near-Death Experience* (New York: Plenum Insight, 1998).

13. Charles T. Tart, "Physiological Correlates of Psi Cognition," *International Journal of Parapsychology* 5 (1963): 375–86; Radin, *Conscious Universe;* Stanley Krippner, ed., *Advances in Parapsychological Research,* vols. 1–7 (New York: Plenum, and Jefferson, N.C.: McFarland, 1977–94).

14. Mark Garvey, *Searching for Mary: An Exploration of Marian Apparitions Across the United States* (New York: NAL/Dutton, 1997); Ingo Swann, *The Great Apparitions of Mary: An Examination of Twenty-two Supra-Normal Appearances* (New York: Crossroad, 1996).

15. Edgar Mitchell, *The Way of the Explorer* (New York: Putnam, 1996); Barbara Ann Brennan, *Hands of Light* (New York: Bantam Books, 1987); Harold Puthoff, "Zero-Point Energy: An Introduction," *Fusion Facts* 3, no. 3 (1991).

16. Nick Herbert, *Quantum Reality* (New York: Anchor Doubleday, 1985).

17. Larry Dossey, *Healing Words: The Power of Prayer and the Practice of Medicine* (New York: Harper, 1993).

18. Ian Stevenson, *Twenty Cases Suggestive of Reincarnation* (Charlottesville: University Press of Virginia, 1980); Stevenson, *Reincarnation and Biology: A*

Contribution to the Etiology of Birthmarks and Birth Defects (New York: Praeger, 1997); Stevenson, *Where Reincarnation and Biology Intersect* (New York: Praeger, 1997); Brian Weiss, *Through Time into Healing* (New York: Simon and Schuster, 1993).

19. James Gleick, "The Doctor's Plot," *New Republic*, 30 May 1994, pp. 31–35.

20. Ron Westrum, "Science and Social Intelligence About Anomalies: The Case of Meteorites," *Social Studies of Science* 8 (November 1978): 461–93.

21. Rudolph Schild, a leading astrophysicist at Harvard's Smithsonian Astrophysics Observatory, when asked in 1992 with other astrophysicists by the journal *Astronomy* what he thought would be the most important discoveries in astronomy in the next twenty years, wrote, "As impressive as the instrumentation and astrophysics are becoming, I expect the greatest advances in our knowledge of the universe to come from completely different fields. The research of Ken Ring on death experiences, and by John Mack on extraterrestrials and abductions, suggest to me that our 4-dimensional thinking is much too limited and that measurements within our space-time continuum will never reveal a more vast universe of higher dimension." Rudolph Schild, 16 December 1992. The journal cut these lines of Schild's statement from the published article that reported the results of its survey.

22. Ted Phillips, *Physical Traces Associated with UFO Sightings* (Evanston, Ill.: Center for UFO Studies, 1975); Roger K. Leir, *The Aliens and the Scalpel: Scientific Proof of Extraterrestrial Implants in Humans* (Columbus, N.C.: Granite Publishing, 1998).

23. At an April 1999 multidisciplinary study conference on anomalous experiences at Harvard, several distinguished scientists and academicians remarked on the fact that scholars and researchers lacked an adequate "science of experience."

24. John Mack, "The Politics of Ontology," *Center Review: A Publication of the Center for Psychology and Social Change* 6, no. 2 (fall 1992): 5, 18.

25. Program for Extraordinary Experience Research (PEER) was founded in 1993 to foster conditions for candid inquiry into anomalous experiences, using careful observation, open dialogue, and the development of a network of compassionate support for experiencers.

26. C. Brooks Brenneis, *Recovered Memories of Trauma: Transferring the Present to the Past* (Madison, Conn.: International Universities Press, 1997). The question of false memory, with or without hypnosis, as applied to the abduction phenomenon is discussed in Appendix A of the paperback edition of John E. Mack, *Abduction* (New York: Ballantine, 1995), pp. 428–29.

27. Stephen Mitchell, ed., *Selected Poems of R. M. Rilke* (New York: Random House, 1984).

28. Robert A. Baker and Joe Nickell, *Missing Pieces* (Buffalo, N.Y.: Prometheus Books, 1992).

29. Alvin H. Lawson, "Perinatal Imagery in UFO Abduction Reports," *Journal of Psychohistory* 122 (1984): 211–39.

30. John E. Mack, *Abduction*, revised paperback edition (New York: Ballantine, 1995), chap. 6.

31. Budd Hopkins, *Witnessed: The True Story of the Brooklyn Bridge UFO Abductions* (New York: Pocket Books, 1996).

32. David E. Pritchard, "Physical Evidence and Abductions," in *Alien Discussions: Proceedings of the Alien Abduction Study Conference Held at MIT*, ed.

Andrea Pritchard, David E. Pritchard, Pam Kasey, and Claudia Yapp (Cambridge, Mass.: North Cambridge Press, 1994), pp. 279–95.

33. Leir, *Aliens and the Scalpel*.

34. Budd Hopkins, *Missing Time: A Documented Study of UFO Abductions* (New York: Marek, 1981).

35. David M. Jacobs, *The Threat: The Secret Alien Agenda* (New York: Simon and Schuster, 1998).

36. Jacques Vallee, *Confrontations: A Scientist's Search for Alien Contact* (New York: Ballantine, 1990); Paul Hill, *Unconventional Flying Objects: A Scientific Analysis* (Charlottesville, Va.: Hampden Roads, 1995).

37. Preston Dennett, *UFO Healings* (Mill Spring, N.C.: Wild Flower Press, 1996).

38. Norman Don and Gilda Moura, "Topographic Brain Mapping of UFO Experiencers," *Journal of Scientific Exploration* 11 (1997): 435–53.

39. For further discussion of the light and energy aspects of the abduction phenomenon, see John Mack, *Passport to the Cosmos* (New York: Crown, 1999), chap. 4.

40. Stephen Larsen, ed., *Songs of the Stars: The Lore of a Zulu Shaman (Vusamazulu Credo Mutwa)*, with a foreword by Luisah Teish (Barrytown, N.Y.: Barrytown, 1996).

41. Dominique Callimanopulos, "Exploring African and Other Abductions," *Centerpiece*, spring–summer 1995, pp. 10–11.

42. Further discussion of this aspect of the abduction phenomenon can be found in Mack, *Passport to the Cosmos*, chap. 5.

43. Personal communication, 10 May 1998.

44. Mack, *Passport to the Cosmos*, chaps. 7–10.

45. E. Slater, "Conclusions on Nine Psychologicals," in *Final Report on the Psychological Testing of UFO "Abductees"* (Mount Rainier, Md.: Fund for UFO Research, 1985); N. Spanos et al., "Close Encounters: An Examination of UFO Experiences," *Journal of Abnormal Psychology* 102 (1993): 624–32; C. McLeod et al., *Anomalous Experience and Psychopathology* (forthcoming), and several other studies referred to in Mack, *Abduction*, pp. 431–32.

46. Kenneth Ring and C. J. Rosling, "The Omega Project: A Psychological Survey of Persons Reporting Abductions and Other UFO Encounters," *Journal of UFO Studies* 2 (1990): 59–98; Kenneth Ring, *The Omega Project: Near-Death Experiences, UFO Encounters, and Mind at Large* (New York: William Morrow, 1992).

47. Richard McNally et al., "Directed Forgetting of Trauma Cues in Adult Survivors of Childhood Sexual Abuse with and Without Posttraumatic Stress Disorder," *Journal of Abnormal Psychology* 107 (1998): 596–601.

48. Questions of the reliability of memory and the possibility of sexual or other forms of abuse as explanations of abduction experiences are discussed more fully in Mack, *Abduction*, pp. 428–34.

10. The UFO Experience: A Normal Correlate of Human Brain Function

1. H. Evans, *Visions, Apparitions and Alien Visitors* (Wellingborough, Northhamptonshire, England: Aquarian, 1984); J. Schnabel, *Dark White* (London: Hamish Hamilton, 1994).

2. J. Nolte, *The Human Brain: An Introduction to Its Functional Anatomy*, 4th ed. (St. Louis: Mosby, 1999).

3. E. R. Kandel, J. H. Schwartz, and T. M. Jessell, *Principles of Neural Science*, 3d ed. (New York: Elsevier, 1991).

4. Nolte, *The Human Brain*; Kandel, Schwartz, and Jessell, *Principles of Neural Science*.

5. K. Henke, A. Buck, B. Weber, and H. G. Wieser, "Human Hippocampus Establishes Associations in Memory," *Hippocampus* 7 (1997): 249–56; A. Martin, C. L. Wiggs, and J. Weisberg, "Modulation of Human Medial Temporal Lobe Activity by Form, Meaning, and Experience," *Hippocampus* 7 (1997): 587–93.

6. P. Gloor, A. Olivier, L. F. Quesney, F. Andermann, and S. Horowitz, "The Role of the Limbic System in Experiential Phenomena of Temporal Lobe Epilepsy," *Annals of Neurology* 12 (1982): 129–44; M. J. Horowitz and J. E. Adams, "Hallucinations on Brain Stimulation: Evidence for Revision of the Penfield Hypothesis," in *Origins and Mechanisms of Hallucinations*, ed. W. Keup (New York: Plenum, 1970), pp. 12–20; L. Nyberg, A. R. McIntosh, R. Cabeza, L. Nilsson, S. Houle, R. Habib, and E. Tulving, "Network Analysis of Positron Emission Tomography Regional Cerebral Blood Flow Data: Ensemble Inhibition During Episodic Memory Retrieval," *Journal of Neuroscience* 11 (1996): 3753–59.

7. D. M. Bear, "Temporal Lobe Epilepsy: A Syndrome of Sensory-Limbic Hyperconnection," *Cortex* 15 (1979): 357–84.

8. E. C. Crosby, T. Humphrey, and E. W. Lauer, *Correlative Anatomy of the Nervous System* (New York: Macmillan, 1962), p. 472.

9. P. Gloor, A. Olivier, L. F. Quesney, F. Andermann, and S. Horowitz, "The Role of the Limbic System in Experiential Phenomena of Temporal Lobe Epilepsy," *Annals of Neurology* 12 (1982): 129–44.

10. P. C. Fletcher, C. D. Frith, and M. D. Rugg, "The Functional Neuroanatomy of Episodic Memory," *Trends in Neuroscience* 20 (1997): 213–18.

11. P. Gloor, V. Salanova, A. Olivier, and L. F. Quesney, "The Human Dorsal Hippocampal Commissure," *Brain* 116 (1993): 1249–73.

12. P. D. MacLean, *The Triune Brain in Evolution* (New York: Plenum, 1990).

13. G. M. Remillard, F. Andermann, G. F. Testa, P. Gloor, M. Aube, J. B. Martin, W. Feindel, A. Guberman, and C. Simpson, "Sexual Manifestations Predominate in Women with Temporal Lobe Epilepsy: A Finding Suggesting Sexual Dimorphism in the Human Brain," *Neurology* 33 (1983): 323–30.

14. H. G. Weiser, "Depth Recorded Limbic Seizures and Psychopathology," *Neuroscience and Biobehavioral Reviews* 7 (1983): 427–40.

15. T. Sutula, G. Cascino, J. Cavazos, I. Parada, and L. Ramirez, "Mossy Fiber Synaptic Reorganization in the Human Temporal Lobe," *Annals of Neurology* 26 (1989): 321–30.

16. N. Geschwind, "Interictal Behavioral Changes in Epilepsy," *Epilepsia* 24 (1983): s23–s30.

17. H. Szechtman, E. Woody, K. S. Bowers, and C. Nahmias, "Where the Imaginal Appears Real: A Positron Emission Tomography Study of Auditory Hallucinations," *Proceedings of the National Academy of Science* 95 (1998): 1956–60.

18. R. G. Fink, H. J. Markowitsch, M. Reinkemeier, T. Bruckbauer, J. Kessler, and W. Heiss, "Cerebral Representation of One's Own Past: Neural Networks Involved in Autobiographical Memory," *Journal of Neuroscience* 16 (1996): 4275–82.

19. J. B. Brewer, Z. Zhao, J. E. Desmond, G. H. Glover, and J. D. E. Gabrieli, "Making Memories: Brain Activity that Predicts How Well Visual Experience Will Be Remembered," *Science* 281 (1998): 1185–90; R. L. Buckner and S. E. Petersen, "What Does Neuroimaging Tell Us About the Role of the Prefrontal Cortex in Memory Retrieval?" *Seminars in the Neurosciences* 8 (1996): 47–55.

20. M. A. Persinger and K. Makarec, "Temporal Lobe Signs and Correlative Behaviors Displayed by Normal Populations," *Journal of General Psychology* 114 (1986): 179–95; M. A. Persinger and K. Makarec, "Psychometric Differentiation of Men and Women by the Personal Philosophy Inventory," *Journal of Personality and Individual Differences* 12 (1991): 1267–71.

21. R. J. Roberts, N. R. Varney, J. R. Hulbert, J. S. Paulsen, E. D. Richardson, J. A. Spriner, J. S. Sheperd, C. M. Swan, J. A. Legrand, J. H. Harvey, M. A. Struchen, and M. E. Hines, "The Neuropathology of Everyday Life: The Frequency of Partial Seizure Symptoms Among Normals," *Neuropsychology* 4 (1990): 65–85; R. J. Roberts, L. L. Gorman, G. P. Lee, M. E. Hines, D. E. Richardson, T. A. Riggle, and N. R. Varney, "The Phenomenology of Multiple Partial Seizure-Like Symptoms Without Stereotyped Spells: An Epilepsy Spectrum Disorder?" *Epilepsy Research* 13 (1992): 167–77.

22. K. Makarec and M. A. Persinger, "Electroencephalographic Validation of Temporal Lobes Signs Inventory in a Normal Population," *Journal of Research in Personality* 24 (1990): 323–37.

23. M. A. Persinger and K. Makarec, "Complex Partial Epileptic-Like Signs as a Continuum from Normals to Epileptics: Normative Data and Clinical Populations," *Journal of Clinical Psychology* 49 (1993): 33–45.

24. M. A. Persinger, "The Tectonic Strain Theory as an Explanation for UFO Phenomena: A Non-technical Review of the Research, 1970–1990," *Journal of UFO Studies* 2 (1990): 105–37; J. S. Derr and M. A. Persinger, "Luminous Phenomena and Seismic Energy in the Central United States," *Journal of Scientific Exploration* 4 (1990): 55–69; J. S. Derr and M. A. Persinger, "Luminous Phenomena and Earthquakes in Southern Washington," *Experientia* 42 (1986): 991–99.

25. P. Devereaux, *Earth Lights Revelation* (London: Blandford, 1989); P. Devereaux and P. Brookesmith, *UFOs and UFOlogy: The First Fifty Years* (London: Blandford, 1997).

26. P. Richards, M. A. Persinger, and S. A. Koren, "Modification of Activation and Evaluation Properties of Narratives by Weak Complex Magnetic Field Patterns That Simulate Limbic Burst Firing," *International Journal of Neuroscience* 71 (1993): 71–85; M. A. Persinger, P. M. Richards, and S. A. Koren, "Differential Ratings of Pleasantness Following Right and Left Hemispheric Application of Low-Energy Magnetic Fields That Simulate Long-Term Potentiation," *International Journal of Neuroscience* 79 (1994): 191–97.

27. M. A. Persinger, P. M. Richards, and S. A. Koren, "Differential Entrainment of Electroencephalographic Activity by Weak Complex Electromagnetic Fields," *Perceptual and Motor Skills* 84 (1997): 527–36.

28. M. A. Persinger, "On the Possibility of Directly Accessing Every Human Brain by Electromagnetic Induction of Fundamental Algorithms," *Perceptual and Motor Skills* 80 (1995): 791–99.

29. C. M. Cook and M. A. Persinger, "Experimental Induction of the 'Sensed Presence' in Normal Subjects and an Exceptional Subject," *Perceptual and Motor Skills* 85 (1997): 683–93.

30. M. A. Persinger, "Vectorial Cerebral Hemisphericity as Differential

Sources for the Sensed Presence, Mystical Experiences and Religious Conversions," *Perceptual and Motor Skills* 76 (1993): 915–30; J. Bancaud, F. Brunet-Bourgin, P. Chauvel, and E. Halgren, "Anatomical Origin of Deja Vu and Vivid Memories in Human Temporal Lobe Epilepsy," *Brain* 117 (1994): 71–90; M. A. Wheeler, D. T. Stuss, and E. Tulving, "Toward a Theory of Episodic Memory: The Frontal Lobes and Autonoetic Consciousness," *Psychological Bulletin* 121 (1997): 331–54.

31. R. G. Fink, H. J. Markowitsch, M. Reinkemeier, T. Bruckbauer, J. Kessler, and W. Heiss, "Cerebral Representation of One's Own Past: Neural Networks Involved in Autobiographical Memory," *Journal of Neuroscience* 16 (1996): 4275–82.

32. M. A. B. Brazier, "Studies of the EEG Activity of Limbic Structures in Man," *Electroencephalography and Clinical Neurophysiology* 25 (1968): 309–18; Brazier, "Evoked Responses Recorded from the Depths of the Human Brain," *Annals of the New York Academy of Sciences* 112 (1963): 33–59.

33. J. Klinger and P. Gloor, "The Connections of the Amygdala of the Anterior Temporal Cortex in the Human Brain," *Journal of Comparative Neurology* 115 (1960): 333–69; A. Parent, *Carpenter's Human Neuroanatomy*, 9th ed. (Baltimore: Williams and Wilkins, 1996).

34. R. E. Bartholomew, "The Quest for Transcendence: An Ethnography of UFOs in America," *Anthropology of Consciousness* 2 (1991): 1–12; A. Budden, *Electric UFOs: Fireballs, Electromagnetics and Abnormal States* (London: Blandford, 1998).

35. L. Labelle, J. Laurence, R. Nadon, and C. Perry, "Hypnotizability, Preference for an Imagic Cognitive Style, and Memory Creation in Hypnosis," *Journal of Abnormal Psychology* 99 (1990): 222–28; J. Schnabel, "Chronic Claims of Alien Abductions and Some Other Traumas as Self-Victimization Syndromes," *Dissociation* 7 (1994): 51–62.

11. Research Directions

1. Cited in David M. Jacobs, *The UFO Controversy in America* (Bloomington: Indiana University Press, 1975), p. 78.

2. Robert Hall, "Sociological Perspectives on UFO Reports," in *UFOs: A Scientific Debate*, ed. Carl Sagan and Thornton Page (Ithaca, N.Y.: Cornell University Press, 1972).

Selected Bibliography

Thousands of books and articles have been written about Ufos, abductions, and the controversy surrounding them. Because of the enormous number, this list will concentrate on some of the most noteworthy and/or representative books to be published in English. Some books may fall within two or more categories. The study of unidentified flying objects and abductions evolved as a grassroots endeavor, and writings on the subject are extremely uneven.

Documents

The National Archives in Washington, D.C., house the bulk of Project Sign, Project Grudge, and Project Blue Book files. Other important documents are at Maxwell Air Force Base, Montgomery, Alabama; the J. Allen Hynek Center for UFO Studies in Chicago, Illinois; and the Fund for UFO Research in Mount Rainier, Maryland.

Reference Books

Undoubtedly, Jerome Clark's *The UFO Encyclopedia*, vols. 1 and 2, 2d ed. (Detroit: Omnigraphics, 1998), is an excellent point to begin for UFO research. Also valuable are Ronald Story, ed., *The Encyclopedia of UFOs* (Garden City, N.Y.: Doubleday, 1980); George Eberhart, ed., *UFOs and the Extraterrestrial Contact Movement: A Bibliography* (Metuchen, N.J.: Scarecrow Press, 1986); Edward G. Stewart, ed., *FSR Flying Saucer Review 1955–1994: An Index* (n.p.: the author, 1995); Edward G. Stewart, ed., *MUFON UFO Network's MUFON UFO Journal and Skylook 1967–1996: An Index* (Sacramento, Calif.: the author, 1996); and Loren Gross, *UFOs: A History* (Fremont, Calif.: the author, 1988). Gross has self-

351

published an extensive multivolume series of reprints of newspaper articles, magazines, official documents, and interviews that extend into the 1960s. Ostensibly a history, the primary material is invaluable for researchers. Lynn Catoe, *UFOs and Related Subjects: An Annotated Bibliography* (Washington, D.C.: U.S. Government Printing Office, 1969); and *Index to the Case Files of Project Blue Book* (Mount Rainier, Md.: Fund for UFO Research, 1997).

Periodicals and Internet

Two peer-reviewed journals serve the UFO community: *The Journal of UFO Studies*, from the J. Allen Hynek Center for UFO Studies, and *The Journal of Scientific Exploration*, published by the Society for Scientific Exploration, Stanford, California.

The two most widely read periodicals in America are *The MUFON UFO Journal*, published by the Mutual UFO Network, Seguin, Texas, and *The International UFO Reporter (IUR)*, from the J. Allen Hynek Center for UFO Studies (CUFOS), Chicago, Illinois. The Fund for UFO Research in Washington, D.C., publishes studies of the UFO and abduction phenomenon, as does CUFOS. *Flying Saucer Review*, published in England, has had a great influence on the UFO research community, especially in the 1960s and 1970s. *The IF Bulletin* from the Intruders Foundation (IF), New York, is dedicated to abduction research. The only peer-reviewed "mainstream" periodical to devote an issue to a debate over abductions was *Psychological Inquiry*, vol. 7, no. 2 (1996).

The Internet has hundreds of sites about UFOs and abductions. The most reliable ones are from the major UFO organizations. For scores of others, caveat emptor. Michael Lindemann's "CNI Newsletter," available on e-mail, represents the best of the newsletters about current events in UFO research.

Proceedings and Papers

A great amount of worthwhile UFO material is in the form of papers presented at UFO conventions and meetings. The quality of the papers varies greatly. Since 1970, the Mutual UFO Network's annual conferences have brought together some of the best people in UFO research; see *MUFON Proceedings* (Seguin, Tex.: Mutual UFO Network). The 1992 MIT conference proceedings are contained in Andrea Pritchard, David E. Pritchard, John E. Mack, Pam Kasey, and Claudia Yapp, eds., *Alien Discussions: Proceedings of the Abduction Study Conference Held at MIT* (Cambridge, Mass.: North Cambridge Press, 1994). Carl Sagan and Thornton Page edited the proceedings from the 1969 AAAS symposium on UFOs in *UFOs: A Scientific Debate* (Ithaca, N.Y.: Cornell University Press, 1972). John Fuller presented papers from the 1968 House of Representatives hearings on UFOs in *Aliens in the Skies* (New York: Putnam, 1969). The Center for UFO Studies has held two UFO conferences in 1976 and 1981: *Proceedings of the 1976 CUFOS Conference* (Evanston, Ill.: Center for UFO Studies, 1976); and Mimi Hynek, ed., *The Spectrum of UFO Research: The Proceedings of the Second CUFOS Conference, Held September 25–27, 1981, in Chicago, Illinois* (Chicago: J. Allen Hynek Center for UFO Studies, 1988). A 1976 Chicago UFO conference is in Curtis Fuller, ed., *Proceedings of the First International UFO Congress* (New York:

Warner Books, 1980). Contactee/New Age–oriented conference presentations
can be read in R. Leo Sprinkle, ed., *Proceedings of the Rocky Mountain Conference
on UFO Investigation* (Laramie, Wyo.: School of Extended Studies, 1980, 1982),
and in *When Cosmic Cultures Meet* (Falls Church, Va.: Human Potential Foundation Press, 1995).

Collections

Selected articles from *Flying Saucer Review* are in Charles Bowen, ed., *The Hu-
manoids* (London: Neville Spearman, 1969). Other noteworthy anthologies are
Hilary Evans and John Spencer, eds., *UFOs: 1947–1987: The Forty-Year Search
for an Explanation* (London: Fortean Tomes, 1987); Hilary Evans and Dennis
Stacy, eds., *UFOs: 1947–1997; From Arnold to the Abductees: Fifty Years of Flying
Saucers* (London: John Brown, 1997); Richard F. Haines, ed., *UFO Phenomena
and the Behavioral Scientist* (Metuchen, N.J.: Scarecrow Press, 1979); James R.
Lewis, ed., *The Gods Have Landed: New Religions from Outer Space* (Albany: State
University of New York Press, 1995); Valerie Vaughn, ed., *UFOs and Science:
The Collected Writings of Dr. James E. McDonald* (Mount Rainier, Md.: Fund for
UFO Research, 1995).

Social, Cultural, Historical Studies

Thomas E. Bullard, "Mysteries in the Eyes of the Beholder: UFOs and Their
Correlates as a Folkloric Theme Past and Present" (Ph.D. diss., University of
Indiana–Bloomington, 1982); Douglas Curran, *In Advance of the Landing: Folk
Concepts of Outer Space* (New York: Abbeville Press, 1985); Jodi Dean, *Aliens in
America* (Ithaca, N.Y.: Cornell University Press, 1997); Charles Emmons, *At the
Threshold: UFOs, Science, and the New Age* (Mill Spring, N.C.: Wild Flower Press,
1997); Leon Festinger, Henry W. Riecken, and Stanley Schachter, *When Prophecy
Fails* (Minneapolis: University of Minnesota Press, 1956); Paris Flammonde, *The
Age of Flying Saucers: Notes on a Projected History of Unidentified Flying Objects*
(New York: Hawthorn Books, 1971); Michael D. Hall and Wendy Connors,
Alfred Loedding and the Great Flying Saucer Wave of 1947 (Albuquerque, N.M.:
Rose Press, 1998); David M. Jacobs, *The UFO Controversy in America* (Bloom-
ington: Indiana University Press, 1975); Paul McCarthy, "Politics and Paradigm
Shifting: James E. McDonald and the UFO Case Study" (Ph.D. diss., Univer-
sity of Hawaii, 1975); June O. Parnell, "Personal Characteristics on the MMPI,
16 PF, and ACI of Persons Who Claim UFO Experiences" (Ph.D. diss., University of Wyoming, Laramie, 1987); Peter Rojcewicz, "The Boundaries of Orthodoxy: A Folkloric Look at the UFO Phenomenon" (Ph.D. diss., University of
Pennsylvania, 1984); Herbert Strentz, "A Survey of Press Coverage of Unidentified Flying Objects, 1947–1966" (Ph.D. diss., Northwestern University, 1970);
Keith Thompson, *Angels and Aliens: UFOs and the Mythic Imagination* (Reading,
Mass.: Addison-Wesley, 1991); Jacques Vallee, *Confrontations: A Scientist's Search
for Alien Contact* (New York: Ballantine, 1990); Vallee, *Forbidden Knowledge: Journals 1957–1969* (Berkeley, Calif.: North Atlantic Books, 1992); Vallee, *Revelations:
Alien Contact and Human Deception* (New York: Ballantine, 1991); Vallee, *Dimensions: A Casebook of Alien Contact* (Chicago: Contemporary Books, 1988).

UFOs in General

The literature on the UFO phenomenon and its meaning is extensive and extremely uneven in quality. Some representative books are Ralph Blum and Judy Blum, *Beyond Earth: Man's Contact with UFOs* (New York: Bantam Books, 1974); Bill Chalker, *The OZ Files: The Australian UFO Controversy* (Potts Point, NSW, Australia: Duffy and Snellgrove, 1996); Roy Craig, *UFOs: An Insider's View of the Official Quest for Evidence* (Denton: University of North Texas Press, 1995); Paris Flammonde, *UFO Exist!* (New York: Putnam, 1976); Daniel S. Gillmor, ed., *Scientific Study of Unidentified Flying Objects* (New York: Bantam Books, 1969 [known as the "Condon Report"]); Richard F. Haines, *Observing UFOs: An Investigative Handbook* (Chicago: Nelson-Hall, 1980); Haines, *Advanced Aerial Devices Reported During the Korean War* (Los Altos, Calif.: LDA Press, 1980); Haines, *Project Delta: A Study of Multiple UFO* (Los Altos, Calif.: LDA Press, 1994); Richard Hall, *The UFO Evidence* (Washington, D.C.: National Investigations Committee on Aerial Phenomena, 1964; reprint, New York: Barnes and Noble, 1997); Allan Hendry, *The UFO Handbook: A Guide to Investigating, Evaluating and Reporting UFO Sightings* (Garden City, N.Y.: Doubleday, 1979); Paul R. Hill, *Unconventional Flying Objects: A Scientific Analysis* (Charlottesville, Va.: Hampton Roads, 1995); Linda Moulton Howe, *Glimpses of Other Realities, vol. 1, Facts and Eyewitnesses* (Huntington Valley, Pa.: LMH Productions, 1993); Howe, *Glimpses of Other Realities, vol. 2, High Strangeness* (New Orleans: Paper Chase Press, 1998); J. Allen Hynek, *The Hynek UFO Report* (New York: Dell, 1977); Hynek, *The UFO Experience: A Scientific Inquiry* (Chicago: Henry Regnery, 1972); J. Allen Hynek and Jacques Vallee, *The Edge of Reality: A Progress Report on Unidentified Flying Objects* (Chicago: Henry Regnery, 1975); Donald E. Keyhoe, *Flying Saucers Are Real* (New York: Fawcett Publications, 1950); Keyhoe, *Flying Saucers from Outer Space* (New York: Henry Holt, 1953); Keyhoe, *Flying Saucers: Top Secret* (New York: Putnam, 1960); Keyhoe, *Aliens from Space: The Real Story of Unidentified Flying Objects* (Garden City, N.Y.: Doubleday, 1973); Gordon I. R. Lore Jr. and Harold H. Deneault Jr., *Mysteries of the Skies: UFOs in Perspective* (Englewood Cliffs, N.J.: Prentice-Hall, 1968); Coral E. Lorenzen, *Flying Saucers: The Startling Evidence of the Invasion from Outer Space* (New York: New American Library, 1966); Coral E. Lorenzen and Jim Lorenzen, *Flying Saucer Occupants* (New York: Signet, 1967); Lorenzen and Lorenzen, *UFOs Over the Americas* (New York: New American Library, 1968); Lorenzen and Lorenzen, *UFOs: The Whole Story* (New York: New American Library, 1969); Charles A. Maney and Richard H. Hall, *The Challenge of Unidentified Flying Objects* (Washington, D.C.: the authors, 1961); James McCampbell, *UFOlogy* (Millbrae, Calif.: Celestial Arts, 1976); Aime Michel, *Flying Saucers and the Straight Line Mystery* (New York: Criterion Books, 1958); Michel, *The Truth About Flying Saucers* (New York: Criterion Books, 1956); Michael A. Persinger and Gyslaine F. Lafreniere, *Space-Time Transients and Unusual Events* (Chicago: Nelson-Hall, 1977); Nick Pope, *Open Skies, Closed Minds: For the First Time a Government UFO Expert Speaks Out* (London: Simon and Schuster, 1996); Kevin Randle, *The Randle Report: UFOs in the 90s* (New York: M. Evans and Co., 1997); Randle, *Project Blue Book Exposed* (New York: Marlowe and Co., 1997); Jenny Randles, *UFO Reality: A Critical Look at the Physical Evidence* (London: Robert Hale, 1983); Edward Ruppelt, *Report on Unidentified Flying Objects* (Garden City, N.Y.: Doubleday, 1956 [1960 revised edition has three additional chapters]); David R. Saunders and R. Roger Harkins, *UFOs? Yes! Where the Condon Committee Went*

Wrong (New York: World Publishing Company, 1968); Peter Sturrock, *Report on a Survey of the Membership of the American Astronomical Society Concerning the UFO Problem*, SUIPR Report no. 681 (Stanford, Calif.: Institute for Plasma Research, 1977); Jacques Vallee, *Anatomy of a Phenomenon: Unidentified Objects in Space—A Scientific Appraisal* (Chicago: Henry Regnery, 1965); Vallee, *Passport to Magonia: From Folklore to Flying Saucers* (Chicago: Henry Regnery, 1969); Jacques Vallee and Janine Vallee, *Challenge to Science: The UFO Enigma* (Chicago: Henry Regnery, 1966); Illobrand von Ludwiger, *Best UFO Cases: Europe* (Las Vegas, Nev.: National Institute for Discovery Science, 1998).

UFO Case Studies

These are case studies of individual cases or groups of sightings investigated by the author: Ted Bloecher, *Report on the UFO Wave of 1947* (Washington, D.C.: the author, 1967); Ellen Crystal, *Silent Invasion: The Shocking Discoveries of a UFO Researcher* (New York: Paragon House, 1991); Isabel Davis and Ted Bloecher, *Close Encounters at Kelly and Others of 1955* (Evanston, Ill.: Center for UFO Studies, 1978); Raymond E. Fowler, *Casebook of a UFO Investigator: A Personal Memoir* (Englewood Cliffs, N.J.: Prentice-Hall, 1982); John Fuller, *Incident at Exeter: The Story of Unidentified Flying Objects over America Today* (New York: Putnam, 1966); J. Allen Hynek, Philip J. Imbrogno, and Bob Pratt, *Night Siege: The Hudson Valley UFO Sightings* (New York: Ballantine Books, 1987); Greg Long, *Examining the Earthlight Theory: The Yakima UFO Microcosm* (Chicago: J. Allen Hynek Center for UFO Studies, 1990); Ted Phillips, *Physical Traces Associated with UFO Cases: A Preliminary Catalog* (Northfield, Ill.: Center for UFO Studies, 1975); Jenny Randles, *The Penine UFO Mystery* (London: Granada, 1983); Peter Robbins and Larry Warren, *Left at Eastgate* (New York: Marlowe, 1997); Mark Rodeghier, *UFO Reports Involving Vehicle Interference: A Catalogue of Data Analysis* (Evanston, Ill.: Center for UFO Studies, 1981); Harley Rutledge, *Project Identification: The First Scientific Study of UFO Phenomena* (Englewood Cliffs, N.J.: Prentice-Hall, 1981); Frank Salisbury, *The Utah UFO Display: A Biologist's Report* (Old Greenwich, Conn.: Devin-Adair, 1974); Edward Walters and Bruce Maccabee, *UFOs Are Real: Here's the Proof* (New York: Avon Books, 1997); Walter Webb, *Encounter at Buff Ledge: A UFO Case History* (Chicago: J. Allen Hynek Center for UFO Studies, 1994); Jennie Zeidman, *A Helicopter-UFO Encounter over Ohio* (Evanston, Ill.: Center for UFO Studies, 1979).

Conspiracy and Cover-Up

For almost the entire history of the UFO controversy, many investigators have felt that the government knows about the UFO phenomenon and is hiding its knowledge. Some representative books are Lawrence Fawcett and Barry Greenwood, *Clear Intent: The Government Coverup of the UFO Experience* (Englewood Cliffs, N.J.: Prentice-Hall, 1984); Stanton Friedman, *Top Secret/Majic* (New York: Marlowe, 1996); Timothy Good, *Above Top Secret: The World Wide UFO Coverup* (New York: William Morrow, 1988); Donald E. Keyhoe, *Flying Saucer Conspiracy* (New York: Henry Holt, 1955); Jim Marrs, *The Alien Agenda* (New York: HarperCollins, 1997); Jenny Randles, *The UFO Conspiracy: The First Forty Years* (New York: Blandford Press, 1987).

Roswell Literature Pro and Con

George M. Eberhart, ed., *The Roswell Report: A Historical Perspective* (Chicago: J. Allen Hynek Center for UFO Studies, 1991); Stanton Friedman and Don Berliner, *Crash at Corona: The U.S. Military Retrieval and Cover-Up of a UFO* (New York: Paragon House, 1992); Philip J. Klass, *The Real Roswell Crashed-Saucer Coverup* (Amherst, N.Y.: Prometheus Books, 1997); William L. Moore and Charles Berlitz, *The Roswell Incident* (New York: Grosset and Dunlap, 1980); Karl T. Pflock, *Roswell in Perspective* (Mount Rainier, Md.: Fund for UFO Research, 1994); Kevin Randle and Donald Schmitt, *The Truth About the UFO Crash at Roswell* (New York: M. Evans and Company, 1994); Bensen Saler, Charles A. Ziegler, and Charles B. Moore, *UFO Crash at Roswell* (Washington, D.C.: Smithsonian Institution Press, 1997).

Abductee Books: Personal Accounts

Personal experience literature has grown rapidly since the late 1980s. While some accounts are relatively accurate, others are based on fragmentary and inaccurate memories, sometimes mixed with channeled information. Nevertheless, they convey the abductees' stresses and pressures as they struggle to come to grips with their situation. Among the most prominent of these accounts are Kim Carlsberg, *Beyond My Wildest Dreams* (Santa Fe, N.M.: Bear and Company, 1995); Beth Collings and Anna Jamerson, *Connections: Solving Our Alien Abduction Mystery* (Newberg, Oreg.: Wild Flower Press, 1996); Leah Haley, *Lost Was the Key* (Tuscaloosa, Ala.: Greenleaf Publications, 1993); Charles Hickson and William Mendez, *UFO Contact at Pascagoula* (Tucson, Ariz.: Wendelle C. Stevens, 1983); Debbie Jordan and Kathy Mitchell, *Abducted! The Story of the Intruders Continues . . .* (New York: Carroll and Graf, 1994); Whitley Strieber, *Communion* (New York: Morrow, 1987); Strieber, *Transformation: The Breakthrough* (New York: Morrow, 1988); Karla Turner, *Into the Fringe* (New York: Berkley, 1992); Ed Walters, *UFO Abductions in Gulf Breeze* (New York: Avon, 1994); Travis Walton, *Fire in the Sky* (New York: Marlowe, 1996); Katharina Wilson, *The Alien Jigsaw* (Portland, Oreg.: Puzzle Publishing, 1994).

Abductee Books: Primary Investigation

Primary investigators have yet to develop a standardized methodology. Thus, these books vary in their ability to ascertain reliable information. Ann Andrews and Jean Ritchie, *Abducted: The True Tale of Alien Abduction in Rural England* (London: Headline Book Publishing, 1998); Richard Boylan, *Close Extraterrestrial Encounters: Positive Experiences with Mysterious Visitors* (Tigard, Oreg.: Wild Flower Press, 1994) (Boylan's own abduction account is contained with others); Anne Druffel, *The Tujunga Canyon Contacts* (Englewood Cliffs, N.J.: Prentice-Hall, 1980); Raymond E. Fowler, *The Allagash Abductions* (Tigard, Oreg.: Wild Flower Press, 1993); Fowler, *The Andreasson Affair* (Englewood Cliffs, N.J.: Prentice-Hall, 1979); Fowler, *The Andreasson Affair—Phase Two* (Englewood Cliffs, N.J.: Prentice-Hall, 1982); Fowler, *The Watchers* (New York: Bantam Books, 1990); Budd Hopkins, *Missing Time* (New York: Marek, 1981); Hopkins, *Intruders: The Incredible Visitations at Copley Woods* (New York: Random House,

1987); Hopkins, *Witnessed: The Brooklyn Bridge Abductions* (New York: Pocket Books, 1996); David M. Jacobs, *Secret Life: Firsthand Accounts of UFO Abductions* (New York: Simon and Schuster, 1992); Jacobs, *The Threat* (New York: Simon and Schuster, 1998); John E. Mack, *Abduction: Human Encounters with Aliens* (New York: Scribner, 1994); Mack, *Passport to the Cosmos* (New York: Crown, 1999); Karla Turner, *Taken* (Roland, Ark.: Kelt Works, 1994).

Secondary Source Abduction Books

These books were written by UFO researchers and other authors who surveyed the primary literature and/or interviewed investigators and abductees. C. D. B. Bryan, *Close Encounters of the Fourth Kind: Alien Abduction, UFOs, and the Conference at M.I.T.* (New York: Knopf, 1995); Thomas E. Bullard, *The Sympathetic Ear: Investigators as Variables in UFO Abduction Reports* (Mount Rainier, Md.: Fund for UFO Research, 1995); Bullard, *UFO Abductions: The Measure of a Mystery* (Mount Rainier, Md.: Fund for UFO Research, 1987); John Fuller, *The Interrupted Journey* (New York: Dial Press, 1966); Coral Lorenzen, *Abducted! Confrontation with Beings from Outer Space* (New York: Berkley Medallion, 1977); Carl Nagaitis and Philip Mantle, *Without Consent: A Comprehensive Survey of Missing-Time and Abduction Phenomena in the UK* (London: Ringpull Press, 1994); Nick Pope, *The Uninvited: An Exposé of the Alien Abduction Phenomenon* (London: Simon and Schuster, 1997); Jenny Randles, *Abduction: Over Two Hundred Documented UFO Kidnappings Investigated* (London: Robert Hale, 1988); D. Scott Rogo, *UFO Abductions: True Cases of Alien Kidnappings* (New York: Signet, 1980); Kenneth Ring, *The Omega Project: Near-Death Experiences, UFO Encounters, and Mind at Large* (New York: William Morrow, 1992); John Spencer, *Perspectives: A Radical Examination of Alien Abduction Phenomenon* (London: MacDonald and Company, 1998).

Critical Literature

As with pro-UFO books, caution must be exercised with debunking literature. Without knowledge of the cases and/or the UFO research community's rejoinders to debunkers' arguments, the subject of UFOs and abductions appears completely illegitimate. Peter Brookesmith, *Alien Abductions* (New York: Barnes and Noble, 1998); Kendrik Frazier, Barry Karr, and Joe Nickell, *The UFO Invasion: The Roswell Incident, Alien Abductions, and Government Coverups* (Amherst, N.Y.: Prometheus Books, 1997); Philip J. Klass, *UFOs—Identified* (New York: Random House, 1968); Klass, *UFOs Explained* (New York: Random House, 1974); Klass, *UFOs: The Public Deceived* (Buffalo, N.Y.: Prometheus Books, 1983); Klass, *UFO Abductions: A Dangerous Game* (Buffalo, N.Y.: Prometheus Books, 1988); Terry Matheson, *Alien Abductions: The Making of a Phenomenon* (Amherst, N.Y.: Prometheus Books, 1998); Donald H. Menzel, *Flying Saucers* (Cambridge, Mass.: Harvard University Press, 1953); Donald H. Menzel and Lyle D. Boyd, *The World of Flying Saucers: A Scientific Examination of a Major Myth of the Space Age* (Garden City, N.Y.: Doubleday, 1963); Donald H. Menzel and Ernest Taves, *The UFO Enigma: The Definitive Explanation of the UFO Phenomenon* (Garden City, N.Y.: Doubleday, 1977); James Oberg, *UFOs and Outer Space Mysteries: A Sympathetic Skeptic's Report* (Norfolk, Va.: Donning, 1982);

Curtis Peebles, *Watch the Skies! A Chronicle of the Flying Saucer Myth* (Washington, D.C.: Smithsonian Institution Press, 1994); Kevin Randle, Russ Estes, and William P. Cone, *The Abduction Enigma* (New York: Forge, 1999); Carl Sagan, *The Demon-Haunted World* (New York: Random House, 1995); Robert Sheaffer, *The UFO Verdict: Examining the Evidence* (Buffalo, N.Y.: Prometheus Books, 1981); Jim Schnabel, *Dark White: Aliens, Abductions, and the UFO Obsession* (London: Hamish Hamilton, 1994).

Contactee Literature

UFO researchers consider the contactee books to be hoaxes, but for many years they had a powerful, albeit negative, influence on public opinion. George Adamski, *Inside the Space Ships* (New York: Abelard-Schuman, 1955); Adamski, *Flying Saucers Farewell* (New York: Abelard-Schuman, 1961); Orfeo Angelucci, *The Secret of the Saucers* (Amherst, Wis.: Amherst Press, 1955); Truman Bethurum, *Aboard a Flying Saucer* (Los Angeles: DeVorse and Company, 1954); Daniel Fry, *The White Sands Incident* (Los Angeles: New Age Publishing Company, 1954); Desmond Leslie and George Adamski, *Flying Saucers Have Landed* (New York: British Book Centre, 1953); Howard Menger, *From Outer Space to You* (Clarksburg, Va.: Saucerian Books, 1959).

Contributors

Stuart Appelle, Ph.D., is Professor of Psychology and Associate Dean of the School of Letters and Sciences at the State University of New York, College at Brockport. He is a research psychologist who has written widely on sensation and perception. He has also published in the mainstream academic literature on ufology, including a chapter on the alien abduction experience in *The Varieties of Psychological Experience,* published by the American Psychological Association. Since 1995 he has been editor of *The Journal of UFO Studies.*

Thomas E. Bullard, Ph.D., is a folklore scholar. His work explores the relationship between UFO reports and traditional beliefs in publications such as *UFO Abductions: The Measure of a Mystery.* He has written many articles on UFOs, abductions, and methodological issues. He is a staff member of the Indiana University library system.

Jerome Clark is a UFO researcher and writer. He is the author of books and articles about UFOs, including the multivolume *UFO Encyclopedia,* published between 1990 and 1998. He has edited *International UFO Reporter,* the quarterly magazine of the J. Allen Hynek Center for UFO Studies, since 1985.

Don Donderi, Ph.D., is Associate Professor of Psychology at McGill University, Montreal, and cofounder and Principal Consultant of Human Factors North, a Toronto-based ergonomics consulting firm. He is coauthor with Donald Hebb of *Textbook of Psychology,* 4th ed., and has published many experimental and theoretical papers in the areas of visual perception, memory, psychological measurement, and the UFO phenomenon.

Budd Hopkins is an artist and abduction researcher. He is Director of the Intruders Foundation and author of many pioneering articles and books on the abduction phenomenon, including *Missing Time; Intruders: The Incredible Visitations at Copley Woods;* and *Witnessed: The True Story of the Brooklyn Bridge Abduction.*

David M. Jacobs, Ph.D., is Associate Professor of History at Temple University. He is the author of numerous articles and books on UFOs and abductions, including *The UFO Controversy in America; Secret Life: Firsthand Accounts of UFO Abductions;* and *The Threat.*

John E. Mack, M.D., is Professor of Psychiatry, Harvard Medical School at the Cambridge Hospital. He is founding director of Program for Extraordinary Experience Research (PEER), which is devoted to studying the clinical, philosophical, political, and spiritual meaning of the UFO abduction phenomenon. His books include the Pulitzer Prize–winning *A Prince of Our Disorder; Abduction: Human Encounters with Aliens;* and *Passport to the Cosmos: Human Transformation and Alien Encounters.*

Michael Persinger, Ph.D., is Professor of Psychology and Neuroscience at Laurentian University in Sudbury, Ontario, Canada. He has written several books and has published more than two hundred technical articles. He is the author of the *Neuropsychological Bases of God Beliefs* and *TM and Cultmania.* Dr. Persinger's clinical practice involves the accurate diagnosis and treatment of patients with acquired brain injuries associated with mild traumas.

Michael Swords, Ph.D., is Professor of Natural Science at Western Michigan University and the author of numerous articles on UFO history and the science of it as it applies to the phenomenon. He is former editor of *The Journal of UFO Studies* and a member of the board of directors of the J. Allen Hynek Center for UFO Studies.

Ron Westrum, Ph.D., is Professor of Sociology and Interdisciplinary Technology at Eastern Michigan University. In addition to articles about the UFO phenomenon, he has written books on the sociology of technology and complex organizations, including *Sidewinder: Creative Missile Design at China Lake.*

Index